Restructuring the French Economy

RESTRUCTURING THE FRENCH ECONOMY

Government and the Rise of Market
Competition since World War II

WILLIAM JAMES ADAMS

The Brookings Institution
Washington, D.C.

Library of Congress Cataloging-in-Publication data
Adams, William James, 1947–
    Restructuring the French economy : government and the rise of
market competition since World War II / William James Adams.
        p.   cm.
    Bibliography: p.
    Includes index.
    ISBN 0-8157-0100-4 (alk. paper)
    1. France—Economic policy–1945–   2. France—Economic
conditions—1945–   3. Industry and state—France.   4. Competition—
France.   I. Title.
HC276.2.A63   1989
338.944—dc19   89-31065
                                                                          CIP

9   8   7   6   5   4   3   2   1

The paper used in this publication meets the minimum requirements of
American National Standard for Information Sciences—Permanence of
Paper for Printed Library Materials, ANSI Z39.48-1984.

Set in Linotron Caledonia
Composition by Monotype Composition Co.
    Baltimore, Maryland
Printing by R.R. Donnelley and Sons, Co.
    Harrisonburg, Virginia
Book design by Ken Sabol

⒝ THE BROOKINGS INSTITUTION

The Brookings Institution is an independent organization devoted to nonpartisan research, education, and publication in economics, government, foreign policy, and the social sciences generally. Its principal purposes are to aid in the development of sound public policies and to promote public understanding of issues of national importance.

The Institution was founded on December 8, 1927, to merge the activities of the Institute for Government Research, founded in 1916, the Institute of Economics, founded in 1922, and the Robert Brookings Graduate School of Economics and Government, founded in 1924.

The Board of Trustees is responsible for the general administration of the Institution, while the immediate direction of the policies, program, and staff is vested in the President, assisted by an advisory committee of the officers and staff. The by-laws of the Institution state: "It is the function of the Trustees to make possible the conduct of scientific research, and publication, under the most favorable conditions, and to safeguard the independence of the research staff in the pursuit of their studies and in the publication of the results of such studies. It is not a part of their function to determine, control, or influence the conduct of particular investigations or the conclusions reached."

The President bears final responsibility for the decision to publish a manuscript as a Brookings book. In reaching his judgment on the competence, accuracy, and objectivity of each study, the President is advised by the director of the appropriate research program and weighs the views of a panel of expert outside readers who report to him in confidence on the quality of the work. Publication of a work signifies that it is deemed a competent treatment worthy of public consideration but does not imply endorsement of conclusions or recommendations.

The Institution maintains its position of neutrality on issues of public policy in order to safeguard the intellectual freedom of the staff. Hence interpretations or conclusions on Brookings publications should be understood to be solely those of the authors and should not be attributed to the Institution, to its trustees, officers, or other staff members, or to the organizations that support its research.

For
Pauline and Walter,
and Barbara, Matthew, and Zachary

Foreword

TWENTY YEARS ago Richard Caves organized for the Brookings Institution a major collection of essays on the British economy. Since then Brookings has sponsored economic profiles of Australia, Canada, Japan, and Sweden, among others, as well as an overview of the economy of Western Europe as a whole. These investigations differ markedly in scope and method, but they share the belief that Americans should study the structure and function of other economies—partly to understand foreign behavior, partly to inform American debates on economic policy. This study of the postwar French economy by William James Adams falls squarely in that tradition.

At the end of World War II, few people predicted the smooth and rapid growth the French economy would experience in the next quarter century. Rigid government regulation of resources, restrictive business practices, and traditional French resistance to change seemed to preclude any dramatic transformation of economic life. Yet by 1985 the gross domestic product had quadrupled and per capita income had doubled. To explain these developments, Adams examines changes in economic conditions, the extent of government aid to industry, and industry responses to the challenges of foreign competition and French membership in the European Communities. Providing information from many sources, the author argues his conclusions while challenging readers to develop their own interpretations of the French experience and its implications for the U.S. economy in the 1990s.

William James Adams is professor of economics at the University of Michigan and affiliate of the Foreign Policy Studies program at Brookings. His research was supported by grants from the Ford Foundation, the German Marshall Fund of the United States, and the John D. and Catherine T. MacArthur Foundation. Also contributing was the Committee on Comparative and Historical Research on Market Economies at the University of Michigan. The final version of the book was written during a sabbatical spent at the Center for Business and Government, Kennedy School of Government, Harvard University.

The author wishes especially to thank his father, Walter Adams, his mentor, Richard Caves, and his former colleague, Joseph Sax, for their inspiration. He also thanks John Steinbruner, who helped launch the investigation; Suzanne Berger, Jacques Mistral, and John Sheahan, who read complete drafts of the book; and Gary Saxonhouse, Alexis Jacquemin, John Meyer, and Raymond Vernon, who offered generous advice. David Gray, Thea Lee, Richard Lopez, Xavier Maret, and Sheila Sadoff assisted with research. James Schneider edited the manuscript, Nancy Erickson verified its factual content, Irita Grierson, Susan Woollen, and Ann M. Ziegler prepared it for publication, and Margaret Lynch prepared the index.

The views expressed in this book are those of the author and should not be ascribed to those persons and organizations whose assistance is acknowledged or to the trustees, officers, or staff members of the Brookings Institution.

BRUCE K. MAC LAURY
President

March 1989
Washington, D.C.

Contents

Tables

1 | The Puzzle of French Economic Growth

AT THE END of World War II, few people predicted that the French economy would grow smoothly and rapidly for the next quarter century. Those who anticipated economic stagnation did not rely on ambient fears of Keynesian-style underconsumption; rather, they argued that fundamental features of French culture were incompatible with rapid growth.[1]

To understand the concerns of the culturalists, one must understand the way an economy grows. Normally companies, industries, and regions expand at different rates. As a result, economic growth entails structural change—change in the *composition* of economic activity.[2] Drawing on his observation of the growth process in a large number of nations, Simon Kuznets explained the concomitance of aggregate growth and structural change in terms of technological progress.[3] Standards of living rise, he claimed, because technologies improve. But technological progress also transforms determinants of supply and demand in particular markets. Hence it affects economic structure as well.

On the supply side, technological change alters the amounts of various inputs needed to produce given quantities of particular outputs. In many cases, according to Kuznets, technological change reinforces

1. Underconsumption is stressed in Hansen, *Economic Policy and Full Employment*; and Svennilson, *Growth and Stagnation in the European Economy*. The cultural argument appears in Landes, "French Business and the Businessman"; and Sauvy, *Histoire Economique de la France entre les Deux Guerres*, vol. 2, chap. 17. Complete references to works cited in footnotes and table notes appear in the bibliography.

2. Structural change is not confined to growing economies: changes in consumer tastes, production technologies, and national comparative advantages can affect economic structure regardless of the rate of growth.

3. Kuznets, *Modern Economic Growth*.

the economies of scale, concentrating production geographically and promoting urbanization. Since consumption patterns differ markedly between urban and rural households, technological progress also changes the composition of demand. Having argued that economic growth depends on technological progress and that technological progress entails structural change, Kuznets concluded that obstacles to structural change impede economic growth: "One basic requirement of modern economic growth is . . . the capacity of society to accommodate itself to the shifts and displacement involved in . . . labor and capital, without putting so high a price on this adjustment as to starve the growing industries of the resources needed for growth."[4] Turned on its head, the argument implies that economies which sustain smooth and rapid growth are economies in which resources flow freely among economic activities.

French Economic Culture

In France, worried the skeptics, resources seemed to be allocated highly rigidly.[5] Restrictive practices of government and business, they argued, distorted market signals, and hyperconservatism inhibited both households and enterprises from responding sensitively to such changes in market opportunities as did occur.[6] The hyperconservative market behavior of households was said to result from a culture in which people derive unusually great satisfaction from regional and occupational identities, from self-employment, and from rural life-styles. In such a culture, opportunities to earn extra income will not always induce people to shed their current activities. To preserve social status, for example, people self-employed in rickety family firms

4. Ibid., pp. 157–58.

5. The term *rigidly* is not devoid of ambiguity. A rigid allocation of resources could be defined as one that fails to differ from its predecessors. Or it could be one that fails to change when (but only when) parameters of cost or demand change. In this book, rigidity is used in the second sense.

6. *Malthusianism* rather than *hyperconservatism* is the word usually employed in the French context. Malthusian behavior, like rigid resource allocation, can be interpreted in several ways. It can mean "repetitious," in the sense that today's behavior blindly follows yesterday's precedent. It can mean "risk-averse." Or it can mean that people enjoy the status quo. In this book Malthusianism is equated with deriving great pleasure from nonmarket goods, such that marginal utilities of income are low (at all utility levels) and fall as income rises.

might resist lucrative but anonymous salaried employment for quite some time.

In agriculture and manufacturing, self-employment meant ownership of a family firm. In many industries family firms supplied the bulk of production. Instead of trying single-mindedly to maximize profit, the owners of such firms attached great weight to preserving direct control over their business operations. This often meant avoiding investments that could not be financed with family funds. As a result, in industries where technological change required modernization of plant and equipment or rapid expansion of production capacity, family firms could be expected to underinvest by the standards of profit maximization. Moreover, to the extent that preservation of family control was considered a major luxury, owners of family firms displayed marginal utilities of money that fell as incomes rose. This led them to behave in risk-averse fashion, a second form of conservatism.

Conservative market behavior remained viable because it was backed by public and private restraints of trade. In a competitive market, companies that fail to invest in best-practice methods of production are vulnerable to competition from productively efficient rivals. Fearing political fallout, however, the governments of the Third Republic worked hard to ensure that such competition did not arise.[7] Arguing that competition had to be organized and managed before it could serve the public interest, government insulated the domestic market from foreign sellers, regulated the prices of domestic sellers, subsidized inefficient firms, and tolerated cartels. In so doing, it blurred the signals of the marketplace and reinforced the conservatism reflected in the negligible sensitivities of individuals to market opportunities.[8] In such an environment, Malthusian enterprises could gratify their inclinations to behave defensively by protecting existing positions in lieu of developing competitive advantages.[9] Fearing government retaliation, even naturally aggressive enterprises failed to

7. See Kuisel, *Capitalism and the State in Modern France*, chap. 1.

8. See the famous study known as the Armand-Rueff report (*Rapport sur les Obstacles à l'Expansion Economique*), commissioned by government during the Fourth Republic; it is reprinted in Rueff, *Combats pour l'Ordre Financier*, especially pp. 371–72.

9. This is the language of strategic management. See Porter, *Competitive Advantage*, pp. 482–536.

Table 1. *Growth of GDP, by Country, Selected Periods, 1950–85*[a]
Percent increase in volume of GDP

Period	France	Germany	Italy	Japan	United Kingdom	United States
1950–58	41	84	54	89	20	27
1958–73	123	108	122	352	63	81
1973–85	28	24	27	56	17	30
1950–85	306	374	334	1,233	129	200
1958–85	187	157	181	606	91	136

Sources: Maddison, *Phases of Capitalist Development*, table A8; OECD, *National Accounts of OECD Countries, 1950–1979*, vol. 1: *Main Aggregates*; and OECD, *National Accounts, 1960–1985*, vol. 1: *Main Aggregates*.
a. Row 4 is derived from rows 1–3; row 5 is derived from rows 2 and 3.

adopt offensive strategies.[10] Few were the firms that innovated or imitated the new products and processes that stimulate growth and structural change.

From the standpoint of the individual household or enterprise, hyperconservatism, risk-aversion, and defensive behavior are not irrational per se. Rationality depends on the tastes of the individual and on the environment created by government regulation. Regardless of its private logic, however, rigid, defensive behavior does not promote structural change. If individuals and companies do not respond sensitively to unsuppressed market opportunities, resources will not flow toward uses considered especially productive in market terms, and sustained growth of market output will be jeopardized.

French Economic Growth

Despite the alleged incompatibility between French economic culture and modern economic growth, the French economy expanded rapidly and smoothly after World War II, quadrupling in size between 1950 and 1985 (table 1). GDP grew especially rapidly between 1958 and 1973. Output per capita also grew rapidly (appendix table A-1), and from 1960 to 1985 real income per capita doubled.[11] Before the first oil shock the growth rate hardly changed from one year to the next, and even afterward, when growth decelerated, it avoided extreme volatility.

10. Landes, "French Business and the Businessman," p. 349.
11. Studies of postwar changes in the standard of living include Fourastié, *Les Trente Glorieuses ou la Révolution Invisible de 1946 à 1975*; and Vangrevelinghe, "Les Niveaux de Vie en France, 1956 et 1965."

Table 2. *Growth of GDP, by Country, 1870–99, 1900–29, 1950–79*[a]
Percent increase in volume of GDP

Period	France	Germany	Italy	Japan	United Kingdom	United States
1870–99	60	116	22	98	86	240
1900–29	57	77	87	146	36	170
1950–79	278	342	299	966	111	173

Source: Maddison, *Phases of Capitalist Development*, tables A6, A7, A8.
a. Source controls for changes in national boundaries.

To appreciate this growth performance, one must compare it with some benchmark. One frame of reference is the French economy before World War II. The figures of Angus Maddison suggest that the best growth performance between 1870 and 1940 occurred between 1921 and 1929, when real GDP grew by 56 percent; in comparison, GDP grew by only 41 percent between 1950 and 1958.[12] During 1922 alone, it grew by 16 percent, far more than in any year after World War II. No wonder some economic historians consider French growth to be a twentieth century, not a postwar, phenomenon.[13] Nevertheless, growth did accelerate after World War II. Starting in 1870 it took forty-two years for GDP to double. Starting in 1890 it took thirty-nine years for GDP to double. After the war the economy doubled in size in a third that amount of time: between 1950 and 1965 and also between 1959 and 1972.[14] And unlike the prewar economy, it grew steadily. Between 1870 and World War I, GDP declined absolutely on twelve occasions; between the two world wars it contracted on seven. GDP was the same in 1948 as it had been in 1939 and 1929. But during the four decades following World War II, it never failed to grow from one year to the next.

All of the large rich economies grew faster after World War II than before, and only the American grew more rapidly at the end of the nineteenth century than after 1950 (table 2). It is important, therefore,

12. Maddison, *Phases of Capitalist Development*, tables A6, A7, A8.
13. Thus Caron, *An Economic History of Modern France*, pp. 266–67, warns against making "too great a contrast between a totally conservative and Malthusian period before 1940 and a post-1945 period which was wholly dynamic." Two historical perspectives on French growth that emphasize early dynamism are Roehl, "French Industrialization"; and O'Brien and Keyder, *Economic Growth in Britain and France, 1780–1914*.
14. Maddison, *Phases of Capitalist Development*, tables A6, A7, A8.

also to compare French postwar growth with its counterparts in comparable countries. Between 1950 and 1985, in terms of GDP and GDP per capita, France occupied a middling slot in the big-six growth league. Its performance rested comfortably above those of the United States and Britain but unmistakably below those of Japan, Germany, and Italy.

To some extent, however, the impressive growth of these last three is attributable to postwar reconstruction.[15] After formation of the EEC, France's relative growth increased sharply. Between 1958 and 1985, France trailed only Japan while tying Italy (see tables 1 and A-1). Germany was close behind—but behind nonetheless. Since the first oil shock, GDP has continued to grow more rapidly in France than in other European countries; in per capita terms, however, Germany has regained the head of the European standings.

International differences in growth rates modify relative standards of living. Both the World Bank and the Organization for Economic Cooperation and Development have compared living standards internationally using purchasing-power-parity exchange rates (appendix table A-2).[16] From 1950 to 1980 France reduced its disadvantage relative to the United States from 100 percent to 20 percent. Relative to the United Kingdom, it converted a 20 percent disadvantage into a 20 percent advantage. By Continental standards, France looked especially good between 1960 and 1975. Italy started and ended the period with two-thirds the per capita income of France. The average German began the period with 15 percent more income than the average Frenchman but ended with the same standard of living. Although French per capita income lost ground to those of Italy and Germany after 1975, it remained larger than the Italian and close to the German mark.

Strong as it was, however, the tendency of the postwar French economy to expand may not be its most impressive feature. Between 1958 and 1985, expansion also proceeded more smoothly than in other

15. The first year after 1944 in which GDP surpassed its pre-1940 maximum was 1945 for the United States and the United Kingdom, 1949 for France, 1950 for Italy, 1952 for Germany, and 1954 for Japan.

16. Because the World Bank has taken great pains to examine consumption patterns in a large number of countries, I shall emphasize its evidence in the text.

large rich countries, with the sometime exception of Japan (see table A-3). Indeed, France's growth was sufficiently stable to appear inevitable. No other European power could claim as much.

Some Hypotheses

Why did the French economy grow smoothly and rapidly for twenty-five years when the bulk of expert opinion believed such growth was impossible? How does one reconcile the economy's alleged lethargy before World War II with its apparent dynamism thereafter? Three broad hypotheses merit careful attention.[17]

HYPOTHESIS 1:
RIGIDITY AND GROWTH ARE COMPATIBLE

To explore the hypothesis that rigidity and growth are compatible, it is useful to distinguish two types of structural change. The first is accomplished through retirements from and new participations in the economy's stock of resources. The second is accomplished through redeployment of resources already in use. I shall refer to these types of structural change as *marginal* and *radical,* respectively. Since strictly marginal change does not require people to change jobs or residential locations, it is compatible with the conservative market behavior attributed to French households and enterprises.[18] Economic growth would not be precluded by hyperconservative economic culture.

There are two reasons to believe that French growth entailed simply marginal doses of structural change—the rapid pace of aggregate growth and the continued importance of traditional products.

The pace at which growth proceeds affects the likelihood that growth-induced structural change will be radical. Imagine an economy composed of two industries. Initially, each industry produces 50

17. A fourth hypothesis, which I shall not explore, asserts that certain forms of rigidity actually promote economic growth and structural change. See Dore, *Flexible Rigidities*; and Hirschman, *The Strategy of Economic Development.*

18. This argument assumes that the proclivities of one generation are not necessarily those of the subsequent generation—that a miner wishes to remain a miner, but a miner's child feels no special attraction to the occupation before choosing his or her first line of work.

percent of national output and employs 50 percent of each national resource. Assume industry A increases its shares of output and all resources by 5 percentage points annually for four years. Accordingly, industry B will experience annual declines of 5 percentage points in its shares of output and resources. After the four years of structural change, the relative importance of the two industries stabilizes, with industry A accounting for 70 percent of economic activity.

If aggregate output and all net resource endowments increase by 1 percent annually in perpetuity, industry B must contract absolutely. During the first year of structural change, output and employment will decrease by 10 percent; by the end of four years, at least 38 percent of its original labor force will have retired or found employment in industry A.[19] The same holds true of other resources.

If aggregate output and resource endowments grow by 10 percent annually, however, industry B will not have to contract as sharply. During the first year of structural change, it will barely contract absolutely; at the end of the transformation period it will employ almost 90 percent as many people as it had before its loss of output share. Thereafter, employment will grow. As a result, fewer of those it employs must contemplate retirement or migration to industry A.

Both these examples involve structural change, but the former is the more radical. Together they suggest that economies growing rapidly in available resources as well as in output may not need to redeploy many resources already in use. As a result, rapid growth may not test an economy's ability to allocate resources flexibly. (I do not wish to suggest, however, that the relationship between pace of growth and likelihood of radical structural change is necessarily negative; very rapid growth might well require great reallocation of resources.) Paradoxically, then, rapid growth may facilitate inertial behavior. In contrast, the degree of structural change probably does affect positively the degree of mobility.

The composition of French output provides a second reason why rigidity and growth might be compatible. At the end of World War II, France devoted more of its resources to agriculture and to small-scale production of differentiated products than did other European

19. Retirement is compatible with the assumptions underlying the example to the extent that labor requirements in industry A can be met through entries into the labor force.

countries. If growth entailed continued emphasis on such goods, only marginal reallocation of resources would have been required.

During the 1950s many believed that France would become the breadbasket of the European Economic Community, exporting agricultural products to Germany in return for heavy manufactures. Economic integration would stimulate growth throughout Europe, so that agriculture would decline in importance for the EEC as a whole. For France, however, the growth inspired by integration would result in continued reliance on the primary sector.

Similar reasoning could be applied to small-scale manufacturing. For EEC members in the aggregate, improvements in the standard of living fostered by economic integration would swell consumption of products with income-elastic demand. Given the favorable image of French luxuries in many lines of mature business, from food to textiles, France could be expected to account for more than its share of community supply. And such luxuries tend to be produced in relatively small plants and companies.

HYPOTHESIS 2:
GOVERNMENT REDESIGNED THE ECONOMY

After World War II the French government implemented a variety of policies designed to promote structural change. Some aimed to channel resources in specific directions. Others tried simply to reduce the risk, or increase the expected net reward, associated with mobility. Perhaps these policies succeeded.

The most famous policy of this sort was indicative planning. Every five years or so, the government convened commissions composed of representatives of government, business, and labor to study the economy. Some were organized by broad line of business; others focused on labor or finance and hence cut across industry boundaries. During the early years of planning, government proposed ambitious rates of growth, and the commissions discussed ways to achieve them. The purpose of these deliberations was to convince business enterprises that expansive behavior was safe. As long as all parties acted according to plan, none would lack for markets or inputs. In other words, government sought to compensate for ingrained risk-aversion by reducing perceived levels of risk.[20]

20. See especially Massé, *Le Plan ou l'Anti-Hasard*. Not everyone shares this

Government also developed industrial and regional policies. The first economic plan (1947–52), drafted before wartime shortages had abated, announced government's intention to promote industries considered critical to general reconstruction and growth. In effect, then, the plan constituted an embryonic form of industrial policy. Throughout the postwar period, but to different degrees at different times, government fostered expansion of specific industries and regions.

Whereas industrial and regional policies were selective, other policies promoted innovation, and hence mobility of resources, throughout the economy. For example, virtually all industrial enterprises qualified for tax breaks that reduced the cost of investing in plant and equipment. Most also qualified for research and development subsidies that reduced both the risk and the expected cost of introducing new products and production methods. The impact of these policies on private decisions is not always easy to judge. For example, government support frequently took the form of lending money to those conducting R&D, with repayment contingent on the success of the project. Such coinsurance encouraged risky research, but it also reduced the incentive to succeed. Structural change results primarily from successful research projects.

Indicative planning, industrial policy, and the more general policies just described all aimed to promote structural change or flexibility in the allocation of resources.[21] Some instruments of policy, such as creation of public enterprises, withdrew decisionmaking entirely from private hands. Others, such as subsidization, aimed simply to modify the parameters of private choice. In all cases, however, the aim was to insert government initiative into the process of resource allocation.

idyllic view of process and result. For example Estrin and Holmes, *French Planning in Theory and Practice*, argue that the plans rarely met their targets exactly and frequently had to be altered in midstream. Nevertheless, to say that uncertainty remained is not to say that it was not reduced; see Carré, Dubois, and Malinvaud, *La Croissance Française*, chap. 14.

21. Other policies, however, implemented for other reasons, also impinged heavily on the mobility of resources. For example, the expansion of the welfare state to protect most of the population from a wide variety of risks may well have reduced the cost and risk of changing jobs because most fringe benefits now traveled with a relocated worker and the failure of a new job to pan out placed a smaller fraction of total remuneration in jeopardy. But the expansion also reduced the penalty for failure to migrate toward work offering higher wages.

HYPOTHESIS 3:

HOUSEHOLDS AND COMPANIES RESPONDED FLEXIBLY
TO CHANGES IN THEIR ENVIRONMENT

For individual households and enterprises, government's structural policies were not the only environmental parameters to change after World War II. Even if government had not attempted to promote structural change, households and businesses might have adopted new patterns of behavior more consistent with flexibility in resource allocation.

In the first place, individual behavior is conditioned by the macroeconomic environment. As the economy continued to grow smoothly and rapidly, conservative and risk-averse households might have come to expect low unemployment.[22] Such an expectation might have encouraged people to change occupations or residential locations in search of better-paying jobs. Similarly, even risk-averse businesses might have perceived the desirability of expanding capacity, creating opportunities for embodiment of technological change.

In the second place, after World War II most French businesses found themselves subjected to increased market competition, and such competition might have encouraged more flexible behavior. French participation in the European Communities meant increased exposure to European competitors, and participation in the General Agreement on Tariffs and Trade meant increased competition from outside Europe. Decolonization forced French businesses to rely less on sheltered foreign markets. And domestic legislation prohibiting refusal to sell promoted competition in certain sectors insulated naturally from international trade.[23]

Not only did competition increase, but it increased in seemingly permanent fashion. France had proposed and then accepted European integration because it had hoped to avoid another war with Germany;

22. For the influence of the macroeconomic environment see Carré, Dubois, and Malinvaud, *La Croissance Française*, p. 608.

23. Caron, *Economic History of Modern France*, goes so far as to argue that the organizing theme of French economic policy since the war has been the dismemberment of the managed economy. For example, he contends that "one of the ideas which inspired [the founding fathers of the European Coal and Steel Community and the EEC] was the wish to make French producers 'restructure' under pressure from foreign competition" (p. 325).

revised calculations of economic costs and benefits were unlikely to provoke withdrawal from the EC. Similarly, French tenacity in Algeria engendered such bitterness and hostility that continued economic contact along quasi-colonial lines was clearly impossible.

The rise of competition might have caused households and enterprises to respond more readily to market signals, even if they remained risk-averse by nature. Public and private restraints of competition often aim to neutralize the effects of shifts in supply or demand. If neither the regulators nor the market mechanism is sure to prevail, the system can breed serious uncertainty for individuals. To the extent that competition clarified and amplified signals emanating from French markets, greater flexibility of individual behavior might be expected.

Increased competition might also have prompted cautious companies to reassess the relative merits of innovative and defensive behavior. Risk-aversion need not prompt individuals to embrace the status quo: in choosing between types of behavior, the cautious person evaluates the risk of each strategy in relation to the other. (For example, consider the effects of inflation on choices among forms of saving. Before World War II the French loved to place their savings in government bonds. After the war, with the onset of serious but imperfectly predictable inflation, households began to place their money in more risky assets. Although inflation might have increased the risk attached to all assets, it probably served to reduce the relative risk of less conservative securities.)[24]

In an oligopolistic or monopolistic market, risk might seem to attach disproportionately to innovation. Powerful firms may perceive the advantages of the familiar strategies that have enabled them to achieve their presently desirable positions, while the ramifications of innovation may appear uncharted and hence relatively risky. Accordingly, they may rely on "the fast second," a strategy of not being the first to rock the boat but of using their resources to reply quickly to moves initiated by others. In a competitive market, however, risk may be distributed more symmetrically between innovative and conservative behavior. The risk of innovation may be great; but unless government can be induced to protect established positions, the risk

24. See Michalet, *Les Placements des Epargnants Français de 1815 à Nos Jours,* as quoted in Boltanski, *Les Cadres,* p. 107, note 7.

of failing to develop competitive advantages may be even greater. Without the opportunity to draw on the assets of power, a firm may find that it cannot respond quickly enough to a rival's innovations unless it has been investing in its own sources of advantage. Once those advantages are developed, the competitive firm is likely to put them to use.

The commitment of the French government to European integration, coupled with its obvious inability to impose neocolonialism on Indochina and Algeria, meant that business could not rely on government to protect established positions. With the onset of vigorous market competition, the prudent firm would appreciate the arms-race analogy and attempt to develop new sources of competitive advantage.

In sum, perhaps the alleged rarity of innovative behavior before World War II should be attributed less to immutable features of French culture than to specific parameters of the French economic environment. When those parameters changed in credibly permanent fashion, behavior changed accordingly. David Landes has summarized clearly and perceptively the two basic views on the relationship between French economic culture and French economic performance:

Roughly speaking . . . the debate has been between two schools. The first feels that the relatively slower industrial development of France by comparison with Britain and, later, Germany from the mid-eighteenth century to World War I can be attributed in significant part to the conservatism, caution, and limited horizons ("Malthusianism") of French entrepreneurs, reinforced by anticapitalist and anticompetitive attitudes on the part of the population as a whole and also by a value system that deprecated business by comparison with more honorific roles. The second school argues that value systems are symptoms rather than causes, that French business behavior has been as effective as conditions have allowed, that growth was more rapid than is commonly admitted, and that insofar as France lagged technologically, she did so because relative factor costs (scarcity of coal, high cost of capital) provided less incentive for adoption of the new industrial machinery. . . . The pace and character of French entrepreneurship was set by family firms, owned and managed by blood relations, whose primary concerns were safety, continuity, and privacy. Not that there were no corporate units mobilizing the capital of strangers; there were, particularly in the capital-intensive branches of transport, metallurgy, mining, and heavy chemicals. But these entrepreneurs preferred the surplus profits of protected markets to price competition and were content to let the less efficient family enterprises lead the way; while this tacit entente was sanctioned by public opinion and sustained by commercial policy.[25]

Plan of the Book

This book examines the plausibility of each of the foregoing explanations of postwar growth. Given the breadth and complexity of each hypothesis, as well as the absence of complete and prefabricated data sets, formal evaluation would quickly degenerate into pseudo-rigor.[26] I therefore rely on less definitive, if still ambitious, procedures designed to illuminate the facts and promote the sophistication of future analysis. Toward this end, I discuss each hypothesis separately, emphasizing the presentation of systematic quantitative information.

Chapter 2 explores the extent of structural change since World War II. The evidence leaves no doubt that French economic structure has changed pervasively during the past four decades, and most of the changes accord perfectly with Kuznets's predictions. Employment in agriculture contracted absolutely as well as relatively. Mining and textiles also contracted sharply, as did self-employment. Until 1975, small plants accounted for decreasing shares of employment, although they have since bounced back. Given the profundity of structural change, it is surprising to find that much of it is marginal in the sense defined above. Nevertheless, personal mobility occurred sufficiently frequently that resources appear to have flowed freely among uses. Although not devoid of merit, the first broad hypothesis—that the French experience demonstrates the compatibility of rigidity and growth—does not appear persuasive.

Chapter 3 examines the government's deliberate efforts to restructure the economy. The first part describes the philosophy and

25. Landes, "Religion and Enterprise," pp. 41–42.
26. This is the methodological conclusion I draw from Carré, Dubois, and Malinvaud, *La Croissance Française*—the most important study in the field.

instruments of intervention. The rest emphasizes the impact of government policy on company behavior and market outcomes. Broadly speaking, I argue that government intervened considerably and subtly in the allocation of resources; in several narrowly defined activities, for better or worse, it determined market performance. Nevertheless, from the perspective of business, government's initiatives rarely impinged decisively on market behavior. Surprisingly, perhaps, government did not enjoy substantial leverage over a broad range of activities. The actual range may well have been too limited to explain the pervasive structural change that occurred after World War II.

Chapter 4 chronicles the rise of competition occasioned by changes in the international environment. After describing the timing and mechanics of the institutional changes associated with the ECSC, EEC, GATT, and decolonization, I attempt to assess the impact of institutional change on the exposure of French firms to foreign rivals and to genuine competition. The evidence suggests that French firms were indeed exposed to foreigners—through international investment as well as through international trade—both at home and abroad. Such exposure did not always create competition of textbook quality, but it unquestionably forced French firms to pursue competitive advantage assiduously. The avalanche of competition that occurred after World War II was powerful and broad enough not only to explain government's indulgence in structural policies but also to overwhelm most effects of such policies on the composition of economic activity.

Chapter 5 explores the rise of competition in retail trade, a sector not heavily exposed to foreign competition. Although changes in domestic economic policy were neither as profound nor as permanent as those in the international environment, they did generate appreciable competition in a sector often vilified for its conservatism.

Chapter 6 presents my conclusions on France's economic prospects and my speculation on their applicability to revitalization of the American economy. To avoid false drama, let me warn the reader not to expect a verdict that attributes all or none of French success to government. To the extent that structural policy worked well, it did so because it was implemented in an environment characterized by credibly permanent exposure to foreign competition. And if the rise of competition seemed to work wonders, it did not occur naturally. Government's behavior, often in pursuit of objectives outside the economic arena, caused competition to thrive. Government leadership definitely mattered, but the task of the open-minded analyst is to establish when and how public artifice mixed with nature to generate high levels of economic performance.

2 | The Extent of Structural Change

IF ECONOMIC growth requires structural change, and if French culture inhibits structural change, then how could the French economy have grown so rapidly and sustainedly after World War II? This chapter explores the possibility that the French pattern of growth did not entail much structural change. In particular, it explores the possibility that economic structure changed only marginally (as defined in chapter 1), so that resources already in use did not have to be redeployed.

Output and Employment at the Industry Level

Between 1959 and 1980, French output increased in the aggregate by 168 percent.[1] At the industry level, output grew on average by 235 percent, and among manufacturing industries it grew on average by 203 percent. Growth was pervasive enough to permit easy rejection of the hypothesis that production tended to remain fixed at the industry level (appendix table A-4). Still, output did not grow proportionately: in five industries it declined (table 3). At the other end of the spectrum, eleven industries grew by more than 500 percent (table 4), and another six produced three to four times as much in 1980 as they had in 1959 (table 3).

Disproportionate growth altered the industrial composition of output. The combined output of the twenty-two industries that failed to double in size fell from 38 percent of the total in 1959 to 23 percent

1. The best information on output structure comes from input-output tables constructed annually since 1959 that decompose the economy into seventy-nine activities. For data on broadly defined industries covering 1949–59, see INSEE, *Comptes Nationaux de la Base 1956, Séries 1949–1959: Séries Longues Macroéconomiques*, pp. 3–13.

Table 3. *Distribution of Industries by Growth of Output, 1959–80*[a]

Percent growth 1959–80	Number of industries	Share of total output 1959[b]	Share of total output 1980[b]
Less than 0	5	1.5	0.3
0–99	17	36.2	23.2
100–199	23	34.4	31.6
200–299	17	18.2	24.6
300–399	6	5.5	9.2
400–499	0	0	0
500 or more	11	4.1	11.1

Source: INSEE input-output tables in 1970 prices, level S (unpublished).
a. Industries defined according to NAP-S79 (see appendix C).
b. *Production distribuée* in 1970 prices.

in 1980. The combined output of the eleven industries that grew by at least 500 percent increased from 4 percent to 11 percent of the total. In manufacturing, the collective output share of the twelve industries that failed to double in size declined from 30 percent in 1959 to 18 percent in 1980; the share associated with the five industries that increased output by more than 500 percent rose from 5 percent to 12 percent.

Given the small number of activities in which output contracted absolutely, one might be tempted to conclude that structural change could occur even if the economic system were undernourished in flexibility. Nevertheless, the Kuznets proposition that production functions change fundamentally during periods of rapid growth compels us to proceed from the realm of output to the allocation of resources.

Social rigidity can be expected to impinge most directly on the mobility of working people.[2] During much of the postwar period, the labor force failed to expand—indeed, it was larger in 1921 than in any census year until 1968.[3] As a result, changes in the composition of employment entailed absolute contraction of certain types of work, increasing the likelihood of radical change in the structure of employment. (The extent to which employed people change jobs depends, of course, on many factors, including interindustry differences in the

2. Readers wishing to study the stock of physical capital should consult Carré, Dubois, and Malinvaud, *La Croissance Française*, chaps. 4, 5; and INSEE, *Le Mouvement Economique en France, 1949–1979*, chap. 1.3.

3. Carré, Dubois, and Malinvaud, *La Croissance Française*, table 9.

Table 4. *Industries with Declining Output or with Output Growth Greater than 500 Percent, 1959–80*[a]
Production *distribuée* in millions of 1970 francs

Code	Industry	Output in 1959	Percent change 1959–80
Declining industries			
051	Crude petroleum	162	−17
451	Leather	1,476	−17
042	Coke	2,425	−35
09	Ferrous minerals	675	−40
041	Coal/lignite	5,882	−71
High-growth industries			
89	Finance	7,187	513
19	Drugs	2,549	535
75	Telecommunications	5,061	546
07	Gas, except natural gas	1,027	576
53	Plastics products	1,987	593
172	Bulk organic chemicals	2,706	614
27	Office equipment, including computers	4,716	631
292	Home electronics	584	651
82-3	Private education and R&D	1,103	690
56	Scrap products	478	810
80	Equipment rental	1,185	1,761

Source: INSEE input-output tables in 1970 prices, level S (unpublished).
a. Industries defined according to NAP-S79 (see appendix C).

growth of labor productivity, in the demographic structure of those employed, and in the rate of voluntary separation.)

Between 1954 and 1975, employment increased by 11 percent in the aggregate and by 22 percent in manufacturing (appendix table A-5).[4] At the industry level, however, rates of growth varied widely around these weighted means. In eight of thirty-two industries, employment fell absolutely; in fourteen of the remaining twenty-four, it increased by 50 percent or more (appendix table A-6). Employment

4. The best information on employment appears in the census of population. Since World War II, censuses have been conducted in 1946, 1954, 1962, 1968, 1975, and 1982. In several important respects, the methods used in 1946 differed from those used thereafter. For example, the 1946 census considered the spouses and adolescent children of farmers as employed in agriculture unless they explicitly declared themselves to be students or employed in another activity. Starting in 1954 such dependents were considered employed in agriculture only if they declared themselves so to be. Comparisons between 1946 and 1954 would thus overestimate the decline in agricultural employment. See INSEE, *Recensement Général de la Population de*

more than doubled in electrical and electronic equipment (148 percent) and in finance and insurance (147 percent). As a result of differential growth, the distribution of employment among industries changed markedly. The fourteen in which employment grew most rapidly increased their share of total employment from 37 percent to 57 percent. Meanwhile, the employment share of the eight in which employment contracted dropped from 41 percent to 18 percent. The frequency and severity of employment contraction make it impossible to reject the hypothesis, for all industries or for manufacturing alone, that employment tended to identical levels in 1954 and 1975 (appendix table A-7).

The pattern of structural change thus differed between output and employment.[5] In the first place, among growing industries, the rate of expansion varied more in terms of output than in terms of employment. Among the twenty-four industries in which employment grew, it doubled in just two cases and tripled in none. Among the seventy-four industries in which output increased, it doubled in fifty-seven and tripled in thirty-four (table 3). In other words, the average product of labor grew at very different rates in different branches of the economy.

Employment and output also differed in the frequency of absolute contraction. Only five of seventy-nine industries, accounting for less than 2 percent of aggregate output in 1959, experienced declining output. In eight of thirty-two industries, accounting for 41 percent of aggregate employment in 1954, employment fell. Despite positive growth of output in most activities, employment declined absolutely in several.

Mai 1954: Résultats du Sondage au 1/20ème, Population-Ménages-Logements, France Entière, p. 9. As a result, I focus on the period starting in 1954. Because of changes in the scheme of industrial classification that occurred in 1974, it is necessary to examine separately the periods 1954–75 and 1975–82. Given my interest here in the long term, I shall emphasize the earlier period. The classification scheme used for this period (MCBCND) decomposes the economy into thirty-seven activities, eighteen of them in manufacturing.

5. Although growth of output is measured for the twenty-two years starting in 1959 while growth of employment is monitored for the twenty-two years starting in 1954, discrepancy in period is unlikely to explain the differences discussed in the text.

Table 5. *Industries in Which Employment Declined, 1954–75*[a]

Code	Industry	Employment 1954	Change 1954–75	Percent change 1954–75
09	Iron ore, iron, and crude steel	226,500	− 3,365	− 1
20	Wood, including furniture	314,700	− 27,335	− 9
19	Leather, including shoes	229,900	− 84,615	− 37
18	Apparel	475,400	− 148,585	− 31
03	Coal	258,100	− 171,605	− 66
17	Textiles	652,900	− 269,910	− 41
36	Household service	593,000	− 273,990	− 46
01	Agriculture[b]	5,043,100	− 3,045,505	− 60

Sources: Praderie and Carré, "La Population Active par Secteur d'Etablissement," pp. 9–17; and INSEE D67, p. 188.
a. Losses net of jobs created. Industries defined according to MCBCND (see appendix C).
b. Includes forest products and fish.

Contractions in employment were often severe. The eight industries in which employment fell suffered a combined net loss of more than 4 million jobs, representing 50 percent of their combined employment in 1954 (table A-6). Agriculture suffered the greatest loss of jobs— over 3 million, or 60 percent of agricultural employment in 1954 (table 5). But agriculture was not the only industry from which employment hemorrhaged: apparel, coal, textiles, and domestic service each lost more than 100,000 jobs. In coal, employment declined by two-thirds.

Although employment declined sharply in a few industries, large numbers of people did not necessarily change jobs. Conceivably death and retirement accounted for most of the contraction, especially if few people entering the labor force or employed in other parts of the economy came to work in declining industries. To assess the need for reallocation of labor resources, one cannot simply measure net declines in employment at the industry level.

On three different occasions since World War II—1964, 1970, and 1977—the Institut National de la Statistique et des Etudes Economiques investigated changes over time in the employment status of particular individuals.[6] In the last of these studies, INSEE asked each

6. See Praderie and Passagez, "La Mobilité Professionnelle en France entre 1959 et 1964"; INSEE D32; and INSEE D91. Preliminary findings from a fourth study (Enquête Formation-Qualification Professionnelle de 1985) appear in "La Mobilité Sociale et la Mobilité Professionnelle."

Table 6. *Labor Mobility, by Sex, Selected Declining Occupations,*
1972–77
Percent

Occupation in 1972	Employment status in 1977			
	Same occupation	Different occupation	Unemployed	Outside labor force
Farm owner				
Male	80.8	4.6	0.3	14.3
Female	71.3	4.1	1.0	23.6
Agricultural laborer				
Male	57.9	26.3	1.7	14.1
Female	36.4	26.9	3.0	33.6
Small shopkeeper				
Male	71.4	15.4	1.8	11.4
Female	70.3	9.3	0.6	19.8
Miner				
Male	49.6	11.5	*	38.9
Female	. . .	. . .	. . .	. . .
Household servant				
Male	65.5	22.5	12.0	*
Female	49.2	17.0	1.9	31.9

Source: INSEE D91, tables 57, 59.
* Less than 0.05 percent.

member of a sample drawn from the entire adult population to
describe both his current job (if any) and the job (if any) held five
years earlier.[7] As a result, this study permits one to compare the
propensity to retire with the propensity to migrate from particular
types of jobs.

Table 6 reveals the mobility between 1972 and 1977 of those
initially employed in occupations of declining importance. Among
men self-employed as farmers in 1972, 81 percent remained so
employed in 1977. On the other hand, only 50 percent of the men
employed as miners in 1972 were still working as miners in 1977. Of
particular interest is the relationship between the fraction of those
employed in the occupation in 1972 who were employed in a different
occupation in 1977 and the fraction of those employed in the occupation
in 1972 who were outside the labor force in 1977. Among men,
retirements outnumbered migrations from farm ownership and min-

7. INSEE's sampling procedure has changed over time. Its first two studies
focused exclusively on people employed at the end of the period observed. Excluded
thereby are people who retired during the period.

ing. In agricultural labor, small shopkeeping, and domestic service, migrations outnumbered retirements. Among women, exits from the labor force outnumbered changes of occupation; but exit from the labor force tends to be less definitive for women than for men. One should not conclude that women leaving jobs in contracting occupations exhibit little occupational mobility.

Even where exits outnumbered migrations, mobility was frequent. More than 25 percent of women employed as agricultural laborers in 1972 had other occupations five years later. Similarly, 17 percent of women working as domestic servants in 1972 had migrated to other occupations by 1977. Only the self-employed in agriculture in 1972 showed low occupational mobility: less than 5 percent of such men and women were employed in different occupations five years later. Although exceptional, this pattern is important because agriculture accounted for most of the absolute decline in employment.

For agricultural occupations, this type of analysis can be extended backward in time.[8] Of the 1,037,000 people who left agriculture between 1959 and 1970, 68 percent retired and 32 percent migrated to other occupations. Among salaried agricultural workers, mobility occurred more frequently: between 1959 and 1964, 50 percent of those who left agriculture remained in the labor force; the corresponding figure for 1965–70 was 54 percent. Granted, not all of these workers left agriculture, for some became self-employed farmers. Nevertheless, the decline of agricultural employment did entail the movement of many workers to new jobs.[9]

The surprisingly low incidence of mobility from agriculture may be explained in a variety of ways. First, redeployment tends to be easier

8. The data in this paragraph are taken from INSEE E46-47, table 13. This volume assembles a wealth of information on the demographic structure of those employed in agricultural occupations; its information on migration is taken from INSEE D32.

9. INSEE assigns occupations to workers on the basis of their principal activity. Thus farmers working part-time in manufacturing are considered farmers. If their manufacturing jobs come to account for the larger amount of their working effort, INSEE considers them to have migrated from agriculture to industry even if they remain and work on their farms. Such movements probably occurred frequently, yet they hardly entail the fundamental restructuring of employment announced in the text. Note, however, that the same logic, working in the opposite direction, implies that at least some of those found to enter agriculture were simply reducing the fraction of their labor time devoted to nonagricultural work. See INSEE E46–47, pp. 31, 34. See also Reignier, "La Pluriactivité en Agriculture."

for younger workers, and farmers tend to be old; 45 percent of those leaving agriculture for other occupations between 1965 and 1970 were thirty-five years of age or older. Second, those leaving agriculture often relocated geographically as well as occupationally: between 1965 and 1970, 50 percent of those leaving agriculture changed *communes,* 20 percent changed départements, and 14 percent changed regions.[10]

Unfortunately, agriculture is the only occupation for which such analysis can be conducted before 1972. It is impossible to present information for 1959–64 and 1965–70 that is comparable to that in table 6 because INSEE's sample for 1965–70 was restricted to people employed in 1970, and the sample for 1959–64 was restricted to people employed in both 1959 and 1964. The best one can do is to focus on those employed at both ends of each five-year period and then calculate the percentage that continued to be employed in their initial occupation. In other words, one cannot compare the frequency of mobility with the frequency of exit from the labor force, but one can compare the frequency of mobility with the frequency of occupational stability.

Table A-8 provides the relevant information for each period. The importance of mobility among those employed at the beginning and the end of each period differed markedly among occupations. Agricultural laborers and household servants tended to change occupations frequently, while self-employed farmers redeployed rarely. Among men self-employed in agriculture the frequency of mobility declined over time; among small shopkeepers it increased. Despite the infrequency of mobility, agriculture still accounted for 15 percent of all people changing occupations between 1959 and 1964.[11]

Turning from occupational to industrial mobility permits examination of such other pockets of contracting employment as coal and textiles (table 7). In coal as in agriculture, outward mobility occurred less frequently than average. In the textiles, apparel, and leather industries, however, it occurred more frequently than average, especially after 1964. Among men employed in this sector as of 1965 and employed somewhere in 1970, 25 percent were employed outside the sector in 1970. In other words, excluding those who left the labor

10. INSEE E46-47, p. 41, and app. table 15; see also Rattin, "Un Chef d'Exploitation Agricole sur Trois A Plus de 60 Ans."

11. Praderie and Passagez, "La Mobilité Professionnelle en France entre 1959 et 1964," table 47.

Table 7. *Labor Mobility, by Sex and Industry, 1959–77*
Percent

		Different industry in t + 5[a]					
		t = 1959		t = 1965		t = 1972	
Code	Industry in year t	M	F	M	F	M	F
01	Agriculture	11.0	6.1	11.0	11.0	9.3	5.5
02	Food	20.2	17.0	24.4	31.2	23.4	19.1
03	Coal	14.7	*	7.2	*	15.3	*
04–05	Electricity, water, byproduct gases	8.6	5.7	3.6	16.2	6.8	11.1
06	Petroleum	25.9	6.2	17.9	53.8	20.7	18.8
07–08	Building materials/glass	24.1	29.2	28.9	41.8	24.2	12.3
09–10	Basic metals/ores	16.8	*	16.2	21.5	10.6	12.7
11	Fabricated metals	n.a.	n.a.	31.1	47.1	21.1	21.9
12–15	Machinery	n.a.	n.a.	19.4	25.2	15.6	17.2
16	Chemicals	15.4	19.0	15.2	30.5	15.7	12.5
17–19	Textiles/apparel/leather	16.1	16.9	24.9	27.5	20.2	21.3
20–23	Wood, paper, miscellaneous	16.4	21.8	20.7	30.0	22.7	26.3
24	Construction	16.1	17.0	19.7	20.0	20.2	28.0
25	Transport	n.a.	n.a.	17.2	24.4	17.4	20.8
26	Telecommunications	n.a.	n.a.	8.0	16.5	5.7	8.3
27–28	Services	14.7	11.8	16.7	14.5	18.9	16.6
29	Wholesale/retail trade	14.9	14.3	22.8	16.2	22.0	17.4
30	Finance/insurance	9.8	10.7	11.1	10.2	10.3	12.4
31–32	National government/army	11.4	4.5	16.1	8.1	11.6	5.2
33	Local government	7.5	7.6	5.3	18.1	6.9	11.2
34	Social security	9.6	6.0	4.6	17.8	3.6	6.0
35	Miscellaneous organizations	11.8	12.9	23.6	25.7	17.2	17.2
36	Household service	20.0	22.1	25.7	30.8	29.1	24.2
	Mean value	15.0	12.0	17.0	23.4	16.0	15.2

Sources: INSEE D32, tables 3.5 bis, 3.6 bis; and INSEE D91, tables 110, 111.
n.a. Not available.
* Less than 0.05 percent.
a. Observation confined to people employed at both ends of the period. Industries defined according to MCBCND (see appendix C).

force or became unemployed, one male textile worker in four changed industries in just five years. The corresponding frequency for women was even higher.

The evidence examined here thus underscores the importance of distinguishing between marginal and radical structural change. In many of the occupations and industries where employment contracted severely, most of those who left chose to retire. Retirement was especially important in agriculture, the activity experiencing the largest decline of employment; and within agriculture the self-employed chose retirement far more frequently than they chose to take a new job. Retirements, unlike migrations between industries or occupations, cannot be counted against the hypothesis of rigidity in the labor force.[12]

Although entries to and exits from the labor force accounted for much of the postwar change in employment structure, they leave a considerable fraction of that change unexplained. Among those employed at both ends of a five-year period, interindustry migration sometimes exceeded 20 percent of initial industry employment. Even in agriculture, plump fractions of those departing took jobs elsewhere in the economy. Changes in the industrial composition of employment were effected in no small measure by personal mobility among industries.[13]

Self-Employment

When farmers leave their land and miners leave their pits to work in urban factories, they experience substantial changes in lifestyle—on and off the job. In such cases, it is plausible to believe that migration indicates flexibility in the allocation of labor resources. Nevertheless, one should not identify flexibility too closely with mobility of workers between industries or occupations. An electrician in the automobile industry does not revolutionize his life merely by becoming an electrician in the farm tractor industry, nor does the automotive electrician who moves to the paint shop of the plant where he already works. Still, profound changes in the allocation of people among employments can occur even if the industrial composition of employment remains unchanged.

Within each industry, some people work for wages while others work for themselves. Because employees tend to experience occupational lifestyles that differ from those of the self-employed, the

12. The psychological and pecuniary cost of mobility depends on the destination. Given the differential likelihood of household displacement, migration from agriculture to urban manufacturing is likely to be more costly than is migration to construction or transport. Those who wish to explore the destinations of mobile workers should consult the appendix tables in Praderie and Passagez, "La Mobilité Professionnelle en France entre 1959 et 1965," pp. 138–41, 144–47.

13. Recent trends in mobility are discussed in Cézard and Rault, "La Crise A Freiné la Mobilité Sectorielle." See also Thélot, "Mobilité Professionnelle Plus Forte entre 1965 et 1970 Qu'entre 1959 et 1964"; and Thélot, "A Propos de la Mobilité Interentreprises."

decision to stop working for oneself and to begin working for another is unlikely to be made lightly. Societies in which labor resources are allocated rigidly are unlikely to display rapid and substantial declines in the importance of self-employment even if economic growth encourages the division of labor and concentration of production.

The census of population allows one to observe changes in the importance of salaried employment between 1954 and 1982.[14] Between 1954 and 1975, salaried employment rose sharply as a proportion of total employment (appendix table A-9). In 1954 fewer than two jobs in three entailed working for others; by 1975 more than four jobs in five involved salaried status. Decreases in the importance of self-employment were felt in most activities. The hypothesis that salaried employment tended not to increase as a percentage of total employment can be rejected at the .01 level of statistical significance (appendix table A-10). Even so, the importance of salaried employment rose especially sharply outside manufacturing: in 1954, only 57 percent of nonmanufacturing jobs were salaried; by 1975 the fraction had risen to 77 percent. Self-employment declined not only in relation to salaried employment but also absolutely. The loss of 2.8 million self-employed jobs during this period amounted to 43 percent of the initial volume of such positions (table A-9). Although the percentage decline in unsalaried jobs was greater in manufacturing, nonmanufacturing industries accounted for 2.6 million of the 2.8 million disappearances.

Turning to the period 1975–82 the economy as a whole, but especially nonmanufacturing, displayed a qualitatively similar if quantitatively muted pattern (table A-9). The ratio of salaried to total employment increased, and the volume of unsalaried employment decreased. In the manufacturing sector, however, the pattern of the previous twenty-two years was reversed. The ratio of salaried to total employment fell slightly, the volume of salaried employment fell 10.5

14. In the evidence that follows, unsalaried workers include spouses and dependent children who help the head of household in a family enterprise. Called *aides familiaux*, they assume particular quantitative importance in agriculture and small shopkeeping. Since the taxes owed and subsidies received by a family are conditioned on whether dependents work as family helpers or as salaried employees, and since the relative benefits of the two categories have changed over time, movement from unsalaried to salaried status, or vice versa, can occur without genuine change in employment status. See Praderie and Passagez, "La Mobilité Professionnelle en France entre 1959 et 1964," p. 34.

percent, and the volume of unsalaried employment rose 0.5 percent. These findings are consistent with other recent observations of return to small-scale and independent employment.[15]

Returning to the period 1954–75, one discovers that the seven industries in which self-employment contributed at least one job in five as of 1954 each experienced a net decline in the volume of unsalaried work (appendix table A-11). In leather and in apparel, unsalaried work declined by roughly 75 percent; in agriculture, it declined by 59 percent. In all except agriculture, where the percentage decline in salaried employment exceeded that in unsalaried employment, the ratio of salaried to total employment rose. The increase was especially dramatic in wholesale and retail trade and in miscellaneous services. In both industries, self-employment accounted for half of all jobs in 1954 but only one-quarter in 1975. Both showed a substantial and simultaneous increase in salaried employment. Although all seven experienced a net loss of unsalaried jobs, agriculture accounted for most of the loss. Wholesale and retail trade was the only other activity in which unsalaried work declined by 100,000 or more jobs. Perhaps farmers and retailers accumulate relatively little industry-specific expertise.

Was the decline of self-employment effected primarily through retirements or primarily through redeployments? Using INSEE's study of labor mobility during 1972–77, one can compare the frequency with which the self-employed left the labor force to the frequency with which they migrated to salaried work (table 8). Among men who had been self-employed and without salaried help in 1972, 6 percent were salaried employees and 15 percent were outside the labor force in 1977. Among men who had employed salaried help in 1972, 7 percent were salaried employees themselves and 12 percent were outside the labor force in 1977. Only those men who were family helpers in 1972 showed a dramatic tendency to exhibit salaried status as of 1977. Otherwise, both women and men were more likely to leave the labor force than to accept a salaried job.

If one wishes simply to measure the frequency with which those employed at both ends of a five-year period had substituted salaried for unsalaried employment, he can examine the periods 1959–64 and

15. See Piore and Sabel, *The Second Industrial Divide.*

Table 8. *Mobility from Unsalaried to Salaried Work, by Sex, 1972–77*
Percent

Position in 1972		Position in 1977			
	Same	Employed in other unsalaried work	Employed in salaried work	Unem-ployed	Outside labor force
Self-employed					
No employees					
Male	74.0	4.8	5.7	0.7	14.8
Female	63.2	3.5	6.8	1.1	25.4
Employed others					
Male	72.7	8.4	7.2	0.2	11.5
Female	68.0	9.2	3.3	0.0	19.5
Family helper					
Male	41.9	33.9	18.3	1.1	4.7
Female	70.1	2.8	5.8	0.7	20.5

Source: INSEE D91, tables 53, 55.

1965–70, as well as 1972–77. For each five-year period—1959–64, 1965–70, and 1972–77—only men initially employed as family helpers showed any substantial tendency to migrate toward salaried work: during each period, one-fifth or so became salaried workers (appendix table A-12). In all other cases, fewer than 10 percent of those initially employed in unsalaried work were salaried five years later.

Although people who continued to work tended to remain unsalaried, many did move to salaried employment. Most of this movement occurred among those leaving agriculture. Among the estimated 44,400 men who were heads of agricultural households in 1959 but employed in nonagricultural occupations in 1964, 78 percent had become salaried. Among the estimated 87,200 men who were family helpers in agriculture in 1959 and employed outside agriculture in 1964, 23 percent had become salaried.

Thus worker mobility played the lesser role in modifications of the distribution of employment by type of remuneration. Absolute and relative declines of unsalaried employment were effected primarily through decisions of the unsalaried to leave the labor force, coupled with decisions of those entering the labor force to choose salaried status.[16] Nevertheless, considerable numbers of people, especially of self-employed farmers leaving agriculture—did go to work for others.

16. This is the conclusion of Praderie and Passagez, "La Mobilité Professionnelle

Size of Establishment

Even among salaried workers in a given activity, professional lifestyle can vary markedly with the size of the establishment in which work is performed. In a society characterized by strong and conservative tastes regarding working life, one would expect many people to be unwilling to abandon salaried positions in the small shops and factories that dominated the country before World War II. To the extent that growth encourages redeployment of labor to large units of production practicing minute division of labor, continued concentration of employment in small-scale production might suggest rigidity in the allocation of labor resources, although such concentration is consistent with other hypotheses as well (the economies of scale may be exhausted at relatively small rates of output; and in a world of open economies, realization of scale economies may not depend intimately on the size and hence growth of the *domestic* market).

Several sources contain information on changes in the distribution of salaried employment by size of plant.[17] Between 1954 and 1972 in most manufacturing industries, small plants accounted for declining shares of total employment (appendix table A-13).[18] This tendency,

---

en France entre 1959 et 1964," p. 49; see also Thévenot, "Les Catégories Sociales en 1975."

17. France has conducted only one true census of manufactures since World War II, the results of which appear in INSEE, *Recensement de l'Industrie, 1963*. But INSEE maintains a directory of industrial and commercial establishments that dates back to 1942. In principle the directory includes all industrial and commercial establishments in France. In practice, according to INSEE, the principal defect of the directory is the tardiness with which disappearing establishments—especially those employing no salaried workers—are removed. During the 1950s and 1960s the contents of the directory were published on various occasions under the title *Les Etablissements Industriels et Commerciaux en France*.

To minimize the possibility that observed changes in the distribution of employment by size of plant would merely reflect changes in the quality of INSEE's directory, I ignore all establishments with fewer than ten salaried workers. In its own annual survey of manufactures, the ministry of industry adopts the same criterion. Thus in this section "total employment" means "total salaried employment in plants with at least ten salaried workers." For 1954–62 the threshold is eleven salaried workers.

18. In this section, manufacturing industries are defined at the two-digit level according to either the *Nomenclature des Activités Économique* (NAE-2) or the *Nomenclatures d'Activités et de Produits* (NAP-100).

NAE-2 divides the manufacturing sector into forty-five two-digit industries. Because

however, was more significant in the statistical sense than it was in the economic sense (appendix tables A-14 and A-16). On average the contribution of small plants to industry employment did not decline appreciably. In some industries, however, the relative decline of small plants was quite pronounced, especially after 1962. From 1962 to 1972 plants with fewer than one-hundred employees lost at least 10 percentage points of employment share in ten industries (appendix table A-15); in no industry did the contribution of such plants to total employment increase by as much as 10 percentage points.

The relative decline of small plants from 1954 to 1962 resulted from the tendency of small plants to maintain employment and the tendency of certain larger plants, those with 51–500 employees and those with more than 1,000, to increase employment (table A-14). From 1962 to 1972, however, employment in the smallest plants, those with 10–19 employees, tended to contract absolutely as well as in relation to industry employment (appendix table A-16). Table A-15 shows the changes in employment levels and shares for plants with 10–99 employees in industries where such plants experienced the greatest relative declines. In all industries but one, plastics products, employment in small plants contracted absolutely as well as relatively. In general, then, pronounced loss of employment share involved absolute as well as relative contraction. Employment did not increase, however disproportionately, in plants of all sizes.

After 1972 small plants acquired a new importance in manufacturing industries. Between 1972 and 1982, plants with ten to forty-nine employees tended to increase not only their volume of employment but also their shares of industry totals (appendix table A-17).[19] Large

---

of changes in definition that occurred in 1959, I have had to exclude two of these industries (miscellaneous manufactures and plastics products) from the evidence covering 1954–62. Again, because of other lacunae in the primary sources, I have had to omit two industries (tobacco products and matches, and miscellaneous manufactures) from the evidence for 1962–72. During both periods the primary sources merge industries 23 and 24, 35 and 36, 17 and 185, and the rest of 18 and 16.

NAP divides the manufacturing sector into forty-four two-digit industries. The primary sources for 1972–82 and 1974–80 omit information on certain of them. Each classification is described fully in appendix C.

19. The data in appendix table A-17 are based on NAP. The primary source omits information on four industries (military products, meat, freshly baked goods, and tobacco products). The table thus reports information on forty industries. Differences

Table 9. *Change in Employment Share of Small and Large Plants, Selected Manufacturing Industries, 1972–82*[a]

Code	Industry	Share of industry employment		Percentage point change 1972–82	Change in salaried employment 1972–82	Change 1972–82 as percent of salaried employment in 1972
		1972	1982			
Small plants (10–49 salaried workers)						
24	Mechanical equipment I	15.1	26.1	10.9	26,068	68
22	Agricultural equipment	12.0	23.7	11.7	4,293	85
53	Plastics products	15.8	27.5	11.7	16,262	108
48	Wood	29.9	42.9	13.0	17,612	73
15	Building material	21.8	36.7	14.9	25,101	71
21	Metallic products	17.4	35.5	18.1	70,682	117
Large plants (500 or more salaried workers)						
27	Office equipment	87.4	61.8	−25.5	−3,508	−11
43	Man-made fibers	88.4	64.0	−24.4	−15,159	−70
11	Semifinished steel	68.2	47.5	−20.7	−27,063	−54
28	Electrical equipment	62.8	45.5	−17.3	−35,896	−27
45	Leather	12.7	1.6	−11.1	−4,359	−89
22	Agricultural equipment	41.1	30.7	−10.4	−5,097	−30

Sources: INSEE E43; and INSEE, *Les Entreprises et Leurs Etablissements au 1er Janvier 1983.*
a. Industries defined according to NAP-100 (see appendix C). Industries are those in which employment in small or large plants as a percentage of employment in all plants changed at least 10 percentage points.

plants tended to suffer decreasing shares of industry employment. By 1982 the distribution of employment by size of plant tended to be the same as it had been twenty years earlier, when the relative decline of small plants was beginning to hit full stride (appendix table A-18). Only plants of medium size exhibited a share of total employment in 1982 that differed significantly from its counterpart in 1962. The resurgence of small plants after 1972 was a general phenomenon (table A-13). The smallest plants increased their shares of employment in thirty-seven of forty industries. The next smallest accomplished the same feat in thirty-five industries. Plants with ten to forty-nine employees increased their shares by more than 10 percentage points in six (table 9). In four of these six, small plants had suffered substantial *decreases* in employment share between 1962 and 1972 (appendix table A-19).

The pervasive vitality of small plants after 1972 dovetails with the apparent vitality, already described, of self-employment after 1975.

in presentation between the sources for 1982 on the one hand and for 1962 and 1972 on the other hand require combination of two categories of plant (500–999 workers and 1,000 or more workers).

It is consistent with the hypothesis of Michael Piore and Charles Sabel that the world has entered a period of decentralizing technological change; but it is consistent with other hypotheses as well.[20]

Between 1972 and 1982, it was the largest plants, those with more than 500 employees, that tended to decline in absolute and relative importance (see table A-17). Table 9 identifies the six manufacturing industries in which the employment share of large plants declined by at least 10 percentage points. It also reports the changes in employment levels that occurred in such plants.

Before 1972, plants of large and intermediate size had not tended to decline. In fact, between 1962 and 1972 plants with 500–999 employees tended to account for increasing shares of industry employment (appendix tables A-16 and A-20). Employment shares of plants with 1,000 or more employees rose in twenty-three of forty industries (table A-13). Only in petroleum and nonelectrical machinery did the employment share of plants with 500 or more employees decline by as much as 5 percentage points. (The corresponding figure for 1954–62 was four industries—petroleum; machinery for agriculture, industry, and railways; tobacco products; and miscellaneous food products.) These cases aside, the decline of the large plant was a phenomenon that began in the 1970s.[21]

The source for 1982 does not distinguish between the very largest plants, those with more than 1,000 employees, and their just-plain-large counterparts with 500–999 employees. As a result, it cannot resolve whether the recent decline of the large plant applied to just one or to both of its subcategories. Fortunately, a different body of information provides the relevant evidence.[22] Between 1974 and 1980,

20. Piore and Sabel, *The Second Industrial Divide*. A second hypothesis emphasizes the potentially spurious nature of the apparent rise of small plants. If plant scale were defined in terms of floor space or output, large plants might not appear to be declining in relation to their smaller counterparts. The apparent demise of the large plant, with size measured in terms of employment, might simply reflect the proliferation of automated factories. For other hypotheses and implications, see Piore, "Historical Perspectives and the Interpretation of Unemployment."

21. This result depends heavily on definition of industries according to NAP-100. If NAE-2 is used instead, then seven of forty activities display large-plant shares of total employment that declined at least 10 percentage points between 1962 and 1972.

22. Ministère de l'Industrie et de la Recherche, *La Concentration dans l'Industrie de 1974 à 1980*. Industries are defined according to NAP-100 (see appendix C). The

employment tended to decline absolutely in plants with 500–999 employees, in plants with 1,000 or more employees, and in both categories combined (appendix table A-21). On the other hand, only when the two groups of large plants are merged did employment *share* tend to decline. In particular industries, the employment shares of large plants, variously defined, sometimes changed markedly. For plants with 500–999 employees, employment share declined by more than 10 percentage points in office equipment and by 5–10 percentage points in eight industries. It increased by at least 5 percentage points in chemical products not elsewhere classified, and in petroleum and natural gas. For plants with 1,000 or more employees, employment share declined by at least 10 percentage points in electrical equipment, glass, and manmade fibers and by 5–10 percentage points in five industries. On the other hand, it increased by at least 5 percentage points in petroleum and natural gas, grain mill products, and miscellaneous foods. In most industries the decline of the large plant during the 1970s applied to large and very large plants alike.

Industry distributions of employment by size of plant have thus experienced substantial modifications since World War II. Between 1954 and 1962 relative decline was concentrated in the small plants; between 1972 and 1982 it was concentrated in large plants. During both periods, relative decline was usually accompanied by absolute contraction. Such contraction is not inconsistent with the need for workers to migrate between plants.[23] Nevertheless, absolute contractions of employment do not guarantee that particular workers migrated from small to large plants between 1954 and 1972 or in the opposite direction between 1972 and 1982. The data presented above are also consistent with other hypotheses. Changes in the distribution of employment may have been achieved through retirements from and entries into the labor force; and individual plants might have migrated

---

source excludes seven of forty-four manufacturing industries (military products, meat, dairy products, preserved foods, freshly baked goods, beverages, and tobacco products).

23. Starting with Stigler, "The Economies of Scale," data of this sort have been used to identify minimum and maximum efficient scales of production. As a result, some readers might be tempted to interpret these findings as suggesting that French plants were inefficiently small until the 1970s, when technological change favoring small-scale operations served to reverse the concentration of production in large plants. For reasons described by Shepherd, "What Does the Survivor Technique Show about Economies of Scale?," such inferences are not generally valid.

Table 10. *Labor Mobility between Plants, by Age Group and Sex, 1959–77*

Percent

Age in year t	Percentage employed in different plant in t + 5					
	Men			Women		
	t = 1959	t = 1965	t = 1972	t = 1959	t = 1965	t = 1972
11–14	21.4	41.5	21.7	32.9	63.5	58.1
15–19	42.1	65.1	68.3	45.8	61.7	57.3
20–24	40.0	57.9	55.1	42.1	54.5	45.1
25–29	27.7	45.0	42.8	22.8	32.4	38.1
30–34	22.1	34.4	34.4	17.2	27.3	29.5
35–39	15.5	27.8	27.4	13.0	24.4	21.2
40–44	17.0	23.8	22.5	11.1	19.5	19.4
45–49	12.2	23.0	19.0	11.9	20.6	16.7
50–54	12.6	20.6	17.0	6.6	18.5	13.3
55–59	10.2	17.1	13.8	8.1	15.4	10.2
60 and older	4.3	9.7	7.1	9.8	9.1	8.6
All	20.5	33.7	32.8	19.4	29.1	28.1

Sources: INSEE D32, table 1.6; and INSEE D91, tables 51, 52.

between size classes while the bulk of their employees remained within them. Consider, for instance, a plant with 1,005 salaried employees. If the plant fires 10 people, the class of plants employing at least 1,000 people loses 1,005 jobs even though only 10 people have left the plant in which they work. More generally, changes in the volume of employment by size of plant do not always convey an accurate picture of the extent to which individuals are leaving the plants in which they work.

With respect to the entry-exit hypothesis, INSEE's studies of mobility provide no evidence. In fact, I am aware of no systematic information at the industry level on the extent to which individuals working in plants of one size have been redeployed to plants of another size. With respect to the second problem—that individual plants might have migrated from one size class to another—something more can be said. INSEE has reported the fraction of people employed at both ends of five-year periods who worked in different plants at the two points in time (table 10). Unlike mobility between occupations, industries, and forms of remuneration, mobility between plants has occurred frequently. Among men of all ages, the chances of changing plants during a five-year period have been at least one in five. Between 1965 and 1970, and then again between 1972 and 1977, they were one in three. In every category of worker age, interplant mobility increased after 1964, a fact not explained by changes in the age structure of the labor force. Although women were less mobile than men, they too tended to migrate between plants, especially after 1964. Changes in the distribution of employment by size of plant have been accompanied by frequent redeployment of individual workers.

Geographic Composition of the Population

Jobs are chosen for location as well as for content. People with strong regional attachments may decide not to change workplaces—despite attraction to the new job's intrinsic characteristics—if the switch requires geographic displacement. (Arguably, regional immobility might also result from the positive correlation between housing prices and level and growth of per capita income.) Even small moves may be considered undesirable if they require substitution of urban for rural living. To the extent that sustained economic growth normally entails geographic mobility of the population, apparent stability in the distribution of people among places might suggest rigidity in the allocation of labor.[24]

Between 1954 and 1982 France's population grew by 27 percent, but some areas grew faster than others.[25] Two regions (appendix table A-22) and sixteen *départements* (table 11) lost population, while one region and fourteen *départements* grew by at least 50 percent. Table 11 suggests that Paris lost population to its suburbs. Between 1954 and 1982, population more than doubled in three of the seven *départements* surrounding Paris. Six of the seven were among the

24. On geographic mobility of the French population, see Boudoul and Faur, "Depuis 1975, les Migrations Interrégionales Sont Moins Nombreuses"; Deville, "Les Migrations Intérieures entre 1968 et 1975"; Desplanques, "Les Migrations Intérieures entre 1968 et 1975: La Ville ou la Campagne?"; Fabre and Taffin, "Qui A Déménagé entre 1973 et 1978, et Pourquoi?"; and INSEE D4.

25. The endpoints of this period are census years. Use of different endpoints would not alter the conclusions that follow. Among *départements* the correlations linking growth between 1954 and 1982 with growth during other census intervals (1946–82, 1962–82, 1946–75, and 1954–75) all exceed 0.96. Among regions the corresponding correlations all exceed 0.89. The data are taken from INSEE, *Recensement Général de la Population de 1982: Population de la France (Métropole et Départements d'Outre-Mer), Régions, Départements, Arrondissements et Cantons*, table C.

ten fastest growing of this period, and all of the four fastest growers were Paris suburbs. Meanwhile, Paris itself lost nearly one-quarter of its population.

With the exception of Paris, however, all *départements* in which population declined were areas where unusually large fractions of the population lived rurally in 1954; and *départements* in which population grew especially rapidly tended to be areas where relatively small fractions of the population lived rurally. Among the eighty-six *départements* for which information is available, the correlation between percentage change in population (1954–82) and share of the population residing rurally (1954) differed negatively from 0 at the .001 level of significance.[26] The relative decline of population in rural areas was also apparent at the regional level (table A-22). The greater the incidence of rural living in 1954, the smaller the growth of population between 1954 and 1982.[27]

In fact the regions growing fastest in population were those with relatively large cities as of 1954. The greater the fraction of 1954 population residing in *communes* of 50,000 or more people, the greater the percentage increase in population between 1954 and 1982.[28]

At the national level, the rural population declined both absolutely and in relation to total population over most of the postwar period. Although 43 percent of the population still lived in rural *communes* in 1954, only 27 percent lived in such areas by 1982. During these twenty-eight years, the number of people in rural areas decreased by 21 percent.[29]

26. In a one-tail *t*-test ($r = -0.58$). In 1982 France was divided into ninety-six *départements*, but in 1954 it had been divided into ninety. The changes involved the division of Corsica into two parts and the division of the three *départements* of the Paris metropolitan area into eight. As a result, information on rural population in 1954 is not available for ten *départements*. Unfortunately, these ten include the entire Paris area. Since the fraction of the population living rurally in 1954 is highly correlated with the corresponding fraction in 1982 ($r = 0.95$, $N = 86$) and since information on rural living is available for all ninety-six *départements* in 1982, it is reassuring to note that the correlation between percentage change in population (1954–82) and rural fraction (1982) also differed negatively from 0 at the .001 level of significance in a one-tail *t*-test ($r = -0.62$).

27. The correlation coefficient ($r = -0.63$) differs negatively from 0 at the .001 level of significance in a one-tail *t*-test ($N = 22$).

28. The correlation coefficient ($r = 0.79$) differs positively from 0 at the .001 level of statistical significance in a one-tail *t*-test ($N = 22$).

29. INSEE, *Recensement Général de la Population de 1982: France Métropolitaine*,

Table 11. *Change in Population, Selected Départements, 1954–82*[a]

| | | Population decreased | | | | | | | Population increased more than 50 percent | | | | |
| | | Population | | Percent change | Percent rural[b] | | | | Population | | Percent change | Percent rural[b] | |
Code	Département	1954	1982	1954–82	1954	1982	Code	Département	1954	1982	1954–82	1954	1982
24	Dordogne	377,870	377,356	0	76	66	60	Oise	435,308	661,781	52	63	43
58	Nièvre	240,078	239,635	0	68	51	94	Val-de-Marne	767,529	1,193,655	56	n.a.	0
19	Corrèze	242,798	241,448	-1	68	52	93	Seine-St.-Denis	845,231	1,324,301	57	n.a.	0
03	Allier	372,689	369,580	-1	55	45	31	Haute-Garonne	525,669	824,501	57	41	27
36	Indre	247,436	243,191	-2	66	51	84	Vaucluse	268,318	427,343	59	37	25
2B	Haute-Corse	134,664	131,574	-2	n.a.	58	38	Isère	587,960	936,771	59	57	32
09	Ariège	140,010	135,725	-3	69	59	13	Bouches-du-Rhône	1,048,762	1,724,199	64	12	7
2A	Corse du Sud	112,331	108,604	-3	n.a.	37	74	Haute-Savoie	293,852	494,505	68	63	39
55	Meuse	207,106	200,101	-3	65	55	06	Alpes-Maritimes	515,484	881,198	71	17	12
43	Haute-Loire	215,577	205,895	-4	76	56	83	Var	413,012	708,331	72	29	16
12	Aveyron	292,727	278,654	-5	67	60	77	Seine-et-Marne	453,438	887,112	96	n.a.	32
32	Gers	185,111	174,154	-6	80	64	95	Val-d'Oise	412,658	920,598	123	n.a.	7
15	Cantal	177,065	162,838	-8	79	65	78	Yvelines	519,176	1,196,111	130	n.a.	11
48	Lozère	82,391	74,294	-10	76	65	91	Essonne	350,987	988,000	181	n.a.	10
23	Creuse	172,702	139,968	-19	86	75							
75	Paris	2,850,189	2,176,243	-24	0	0							

Sources: INSEE, *Recensement Général de la Population de 1982: Population de la France (Métropole et Départements d'Outre-Mer), Régions, Départements, Arrondissements, et Cantons,* table C; INSEE, *Recensement Général de la Population de Mai 1954: Population Légale (Résultats Statistiques),* table PL10; and INSEE, *Recensement Général de la Population de 1982: Métropole, Tableaux Statistiques de Population Légale,* table 4.

n.a. Not available.

a. *Département* boundaries as of 1982. Between 1954 and 1982 four *départements* were divided into ten. For these ten, rural population in 1954 is not available.

b. Rural population of a *département* is population of its rural *communes.* A commune is rural if fewer than 2,000 people inhabit the communal seat.

Differences among areas in population growth can occur for many reasons, including variations in rates of birth, death, emigration, or immigration. In fact, apparent differences in growth can even be spurious. For example, if many communities are reclassified from rural to urban status, then urban areas may appear to grow in importance even if no one changes residence.

Starting with the 1962 census, INSEE asked each resident to divulge his or her residential location on January 1 of the previous census year. In the 1982 census, INSEE also asked for information on location at birth. As a result, for most of the postwar period it is possible to observe the fraction of the population (excluding those who leave the country) residing at different locations at each end of census intervals. Appendix table A-23 shows the frequency of geographic migration between successive censuses since 1954. Mobility has been very high between dwelling units and between *communes*. Migrations between *départements* ranged from 11 percent to 15 percent, while those between regions fluctuated around 8 percent.[30]

Geographic mobility clearly increased between the late 1950s and the early 1970s, although comparisons are complicated by differing intervals between censuses. Whether between *communes*, between *départements*, or between regions, the incidence of mobility during the seven years ending in 1975 exceeded the incidence of mobility during the eight years ending in 1962. The one exception involved immigration at the national level. Largely because of the influx of people from Algeria in 1962, the incidence of international immigration was greatest from 1962 to 1968.

As significant, perhaps, as the increase in mobility before 1975 was its failure to atrophy thereafter. Although economic growth slowed considerably, demographic mobility declined only slightly, as if locational attachments had abated over the postwar period.

Structure de la Population Totale, table R1, new definition of urban *communes.* In absolute terms the rural population shrank in 1954–62, 1962–68, and 1968–75. In 1975–82, it rose by 1 percent.

30. Conceivably, examination of mobility in other countries could help us to decide whether mobility between broadly defined areas is great or small in France. Unfortunately, as the data in table A-23 suggest, the incidence of mobility depends heavily on the size of the territory in question, and countries differ in terms of the size of their administrative units.

My principal concern is with the labor force. For this segment of the population, the only form of migration that has been monitored throughout the postwar period is that between regions (table 12). Broadly speaking, mobility of the labor force resembled mobility of the population as a whole. Until the mid-1970s the frequency of migration tended to increase; thereafter, it tended to decrease. Regions of especially great emigration during one census interval tended also to incur great emigration during other census intervals.[31] Before 1975, and especially between 1954 and 1962, the frequency of emigration depended positively on the importance of rural living and negatively on the existence of large towns (appendix table A-24). Despite these similarities, however, patterns of mobility did differ between the labor force and the population as a whole. Starting in 1968 the labor force displayed the greater mobility. And the decline in migration that accompanied economic slowdown hit the labor force more than the population.

Conclusion

I have examined changes over time in the allocation of a single resource: labor. A general appraisal of flexibility in the allocation of French resources would require examination of other durable resources, including plant and equipment. Such an exercise is beyond the scope of this book.[32] In the context of the hypotheses discussed at the beginning of this chapter, labor is the most important resource to analyze, partly because of its durability and relative lack of industrial specificity, but mostly because of the potential impact of nonpecuniary objectives on its deployment.

Between 1954 and 1982, the structure of the French labor force changed profoundly. Structural change did not always entail reallo-

31. The pairwise correlations between migration rates for 1954–62, 1962–68, 1968–75, and 1975–82 all differ positively from 0 at the .01 level of significance in one-tail t-tests. All but the correlation between first-period and last-period migration differ positively from 0 at the .001 level of significance.

32. Published information on changes in the composition of capital is sketchy and fragile. Partly because of the absence of systematic information on true economic depreciation, the capital stock requires special study. See Carré, Dubois, and Malinvaud, *La Croissance Française*, pp. 143–212; and INSEE, *Le Mouvement Economique en France, 1949–1979*, pp. 35–68.

Table 12. *Geographic Mobility of Labor Force between Census Years, by Region, 1954–82*
Percent

Initial residence	Different region at end of period[a]			
	1954–62	1962–68	1968–75	1975–82
Ile de France	5.1	5.6	9.1	10.2
Champagne-Ardenne	9.3	8.6	11.6	10.3
Picardie	10.5	8.9	11.7	10.4
Haute-Normandie	8.1	6.7	8.9	8.7
Centre	10.2	8.8	11.4	10.1
Basse-Normandie	12.0	9.5	11.6	9.9
Bourgogne	10.4	8.7	11.5	10.3
Nord-Pas de Calais	4.5	5.0	7.4	7.0
Lorraine	6.1	6.7	9.7	9.3
Alsace	4.0	3.9	5.5	5.5
Franche-Comté	7.5	6.8	10.9	9.2
Pays de la Loire	8.1	7.1	8.5	7.5
Bretagne	9.2	7.1	8.3	7.2
Poitou-Charentes	9.9	9.9	11.8	10.0
Aquitaine	7.1	7.1	9.5	7.7
Midi-Pyrénées	7.7	7.7	9.9	8.3
Limousin	9.7	8.7	11.0	9.4
Rhône-Alpes	3.9	4.2	6.3	5.9
Auvergne	8.1	7.4	10.0	8.6
Languedoc-Roussillon	10.0	9.7	12.8	9.5
Provence-Alpes-Côte d'Azur	6.3	6.7	8.5	7.9
Corse	16.9	9.2	15.5	9.6
All	7.1	6.8	9.3	8.6

Sources: INSEE, *Annuaire Statistique de la France, 1967*, p. 70; and INSEE D97, pp. 48–51 and erratum pp. 4–5.
a. For 1954–62, labor force is defined as people employed in France at both ends of the period. For other periods, labor force is defined as French labor force at period end.

cation of labor already deployed: to an important degree, it was accomplished through exits from and entries into the labor force. Even so, people who were already employed moved frequently. Whether or not this mobility was as great as that observed in other rich countries, the radical elements of French restructuring can hardly be ignored.[33] Although much of the structural change occurred before 1975, the process definitely continued thereafter. It cannot be argued that French employment structure crystallized after the first oil shock.

33. It would be interesting to compare INSEE's data with those in the U.S. census

One is left, then, with another question rather than with an answer to the original paradox. Now to be explained is why alleged conservatism of the private sector, reinforced by alleged public-sector jamming of market signals, prevented neither economic growth nor reallocation of labor resources.

---

of population. See, for example, U.S. Department of Commerce, Bureau of the Census, *1970 Census of Population: Mobility for States and the Nation*; and *1970 Census of Population: Occupation and Residence in 1965*. For an early attempt to compare mobility internationally, see Madinier, "La Mobilité du Travail aux Etats-Unis et en France."

3 | Restructuring by Government Design

As THE French economy grew after World War II, its structure changed substantially. Important fractions of the labor force migrated geographically and occupationally during fairly short intervals of time. The conservative market behavior of prewar France described by David Landes and by Alfred Sauvy seemed to recede if not disappear.[1] How does one explain the new predilection for flexible market behavior? Why should the decade after World War II have marked a rupture in patterns of conduct?

Knowledge of French history and institutions tempts one to explain postwar behavior as a response to government initiative. As early as the seventeenth century, dissatisfied with national economic performance and skeptical of the ability or willingness of private parties to improve that performance, many public officials advocated energetic intervention in the microeconomy. Dormant before World War I and only fitfully active during the two decades that followed, their ideas awoke after the Liberation in such guises as public enterprise, government procurement, indicative planning, and industrial policy.[2] Arguably, these policies affected economic structure in two ways: they nudged private parties toward elastic responses to market signals, and they compensated for remaining private conservatism by escalating direct government participation in the allocation of resources.

This chapter explores government initiative as an explanation of structural flexibility. After describing the historical and philosophical origins of postwar policies, it examines government's behavior in each

---

1. Landes, "French Business and the Businessman"; and Sauvy, *Histoire Economique de la France entre les Deux Guerres*, vol. 2, chap. 17.
2. Kuisel, *Capitalism and the State in Modern France.*

of several capacities: seller, buyer, tax collector, regulator, and propagandist.

Methodologically, the chapter embraces two basic principles. The first is the importance of viewing government action from the perspective of a company or an industry. Without such a perspective, it is difficult to gauge the likelihood that government policy did much to affect behavior. The second principle is the importance of complementing studies of particular policies or industries with comprehensive chartings of government-business relationships. Case studies help one to understand the physiology of government involvement in the economy. Without them, one loses touch with complexities of behavioral choice in the public and private sectors. One also loses the ability to specify partial-equilibrium models of government impact. On the other hand, by design, case studies fail to illuminate fully government's involvements elsewhere in the economy. Since the effects of each policy depend critically on all the rest, including those aimed at other economic actors, failure to appreciate the full spectrum of government involvement also condemns efforts to measure how and how much government affects particular economic activities. Given the recent proliferation of excellent industry studies, I pursue the broader approach here.[3]

At the end of the chapter, I suggest that government devoted considerable money and energy to promoting structural change. In certain lines of business its actions accelerated expansion of output, introduction of new products and technologies, and improvement of productive efficiency.[4] Nevertheless, it is far from obvious that government initiatives affected enough activities to account for the pervasive structural change observed in chapter 2. Government's ability to alter the market decisions of buyers and sellers might not have been commensurate with its appetite for and rhetoric of intervention.

---

3. See, for example, Zysman, *Political Strategies for Industrial Order*; Padioleau, *Quand la France S'Enferre*; and Jublin and Quatrepoint, *French Ordinateurs*.
4. See especially Sheahan, *Promotion and Control of Industry in Postwar France*.

Some History

COLBERT

In 1661 Jean-Baptiste Colbert became the principal advisor of Louis XIV. During his twenty-two years in power, he served a monarch bent on wresting European supremacy from the Dutch.[5] As a mercantilist, Colbert believed that French success depended critically on national economic strength, as measured by royal accumulation of monetary resources. Fearful that the unaided behavior of private parties would not conduce to such strength, he implemented an elaborate program of economic development.

Promotion of domestic industry was an important part of the program, for Colbert saw many virtues in industrialization. First, it would erode the autarky and barter that prevailed in contemporary peasant economies, facilitating tax collection and centralization.[6] Second, it would help French goods displace foreign competitors in French and other markets. The less France imported, the more of its money would remain within the country for government to tax, and the less of it would end up in the hands, and hence the armies, of its foes. Finally, industrialization would permit France to avoid reliance on foreigners for up-to-date military products.

Most of Colbert's promotional schemes used the lure of expected profit to develop private initiative in particular lines of business; the state owned only a few enterprises. Many schemes relied on cash expenditure—outright gifts to prospective entrepreneurs, pensions and interest-free loans, bounties, payments to attract skilled foreign workers, payment of rent on buildings, and harrassment of foreign ships in the Mediterranean. Others depended on tax expenditure; these included exemption from import, export, and transit duties; exemption of the entrepreneur and his employees from salt, wine,

---

5. This discussion draws heavily on Cole, *Colbert and a Century of French Mercantilism*, especially chaps. 1, 6, 7, and 9–14. See also Colbert, *Testament Politique*; Goubert, *Louis XIV et Vingt Millions de Français*; Usher, "Colbert and Governmental Control of Industry in Seventeenth Century France"; and Boissonnade, *Colbert*.

6. Goubert, *100000 Provinciaux au XVIIe Siècle*, pp. 160–73.

and income taxes; and exemption from the obligation to house and feed soldiers. Other schemes involved protection from foreign competition and still others the manipulation of the domestic regulatory environment—as in creation of legal monopolies, prevention of interference by local guilds in production and marketing decisions, delegation of the power of eminent domain, and requirement that legal suits against favored enterprises be brought exclusively in (friendly) royal courts. On paper, many of Colbert's methods differed little from their modern counterparts.

Colbert believed that product quality would determine French success in export markets. Since merchandise was identified primarily by national origin, brand loyalty was an industrywide public good. If a few French enterprises cut corners, all would suffer. Hence the alleged need for regulation. In textiles, for example, Colbert established standards for the length and width of particular fabrics, for thread count, and for ability to withstand shrinkage.[7] Inevitably, such regulations were industry-specific.

Colbert's program was so ambitious that *colbertisme* is still a popular term for pervasive government initiative at the microeconomic level. Nevertheless, Colbert's ideas were hardly novel. Richelieu and Sully, ministers to Louis XIII and Henri IV, had pursued similar strategies, and the composition of national output had received explicit attention for decades.[8] Although the content of colbertisme is easy to describe, its impact on the economy has proved difficult to measure. Historians seem to agree that Colbert's predecessors failed to achieve lasting effects. The enterprises they promoted usually disappeared quickly after removal of their privileges. Regarding Colbert's own achievements, however, historians continue to disagree. Abbot Usher and Charles Cole argue that Colbert's policies did contribute, however partially, to long-term economic development. Pierre Goubert contends that neither the design nor the impact of Colbert's initiatives can be distinguished from those of his ineffectual predecessors: in Goubert's view, enduring industrial development did not occur until

7. Such regulations applied only to urban producers. Rural enterprises, which accounted for a larger share of output (at least in textiles), remained unregulated. Goubert, *100000 Provinciaux au XVIIe Siècle*, pp. 150–55.

8. See Cole, *French Mercantilist Doctrines before Colbert*; and Nef, *Industry and Government in France and England, 1540–1640*, especially pp. 85–88.

the eighteenth century and should not be attributed to Louis XIV's famous advisor.[9]

THE PSYCHOLOGY OF 1945

Historical distance is not the only reason why the impact of colbertisme has been difficult to assess. No less discord exists in evaluations of French industrial policies since World War II.[10]

On May 8, 1945, the European phase of World War II was over. The French had won the war; but even ultimate victory could not mask the events of June 1940, when German tanks had swept effortlessly across the French countryside and the French army had suffered a humiliating defeat. The collapse had come so swiftly and decisively that few people blamed the army alone. The basic fabric of French society appeared ready for reexamination; in the eyes of most, it would need more than mending.

To begin with, France would have to develop a commitment to economic growth. The outcomes of modern wars were seen to depend as much on the sizes of economies as on the sizes of armies. France was unprepared for World War II, it was argued, because its economy had been stagnating.[11] Rightly or wrongly, perhaps by extrapolation, many argued that between the wars, and even during the nineteenth century, the French economy grew very slowly by international standards. If France was to preserve its independence, its economy would have to grow at least as rapidly as did the economies of its rivals.

But growth alone would not suffice. Modern military methods required modern military equipment, which could not be produced easily by a traditional economy, whatever its size. The image of French cavalry fighting German tanks symbolized the persistence in France of a rural economy at a time when Germany had already become an industrial society. The French economy would have to undergo structural transformation. It would have to produce more

9. Cole, *French Mercantilist Doctrines before Colbert*; and Goubert, *Louis XIV et Vingt Millions de Français.*

10. Compare, for example, Aujac, "An Introduction to French Industrial Policy," pp. 13–35; Stoffaës, "Industrial Policy in the High-Technology Industries," pp. 36–73; and Mentré, "The French Economy Should Be Deregulated," pp. 143–55.

11. The economic dimension of the "never again" attitude is expressed in many places, including the opening lines of Albert, *Le Pari Français,* p. 9.

manufactures and fewer primary products. Within the manufacturing sector, it would have to develop heavy industry—metallurgy, chemicals, machinery—and reduce the importance of food and textiles. In so doing, it might shed its image as an economy devoted to production of high-quality merchandise under artisanal conditions. Without structural modernization, it was argued, economic growth could not be expected to guarantee French independence.

Most importantly, it was believed that economic growth and transformation would not occur unless government assumed responsibility for economic policy. Between the Franco-Prussian War and World War II, the French government, like other governments, tended to rely on business enterprise to determine what was best for the economy. For the most part, business advocated laissez-faire. Hence government owned few business enterprises, collected a slender fraction of GNP in taxes, and even refrained from systematically collecting and studying information on what was happening in the private sector. When business and agriculture asked for protection from foreign goods, however, government erected barriers to imports that seemed as formidable as the Maginot Line itself. Although government's philosophy has been described as economic liberalism, the practice of that philosophy entailed neither laissez-faire nor perfect competition. It merely resulted in abdication of economic initiative to private enterprise.[12]

At the time of the Liberation, the record of private enterprise seemed wanting. Before the war, under the stewardship of the business community, the economy had stagnated. During the war the business community had exhibited unseemly enthusiasm for collaboration with the Germans. Since neither the economic nor the political judgments of the old elite could be trusted, a new class of leaders would have to be mobilized. The public sector seemed the place to do it.[13]

As memories of interwar stagnation and wartime collaboration gave

---

12. Kuisel, *Capitalism and the State in Modern France*, chaps. 2–5, traces the twentieth century origins of postwar government activism.

13. Monnet, *Mémoires*, p. 276, argues that slow interwar growth could be imputed to insufficient productive investment caused by anemic entrepreneurship. Just after World War II, in a discussion with Charles de Gaulle, Monnet broached the importance of convincing the French people that production methods had to be modernized; de Gaulle responded, "That is the role of government." Ibid., p. 278.

ground to experiences of rapid growth, government initiative had to be justified in new ways. Some people believed laissez-faire would effect all desirable economic change but not soon enough. Government would have to intervene if France was to hold or gain position vis-à-vis its rivals. Others believed laissez-faire might fail even in the long run. Anxious to maintain control of family enterprises, backward entrepreneurs might go bankrupt before they accepted the need to seek outside funds for expansion and modernization. Given the perceived shortage of spontaneous entrepreneurship, government initiative would be required to promote new activities and modern methods of production. Despite the appearance of arguments like these, however, advocates of structural change worried mostly about what constitutes optimal economic structure, taking for granted the proposition that structural change required government initiative.

The Logic of Structural Policy

Dissatisfaction with economic performance does not imply dissatisfaction with the microeconomy, and dissatisfaction with the microeconomy does not engender automatic belief in the intrinsic value of particular economic activities. Within a Paretian framework, for example, the latter dissatisfaction could stem from a perceived need to correct market failures wherever they occur. Or, within a cultural framework, it could result from a perceived need to transform the outlooks of those who fail to respond elastically to market opportunities. How did the psychology of 1945 express itself in a perceived need for government intervention in the composition of economic activity?[14] Like Colbert, many postwar policymakers believed that government should identify desirable features of economic structure and then, either directly or by amplifying market signals, secure their achievement. Although structural policy as practiced did not always dovetail with structural policy as debated, the economic ideas wafting through the policy community surely affected the formulation and implementation of government intervention.

14. The psychology of 1945 affected other dimensions of economic thought as well. See Fourquet, *Les Comptes de la Puissance*; Boltanski, *Les Cadres*; and Kuisel, *Capitalism and the State in Modern France*, chaps. 7–9.

Some advocates of structural policy urged a comprehensive approach to structure, offering as blueprints the allocations of resources exhibited by France's designated rivals. In the seventeenth century, Holland was the principal lightning rod of envy; since World War II, Germany has occupied that position. Others simply urged identification and promotion of "strategic" activities deemed critical to military preparedness or to sustained economic growth. [15] But whether concerned about economic structure in general or about certain activities in particular, few supported the criteria of Pareto optimality. Few argued that seventeenth century Holland or nineteenth century Germany had become rich and safe by embracing textbook prescriptions to compete domestically and specialize internationally. They considered the enjoyment of economic power, not economic efficiency, to be the primary explanation of different standards of living and military security. [16]

After World War II, the debate over which activities deserved strategic status proceeded along three lines: one related to the regional composition of activity, a second to its industrial composition, and the last to its distribution by size of firm.

REGIONAL POLICY

In the seventeenth century, regional policy meant annexation of territory belonging to a foreign country. It was rightly considered a strategy to promote national strength. Postwar regional policy served a different set of purposes. Early on it consisted of discouraging economic expansion of the Paris metropolitan area and promoting industrialization in the western half of the country. [17] More recently government has emphasized creating jobs in regions heavily reliant on shrinking industries, especially in Lorraine and the Nord.

The current concern with regional balance does not spring directly from pursuit of national economic strength. It reflects instead a desire to ensure social stability by seeing to it that poor and troubled regions share in the fruits of growth even if national growth is slowed thereby.

15. A systematic approach to the identification of strategic industries appears in Aujac, "La Hiérarchie des Industries dans un Tableau des Echanges Inter-Industrielles."

16. See Perroux, *Pouvoir et Economie.*

17. Gravier, *Paris et le Désert Français*, seemed to inspire government reflection on the alleged imbalance between Paris and the rest of the country.

Because it is designed as much to retard as to promote structural change, I shall not examine it here.

INDUSTRIAL POLICY

The second structural policy, industrial policy, is usually defined in France as stimulation of the industrial sector in general (manufacturing, mining, public utilities, and construction) or of particular manufacturing industries at the expense of agriculture, commerce, and services. For my purposes, industrial policy is better defined as actions designed to alter the distribution of output among lines of business. On this definition, industrial policy can aim to promote activities outside the industrial sector, but it cannot aim simply to expand the economy without regard to its industrial composition. Although it is more American than European in flavor, this definition of industrial policy is compatible with both French uses of the term.

As the strengths of various economic interests and ideas changed over time, so did the apparent logic of industrial policy. One dimension of apparent change involved the types of industries to promote. Immediately after World War II, structuralists tended to believe in modernizing and expanding mature industries deemed essential to industrialization of the economy. The first economic plan (1947–52) promoted six industries of varying breadth: coal, electricity, steel, cement, agricultural equipment, and internal (especially rail) transport. Although the plan talked of reconstruction, as if it were merely organizing the replacement of capacity destroyed in war, government actually wished to expand and modernize the capital stock. Because of the shortages that prevailed throughout Europe, France could not count on importing quantities of these products sufficient to ensure the macroeconomic growth desired by government. As for the long term, the advantages of German-style industrialism based on heavy industry seemed obvious. By the mid-1960s, however, the concerns of many structuralists had migrated to development of native technology in the nuclear, electronic, and aerospace arenas. The early 1980s brought renewed concern for supporting mature industries but no diminution of interest in their emerging counterparts.

Another change in the logic of industrial policy involved the selectivity of promotion. During the late 1940s and the late 1970s, the prevailing view favored focus on a fairly small number of industries.

The 1970s advocates referred to their position as a strategy of niches (*politique des créneaux*), a strategy of promoting narrowly defined activities in which France could realistically hope to achieve world preeminence and static comparative advantage. During the late 1950s and the early 1980s, conventional wisdom favored a more general style of intervention. Advocates of broad intervention in the late 1950s may have believed that large segments of industry required help in preparing for the impending economic integration of Europe.[18] In the early 1980s, advocates of generality argued that a strategy of niches would leave France with far too limited a range of opportunities to absorb high-wage labor and hence nourish prosperity. Rather than appear to abandon so many choice lines of business to foreigners, government should develop for each vertical stream of production a strategy designed to ensure continued French production. This approach (*politique des filières*) would intervene at tactical points in each vertical stream to eliminate bottlenecks and cost disadvantages.[19]

During the mid-1980s, the modal sentiment on selectivity lay somewhere between market niches and vertical streams and was sometimes labeled a strategy of technological clusters (*grappes technologiques*).[20] The idea was to promote French expertise in narrowly defined but economically interactive technologies. Viewed from a particular market, this appeared to be a strategy of niches: France would not attempt to cover a market in its entirety, but only that part of demand that could be satisfied by certain technologies. Viewed macroscopically, however, technological clusters could appear to be a strategy of vertical streams. Clustering would depend on economic as well as technological complementarity. Promotion of carefully selected clusters could generate a dense network of comparative advantage.

How does one explain the evolution of conventional wisdom? Why, for example, was it fashionable to advocate narrow intervention in some periods but broad intervention in others? Conceivably, the relative appeals of the two approaches may have depended on momentary budget constraint: the tighter the constraint, the greater

18. Fourquet, *Comptes de la Puissance*, p. 234.

19. Monfort, "A la Recherche des Filières de Production"; and Jacquemin and Rainelli, "Filières de la Nation et Filières de l'Entreprise."

20. See Stoffaës, *Fins de Mondes*, pp. 324–26.

the apparent virtue of selectivity. Against this hypothesis, one might argue that constrained government budgets do not compel selective industrial policy. Taxation or regulation of nonpriority activities could be used in lieu of subsidies to alter the composition of output, and such policies do not bite deeply into the budget. Nevertheless, the political attractiveness of promotion relative to control limits recourse to the restrictive approach.

Although industrial policy evolved in these and other ways, it remained predicated on the belief that static comparative advantage is not the appropriate arbiter of international specialization. France's role in the global division of labor should be determined as much by the nation's goals as by its natural endowments.

FIRM SIZE

The second structural policy inspired by preoccupation with economic strength involved the distribution of economic activity by size of firm. For three decades after World War II, most French observers believed that French firms were too small to support a strong economy. Unless government also promoted bigness, its efforts on behalf of certain industries would fail to improve economic performance.

Initially, the importance of size was justified in terms of static economies of scale. Historically, it was suggested, French firms tended to produce high-quality, high-cost goods in quasi-artisanal plants. Such a strategy might have suited a society in which nobles and clergy controlled most discretionary income, but it hardly conduced to bulky positions in modern markets. Mass production was now required, and in that segment of most industries French firms wallowed well below minimum efficient scale. By the mid-1960s, increased ability to perform research and development replaced mass production as the rationale for large firms. Technology appeared to be changing rapidly and growing in sophistication. A strong economy required firms capable of holding their positions on the technological frontier. As economies of scale were perceived to apply as much to inventive as to productive activity, promotion of large-scale enterprise continued to appear desirable.[21]

Whether inventive or productive, economies of scale might seem related to economic efficiency. Thus the philosophy of promoting

21. Adams, "Firm Size and Research Activity: France and the United States."

large-scale enterprise might appear to be rooted in the norms of Pareto optimality. Such, however, was not the case. Just as comparative advantage was not viewed as depending on exogenous natural factors, so the advantages of size were not considered to depend definitively and exclusively on real economies of scale. Uppermost in the minds of many believers in bigness was the weight needed by a firm to elbow foreign corporations aside in markets beyond French borders. In other words, economies of scale were presumed to exist wherever profit rose with firm size. The source of the profit—efficiency or market power—was not critical. Once again, the needs of France were defined largely in terms of what existed in countries considered to be major rivals.

Promoting one or two large firms per industry became known as the strategy of national champions. By the late 1970s, following dramatic macroeconomic shocks and pervasive technological change, the popularity of national champions waned.[22] Large-scale operation was perceived to breed rigidity at a time when adaptability was considered essential. Small and medium-size firms were recognized as potentially important beyond the niche of high-quality consumer goods. They, too, deserved the patronage of government. A strong economy, it was concluded, required a dense industrial fabric, and such a fabric cannot be woven without threads gathered from enterprises of all sizes.

Doctrine, of course, is not the same thing as policy. Actual government initiatives were undertaken by a wide variety of officials in many semiautonomous organizations. Even when a single conventional wisdom seemed to prevail, actual promotion and control pulled simultaneously in multiple directions. To assess the effects of structural policy on structural change, one must proceed beyond economic ideas to government actions. One must also establish a framework for measuring the impact of such actions.

Measuring Impact

Intervention does not imply impact. Granting government's appetite for shaping economic structure, even numerous and bulky

22. Hall, *Governing the Economy*, pp. 149–50.

structural policies need not impinge radically on the allocation of resources among industries, enterprises, or regions. Before proceeding, one must decide how to measure the effect of postwar structural policy on the composition of domestic activity.

IMPACT OF SUBSIDIES

Ultimately, structural impact consists of shifts in supply, in demand, or in rules governing buyer-seller interactions. Policies affecting supply or demand are tantamount to positive or negative subsidies, and their importance can be evaluated using familiar economic tools. To analyze the impact of a particular subsidy on the distribution of output among industries, I consider the following model of a subsidy's effect on the behavior of its recipients. Suppose that government wishes to expand the output of a specific profit-maximizing firm. Suppose further that the enterprise takes its selling price (P) as given, such that $P = a$, where a is a parameter. (The argument also applies to a monopolist, as can be verified by substituting a linear demand curve with negative slope for the parameter a.) Suppose finally that $TC = b + cQ^2$, where TC denotes total cost, b and c are parameters, and Q denotes the output and market supply of the enterprise. If the government fails to intervene, the enterprise sells $Q^* = \frac{1}{2}(a/c)$ and receives net revenue of $NR^* = \frac{1}{4}(a^2/c) - b$, where asterisks denote equilibrium values.

Subsidy 1. Government seeks to expand the firm's output by offering a subsidy of $S = \frac{1}{2}cQ^2$. The enterprise now sells $Q^* = a/c$ and realizes profit of $NR^* = \frac{1}{2}(a^2/c) - b$. Effectively, government reduces marginal cost by 50 percent $(TC = b + cQ^2 - S = b + \frac{1}{2}cQ^2)$, inducing the firm to increase output by 100 percent. The cost to government in terms of subsidy paid is $S^* = \frac{1}{2}(a^2/c)$.

Subsidy 2. Identical in amount to subsidy 1, subsidy 2 is structured as a lump-sum transfer. Output settles at the nonintervention level $\frac{1}{2}(a/c)$, and the firm realizes profit of $NR^* = \frac{3}{4}(a^2/c) - b$.

Subsidy 3. Like subsidy 1, subsidy 3 is contingent on the amount sold. Specifically, $S = \frac{1}{4}cQ^2$. In this case, the firm produces $Q^* = \frac{2}{3}(a/c)$ and realizes profit of $NR^* = \frac{1}{3}(a^2/c) - b$. Government pays a subsidy of $S^* = \frac{1}{9}(a^2/c)$, 2/9 the value of subsidies 1 and 2.

Comparison of these subsidies reveals the two basic determinants of government's influence on company output. First, given the terms on which it is granted, the effect of a subsidy depends on its amount: subsidies 1 and 3 carry similar designs (both depend quadratically on the rate of output), and the larger subsidy generates the larger increase in output. Second, however, given its amount, the impact of a subsidy depends on its terms: subsidies 1 and 2 are identical in amount, but only one affects the rate of output.[23] Thus the amount of subsidy may measure government's commitment to intervention, but it does not measure the impact of that intervention on output.[24]

Unfortunately, the simplicity of this example masks the difficulty in practice of measuring the effect of structural policy on the composition of economic activity. In the first place, the underlying model is partial-equilibrium in nature, designed to predict change in the subsidized output. Without a general-equilibrium model, however, changes in other outputs and thus the full effect on economic structure cannot be predicted—and the informational hunger of general-equilibrium models is difficult to sate. In the second place, this example focuses on a single subsidy. In reality, economic structure is influenced by multiple subsidies and myriad enterprises; practically speaking, it is impossible to specify the terms on which each and every subsidy is granted. As a result it is impossible to model satisfactorily the extent to which government intervention hits the elastic regions of supply and demand.

The best one can do in a broad study such as this is to compare each industry's dependence on government with its dependence for the same purpose on private parties. For example, to measure the impact of government procurement on each of several industries (or enterprises) one examines the ratio of government purchases to industry sales. Or to measure the impact of government subsidies on industry investment, one examines the ratio of subsidies received to the cost of projects undertaken. Ratios of this sort have two major

23. The fraction of a subsidy that rewards inframarginal activities will not affect the recipient's behavior. As a result of its lump-sum nature, all of subsidy 2 rewards inframarginal activity.

24. Note the importance of specifying what one means by impact. In this example, dQ/dS is twice as large for subsidy 3 as for subsidy 1. Arguably, therefore, subsidy 3 displays the larger *policy* impact, even though its *structural* impact is smaller.

defects. First, they fail to take account of the elasticity of private response to public policy. The formal example discussed above shows clearly that changes in output do not vary directly with ratios of subsidy received to either sales revenue (S/PQ) or production cost (S/TC). Both ratios are larger with subsidy 2 than with subsidy 1 (in equilibrium, S/PQ is twice as large), and yet subsidy 1 has infinitely more effect on output. Second, these ratios fail to take account of the possibility that those most affected by a subsidy are not those who receive it directly.

While awaiting systematic information on elasticities of response to subsidies and their equivalents, one may draw provisional inferences from ratios reflecting dependence on government; but the willingness to do so should depend on the degree of apparent government leverage. For example, if government subsidizes an industry heavily, then one might wish to avoid even tentative conclusions until the relevant elasticities of response have been estimated. But if government subsidizes an industry lightly, one might reasonably accept as a working hypothesis that government's intervention failed to alter behavior appreciably (remembering all the while that a subsidy of one dollar can theoretically make the difference between building and not building a grand dam such as Serre-Ponçon, and a subsidy of one billion dollars can fail to affect the same decision). This procedure is hardly perfect, but the smaller the ratio of subsidy to activity, the smaller the likelihood that small subsidies might suffice to tip the balance in one direction or another. As for the problem of general-equilibrium effects, one can employ input-output relationships to hazard guesses as to which activities were affected ultimately by government policies.

IMPACT OF REGULATIONS

In theory, regulations, like taxes, can be distilled to their subsidy equivalents, permitting combination or comparison of rules with government's other influences on economic structure. Unfortunately, measuring subsidy equivalence can be difficult. Regulations are not always enforced. In fact, some regulations are *designed* to be threats—cards dealt by government to itself for the purpose of bargaining with private parties on issues unrelated to the substance of the rules. For each card that government plays, for each regulation enforced, several remain hidden in its hand. Unenforced regulations, no less than their enforced counterparts, can influence the behavior of private parties; and yet even their presence, not to speak of their impact, is difficult to discern.

Theoretically, the effect of government's decision to enforce rules in one area (pollution control, say) on private behavior in another area (shedding workers, say) depends critically on the private party's perception of what triggers government's action. Consider three possible reactions of a company to the news that it must pay a fine for polluting. The company may treat the fine as a lump-sum tax, devoid of implications for future behavior. Or it may accept the nominal justification for government's action, treating the penalty as information on the probability with which government will attack those who contravene pollution rules. Depending on its updated parameters, the company may or may not respect pollution rules in the future, but it will not change such assumedly unrelated decisions as whether or not to reduce employment. Finally, the company may believe it has been singled out for punishment under pollution rules because it contravened government's desire that businesses not release workers. If it is cheaper to retain workers than it is to cut pollution, the company might respond to government's action by maintaining employment, continuing to pollute, and expecting to avoid pollution fines. Without sophisticated institutional knowledge, one would be foolhardy indeed to predict the impact of a regulatory *system* on supply and demand, and hence on economic structure.

In a society in which government regulates private behavior extensively, violations of government's proscriptions will occur routinely. To the extent that enforcement of all rules against all violators is economically and politically impractical, the hidden cards will be credible threats only if government is considered able to play them selectively. In other words, without administrative and prosecutorial discretion, government's ability to place everyone in violation of the rules will not create effective leverage on their behavior.

The concept of horizontal equity, of treating similarly situated people in similar manners, does not appear frequently in French law. By American standards, administrative discretion is especially broad. Since World War II, according to Peter Hall, government burdened French companies with so many restrictive regulations that "few could survive without selective exemptions that rendered them dependent on the goodwill of the industrial policy-makers."[25] Selective criminal prosecution has also been used to the same end. (In both countries, certain laws appear to be used frequently to punish people who cannot be prosecuted directly, or have not been prosecuted successfully, for allegedly noxious behavior. In the United States, mail fraud, wire fraud, and violation of civil rights fall in this category.) Consider the case of Pierre Moussa, head of Paribas on the eve of its nationalization in 1982. To prevent the Swiss and Belgian subsidiaries from falling into government hands when the parent company moved to the public sector, Moussa arranged for each subsidiary to gain control of the other. His actions violated no law, but they contravened the spirit of the nationalization. The government retaliated by prosecuting him for helping clients of the bank withdraw their money illegally from France, even though other bankers engaging in comparable activities were left alone.[26]

Given the importance of hidden cards in the government's hand, French companies may respond more to fear of attack than to receipt of subsidies. If so, government's structural leverage would be frustratingly difficult to model, and one would have to be very tentative in any conclusions regarding its effect on economic structure.

Government as Seller

The state has owned business enterprises since the seventeenth century. At the end of World War II, however, the number and scope of its holdings were modest.[27] Shortly after the Liberation,

25. Hall, *Governing the Economy*, p. 153. Hall refers to selective enforcement as a strategy of "exceptionalism," and to demonstrate its hallowed place in French administrative practice, he cites Tocqueville: "'In point of fact, there were no royal edicts or decrees, no letters patent duly embodied in the code book that did not lend themselves to a host of differing interpretations when they were applied to particular cases. Letters from the Controller-General and the Intendants show that government was always ready to countenance deviations from the orders issued by it. . . . There we have the old régime in a nutshell: rigid rules but flexibility, not to say laxity, in their application.'"

26. See Kramer, "Letter from Europe," pp. 49–59. Eventually, Moussa was acquitted; see *Economist*, April 28, 1984, p. 71.

27. Historical background on French public enterprise appears in Sheahan, "Experience with Public Enterprise in France and Italy"; Chenot, *Les Entreprises Nationalisées*; and Dufau, *Les Entreprises Publiques*.

partly to punish collaborators, partly to foster democracy in the workplace, but mainly to increase government's ability to influence the economy, the state acquired a number of enterprises and created others (table 13).[28] Some of the acquisitions engaged in manufacturing, but most specialized in energy or finance. A few of the creations combined the functions of a government agency with those of a business enterprise, performing basic research of the sort undertaken in government laboratories and sometimes setting product standards for the private enterprises around them, but also engaging in ordinary commercial activities.

From 1950 to 1980 the public sector changed little in scope, although toward the end of the period the state acquired important equity positions in the steel and computer industries, and certain existing public enterprises were allowed to develop new lines of business. Then in 1982, state ownership expanded dramatically. The new members included a number of manufacturers, five of which (Compagnie Générale d'Electricité, Pechiney-Ugine Kuhlmann, Rhône-Poulenc, Saint Gobain-Pont à Mousson, and Thomson-Brandt) were acquired through legislation, another four of which (Dassault, Matra, Roussel Uclaf, and the French subsidiary of ITT) were acquired through voluntary negotiations with existing owners, and several more of which were acquired indirectly in their capacities as subsidiaries of acquired enterprises. (For example, Saint Gobain brought with it CII-HB, the second largest manufacturer of computers in France.) Also acquired were two large investment banks and thirty-six commercial banks, leaving only a few small companies, many with foreign parents, in private commercial banking.[29]

Since World War II, then, the French state has owned a multitude of business enterprises. In principle these could have shaped economic structure directly through their production decisions and indirectly through their pricing decisions. In which industries did they contribute large shares of output? To which industries, if any, were they major suppliers of intermediate products or capital goods?

28. "Les Entreprises Publiques," *Cahiers Français*, no. 150 (September 1971), p. 6.

29. Blanc and Brulé, *Les Nationalisations Françaises en 1982*.

Table 13. *Chronology of Selected Public Enterprises, 1667–1980*[a]

Year	Enterprise
1667	Manufacture des Gobelins becomes state-owned Manufacture Royale des Meubles de la Couronne
1816	CDC created
1837	CDC manages funds collected by Caisses d'Epargne
1878	Beginnings of state railway system
1881	Postal savings system created
1918	Postal checking system created
1919	Crédit National created
1920	Crédit Agricole and BFCE created
1921	CNR created
1924	MDPA nationalized; CFP and ONIA created; state casts 40 percent of votes in CFP
1933	Air France, CGT, partly owned by state
1936	Nationalization of most production of military equipment; forerunners of SNIAS, DTCN, DTAT, and DTCA created. Office du Blé and CNME created
1937	SNCF formed from 2 public and 5 private railroads
1939	RAP created
1940	Havas acquired
1941	SNPA created
1944	ATIC and CEA created
1945	BRP created; Renault, Moteurs Gnôme et Rhône (renamed SNECMA), Banque de France, BNCI, CNEP, Crédit Lyonnais, Société Générale, Air France, Air Bleu, and Air France-Atlantique acquired
1946	ONERA created; CDF, EDF, and GDF formed from acquisitions; 34 insurance companies acquired
1948	CGT and Messageries Maritimes owned primarily by state; COFACE created
1949	TRAPIL created
1955	FDES formed from various public financial enterprises; SDR created
1960	UGP created
1961	CNES created
1966	ERAP formed from RAP and BRP; BNP formed from BNCI and CNEP; CDF-Chimie regroups CDF's chemical operations
1967	EMC formed from MDPA and ONIA
1968	AGF, GAN, MGF, and UAP formed from existing public insurance enterprises
1970	SNIAS formed primarily from NORD and SUD; IDI created
1975	CII and Bull merge and become partly state-owned
1977	SNEA formed from ERAP and SNPA
1978	Avions Marcel Dassault partly state-owned
1980	CEPME formed from CNME, CCCHCI, and Groupement Interprofessionnel des Petites et Moyennes Entreprises

Sources: Bellon and Chevalier, eds., *L'Industrie en France;* Catherine and Gousset, *L'Etat et l'Essor Industriel;* Chenot, *Les Entreprises Nationalisées;* Choinel and Rouyer, *Le Système Bancaire Français;* Dufau, *Les Entreprises Publiques;* and Stoffaës, *Politique Industrielle.*
a. Abbreviations explained in appendix B.

GOVERNMENT SUPPLY OF NONFINANCIAL PRODUCTS

Before 1982, state-owned enterprises (SOEs) played little or no part in most nonfinancial activities. In both 1959 and 1969 they accounted for less than 5 percent of value added in nineteen of twenty-nine such industries (appendix table A-25). In 1980, on the eve of the Mitterrand acquisitions, they accounted for less than 5 percent of output in twenty-nine of thirty-eight industries (appendix table A-26). After 1982 they increased their industrial presence: in only fourteen of forty industries did they contribute less than 5 percent of output. This change occurred too late, however, to affect the course of structural change during the quarter century following World War II.

Although state-owned enterprises existed in few industries before 1982, they tended to dominate those to which they belonged. When nonfinancial industries are defined broadly, as in tables A-25 and A-26, SOEs dominated coal, electricity, gas distribution, and telecommunications. When industries are defined narrowly, they dominated other lines of business as well: in 1962, they contributed 100 percent of the crude natural gas, virtually 100 percent of the tobacco products and matches, 65 percent of the miscellaneous minerals, 62 percent of the military products, 47 percent of the aircraft, and 37 percent of the health services produced in France.[30] They also supplied all nuclear fuels, all television service, and virtually all intercity rail service. An SOE such as Renault, which accounted for less than 40 percent of its industry's output (and even less of domestic consumption) in 1982, was exceptional.

The impact of SOEs on economic structure does not depend alone on their control of market supply.[31] Among the many determinants of such influence, the most direct are price elasticities of demand for their products, together with the pricing strategies they adopt. (Product innovation and product quality also matter. So do price elasticities of demand upstream and downstream.) Unfortunately, systematic evidence on price elasticities of demand does not exist. To

30. INSEE E11, p. 29.

31. SOEs can affect many features of the economy besides the composition of output. They might pioneer new styles of labor-management relations or facilitate implementation of macroeconomic policy. On the latter, see Durand and Passeron, "L'Incidence Macroéconomique des Dépenses d'Investissement."

complement information on SOE pricing, I shall simply identify industries that purchase large fractions of their physical inputs—current and capital—from industries dominated by SOEs.

In what respects, if any, did the prices of public enterprises diverge from the prices that would have been charged by comparable private enterprises? In principle, by charging relatively high prices SOEs can curtail consumption by final consumers and the output of business clients. By charging relatively low prices they can accomplish the opposite. By charging high prices to some customers and low prices to others, they can pursue both strategies simultaneously. To policymakers, discriminating among customers is especially attractive because it reduces the need for government to subsidize promotional activities. The feasibility of discrimination is limited, however, by arbitrage between buyers and by opportunities for business clients facing high prices to substitute other inputs for the products of state-owned enterprises.

SOE pricing may be analyzed along two dimensions: the extent of discrimination and the extent to which average price diverged from average cost. Presumably, comparable private enterprises would have maintained average price above average cost, and they would have discriminated among buyers to maximize profit.

Many SOEs did charge different prices to different buyers. Some of these differences can be interpreted as marginal cost pricing. In 1956, for instance, Electricité de France introduced time-of-day, time-of-year, and distance-from-generator prices for its high-voltage (industrial) customers. Similarly, in 1962 SNCF changed its pricing system from a flat rate per ton-kilometer of freight traffic on all routes to one that varied according to electrification, grade, and curvature of the line.[32] Other differences clearly involved charging what the traffic would bear, as when EDF moderated the price of electricity for clients who might build their own power plants, and when SNCF inflated its price for rail services to clients without recourse to other modes of transport.[33] The discriminatory features of the system were not entirely dissimilar to the practices of private but regulated

32. Lévy-Lambert, *La Vérité des Prix*, pp. 26–33; and Nelson, *Marginal Cost Pricing in Practice*, pp. 29–156.

33. Sègre, *Les Entreprises Publiques en France*, p. 161; and Lévy-Lambert, *La Vérité des Prix*, pp. 26–27.

counterparts in the United States. Nevertheless, differences did exist. Government occasionally used its power of ownership to establish SOE prices that supported particular government policies. For example, "when the steel industry increased its prices against the will of the authorities, the cost of transportation and coal was immediately raised for the steel companies by means of price increases put into effect by the relevant nationalized suppliers. This experience made the steel companies understandably more wary of independent pricing decisions in the future."[34] (Although government behavior of this sort sounds alien to the American system, recall the willingness of Lyndon Johnson to sell copper and aluminum from strategic stockpiles until private enterprises moderated their intended price increases.) Of the numerous similar actions undertaken in various industries, many have employed carrots rather than sticks. For example, in a 1966 arrangement with the steel industry, government "agreed that it would take measures to reduce the cost of domestic coking coal and coke, thus bringing these costs into line with world prices. This involved an increased subsidy of some kind by the State to Charbonnages de France." Similarly, government "agreed to explore ways to reduce the cost of transportation used by the steel industry, and to 'consult' with the industry on proposed transport cost increases affecting steel."[35]

With respect to average prices, French practice differed sharply from that of corresponding private enterprises; average prices in France were often low enough to require government subsidies.[36] SOEs tended to price their products more to promote than to discourage consumption.

The prices charged by SOEs did not necessarily impinge greatly on the production decisions of client companies. In particular, a

34. McArthur and Scott, *Industrial Planning in France*, p. 298.
35. Ibid., p. 374. Dumez and Jeunemaître, "Le Jeu des Tarifs Publics en France," p. 142, report that the technical ministries (industry, telecommunications, and transport, for example) exercised primary control over SOE price *structures*.
36. Dufau, *Les Entreprises Publiques*, pp. 190–91; and *Rapport sur les Entreprises Publiques* (the Nora report). According to Dumez and Jeunemaître, "Le Jeu des Tarifs Publics en France," three branches of the finance ministry (treasury, budget, and prices) exercised primary control over average prices. Hoping to curb subsidies and borrowing, the first two argued for high prices; hoping to dampen inflation, the last argued for low prices.

company able to purchase inputs cheaply from a public enterprise was unlikely to expand output markedly unless the inputs in question accounted for a large fraction of the company's total purchases. In other words, the elasticity of output with respect to specific input prices may be small, especially when those inputs are used sparingly by the producer.

Before 1982 most business purchases of goods and services from SOEs involved nondurable inputs. In accounting terms they involved intermediate consumption, not capital formation. As a result, using a two-step procedure, it is possible to construct for each branch of the economy a rough indicator of sensitivity to SOE pricing. First, one identifies the industries in which SOEs contributed most of the output and hence presumably controlled the prices the industries charged.[37] Second, using input-output tables, one calculates the share of each industry's intermediate consumption that was contributed directly by industries identified in step 1 as controlled by SOEs. In other words, the leverage of SOEs on economic structure is estimated by determining which industries relied heavily on inputs supplied by industries that SOEs dominate. Only industries that bought large fractions of their intermediate products from industries controlled by SOEs can be expected to have expanded as a result of favorable SOE prices. If those who bought heavily from SOEs had low elasticities of substitution among inputs, then this procedure also identifies industries that might have contracted as a result of unfavorable SOE prices.

Before 1982, SOEs controlled large fractions of output in several lines of nonfinancial business (see tables A-25 and A-26). Chief among these were coal, gas, electricity, rail transport, telecommunications, aerospace equipment, and petroleum. For which industries did these products contribute relatively large fractions of intermediate consumption in 1981? Few industries spend very much of their intermediate-product budgets on coal, gas, rail transport, or aerospace equipment. Petroleum accounted for at least 5 percent of intermediate consumption in thirty-five of seventy-nine industries, and in nineteen it accounted for more than 10 percent of such consumption (appendix table A-27); but in many activities the share of petroleum in nominal intermediate consumption was probably much smaller before the first

37. Merrill and Schneider, "Government Firms in Oligopoly Industries."

oil shock. Electricity and telecommunications were also important intermediate products for several industries.

Enterprises that bought heavily from SOEs were often state-owned themselves. Coal and petroleum were important inputs to electricity.[38] Electricity and petroleum were important to both coal and rail transport, petroleum was important to air transport, and telecommunications was important to financial services. Aside from the petroleum industry, most SOE leverage on the output of client industries involved other industries dominated by SOEs.[39]

GOVERNMENT SUPPLY OF FINANCIAL SERVICES

Since 1946 the state has owned much of the French financial system.[40] Among registered banks, for example, three large public enterprises accounted for 62 percent of deposits in 1980, and the ensemble of SOEs accounted for 93 percent of deposits in 1982.[41] Similarly, just after World War II SOEs accounted for 40 percent of the insurance business.[42] By 1980 four large SOEs received 33 percent of all insurance premiums not covered by the social security system.[43]

38. So were nuclear energy activities (research, mining, fuel enrichment, and waste processing), activities dominated by CEA but too narrow to appear separately in these data.

39. Since SOEs were relatively unimportant suppliers to most private enterprises, debates over government subsidies to SOEs, inspired by foreign claims of unfair advantages to SOE clients, may seem moot. Nevertheless, it is interesting to note in anticipation of my examination of subsidies that EDF and PTT, the SOEs appearing to enjoy the greatest commercial leverage over private enterprises (not only did both dominate domestic production of products used relatively heavily in several lines of business, but neither faced consequential competition from abroad) were among the least subsidized of the public enterprises (tables A-39 and A-40). Symmetrically, heavily subsidized SOEs tended to enjoy little commercial leverage over private enterprise.

40. In the taxonomy of the 1971 SNA the financial system includes credit institutions (S40) and insurance companies (S50). Credit institutions include lenders who create money (S41) and lenders who do not (S42). S41 includes the central bank (S411) and other creators of money (S412), while S42 includes the Caisse des Dépôts (S421) and other nonmonetary credit institutions (S422).

41. Blanc and Brulé, *Les Nationalisations Françaises en 1982*, p. 57.

42. Delion and Durupty, *Les Nationalisations, 1982*, p. 16.

43. I arrive at this figure as follows: Loustalet, "L'Assurance," pp. 402–03, 405, presents data on premiums received by fourteen groups of insurance companies accounting collectively for 70 percent of premiums received. The four public enterprises account for 46.7 percent of premiums received by the group of fourteen.

Even if it had exercised no regulatory powers over private financial enterprises, government might be expected to have controlled postwar markets for financial services.[44]

Government and its financial enterprises supplied three types of services to the rest of the economy: loans, infusions of equity capital, and insurance. Prices had to be set in each area.

Many financial SOEs loaned their money on attractive terms, ones more desirable to the user than ones based strictly on the cost and risk characteristics of the use. Financial SOEs tended to offer longer terms, lower rates, and more comforting periods of grace before repayments of principal. For example, the Bank of France tended to discount receivables at rates well below those charged by other financial enterprises. Similarly, many loans from Crédit National and Fonds de Développement Economique et Social (FDES) carried some type of advantage to the borrower.[45] In 1975, when the prime rate was 10.3 percent, medium-term export credit could be obtained for as little as 6 percent, long-term business credit was available from Crédit Agricole at 4.5 percent and from FDES at 9.75 percent, and housing credit could be had for as little as 5 percent. This diversity of interest rates, associated with public-sector financing, persisted. In the mid-1980s, when the market rate of interest was close to 15.75 percent, loans qualifying for interest subsidies could be obtained at rates ranging from 9 percent to 14.75 percent. During 1984, Fr 287.5 billion were loaned at preferential rates to various categories of borrowers.[46]

Typically, government required less of a dividend from recipients of equity infusions than would have been demanded by private investors. Between 1970 and 1974, for example, none of the *grandes*

44. The banks and insurance companies acquired by government from private owners functioned much like private enterprises. In contrast, certain specialized credit institutions created by government had no counterpart in the private sector. Readers unfamiliar with these enterprises may wish to consult the illustrative descriptions in appendix E.

45. In 1982, for example, 60 percent of Crédit National's direct loans to nonfinancial enterprises included some type of interest subsidy; see Choinel and Rouyer, *Le Système Bancaire Français*, p. 100. On the practices of FDES, see Philippe, *Le Rôle de l'Etat dans le Financement de l'Entreprise*, p. 77.

46. Lévy-Lambert, *La Vérité des Prix*, p. 108; and Ministère de l'Economie, des Finances et du Budget, *Livre Blanc sur la Réforme du Financement de l'Economie*, p. 56 (henceforth, Ministère des Finances, *Livre Blanc*).

entreprises nationales, or GEN (see appendix table F-6), paid any dividends to government.[47] Between 1975 and 1980, for the eight combined, dividends paid during year t never amounted to as much as 4 percent of equity infusions received from government during that year.[48]

Insurance of bond repayments was usually provided free of explicit charge, but public and private exporters were supposed to pay for the insurance they received. Until the first oil shock, premiums paid by exporters did cover indemnities received in several categories of insurance.[49] Even then, however, export insurance against increases in the cost of production and against unsuccessful prospecting abroad were provided at a loss. After 1974, in most types of export insurance, premiums failed to cover indemnities, and some of the shortfalls were substantial.[50]

Financial SOEs priced their services to promote favored investment projects. Compartmentalization, or *cloisonnement*, of the financial system, in which nominal access to favorably priced funds was limited to certain categories of investors and investments, reveals an intent not simply to stimulate investment generally but also to provoke changes in its composition.

The net impact of SOEs on the composition of investment is very difficult to measure. In the first place, it is difficult to identify the ultimate beneficiaries of the system. In the second place, it is difficult to determine the extent to which beneficiaries used funds obtained at preferential prices merely to finance inframarginal investments. Ideally, using information embodied in the marginal-efficiency-of-investment schedule associated with each industry, one could deter-

47. Dividends as defined in the 1971 SNA. See INSEE E57; and INSEE, *Rapport sur les Comptes de la Nation* (annual).

48. Dividends paid is variable R44 and external equity received is variable F50 in the 1971 SNA. In comparison, this ratio never amounted to less than 200 percent for other nonfinancial enterprises (S12) between 1970 and 1980.

49. Freyche, "Export Promotion as Industrial Policy," p. 83.

50. During the first half of the 1980s the balance between premiums and indemnities disappeared for insurance against fluctuations in exchange rates. See Ministère des Finances, *Livre Blanc*, pp. 100–01. Between 1974 and 1982, indemnities exceeded premiums by 44 percent for insurance against nonrepayment of loans to foreign clients. See *Rapport au Parlement sur les Fonds Publics Attribués à Titre d'Aides aux Entreprises Industrielles, Annexe au Projet de Loi Portant Règlement Définitif du Budget de 1981 et 1982*, p. 147.

mine which investment projects would have been funded if existing markets had allocated saving, and one could then compare that set of projects with the one implemented in fact; differences between the two would constitute the impact of government initiative. Unfortunately, in a study of this breadth, it is impossible to distinguish inframarginal from marginal projects or to identify the ultimate beneficiaries of public-sector pricing. Recognizing the limitations of the approach, I simply examine variations among industries in the ratio of subsidized to total investment. Prima facie, activities that relied heavily on subsidized funds can be expected to have received the greatest incentive to expand.

In 1984, loans at preferential rates amounted to 21 percent of gross investment in plant and equipment and to 30 percent of medium- and long-term borrowing from credit institutions; in all probability the corresponding figures for earlier years were even larger.[51] Not only did a considerable fraction of bank loans carry below-market rates of interest, but they financed a major share of investments by nonfinancial enterprises. Between 1953 and 1972, financial credit funded one-fifth to one-third of such investments (appendix table A-28).[52] In comparison, only once, during the 1963 credit crunch, did new issues of stocks and bonds ever account for as much as 15 percent of financial requirements.

At the industry level, complete information on business finance has been published only for 1951. These data permit observation of business reliance on financial credit during the heyday of government activism in financial markets. Many industries relied almost exclusively on internal funds—thirteen of thirty-seven employing them to meet at least 80 percent of their financial needs. Nevertheless, certain industries did rely heavily on financial credit, especially that extended by Fonds de Modernisation et d'Equipement, the forerunner of FDES (appendix table A-29). Only one industry, chemicals, satisfied more

51. See Ministère des Finances, *Livre Blanc,* p. 88; and the annual reports of the Conseil National du Crédit.
52. Externally supplied funds were the marginal source of saving available to most industries; to the extent that such funds were unrestricted in use, their price, in concert with the investor's marginal efficiency of investment, would determine the volume of investment. For data based on stocks, rather than flows, of liabilities, see Goldet, Nicolas, and Séruzier, "L'Endettement des Entreprises et des Ménages de 1954 à 1974," tables 1, 2.

than 5 percent of its requirements through flotation of equity. Of the small number that raised at least 5 percent of requirements on the bond market, most were dominated by SOEs. In general, this pattern is consistent with the hypothesis that government attempted to reserve for priority uses the part of national saving that it controlled.

After 1951, for nonfinancial enterprises, the best financial information at the industry level relates internal funds to investment. In effect, it ignores the breakdown of external funds into financial credit and securities. Given the unimportance of securities as a source of funds, it is reasonable to suppose that financial credit was important wherever internal finance was not.

Table 14 presents industry-level rates of internal finance for private nonfinancial enterprises from 1959 to 1969.[53] In thirteen of twenty-eight industries, gross saving amounted on average to at least 80 percent of investment in tangible assets. In another ten the ratio ranged from 67 percent to 80 percent. In only five industries did internal saving fail to generate at least two-thirds of the funds invested in plant, equipment, and inventory. These were the industries most likely to have felt incentives to expand as a result of pricing policies pursued by financial enterprises.

Table 14 also presents rates of internal finance for nonfinancial SOEs. In certain lines of business, SOEs tended to generate more funds internally than they invested in tangible assets. (To some extent, subsidies received directly from government, as opposed to cash flow from operations, explains the excess of cash flow over investment.) But SOEs in real estate; electricity, gas, and water; wholesale and retail trade; and ships, planes, and weapons tended to spend substantially more on tangible assets than they generated in cash flow. (Note that both public and private enterprises display low rates of internal finance in real estate, wholesale and retail trade, and ships, planes, and weapons.) These are the SOEs most likely to have expanded in response to financial credit received at attractive rates.

53. Gross cash flow denotes gross saving (categories 8A and 79 of the 1962 SNA). Gross investment comprises expenditure on inventory, plant, and equipment (categories 6c and 6d1 of the 1962 SNA). Had gross investment in financial assets been available, I would have included it, too, in the denominator. Between 1953 and 1959 (1956 SNA), on average, investment in financial assets accounted for 17 percent of all investment by nonfinancial enterprises; the corresponding figure for 1959–72 (1962 SNA) was 11 percent. See INSEE E31–32, vol. 2, table VII.2.

Table 14. *Gross Saving as Percent of Gross Investment, by Industry and Type of Enterprise, 1959–69*[a]

Code	Industry	Gross saving as percent of gross investment[b]			Gross saving less measured subsidies received as percent of gross investment[b]		
		All	Private	State-owned	All	Private	State-owned
10A	Real estate	17	9	23	11	6	16
03B	Electricity	47	88	46	44	77	43
05E	Ships/planes/weapons	52	48	65	23	7	48
11	Wholesale/retail trade[c]	60	59	51	23	42	850
10B	Hotels/restaurants	62	62	. . .	61	61	. . .
07E	Paper	70	70	. . .	65	65	. . .
07D	Wood	70	70	. . .	70	70	. . .
05B	Mechanical equipment	72	72	. . .	71	71	. . .
08A	Building material	72	72	. . .	72	72	. . .
02	Food/tobacco	73	69	305	46	42	305
05C	Electrical equipment	73	73	. . .	72	72	. . .
07C	Leather	74	74	. . .	73	73	. . .
01	Agriculture	79	79	. . .	64	64	. . .
06A	Glass	80	80	. . .	80	80	. . .
04A	Ferrous minerals/metals	82	82	. . .	79	79	. . .
07B	Apparel	82	82	. . .	82	82	. . .
07A	Textiles	83	83	. . .	83	83	. . .
06B	Chemicals/rubber	84	74	96	43	73	8
09B	Telecommunications	84	. . .	84	76	. . .	76
05A	Fabricated metals	85	85	. . .	84	84	. . .
10C	Services, miscellaneous	85	79	108	71	73	64
09A	Transport services	85	98	78	16	95	−23
05D	Road vehicles	86	90	77	86	90	77
08B	Construction	86	86	. . .	85	85	. . .
07G	Miscellaneous manufactures	87	87	. . .	87	87	. . .
03A	Coal	88	25	90	8	18	7
04B	Nonferrous minerals/metals	89	89	. . .	87	87	. . .
07F	Publishing	96	96	150	93	93	130
03C	Petroleum	105	87	201	88	82	133
	Weighted average	70	n.a.	n.a.	52	n.a.	n.a.

Sources: INSEE C4; INSEE C20.
n.a. Not available.
a. Industries defined according to ENF (see appendix C). Mean values for the period.
b. Gross investment in inventory, plant, and equipment.
c. Mean for public sector relates to 1960–69.

For monetary and nonmonetary credit institutions, the sources of finance can be ascertained since 1970 (appendix table A-30). In both types of enterprise, deposits were the chief source of funds, but financial credit was also important to nonmonetary institutions. Bonds accounted for surprisingly small fractions of financial resources.

Between 1959 and 1968 most nonfinancial SOEs received no new external equity (appendix table A-31). (In the flow-of-funds statistics associated with the national income accounts, injections of equity by government are classified as new external equity.) Manufacturers of aircraft and Air France received modest infusions, while Gaz de France and Electricité de France relied more heavily on them. Between 1959 and 1976 most of the grandes entreprises nationales received infusions of equity, but Gaz de France, Electricité de France, and perhaps Air France were the only ones to finance considerable fractions of their investments with such equity (appendix table A-32). Among financial enterprises, the importance of new external equity varied considerably. Banks narrowly defined (sector S412 of the 1971 SNA) and the Caisse des Dépôts relied lightly if at all on such equity, but certain specialized credit institutions (sector S422) received 10 percent of their funds on average in the form of new equity, injected undoubtedly by government. (New external equity was especially important between 1966 and 1973, ranging from 10 percent in 1966 to 24 percent in 1968.)[54]

In sum, only a few SOEs, virtually all of them specialized credit institutions, relied heavily on government infusions of equity.

CONCLUSION

Among the many enterprises owned by the state before 1982, a few specialized purveyors of financial credit were the most likely to shape economic structure. Certain nonfinancial enterprises—public and private alike—relied heavily on financial credit. Much of that credit was supplied on better than market terms. This evidence supports the view that French industrial policy was conducted primarily through the financial system. In the words of John Zysman, "Interventionist strategies of development pursued by the French

54. See Bourdon and Sok, *Tableaux des Opérations Financières et Endettement des Entreprises par Secteur, 1959–1976*; and INSEE, *Rapport sur les Comptes de la Nation*.

bureaucracy and executive would not have been possible without the capacity for action created by the financial system. A credit-based, price-administered financial system made possible administrative influence and often discretion in the allocation of capital . . . finance was crucial in shaping the state bureaucracy's capacity to intervene in industrial affairs."[55]

Nevertheless, one must remember the distinction between subsidy and influence. Some observers believe that interest and insurance subsidies had little impact on economic structure: they argue that many borrowers had decided to invest before learning of their qualification for preferential interest rates, that borrowers frequently reneged on promises made at the time they applied for preferential rates, and that subsidies were available for so many purposes to so many borrowers that the system lacked structural intent and effect.[56]

To the extent that public financial enterprises did alter the allocation of saving among industries, the chief beneficiaries appear to have been producers and users of housing, not producers or users of plant and equipment. (It is generally believed that the credit system also stimulated exports.) In the first place, not only did postwar investment in living space grow far more rapidly than investment in plant and equipment, but especially attractive rates of interest applied to housing.[57] In the second place, although manufacturers did receive loans at preferential rates, they also provided substantial commercial credit—at rates below market levels—to wholesalers and retailers.[58] In some measure, then, they served as intermediaries between state-owned financial enterprises and their own customers. The compartments of the financial system may have been more porous than some observers recognized or some public officials desired.

Throughout this section, I have assumed implicitly that government in fact controlled the behavior of enterprises owned by the state. The advisability of such an assumption is by no means obvious. Many

55. Zysman, *Governments, Markets and Growth*, pp. 168–69.
56. Ministère des Finances, *Livre Blanc*, p. 83.
57. See Goldet, Nicolas, and Séruzier, "L'Endettement des Entreprises et des Ménages de 1954 à 1974"; and Ministère des Finances, *Livre Blanc*.
58. Vannoise, "Le Crédit Commercial Interentreprises." See also Dietsch, "La Fonction Financière du Crédit Commercial Interentreprises"; and INSEE E103. One cannot be sure, of course, that reduction in preferential access to funds would have prompted manufacturers to lend commensurately less to wholesalers and retailers.

SOEs, especially those selling to clients other than government and those covering expenses with sales revenue, may have behaved as independently of government as did their private counterparts.[59] To the extent that public as well as private enterprises show some separation of ownership and control, one must explore means other than ownership by which government could have shaped economic structure.

Government as Buyer

To measure the impact of government procurement on economic structure, one would have to determine who would control the purchasing power now enjoyed by government and how those parties would have spent it. In a study of this breadth, however, the best one can do is to examine for particular industries the ratio of government purchases to sales. The larger the ratio, the greater the possibility that government promoted the industry's expansion.

PURCHASES OF GOODS AND TRADITIONAL SERVICES

Government's importance as a buyer depends on how government is defined. Construed narrowly, it encompasses just the activities of the state. Construed broadly, it embraces other agencies of national government, local governments, and public enterprises.

Between 1959 and 1980, on average, government broadly defined accounted for 11 percent of aggregate intermediate consumption and 25 percent of aggregate investment in fixed capital (appendix table A-33).[60] In the case of intermediate consumption, national government accounted for half the government total and the grandes entreprises nationales (GEN) for one-third.[61] Over time the importance of each segment of government changed only slightly. The GEN and local

---

59. Dumez and Jeunemaître, "Le Jeu des Tarifs Publics en France," p. 142, argue that SOEs enjoyed more independence in pricing the less they relied on borrowing or government subsidies to finance their activities.

60. More recent information appears in Ministère de l'Economie, des Finances et du Budget, "Le Recensement Economique des Marchés Publics." The impact of procurement on economic performance is discussed in Ponssard, "Marchés Publics et Innovation," and Dupoux and Grosgeorge, *Les Marchés Publics en France*.

61. The national accounts treat all military expenditure as intermediate consumption; see Camus and others, *La Crise du Système Productif*, p. 156.

government each accounted for roughly 40 percent of government's gross fixed capital formation, with national government responsible for most of the remaining 20 percent. The GEN and national government experienced declining shares of aggregate investment in fixed capital, while local government's share increased: the GEN accounted for 16 percent in 1959 and 12 percent in 1980, national government accounted for 6 percent in 1959 and 3 percent in 1980, and local government accounted for 7 percent in 1959 and 10 percent in 1980.[62]

Among manufacturing industries broadly defined, government was rarely an important client.[63] In 1974, for example, in eighteen of twenty industries, government bought no more than 5 percent of output (table 15). In the two remaining industries, however, government purchased 17 percent (electrical and electronic equipment) and 38 percent (ships and planes) of output. Government's importance among buyers also varied across narrowly defined manufacturing industries. During 1974, in the case of ships and planes, the government bought 43 percent of the aerospace equipment but only 6 percent of the ships. Within aerospace equipment, it purchased 57 percent of the aircraft fuselages but only 22 percent of the outer space equipment. In electrical and electronic equipment, it bought 51 percent of telephone and telegraph equipment, 46 percent of professional electronic equipment, and 44 percent of high-voltage electrical equipment; but it purchased only 11 percent of low-voltage electrical equipment and less than 10 percent of computer equipment.[64]

62. INSEE C67–68; and INSEE, *Rapport sur les Comptes de la Nation*, tableaux économiques d'ensemble and comptes détaillés des secteurs institutionnels.

63. The evidence reported in the remainder of this section is based on ministry of industry data for 1974; see Ministère de l'Industrie et de la Recherche, *Les Marchés Publics en 1974 dans l'Industrie*; and Mathieu and Suberchicot, *Marchés Publics et Structures Industrielles*. These studies report for most industries the ratio of government procurement to industry sales. "Government" includes national government, local government, and SOEs (not just the GEN). "Procurement" excludes expenditures falling outside the scope of purchasing rules laid down by government (the code des marchés publics, for example). Such rules apply primarily to large contracts (Fr 30,000 per contract in 1974); hence the procedure employed by the ministry tends to exclude purchases of nondurable goods. In 1972, procurement amounted to roughly 80 percent of total government purchases; Ministère de l'Industrie et de la Recherche, *Les Marchés Publics en 1974 dans l'Industrie*, p. 8. "Industry sales" excludes sales of companies employing fewer than ten people.

64. The figure for computer equipment is taken from ibid., table C1.

Table 15. *Government Purchases as Percent of Sales,*
by Industry, 1974[a]

	Broadly defined industries[b]			Narrowly defined industries[c]		
Code	Name	Percent of industry shipments	Code	Name	Percent of industry shipments	Percent of shipments by firms doing business with government
T11	Bulk chemicals	0.2	3301	Aircraft fuselages	57.3	57.3
T10	Glass	0.4	2911	Telephone/telegraph equipment	51.2	53.2
T19	Leather/shoes	0.7				
T21	Paper	0.7	3302	Aircraft engines	48.1	48.3
T18	Textiles/apparel	0.8	2914	Professional electronic equipment	46.1	48.2
T22	Printing/publishing	0.9				
T23	Rubber/plastics	1.1	3303	Special equipment for aircraft	44.0	44.5
T09	Building materials	1.2	2811	High-voltage electrical equipment	43.9	44.3
T20	Wood/miscellaneous mfg.	1.2				
T06	Electricity/water	1.4	1803	Explosives	41.5	46.7
T08	Nonferrous minerals/metals	2.0	3121	Railway rolling stock	29.5	31.1
T12	Chemical products	2.0	2406	Pumps/compressors	25.4	30.6
T07	Ferrous minerals/metals	2.8	3201	Warships	23.0	28.1
			3304	Outer space equipment	22.3	22.3
T13	Metallic products	2.9	2504	Mining equipment	21.8	24.7
T16	Ground transport equipment	3.0	2818	Insulated electrical cable	18.9	22.2
T04	Coal	3.7	0521	Natural gas	16.1	16.2
T05	Petroleum	4.9	2408	Boilers	15.6	23.2
T14	Mechanical equipment	5.0	3203	Miscellaneous ships	15.0	30.2
T15	Electrical equipment	17.2	4523	Miscellaneous leather goods	14.5	21.1
T17	Ships/planes	38.4	2814	Insulators, electrical	13.2	15.5
			1502	Gravel	11.9	15.0
			2810	Low voltage electrical equipment	10.7	13.8
			2812	Electrical equipment for industry	10.1	11.1

Source: Mathieu and Suberchicot, *Marchés Publics et Structures Industrielles*, tables 1, 4.

a. Government comprises state-owned enterprises as well as national and local governments.

b. Industries defined according to NAP-T (see appendix C). Source omits government purchases of water (part of T06), weapons (part of T17), and food (all of T02 and T03). See note 62 in text.

c. Industries from which government purchased more than 10 percent of shipments. Industries defined according to NAP-600. Source omits NAP-100 industries 08, 26, and 35–42. See note 62 in text.

Even if defined narrowly, industries comprise a variety of companies producing a variety of products. For example, aircraft fuselages includes balloons and gliders as well as jet aircraft. Such heterogeneity makes it useful to calculate a second measure of government's position among buyers: the ratio of government procurement to total shipments of companies from which government buys. The greater the difference between this and the initial measure, the greater the possibility that industrial heterogeneity obscures the importance of government procurement. In fact, however, the two measures fail to diverge appreciably for most of the narrowly defined industries appearing in table 15.

The direct impact of government procurement also differed by size of seller. In 1974, in six of nine industries for which it was a major client, government affected the largest sellers more than the rest (appendix table A-34). These figures must be interpreted with care. Because small companies are often owned by large companies, they might function as operating divisions of their large parents. Even when they enjoy legal independence, small companies might earn their livelihood from subcontracting that trickles their way from government purchases. Thus small companies might be influenced by government purchases to an extent greater than that suggested in table A-34. In terms of direct influence, however, it remains the case that government procurement affected the big more than the small.

The importance of government as a buyer would be especially likely to translate into structural leverage if procurement decisions were concentrated in a few purchasers. In two respects, such concentration was in fact achieved. First, local governments played a minor role in procurement of industrial products, spending just Fr 7 on procurement for each Fr 1,000 spent by national government.[65] Second, although SOEs spent 82 percent as much on procurement as did national government, they targeted their expenditure relatively little on products susceptible to government leverage. National government spent three-quarters of its procurement funds on electrical and electronic equipment and on ships and planes, precisely the industries over which government in general exercised most leverage.

65. The figures in this paragraph are based on Mathieu and Suberchicot, *Marchés Publics et Structures Industrielles*, table 2. The weight of local governments was felt primarily in the construction business, which lies outside the data set employed here.

(If industries are defined narrowly, it is national government that buys the major share of aircraft, of professional electronic equipment, and of explosives, three product lines where the ratio of government procurement to industry output is large.) In contrast, SOEs spent less than 29 percent of their procurement funds on the products of these two industries. Some 60 percent were spent on petroleum, ferrous minerals and metals, mechanical equipment, and ground transport equipment, industries that sold 5 percent or less of their output to government. Only in narrowly defined industries did SOEs account for large shares of government purchases of products supplied primarily to the public sector.[66] Even in those cases, the number of government organizations involved in procurement remained small; a coherent procurement strategy, designed to support structural policy, was not obviously infeasible.

One of the important services purchased by government was development of science and technology.[67] Government maintained two types of programs, one with specific industries and technologies in mind, the other to promote research in general. Support of aerospace research illustrates the first approach.[68] The activities of Fonds de la Recherche et de la Technologie (FRT) and Agence Nationale de Valorisation de la Recherche (ANVAR) exemplify the second. FRT financed up to 50 percent of a research and development project undertaken by a business enterprise and up to 100 percent of a project undertaken by a quasi-governmental laboratory. Typically, FRT did not require repayment, so the national income accounts considered its support a form of subsidy. Like FRT, ANVAR covered up to 50 percent of a project undertaken in a business enterprise; unlike FRT, however, ANVAR required repayment if the project bore commercial fruit (the amount repaid depended on the output and profitability of

66. In the case of electrical and electronic equipment, for example, PTT bought important fractions of telephone and telegraph equipment; EDF and, to a lesser extent, SNCF and RATP, bought important fractions of high-voltage equipment. See ibid.

67. Linkages between investment in R&D and gain in productivity are explored in Cunéo, "L'Impact de la Recherche et Développement sur la Productivité Industrielle."

68. *Rapport au Parlement sur les Fonds Publics Attribués à Titre d'Aides aux Entreprises Industrielles, Annexe au Project de Loi Portant Règlement Définitif du Budget de 1980*, pp. 107–16.

the new product).[69] In the national income accounts, support of innovation administered by ANVAR was classified under loans, not subsidies; but the extent to which government advances were repaid is difficult to determine.[70]

Government concentrated its support of industrial research on a few activities.[71] In 1975, 65 percent went to the aerospace industry and 24 percent to electronics; the next largest recipient, office equipment, received just 6 percent of the total.[72] These were precisely the industrial activities in which R&D accounted for the greatest share of sales revenue (appendix table A-35). Government might thus have exerted great influence on the industrial composition of research activity, although the actual effect depended on the extent to which it rewarded projects that would have been undertaken even without its assistance.

Government concentrated its support of research by company as well as by industry. In 1975 the top twenty enterprises ranked

69. *Rapport au Parlement sur les Fonds Publics Attribués à Titre d'Aides aux Entreprises Industrielles, Annexe au Projet de Loi Portant Règlement Définitif du Budget de 1981 et de 1982*, pp. 63, 68–71.

70. In any given year, government advances exceeded reimbursements by a substantial margin; but government support has been growing and repayments, if they occur at all, do not begin until five to ten years after the receipt of support. See *Rapport au Parlement sur les Fonds Publics Attribués à Titre d'Aides aux Entreprises Industrielles, Annexe au Projet de Loi Portant Règlement Définitif du Budget de 1977*, p. 68.

71. The Commissariat à l'Energie Atomique (CEA), Centre National d'Etudes Spatiales (CNES), and other quasi-governmental laboratories were classified as government agencies in the 1971 SNA. As a result, their research activity was likely to have been excluded from the industrial category. To appreciate the importance of such laboratories, consider the structure of national government's budget for civilian research in 1984: FRT, 4.1 percent; ANVAR, 4.9 percent; the electronics program, 6.2 percent; the civilian aerospace program, 12.3 percent; CEA, 9.2 percent; CNES, 17.9 percent. See *Rapport Annexe sur l'Etat de la Recherche et du Développement Technologique: Activités en 1982 et 1983, Perspectives 1984*, pp. 302–05; the figures relate to *crédits de paiement*.

72. Ministère de l'Industrie, *La Recherche Développement dans les Entreprises Industrielles en 1975*, table 1. These figures probably understate government support of computers. Much of the relevant research may be classified as electronics. On the same reasoning, support of nuclear power and weapons may entail flows of funds to chemicals, to electrical equipment, or to mechanical equipment. Nevertheless, the figures do reveal that companies such as CII that engage primarily in the computer business did not receive the same intensity of public funding as did companies engaged primarily in certain other lines of business.

according to their intramural expenditure on research accounted for 50 percent of all industrial research. When ranked according to government support, the top twenty received 88 percent of the total. Membership in this group of special beneficiaries changed little over time.[73]

Finally, government support of research was handled by a small number of agencies. In 1975 three ministries allocated 99 percent of government funds for industrial research—defense accounting for 66 percent, industry for 26 percent, and telecommunications for 7 percent. At the industry level, however, these averages can be misleading. In the case of public funds destined for aerospace equipment, defense accounted for 79 percent, and industry for 21 percent; in the case of electronics, defense accounted for 52 percent, telecommunications for 29 percent, and industry for 15 percent; and in the case of office equipment, defense accounted for 10 percent, telecommunications for 0.2 percent, and industry for 90 percent. In other words, defense oversaw aerospace, industry managed computers, and all three participated in electronics. To most industries displaying low ratios of research expenditure to sales revenue, the ministry of industry was the principal supplier of public research funds. To industries displaying relatively high ratios, however, the ministry of defense tended to dominate—as illustrated by miscellaneous chemical products, including explosives; ground transport equipment, including military vehicles; building materials, including ceramics; precision goods; and rubber products.[74]

PURCHASES OF POLICY SERVICES: SUBSIDIES

Because government rarely offers a cash subsidy without asking the recipient to modify his behavior, cash subsidies may be viewed as government purchases of policy services. For example, when government provided cash to the SNCF in return for a promise of low passenger fares for large families, it was really purchasing railway services for certain members of the population. (For this reason, perhaps, in the 1971 SNA several government transfers to SNCF were excluded from the railway's measured subsidies. See appendix F.)

73. Ibid., pp. 35–38.
74. Ibid., table 7.

Not all subsidies succeed in modifying the behavior of their recipients, because the impact of a subsidy depends on its magnitude and the elasticity of response to it. Where demand is inelastic, subsidizing output will not expand the quantity sold; where supply is inelastic, subsidizing consumption will not expand the quantity sold. Even where supply and demand exhibit the requisite properties, the effect of a subsidy on output depends on the criteria governing subsidy awards. It is also the case that not all influential subsidies serve to alter economic structure. Some subsidies are designed with macro-economic stabilization in mind. Others aim to alter more the methods of production than the volumes of output. Given its amount, a subsidy tied explicitly to the volume of output is more likely to alter the industrial composition of economic activity than is a subsidy tied to the use of certain factors of production or to the location of productive capacity in certain regions. Nevertheless, the distribution of subsidies among enterprises might affect the composition of economic activity profoundly.

Distribution of Measured Subsidies among Activities. Between 1959 and 1980, nonfinancial enterprises received virtually all subsidies tied explicitly to investment in plant and equipment (table 16).[75] Initially, unincorporated enterprises accounted for most of the non-financial total, but by the end of the period, corporations (GEN excluded) took the lion's share. Operating subsidies, linked either to production or to expenses other than plant or equipment, also went primarily to nonfinancial enterprises (table 17). Nevertheless, by 1980 the share devoted to credit institutions had risen from 3 percent to 13 percent. The shares accorded to insurance companies and unin-corporated nonfinancial enterprises also grew, albeit modestly, while the combined share of GEN and other nonfinancial corporations fell from 91 percent in 1959 to 77 percent in 1980.

Among nonfinancial enterprises, subsidies were dispensed reason-ably selectively. In the first place, they were concentrated in state-owned enterprises. Between 1959 and 1969, on average, SOEs received 71 percent of the nonfinancial total (appendix table A-36).[76]

75. For a study of recent subsidy patterns, see Dutailly, "Aides aux Entreprises."
76. Table A-36 is based on the 1962 SNA, tables 16 and 17 on the 1971 SNA. The significance of this distinction is discussed in appendix F.

Table 16. *Share of Capital Subsidies, by Type of Enterprise, 1959–80*[a]
Percent unless otherwise specified

	Nonfinancial			Financial		
Year	Grandes entreprises nationales (S11)	Other corpora- tions (S12)	Unincor- porated enterprises (S81)	Banks (S40)	Insurance companies (S50)	Total subsidies (millions of francs)
1959	5.1	41.0	54.0	*	*	752
1960	4.2	49.5	46.3	*	*	818
1961	5.6	51.8	42.6	*	*	939
1962	6.4	52.5	41.1	*	*	927
1963	6.1	54.4	39.5	*	*	1,050
1964	7.3	51.8	40.9	*	*	1,359
1965	11.0	55.5	33.5	*	*	1,603
1966	14.1	60.2	25.7	*	*	2,423
1967	13.6	60.6	25.8	*	*	2,870
1968	17.4	62.9	19.7	*	*	2,742
1969	17.2	60.8	22.0	*	*	3,017
1970	12.8	70.7	16.5	*	*	2,847
1971	10.0	71.7	18.2	*	*	2,697
1972	10.8	73.0	16.2	*	*	3,161
1973	11.6	70.9	17.5	0.1	*	3,653
1974	11.6	74.6	13.8	*	*	4,206
1975	12.4	70.5	17.1	*	*	6,427
1976	6.7	74.7	18.6	*	*	14,099
1977	12.4	75.1	12.4	*	*	7,164
1978	12.1	75.5	11.3	0.4	0.7	6,930
1979	12.4	76.4	11.2	*	*	7,310
1980	11.1	76.1	12.5	0.3	*	8,118

Sources: INSEE C67–68; and INSEE, *Rapport sur les Comptes de la Nation* (annual), comptes détaillés des secteurs institutionnels.

* Less than 0.05 percent.

a. 1971 SNA. Capital subsidies are *aides à l'investissement* (R71).

In the second place, most subsidies were granted to a small number of industries. Between 1959 and 1969 three industries received 68 percent of all subsidies distributed to nonfinancial enterprises (appendix table A-37). The ten largest recipients accounted for 96 percent; the remaining 4 percent was spread among nineteen other lines of business.

Thirteen of twenty-nine nonfinancial industries contained SOEs. Three of these accounted for 81 percent of all subsidies to SOEs. Rail transport (RATP and SNCF), nuclear weapons and power (CEA, classified under chemicals), and agricultural stabilization (ONIC and FORMA, classified under wholesale and retail trade) were the specific beneficiaries of government aid. Twenty-eight of the industries con-

Table 17. Share of Operating Subsidies, by Type of Enterprise, 1959–80[a]

Percent unless otherwise specified

| Year | Nonfinancial | | | | Financial | | | Total subsidies (millions of francs) |
	Grandes entreprises nationales (S11)	Other corporations (S12)	Unincorporated enterprises (S81)	All	Banks (S40)	Insurance companies (S50)	All	
1959	33.9	57.4	3.2	94.5	3.0	2.6	5.5	3,912
1960	32.9	56.7	4.5	94.1	4.2	1.7	5.9	4,410
1961	28.6	59.7	5.7	93.9	4.3	1.8	6.1	5,263
1962	33.0	56.2	4.0	93.1	5.7	1.2	6.9	6,737
1963	44.9	43.7	5.7	94.4	4.4	1.2	5.6	8,079
1964	46.5	42.3	3.9	92.7	5.9	1.4	7.3	8,175
1965	48.6	40.1	3.4	92.0	6.3	1.6	8.0	9,445
1966	44.5	44.2	2.5	91.2	7.4	1.4	8.8	10,270
1967	45.0	43.6	3.0	91.6	6.6	1.8	8.4	11,412
1968	47.2	43.5	2.4	93.1	5.9	1.0	6.9	13,736
1969	44.6	42.2	4.0	90.8	8.0	1.1	9.2	14,495
1970	35.5	48.4	3.4	87.3	10.4	2.2	12.7	14,036
1971	35.4	42.7	4.4	82.5	13.8	3.7	17.5	15,651
1972	30.9	45.4	4.4	80.8	14.9	4.3	19.2	17,692
1973	33.2	44.4	3.7	81.4	14.8	3.9	18.6	20,988
1974	30.4	36.6	15.1	82.2	14.1	3.7	17.8	23,798
1975	27.9	40.7	13.3	81.9	12.8	5.3	18.1	31,355
1976	27.2	41.3	11.2	79.8	14.0	6.3	20.2	39,578
1977	31.6	41.7	10.2	83.4	11.5	5.0	16.6	46,991
1978	28.6	46.7	6.5	81.7	14.6	3.6	18.3	51,661
1979	28.5	46.8	4.4	79.6	13.4	7.0	20.4	58,156
1980	27.2	49.6	6.6	83.4	12.7	3.9	16.6	62,269

Sources: INSEE C67-68; and INSEE, *Rapport sur les Comptes de la Nation* (annual), comptes détaillés des secteurs institutionnels.

a. 1971 SNA. Operating subsidies are *subventions d'exploitation* (R30).

tained private enterprises. The largest three recipients of subsidy represented three stages in the production of food: agriculture, food processing, and wholesale and retail trade. (The private manufacturers receiving subsidies were those obliged to buy inputs from domestic sources at prices above world market levels. They received substantial fractions of their subsidies from ONIC and FORMA, the two public enterprises in wholesale and retail trade.) Collectively, food-related activities accounted for 74 percent of all subsidies to private nonfinancial enterprises. Ships, planes, and weapons (mostly ships) and miscellaneous services (mostly healthcare) were the only others to account for at least 5 percent of subsidies to private nonfinancial activities. Neither transport services nor chemicals—both important beneficiaries of aid to SOEs—received a large fraction of the subsidies, hardly surprising, since the SOEs in these sectors supplied rail transport, nuclear power, and nuclear weapons, none of which was produced by the private enterprises in these sectors.

For 1967–81, available data relate to nonfinancial enterprises other than the grandes entreprises nationales.[77] During these years, agriculture and food wholesaling received the largest amounts of subsidies, accounting for 43 percent of the nonfinancial total, GEN excluded (appendix table A-38).[78] Combined with food processing, their share approached 54 percent. The only other activities to account for more than 5 percent of the total were consumer services (healthcare), transport services, and real estate (public housing). The remaining twenty-nine activities accounted for just 22 percent of subsidies received by nonfinancial enterprises, again GEN excluded.

In sum, measured subsidies were indeed focused on a few activities, but the principal beneficiaries violated most people's preconceptions of sunrise industries. Most were not even engaged in manufacturing.

The Degree of Subsidy. The impact of a subsidy on its recipient will depend partly on its importance relative to other sources of revenue. As a result, it is useful to examine the degree of subsidy—

77. The GEN are identified in appendix table F-6. Among the GEN, most subsidies were received by RATP, SNCF, and CDF; see INSEE E57.

78. Because table A-38 is based on the 1971 SNA, it excludes subsidies paid to such important recipients as CEA, ONIC, and FORMA (see appendix F).

the ratio of subsidy received to cost of subsidized activity—for particular companies and industries (see appendix F). High ratios of subsidy to outlay signal potentially great effects of the donor on the recipient's market behavior. (A contingent subsidy of $50 would induce many people to purchase a pocket calculator but few to indulge in a luxury automobile.) Clearly, however, enough other factors intrude on the relationship between donor and recipient to jeopardize strong inferences from such ratios. (A subsidy in excess of 100 percent may be required to prompt possessors of multiple calculators to buy another.) In the first place, not all subsidies paid by government succeed in altering behavior: intentionally or not, government's efforts might serve simply to transfer income in the direction of subsidy recipients. In the second place, the recipient's response may be elastic in some dimensions but inelastic in others. Consider, for example, a government that subsidizes a monopolist to alter the geographic distribution of output. Even if the monopolist modifies the spatial composition of his activity, he may choose not to change overall output consequentially. If the firm adopts this strategy, national output of its product will appear inelastic with respect to the subsidy.

Some nonfinancial state-owned enterprises have been subsidized lavishly. Between 1959 and 1969 ONERA received aid amounting to 76 percent of its outlays (appendix table A-39). Both CEA and the combination of ONIC and FORMA financed two-thirds of their outlays from subsidies. SNCF, RATP, and public enterprises in the petroleum industry used subsidies to pay for at least 20 percent of their outlays.[79] But not all public enterprises experienced government's largesse. Eleven such nonfinancial enterprises received virtually no subsidies between 1959 and 1969, and another seven relied on subsidies to cover no more than 5 percent of expenses. These eighteen included all manufacturers assigned to the aerospace industry and Renault, Air France, EDF, and PTT.

Most public enterprises diplayed degrees of subsidy that varied over time, but few experienced radical changes in the intensity of aid (tables A-39 and A-40). One exception was coal. In the nationalized

79. Five public enterprises were assigned to the petroleum industry (appendix table F-5). Principal among them were SNPA and ERAP. SNPA (and TRAPIL) received virtually no subsidies (table A-39). Therefore, despite the absence of direct evidence, it may be assumed that ERAP was subsidized substantially.

segment of the industry, the ratio of subsidies to outlays rose steadily and sharply between 1959 and 1969. Thereafter, the increase seemed to abate. Two other exceptions were Imprimerie Nationale and PTT, both of which registered relatively large rates of subsidy during brief periods. Compagnie Nationale du Rhône was subsidized modestly before 1966, but during the four remaining years of observation, subsidies accounted for as much as 14 percent of outlays.

Thus between 1959 and 1969 measured subsidies did finance a large share of outlays, but only in a few nonfinancial enterprises. These belonged to one of four groups: military research and development (ONERA and CEA), agricultural stabilization (ONIC and FORMA), rail transport (RATP and to a lesser extent SNCF), and petroleum (ERAP).[80] Subsidies to public enterprises impinged inconsequentially on most of manufacturing and much of energy, transport, and telecommunications.

Measured subsidies affected private nonfinancial enterprises very little during these years (appendix table A-41). With all private nonfinancial activity divided into twenty-eight industries, none received subsidies of as much as 5 percent of outlays during the period as a whole, and only ships, planes, and weapons, with 6.2 percent in 1959, and coal with 6.4 percent in 1968, achieved more than 5 percent in a single year. (The private component of the coal industry is trivially small, though.)

Between 1967 and 1981, measured subsidies continued to impinge lightly on nonfinancial enterprises, excluding GEN (appendix table A-42). With nonfinancial activity divided into thirty-six industries, only real estate attained a mean degree of subsidy of at least 5 percent. Among manufacturing industries, ships and planes were subsidized to the greatest degree, but subsidies amounted to just 3 percent of outlays. In no year between 1967 and 1981 did ships and planes exhibit a degree of subsidy in excess of 5 percent. The only other manufacturing industries to exceed 1 percent during at least one of these fifteen years involved food or electrical and electronic equip-

80. In its youth CEA engaged heavily in development of nuclear weapons but also in design of nuclear power plants. During the 1970s, after deciding to abandon the graphite-gas process developed by CEA, Georges Pompidou allowed the agency to expand its involvement in such commercial activities as uranium mining, fuel enrichment, and waste processing. Stoffaës, *Politique Industrielle*, p. 527.

ment. The others with relatively high degrees of subsidy were agriculture; electricity, gas, and water; consumer services; and food wholesaling.

Only since 1959 do the national income accounts provide information on degrees of subsidy at the industry level. And yet the era of plentiful support might well have preceded that year. Not only did the Marshall Plan provide governments of the late 1940s and early 1950s with the means to subsidize indulgently (between 1948 and 1954 American aid accounted for 10 to 20 percent of national government receipts), but the Treaty of Rome, with its provisions curbing government promotion of domestic enterprises, had yet to be implemented.[81]

The detailed economic portrait of 1951 offers the best glimpse of subsidies during the early postwar years.[82] Both measured subsidies and indemnities for wartime damage, then an important component of government aid, were concentrated in a few activities (appendix table A-43). Railroads, wholesale and retail trade, services, nonelectric machinery, and agriculture received 86 percent of allocated subsidies. Meanwhile, agriculture, maritime transport, railroads, petroleum, and fish or textiles (the two tie for fifth place) received 90 percent of allocated indemnities. Railroads captured one-third of allocated subsidies, while agriculture received 40 percent of allocated indemnities. But most industries were subsidized to only a slight degree (appendix table A-44). In twenty-five of the thiry-seven, subsidies (including indemnities) amounted to less than 1 percent of expenditures. Eight industries, none of them in manufacturing, received subsidies covering at least 5 percent of expenditures. Among manufacturing industries, mechanical equipment, petroleum, and aircraft were subsidized to the greatest degree.

In certain respects, then, degrees of subsidy during 1951 resembled degrees of subsidy in later years: rail transport and agriculture were subsidized heavily, and manufacturing industries were not. In other respects, however, the situation differed. Water transport, as well as water and steam, were subsidized heavily, and coal had yet to display

81. See INSEE, *Le Mouvement Economique en France, 1949–1979*, pp. 233–34; and Balassa, "Whither French Planning?"

82. Ministère des Affaires Economiques et Financières, *Tableau Economique de l'Année 1951.*

the intensity of subsidy that characterized the late 1960s. The most important conclusion to be drawn from table A-44 is that even as early as 1951, degrees of subsidy did not vary substantially among manufacturing industries.

Government has also subsidized the activities of credit institutions and insurance companies. If degree of subsidy is measured in the manner already applied to nonfinancial enterprises, government aid impinged only modestly on both types of financial enterprise (appendix table A-45). Between 1959 and 1980, measured subsidies never amounted to as much as 5 percent of outlays.

Government helped financial enterprises primarily through interest subsidies (*bonifications*). Enterprises received subsidies on the basis of two rates of interest: that paid by the financial enterprise to acquire funds on the bond market and that at which the treasury desired funds to be loaned. From the perspective of the recipient, *bonification* weakened the relationship between interest paid and interest received.[83]

If one assumes that all operating subsidies received by financial enterprises took the form of interest subsidies, then degree of subsidy should be calculated as the ratio of operating subsidies received to interest paid. Appendix table A-46 shows such ratios for 1959–80. The degree of subsidy is only slightly greater than that displayed in table A-45; over the period as a whole it amounted to 5 percent, and its maximum value was 7 percent. Financial institutions were subsidized relatively heavily between 1962 and 1967 and then again during 1971 and 1972. The first of these periods corresponded to the era when treasury was abandoning its role as direct financier of the economy. From 1970 to 1980, degree of subsidy can be measured separately for monetary and nonmonetary credit institutions (table A-46). During each of these eleven years, the former were subsidized

83. Because receipt of interest subsidies did not usually constrict the freedom of lenders to set their own terms, *bonification* did not guarantee that rates charged to borrowers would be lowered as subsidies increased. Some subsidies, however, were linked explicitly to the rates at which loans were made. In 1980 three-quarters of government expenditure on *bonification* was governed by procedures leaving lenders free to price their loans as they pleased. *Rapport au Parlement sur les Fonds Publics Attribués à Titre d'Aides aux Entreprises Industrielles, Annexe au Project de Loi Portant Règlement Définitif du Budget de 1980*, pp. 165–68.

to a greater degree than were the latter, but the ratio of operating subsidy received to interest paid never exceeded 10 percent for either.

In recent years, only a few financial enterprises have received interest subsidies. In 1980, for example, Crédit National, CEPME, and the Sociétés de Développement Régional (SDR) accounted for more than 75 percent of subsidies received. In 1984 the SDR, together with Crédit National, CEPME, and Crédit Coopératif, distributed 100 percent of relevant loans (those for industry, trade, and tourism) to those qualifying for interest subsidies.[84]

Given the concentration of interest subsidies in a few recipients, it is important to measure the degree of subsidy experienced by those particular financial enterprises. Crédit National received a subsidy equal to 1 percent of its debt outstanding on the bond market, while CEPME received a corresponding subsidy of 1.2 percent; the SDR, which lend to companies they wish to attract to their regions, received subsidies equal to 2 percent of their total debt outstanding.[85]

Government subsidies—those that qualified for the name in France's national income accounts—were thus focused on a few beneficiaries, and the money involved was considerable. Nevertheless, even the major beneficiaries did not rely on subsidies to pay most of their bills. Whether one focuses on allegedly favored mature industries such as steel or allegedly favored young industries such as computers, government subsidies generally represented little of the money expended by private enterprises between 1959 and 1980.

Government as Tax Collector

Taxes are negative subsidies and tax expenditures are positive subsidies. In principle, government could have used selective fiscal policy to shape economic structure. In practice, little information exists on the microeconomic aspects of fiscal policy.

Only a few tax expenditures, such as the credit allowed against the value-added tax to those who increased their investment during 1975, appear as subsidies in the national income accounts. Even the tax expenditures listed in parliamentary reports on industrial subsidies

84. Ministère des Finances, *Livre Blanc*, p. 82.
85. Conseil National du Crédit, *Rapport Annuel, 1981*, annexe, pp. 165–68.

usually escape the subsidy heading in national income accounts.[86] The ministry of finance has published studies of a handful of tax expenditures, but the most comprehensive information on the subject appears in a 1982 report from the Commissariat Général du Plan on industrial subsidies.[87]

Unlike most studies of tax expenditure, that of the commission sought to quantify relief not only to large industrial corporations, but also to agriculture and small business. It found, for example, that during 1980 industrial corporations gained Fr 2.4 billion from accelerated depreciation, Fr 2.2 billion from provisions against possible increases in raw material prices, Fr 2.0 billion from general incentives to invest in plant and equipment, Fr 3.2 billion from consolidated reporting of domestic subsidiaries, Fr 1.4 billion from consolidated reporting of foreign subsidiaries, Fr 1.3 billion from reduction of value-added tax on television sets, Fr 1 billion from provisions for risk in lending to foreign buyers, Fr 0.8 billion from advantages to publishers of periodicals, Fr 0.6 billion from depletion allowances, and Fr 0.5 billion from incentives to locate investments in particular regions. Meanwhile, farmers gained Fr 2.5 billion from taxation of estimated rather than actual income, Fr 1.9 billion from reductions of value-added tax on intermediate consumption (feed and fertilizer), and Fr 1.4 billion through exemptions from or reductions of value-added tax on agricultural products. Finally, small business gained Fr 1.4 billion through exemptions from or reductions of value-added tax on their products. Although rough enough to scar anyone attempting strong conclusions, this evidence suggests the importance of extending measurements of tax expenditure beyond the boundaries of the industrial sector.

To proceed from amounts of tax expenditure to impact on recipients, the best one can do in a comprehensive study such as this is to

86. *Rapport au Parlement sur les Aides à l'Industrie, Annexe au Projet de Loi Portant Règlement Définitif du Budget de 1984*. See also Ministère de l'Economie, des Finances et du Budget, "Les Dépenses Fiscales" (1985); Ministère de l'Economie, des Finances et du Budget, "Les Mesures Fiscales Nouvelles"; and Ministère de l'Economie, des Finances et du Budget, "Les Dépenses Fiscales" (1981).

87. An example of the work of the Ministère de l'Economie, des Finances et du Budget is "Les Statistiques de la Direction Générale des Impôts pour 1980," pp. 28–32. The report of the Commissariat Général du Plan is "Aides à l'Industrie," app. 5, pp. 105–17.

calculate effective rates of taxation at the industry level. I shall perform such calculations separately for indirect and direct business taxes.

INDIRECT TAXES

Between 1959 and 1980 government derived either 44 percent or 81 percent of its fiscal receipts from indirect taxes, depending on whether social security contributions are considered part of the category (table 18).[88]

The value-added tax (VAT) was introduced to the industrial sector in 1954, and by 1979, in most important sectors of the economy, it had replaced the general sales tax of 1920.[89] From 1954 until 1968 the standard rate of tax was 25 percent, and on July 1, 1982, it was 18.6 percent.[90] But not all products were taxed at the standard rate. As of July 1, 1982, four other rates existed: 33.33 percent, 7 percent, 5 percent, and 0 percent. In theory the government taxed luxuries at the highest rate and necessities at one of the reduced rates. In fact, however, the assignment of rates to products was not that simple. Automobiles as well as jewelry, and tobacco as well as furs, were taxed at 33.33 percent. Moreover, although most foods were taxed at a reduced rate, such necessities as clothing were not. Symptomatic of the loose fit between rate of tax and necessity of product was a finding that the ratio of VAT to consumption expenditure failed to vary among households either by social class or by amount consumed.[91] VAT was not the only indirect tax to vary in rate among industries. Heavy excise taxes were levied on products such as gasoline and tobacco; and since government paid all or part of certain employers' social security taxes, the effective rate of that obligation also differed among enterprises.[92]

88. Musgrave, *Fiscal Systems*, pp. 174–75, classifies social security contributions (or *cotisations*) as indirect taxes when paid by employers and as direct taxes when paid by employees. Employers alone contributed to the family allowance and workman's compensation systems; employers and employees both contributed to all other branches of the social security system. See Direction de la Sécurité Sociale, *La Sécurité Sociale*, p. 73.

89. Balladur and Coutière, "France," p. 20.

90. Mehl and Beltrame, *Le Système Fiscal Français*, p. 70. Current rates, together with European comparisons, appear in Ministère de L'Economie, des Finances et de la Privatisation, "La Réforme Fiscale, 1986–1988," pp. 19–20.

91. Balladur and Coutière, "France," pp. 20, 25.

92. Government frequently helped to finance social security benefits, especially

Table 18. *Tax Receipts, by Source, as Percent of All Tax Revenue, 1959–80*[a]

	Indirect taxes				Direct taxes		
Year	VAT (R21)	Import duties (R29)	Other indirect (R22)	Social security (R62)	Corporate income (R611)	Personal income (R612)	Other direct (R613)
1959	20.6	1.3	28.9	29.6	6.6	8.0	5.1
1960	21.1	1.5	28.3	29.9	6.0	7.9	5.4
1961	20.7	1.4	27.8	31.6	5.8	7.7	5.0
1962	20.8	1.5	27.7	32.7	5.2	7.7	4.5
1963	21.1	1.6	26.9	33.6	4.7	7.8	4.3
1964	21.1	1.6	26.2	33.3	4.9	8.8	4.2
1965	20.4	1.5	26.1	33.6	5.0	9.2	4.1
1966	20.9	1.4	25.9	33.9	4.2	9.3	4.3
1967	20.5	1.3	25.3	35.1	4.5	9.0	4.3
1968	23.9	1.0	20.4	35.5	4.1	10.2	4.8
1969	27.0	0.9	17.1	35.7	4.7	10.1	4.4
1970	25.6	0.9	16.5	36.5	5.9	9.8	4.7
1971	26.2	0.5	16.1	37.9	5.5	9.5	4.3
1972	26.3	0.3	16.1	37.9	5.6	9.7	4.2
1973	24.3	0.2	17.5	38.0	5.8	8.8	5.4
1974	25.0	0.1	15.1	39.1	7.7	10.2	2.8
1975	23.3	*	15.5	41.4	5.1	9.4	5.2
1976	23.7	*	14.3	40.7	5.6	10.3	5.4
1977	21.2	*	15.0	42.5	5.4	10.8	5.1
1978	21.7	*	15.3	42.7	4.5	10.7	5.1
1979	21.6	*	15.4	43.3	4.5	10.4	4.8
1980	21.1	*	14.8	43.7	4.8	10.4	5.2
Mean	22.6	0.8	20.6	36.7	5.3	9.3	4.7

Sources: INSEE C67–68; and INSEE, *Rapport sur les Comptes de la Nation* (annual, 1970–80).
* Less than 0.05 percent.
a. 1971 SNA. Includes national government, local government, and the social security system (S60C).

Given the quantitative importance of indirect taxes, it would not be surprising to learn that some of the interindustry variation in rates

in the public sector. For example, as part of a 1971 agreement with SNCF, government paid Fr 2.5 billion into retirement funds associated with the railways. It adopted similar programs for miners. See Dufau, *Les Entreprises Publiques*, pp. 195–96. In the private sector, it has contributed to the social security system on behalf of the textile industry; see Commission of the European Communities, *Thirteenth Report on Competition Policy*, p. 285; and de la Torre, *Clothing Industry Adjustment in Developed Countries*, pp. 151–57.

can be explained in terms of government's desire to influence the composition of output. During the 1960s, when government wished to promote the electronics industry, it recognized the irony of subsidizing industry members while treating some of their products to the highest VAT rate. Accordingly, VAT on television receivers was reduced to the normal rate of the day (17.6 percent).

If particular industries supply several products, some of which are taxed at high rates and others at low rates, then variations in rate at the product level do not necessarily alter the industry-level composition of economic activity. To determine, therefore, whether variations in rate affected industrial structure, I examine differences among industries in the importance of indirect taxes. Because payroll taxes are based on payrolls and VAT is based on sales, I examine the ratio of social security contributions to payroll and the ratio of other indirect taxes to value of output.[93]

Between 1962 and 1969 most industries contributed to the social security system at nearly the same rate (appendix table A-47). On the low side were hotels, cafes, and restaurants; agriculture; and telecommuncations. On the high side were SOEs in electricity, gas, and water and in transport services. Neither such likely beneficiaries of a progressive industrial policy as electrical equipment, autos, and ships, planes, and weapons nor such likely beneficiaries of conservative strategies as textiles and apparel paid tax at especially low rates.[94]

Between 1959 and 1969, for all nonfinancial industries combined, indirect taxes amounted to 6.6 percent of output (appendix table A-48). Only a few activities were taxed at rates below 3 percent or above 10 percent. In the private sector, indirect taxes impinged most forcefully on the petroleum industry. In the public sector the tobacco monopoly, together with the Régie des Alcools, paid indirect taxes amounting to more than twice the value of output. Private agricultural enterprises and the government printing office, however, paid indirect taxes at rates less than 2 percent, and public enterprises in telecom-

93. In the 1971 SNA, all industry-level variables are measured net of VAT. As a result, I confine myself here to data based on the 1962 SNA. Indirect taxes are defined comprehensively to include VAT (735) and sales (736), excise (737), and payroll (738) taxes. Output includes increases in inventories and excludes indirect taxes.

94. Before controlling for the interindustry variation in wage structures. As in the United States, an upper limit exists on each person's wages subject to payroll tax. See Direction de la Sécurité Sociale, *La Sécurité Sociale en France*, p. 74.

munications, chemicals, and miscellaneous services paid at rates between 2 percent and 3 percent.

In sum, government clearly sought to limit consumption of petroleum and tobacco products and to promote consumption of products supplied by such other industries as agriculture, telecommunications, government documents, public drama and operas, and healthcare in public institutions. The existence of extreme values notwithstanding, variations among industries in the rate of tax occurred infrequently.[95]

DIRECT TAXES ON BUSINESS INCOME

Between 1959 and 1980 government derived 5 percent of its fiscal receipts from a tax on corporate income (see table 18). Such a tax affects corporate saving and hence the ability of nonfinancial enterprises to finance investment internally. If the ratio of tax paid to cash flow varies appreciably among industries, the tax might alter the industrial compositions of investment and output.

As a proportion of cash flow, income tax depends on the rate at which income is taxed and on the distribution of cash flow between expenses and income. With respect to the rate of tax, the ministry of finance treated all corporations alike: after 1958 government took one-half of corporate income.[96] With respect to the division of cash flow between income and expense, however, corporations varied appreciably. Because much of the variation corresponded to differences in the magnitude of depreciation, it is important to examine how depreciation has been determined in the French system.[97]

The fiscal treatment of depreciation contained provisions that applied equally to all corporations and provisions that applied only to

95. Since VAT is not levied on exports, industries exporting large parts of their output have low ratios of indirect taxes to value of shipments.

96. Mehl and Beltrame, *Le Système Fiscal Français*, p. 28. Recent reductions in corporate tax rates are described in Ministère de l'Economie, des Finances et de la Privatisation, "Les Mesures Fiscales Adoptées au Cours de l'Année 1987"; and Ministère de l'Economie, des Finances et de la Privatisation, "La Réforme Fiscale, 1986–1988," pp. 11–18.

97. Fixed assets were usually valued at historical cost less accumulated depreciation. Between 1945 and 1959, however, French firms were allowed to revalue their assets upward to take account of inflation. As a result, firms could accumulate depreciation beyond the amount originally spent to acquire their assets. Since 1959 such revaluations have been prohibited in theory but, thanks to favorable rulings of the Conseil d'Etat, practiced occasionally. Price Waterhouse, *Accounting Principles*, p. 24.

some. Before 1960 all corporations were obliged to depreciate their assets according to the straight-line method. Starting in 1960 they were allowed to adopt the declining balance alternative (*amortissement dégressif*). Although applicable to only certain kinds of assets, declining balance was available to all industrial and commercial corporations. As of 1975, about half of such enterprises took advantage of the option. In contrast, to promote regional development and redevelopment, certain companies were allowed to depreciate certain assets by 25 percent during their first year of use. Such depreciation was not available to all corporations; it required advance approval by the ministry in charge of the budget. During 1980 two industries (automobiles and food) accounted for 52 percent by value of the favored investment.[98] Even those depreciation provisions that applied equally in theory may have provided fiscal relief to some corporations more than to others. The quantitative consequences of these practices should not be underestimated. According to Anicet Le Pors, accelerated depreciation alone cost the government Fr 18 billion in 1975.[99] This was a considerable sum when compared with the amount of income tax actually paid by corporations that year (Fr 27 billion according to the national income accounts).

Despite its importance, the treatment of depreciation was just one of many fiscal practices that governed variations among activities in the effective rate of income tax. The combined effect of these practices is discernible in appendix table A-49, which shows the ratio of corporate income tax to corporate cash flow between 1962 and 1969. In the private sector, steel corporations paid 4 francs in tax from each 100 francs in cash flow, while corporations in real estate and in wholesale and retail trade paid more than 20 francs per 100. In the public sector, income tax impinged trivially if at all on most industries; only the tobacco monopoly (classified in food) paid more than 5 percent of cash flow in income tax.

As long as government allowed any form of deduction for depreciation, one would expect the ratio of income tax to cash flow (t) to vary inversely with the ratio of capital to output (k). Therefore, one

98. Ibid., p. 68; and *Rapport au Parlement sur les Fonds Publics Attribués à Titre d'Aides aux Entreprises Industrielles, Annexe au Projet de Loi Portant Règlement Définitif du Budget de 1980*, p. 35.

99. Le Pors, *Les Béquilles du Capital*, p. 29.

must control for capital intensity of production when examining the use of income tax to shape economic structure. Toward that end, for twenty of the industries in table A-49, I regressed t on a measure of k and then ranked industries on the basis of differences between observed and predicted values of t.[100] The regression is

$$\hat{t} = 18.56 - 0.54\,k$$
$$(1.75)\quad(0.23)$$
$$R^2 = 0.24;\; F = 5.64;\; N = 20$$

(standard errors in parentheses), and the residuals appear in appendix table A-50. As expected, the tax rate depended negatively on the capital intensity of production (at the .05 level of significance in a one-tail t-test). After controlling for capital intensity, however, steel corporations still appeared to be taxed relatively lightly. To lesser extents, corporations manufacturing ships, planes, and weapons, nonferrous minerals and metals, automobiles, and petroleum also tended to pay unexpectedly low taxes. In contrast, corporations in building materials, glass, coal, mechanical equipment, and miscellaneous manufactures tended to pay more in taxes than would be expected from their capital intensity.

Table A-50 shows just one of many possible effects of corporate income tax on economic structure. It does suggest, however, that several beneficiaries of the system were mature industries. (The explanatory variable, k, is measured in flow rather than stock terms. The relative frequency with which mature industries appear to benefit from depreciation rules may be spurious—attributable simply to their relatively low ratios of investment to assets.) It also suggests that certain nominal targets of government promotion, especially in electrical and electronic equipment, were not among the advantaged.

DIRECT TAXES ON PERSONAL INCOME

Certain types of interest received were exempt from personal income tax. For example, starting in 1983 individuals could deposit

100. The sample consists of all industries engaged in the production of goods rather than services. Conventionally measured, output, and hence the ratio of capital to output, is difficult to compare between suppliers of goods and suppliers of services. Actually, k is measured as the ratio of gross investment in plant and equipment to production. In other words, the numerator measures gross additions to, rather than the existing stock of, capital.

up to Fr 10,000 in special bank accounts (called CODEVI) bearing 7.5 percent interest tax free. Banks were then required to lend these funds to business at the rate of 9.75 percent. The funds had to be used for designated types of investment. In 1984, when the corresponding market rate of interest was roughly 15.75 percent, nonfinancial enterprises borrowed Fr 13.5 billion under this program.[101]

The fiscal treatment of personal income undoubtedly affected the volume of investment. Since marginal investment projects are distributed unequally among activities, such treatment undoubtedly affected the future composition of output. With one exception, however, it is unlikely that the personal income tax was used consciously to shape the allocation of saving among business uses. That exception was the favorable tax treatment of interest on saving earmarked for down payments on housing; such treatment certainly served consciously to expand the residential construction industry.

CONCLUSION

In comparison with its German and American counterparts, the French government relied more on cash subsidies and less on tax expenditures when attempting to modify the behavior of nonfinancial enterprises. Even so, it did deprive itself of considerable receipts.[102] The ministry of finance did engage in tax expenditure, and it did so in a deliberately selective manner. Many tax breaks, especially those permitting payment on the basis of expected rather than actual income, were established through bargaining between individual companies and the Direction Générale des Impôts (DGI). This gave DGI the power to alter the relative profitability of various industries.

To what extent, however, did tax expenditures affect the composition of economic activity? Although effective rates of taxation differed among industries, the pattern of variation did not always reveal a desire to promote structural change. Traditional enterprises in mature industries enjoyed substantial and evident tax advantages; few emerging activities could say the same.[103]

101. This was 2.8 percent of all uses of funds, 4.8 percent of investment in tangible assets. See Ministère des Finances, *Livre Blanc*, pp. 80, 82, 87.

102. Le Pors, *Les Béquilles du Capital*, pp. 44, 95, 109.

103. I have limited the discussion of taxes to variations in rates among industries, but I might also have described corresponding variations by size of enterprise. Under

Government as Regulator

Regulation permits government to assume an activist economic stance without spending (and therefore raising) large sums of money. For this reason, perhaps, the French government has often placed unusually pervasive constraints on the behavior of households and enterprises. Since World War II, some of these have been designed, however partly, to facilitate alterations of economic structure.

REGULATION OF PRODUCT MARKETS

From the end of World War II until the end of 1986, government enjoyed broad standby authority to regulate prices. Occasionally, prices were frozen across the board, but usually, different degrees of control were applied to different sectors of the economy.[104] Undifferentiated oligopolies such as steel were regulated especially assiduously, but luxuries, exports, companies with fewer than twenty employees, and goods heavily exposed to foreign competition were often controlled rather lightly.

Most advocates of price control hoped it would moderate inflation. Although macroeconomic, this hope might prompt disparate treatment of industries. First, input-output linkages may be such that regulation of certain key prices would prevent other prices from rising rapidly.[105]

---

both VAT and the tax on corporate income, enterprises are treated in one of three ways: exemption, obligation to pay in regular fashion, or opportunity to pay a fixed sum (*forfait*), negotiated with DGI in lieu of regular treatment. In practice, the rate of tax implicit in the fixed sum tended to lie well below the standard rate. Typically, exemption applied only to the smallest companies, while the fixed-sum alternative to regular treatment was available to slightly larger companies. The system thus favored permanently small enterprises. Companies paying VAT, however, were entitled to deduct the VAT they paid when purchasing plant and equipment from the VAT they owed. In this respect, the tax favored dynamic companies. Enterprises investing heavily in tangibles sometimes submitted voluntarily to it.

104. Prices were frozen in 1952, 1954, 1957, 1963, and 1969. Two brave ministers (Paul Ramadier in 1947 and Jean-Pierre Fourcade in 1974) even tried to decrease prices by fiat. See Bloch-Lainé and Moschetto, *La Politique Economique de la France*, p. 112; and Philippe, *Le Rôle de l'Etat dans le Financement de l'Entreprise*, p. 17. Lévy-Lambert, *Vérité des Prix*, describes eleven distinct regimes.

105. A cynical variant of this argument suggests that government cared less about actual than about perceived inflation. To ensure domestic political tranquility, it focused regulation on products weighty in the official price index. In this connection, it is interesting to note that 10 percent of the 1986 index involved prices of state-

Second, the administrative burden of regulation could have encouraged focus on certain industries: prices in tight-knit oligopolies are relatively easy to monitor; and prices of homogeneous products require little rethinking over time, because industries with homogeneous products tend to experience relatively little product innovation and relatively little brand proliferation.

Although price controls were adopted primarily to curb inflation, certain public officials probably recognized their utility for other purposes. One French expert has summarized French price controls as "both an extension of incomes policy to the arena of profit and the foundation of France's ability to compete with foreign rivals. Through their impact on internal finance, price controls leave companies in growth industries with sufficient investment funds, while obliging other companies to increase their productivity so as to develop adequate financial resources."[106] In the context of economic structure, selective severity of price controls could be used to shape the composition of business investment. The tighter the control of an industry's prices, the greater its difficulty in financing desired investment with internal funds alone.[107] Since government controlled access to many types of external funds, especially financial credit, business recourse to external finance gave government an opportunity to curb types of investment that it disfavored.

The financial history of the steel industry accords well with the structural interpretation of price control.[108] During the mid-1960s

owned public utilities; see Dumez and Jeunemaître, "Le Jeu des Tarifs Publics en France," p. 140.

106. Philippe, *Le Rôle de l'Etat dans le Financement de l'Entreprise*, p. 19.

107. Desired investment can change as a result of price control. In a closed economy, binding price constraints serve to increase output in monopolistic industries and to decrease output in competitive ones. If capacity is utilized fully when controls are implemented, desired investment is likely to change in the same direction as output. In an open economy, regulation's impact on investment is more complex. To the extent that domestic producers anticipate a booming and expanding foreign market, they might wish to augment capacity even if their domestic market is competitive. On the importance of internal finance, recall tables 14 and A-28. Family-owned companies are especially likely to avoid external finance wherever possible, and French industry sported many such companies. As recently as 1971, half of France's 200 largest industrial corporations were controlled by family owners. See Morin, *La Structure Financière du Capitalisme Français*, table 9.

108. See McArthur and Scott, *Industrial Planning in France*; and Lévy, "Industrial Policy and the Steel Industry."

many public officials considered the industry overpopulated: until rival sellers merged, French companies were allegedly doomed to compete unsuccessfully in world markets. Government also believed (with more justification) that most steel companies opposed the idea of merger. Thus steel prices were kept low to force the companies to seek financial credit, and extension of such credit was made contingent on the mergers desired by government.

Any general conclusion on the structural impact of price controls must take account of the fact that French rates of inflation often exceeded those of other large OECD countries. This could be interpreted as revealing the unimportance of studying price controls, but it could also be interpreted as revealing the importance of objectives other than macroeconomic price stability in their design.

In addition to regulating domestic prices, government controlled access to foreign exchange, importation of goods, and anticompetitive methods of business. I shall discuss exchange controls and import quotas in chapter 4, and the rules of competition in chapter 5.

REGULATION OF FINANCIAL MARKETS

Between 1947 and 1955 government exercised tight control over issues of new securities. The budget act (*loi de finances*) of 1947 authorized the treasury to veto almost any new offering of bonds or equities. In exercising this veto the treasury was to consider the timing of the flotation and the use of the funds. According to François Bloch-Lainé and Pierre de Vogüé, "this procedure permitted an allocation of funds to those most likely to use them in the public interest."[109] In other words, the treasury used its power with the intention of influencing the composition of investment.

Over the past quarter century, government has relaxed its control of the market for equities. It no longer intervenes selectively in new issues. It allows all companies a stock exchange listing, provided only that they comply with a standard set of technical requirements, the most important of which involve the fraction of voting stock to be quoted on the exchange, the methods used to construct financial accounts, and the amount of information disclosed to the public. It promotes the equity market generally by offering fiscal advantages to

109. Bloch-Lainé and Vogüé, *Le Trésor Public et le Mouvement Général des Fonds*, p. 185.

small investors, by creating a special compartment of the stock exchange for companies not yet qualified for full listing, and by allowing SOEs to issue nonvoting certificates of participation.[110]

In the case of bonds, however, deregulation definitely lagged. Even after 1955, when setting the calendar of offerings, treasury did not adopt the principle of first-in-time, first-in-line. Rather, it accorded priority first to government bodies, then to SOEs. Frequently, private enterprises found themselves postponed out of the market. Although prior approval by treasury had supposedly disappeared by 1969, John Zysman found as late as 1983 that "none of our interviewees suggested that this change had altered the pattern of access."[111]

Companies can avoid regulation of domestic securities markets by floating new issues abroad. Until the 1960s, however, government constrained this option by regulating access to foreign exchange, believing evidently that the initial inflow of capital, which would affect the balance of payments salutorily, would be outweighed by future, potentially unpredictable debits on that account. Exchange controls were employed not only to ensure balance of payments equilibrium but also to ensure that priority activities received preferential access to foreign currencies. Although weakened considerably by implementation of the EEC, exchange controls remained in force until 1986.[112] By curtailing the domestic supply of new bonds, government placed upward pressure on their prices and downward pressure on their rates of interest. As a result, those who did gain access to the market paid less for the right to borrow than if the supply of new issues had not been regulated.

Apart from government itself, the nominal beneficiaries of this policy—nominal because these enterprises often passed their savings on to customers in the form of lower rates of interest—were financial SOEs engaged in long-term lending. Not only did such enterprises

110. Défossé and Flornoy, *La Bourse des Valeurs.*

111. Zysman, *Governments, Markets, and Growth,* pp. 123–24. Compare Dony, Giovaninetti, and Tibi, *L'Etat et le Financement des Investissements Privés,* p. 306.

112. Information on the foreign bonds of French enterprises appears in INSEE, *Le Mouvement Economique en France, 1949–1979,* pp. 359–63. In 1959, for example, when nonfinancial enterprises had Fr 1,861 million worth of bonds outstanding at home, they had Fr 46 million worth outstanding abroad. On the abolition of exchange controls, see Ministère de l'Economie, des Finances et de la Privatisation,"1987: Une Année d'Action Economique et Financière," pp. 20–21.

account for a large fraction of domestic bond issues, but bonds constituted the principal source of their funds. Along with interest subsidies, regulation of access to the bond market permitted designated financial institutions to offer credit on attractive terms to their segmented clienteles. (As in the case of interest subsidies, government ownership of the relevant financial enterprises helped ensure that economies in the acquisition of funds were passed along to nonfinancial borrowers.) To government, however, interest subsidies and flotation control differed in one important respect: the latter entailed only trivial expenditure of government funds. In fact, effective flotation control reduced the amount of interest subsidy required to induce a lender to offer funds at a given rate of interest. Hence it reduced the budgetary commitment required to effect major reallocations of saving among investments.

A second form of financial regulation involved the portfolios of banks and insurance companies. Most governments regulate portfolio compositions to prevent financial panics, and some further regulate them to augment artificially the demand for government securities. In France, however, the goals of portfolio regulation extended beyond these traditional domains. To ensure compartmentalization of the financial system, and hence low rates of interest on select uses of saving, government required certain banks to limit their clienteles in specific ways and required other financial institutions to devote minimum fractions of their portfolios to certain kinds of assets.[113]

A general manifestation of this policy early in the postwar period consisted of requiring various financial enterprises to devote ample parts of their portfolios to government securities—not only to finance government expenses but also to permit the treasury, through FDES, to direct saving to certain uses. Crédit Agricole illustrated the policy of compartmentalization as applied to a particular financial institution.[114] As of 1971, although it could receive deposits from anyone, the bank was obliged by government decree to restrict most of its lending to people who lived or worked in rural settings, to agricultural cooperatives, and to local governments. In 1978, in return for relinquishing its exemption from income tax, Crédit Agricole gained

113. In general, see Hodgman, *National Monetary Policies and International Monetary Cooperation*, chap. 3.
114. Choinel and Rouyer, *Le Système Bancaire Français*, pp. 59–61.

the right to lend first to small companies engaged in the manufacture of food and then, as of 1981, to all companies with fewer than 100 employees. Finally, in 1982 Crédit Agricole was authorized to lend to all households and to all enterprises employing fewer than 500 people and located in metropolitan areas with populations less than 65,000.

The structural significance of these regulations depends partly on their effectiveness, and that effectiveness is open to question. Few compartments of the financial system had hermetic seals, but segmentation was sufficiently pronounced to prevent the exercise of monetary policy through manipulation of "the" rate of interest.[115]

During much of the postwar period, French monetary authorities also imposed ceilings on loans outstanding (*encadrement du crédit*) at individual financial enterprises. During periods of credit control, the Bank of France would note the volume of loans outstanding at each regulated enterprise on some reference date and establish for each such enterprise a target rate of increase for loans outstanding. (Credit controls existed from February 7, 1958, to February 5, 1959; February 27, 1963, to June 24, 1965; November 12, 1968, to October 27, 1970; and December 12, 1972, to January 1, 1985.)[116] Strictly speaking the targets were guidelines rather than orders, but violators were penalized. During the first three episodes of control, they suffered decreased opportunities to discount at the central bank (and throughout this period, the Bank of France rediscounted on better than market terms). During the fourth episode, they suffered even harsher penalties, as they were obliged to increase their reserve ratios and to deposit the supplementary reserves in non-interest-bearing accounts at the central bank. The required supplement rose geometrically with the difference between actual and target rates of increase in loans outstanding.

In principle, credit ceilings served two purposes. On the macroeconomic level they complemented open market operations as a way to effect stabilization.[117] On the microeconomic level they permitted

115. Ministère des Finances, *Livre Blanc*, p. 17.

116. Castel and Masse, *L'Encadrement du Crédit*, pp. 29–37; Hodgman, *Selective Credit Controls in Western Europe*; and Ministère de l'Economie, des Finances et du Budget, "La Politique Monétaire en 1985."

117. In comparison with foreign counterparts, French monetary policy has not

certain types of investment to be financed at low rates of interest while the central bank was constricting the aggregate supply of credit. In other words, investments desired by government could be sustained through regulatory segmentation of the credit market.

The microeconomic content of the system appeared in its mechanics. Not all financial enterprises were regulated; the system applied primarily to *institutions de crédit monétaires*—for the most part banks that created money as defined in M2. And certain loans of regulated enterprises were exempt (*désencadré*) in the sense of being excluded from the credit outstanding to be juxtaposed with the enterprise's credit ceiling. Moreover, credit ceilings rose more rapidly at some financial enterprises than at others. During 1980, for instance, the rate of increase ranged from 2.5 to 4.5 percent. It depended on how the enterprise was expected to distribute its credit among uses and users: "Some French officials maintain that the purpose of this variation is to increase the market share of smaller institutions and thereby stimulate financial competition. However this explanation is not widely accepted by French bankers, who point out that some institutions receiving the higher limits are, in fact, subsidiaries of the largest business banks. Bankers point, instead, to differences in the composition of the lending business conducted by various institutions."[118]

During the era of credit ceilings, unregulated financial enterprises—those exempt from quantitative control of credit expansion—increased their share of lending activity, and unregulated credit increased its share of financial credit outstanding.[119] By 1981 unregulated credit amounted to 33 percent of all credit used by households and nonfinancial enterprises; many of the unregulated loans financed exports, direct foreign investments, or domestic investments in plant and equipment. Between 1972 and 1981, however, households maintained their share of loans from regulated purveyors of credit (banking and

---

relied heavily on open market operations. Aftalion, "The Political Economy of French Monetary Policy."

118. Cohen, Galbraith, and Zysman, "Credit Policy and Industrial Policy in France," p. 19.

119. The evidence in this paragraph is taken from Castel and Masse, *L'Encadrement du Crédit*, pp. 25, 40–41, 84, 88. It relates to changes in the allocation of credit, which need not correspond closely to changes in the gap between actual and desired allocation of credit. Nevertheless, I know of no expression of industrial policy that suggests that housing received ex ante an insufficient share of credit.

leasing institutions), and loans from such financial enterprises also came increasingly to finance exports or housing at the expense of investments in plant, equipment, and working funds. Between 1972 and 1981, banking and leasing institutions increased their finance of exports by 495 percent, their finance of housing by 382 percent, and their finance of investment in plant and equipment by 168 percent. Funds devoted to the combination of exports and investment increased by 243 percent. Among the funds used to finance investment, credit associated with leasing increased by 339 percent.

REGULATION OF LABOR MARKETS

Government regulated the labor market in two major ways: it placed a floor on permissable wage rates, and it required government approval for many forms of economic layoff. The latter served mainly as an adjunct to regional policy, and so I shall not discuss it here.

The minimum wage was introduced for all adult employees in 1950. (Originally known as the *salaire minimum interprofessionnel garanti*, or SMIG, the minimum wage has been known since 1970 as *salaire minimum interprofessionnel de croissance*, or SMIC.) Shortly after its introduction, the minimum wage was tied by law to variations in the consumer price index. Not infrequently, the index was manipulated to prevent automatic increases in SMIG. Despite periodic adjustments based on other criteria, SMIG fell rapidly and far behind other wages. Under the Grenelle agreements of 1968, however, it quickly jumped 35 percent. Then in 1970, SMIC was linked not only to the cost of living but also to the average wage. Minimally, SMIC was to rise at a rate equal to the rate of increase in the cost of living plus one-half the rate of increase in the average real wage. Relative to the period before 1968, the ratio of minimum to average wage rose sharply.

During the early 1980s, some 4 percent of salaried employees were paid the minimum wage, but the percentage differed among activities.[120] In the clothing sector, 38 percent of salaried employees were remunerated at or close to the minimum wage; in textiles and leather, the comparable figure was close to 30 percent. In contrast, fewer than 5 percent in energy, fabricated metals, transportation, and telecom-

120. Les Echos, *L'Economie de A à Z*, p. 185; and Padieu, "Les Bas Salaires," p. 27.

munications were paid at or near the minimum wage. At 10 percent of salaried employees, the electrical equipment sector lay between the two extremes. The importance of the minimum wage also differed by size of company. In companies with more than 2,000 employees, only 4 percent received something close to it; however, more than 17 percent of those in companies with fewer than 50 employees received close to the minimum wage.

The most important reason for increasing the ratio of minimum to median wage was sensitivity to the plight of low-wage workers. Nevertheless, many public officials were surely aware of minimum wage's impact on the structure of economic activity. Those who advocated structural change would not have been unhappy to learn that relative increases in the minimum wage had bridled production of mature goods in small companies.[121] They might have supported such changes in SMIC for structural reasons.

Government as Propagandist

Jean Monnet, the father of French economic planning and a vigorous proponent of active government, did not view himself as a manipulator of subsidies and regulations. Rather, he felt his task was to change the attitudes of private parties, to persuade business leaders in particular that expansion and modernization were in their interest.

> Existing regulations—covering the allocations of raw materials and credit—created substantial opportunities to influence private behavior. And yet, ours would not be an attempt to direct the economy. . . . In the first place, the regulatory apparatus of government was not to be placed in the hands of the planners; and those with the nominal authority to regulate were unlikely to surrender it to us in practice. In the second place, however, and probably more important, I continued to believe that nothing is more powerful than persuasion."[122]

Under Monnet's direction the planning agency was lean in staff and budget.

---

121. Insofar as government restricted imports of mature products from developing countries, however, it contravened this effect of SMIC's evolution.

122. Monnet, *Mémoires*, p. 305.

Monnet was not alone in his focus on states of mind. According to Richard F. Kuisel,

> modernizers were found among public officials, politicians, labor leaders, industrialists, and academics. Both left and right contributed to the trend. . . . Some prescient individuals anticipated the trend as early as 1900. At the end of the First World War reformers like Albert Thomas and Etienne Clémentel tried to force the pace, overreached themselves, and failed. Between the wars, critics of the existing order proposed more radical alternatives than economic management and modernization. There were corporatists, technocrats, syndicalists, and socialists, but their designs were too daring or sectarian to be successful. By the end of the Second World War, however, the French were ready to listen to the partisans of management and expansion.[123]

Under the Marshall Plan, France dispatched large numbers of business executives, trade unionists, civil servants, and politicians to the United States with an eye toward absorption of American productivity. They returned not only with such trimmings as butch haircuts and wineless lunches but also with an appreciation of how business was conducted in a relatively dynamic, seemingly disorganized setting.[124] Meanwhile, at home the proliferation of large private organizations was creating a new component of the labor force, what John Kenneth Galbraith dubbed the technostructure and what in France is called the *cadres*. By economic interest, and therefore by belief, this burgeoning group of middle managers in large bureaucratic enterprises echoed Monnet's call for vigorous modernization.[125]

Anyone who has been exposed to people as charismatic as Jean Monnet understands that exhortation alone can change behavior. And anyone who has parachuted into a foreign culture understands the

123. Kuisel, *Capitalism and the State in Modern France*, p. 279.

124. These missions to the United States affected government's activities, too. Sent by Jean Monnet to meet David Lilienthal and to observe the Tennessee Valley Authority, Libert Bou returned with plans to tame the Rhône river; see Monnet, *Mémoires*, p. 327. Charles Prou came back with the idea of constructing an input-output table, one I employ in this book (the tableau économique de 1951); see Fourquet, *Les Comptes de la Puissance*, p. 162.

125. Boltanski, *Les Cadres*.

importance of such personal confrontations with alien styles of conduct as occurred during productivity missions to the United States. Although economic planning might have worked best during its early years because it was backed with Marshall money, it might also have worked especially well because, in comparison with subsequent periods, it focused more on the conception than on the finance of modernization.[126]

While recognizing the importance of mind set as a conditioner of action, one might still wonder whether government initiative was necessary to change private optics at the end of World War II. The prewar presence of modernizers may not have sufficed to effect change, but it surely sensitized private parties to the need for reform. The war affected the attitudes of many people, not just the new government elite. The emergence of a technostructure reduced the social and political strength of the traditionalists. Most importantly, however, given the myriad changes occurring in the environment of households and businesses, even the old fundamental objectives of private parties might have resulted in changed modes of behavior. In other words, changes in behavior do not stem solely from changes in world view. While recognizing government leadership in the effort to modernize minds, one must examine the possibility that private behavior evolved largely of its own accord. Such is the goal of the next two chapters of this book.

Conclusion

Charles Schultze has made three telling observations on industrial policy. First, from an economic perspective, it is extremely difficult to identify industries worthy of support. Second, from a political perspective, it is extremely difficult to limit support to worthy industries. Finally, from a historical perspective, the postwar economic success of countries that rely heavily on industrial policy should not

126. Writing in 1963, Charles Kindleberger argued that "the basic change in the French economy is one of people and attitudes"; see "The Postwar Resurgence of the French Economy," p. 157. Eighteen years later, Richard Kuisel opined that "changing national consciousness" was the key to France's renovation; *Capitalism and the State in Modern France*, p. 275. See also Carré, Dubois, and Malinvaud, *La Croissance Française*, p. 608.

be attributed primarily to that form of government initiative. [127] The study of French structural policies bears directly on each of these observations.

ECONOMIC THEORY: PICKING WINNERS

Structural policy is a form of surgery. It puts an external actor to work on the anatomy of a complex organism. Intent on curing a relatively macroscopic and seemingly well defined disease or condition, the actor quickly becomes involved in the physiology of the system, in the behavior of the myriad components internal to it. Although many of these components are barely perceived from the outside, they interact so pervasively and importantly that successful surgery requires extravagantly detailed knowledge of how the system functions. [128]

In a static world, the problems associated with intervention tend to be practical rather than theoretical. Once the goals have been established, it is the tedium of detecting and controlling relevant factors that hinders success. In time, the techniques of detection and control can improve enough that previously daunting interventions can be made without fanfare. [129] Such was the case in French structural policy when the early planners restored several mature industries to health. In general, when government operated on industries charac-

127. Schultze, "Industrial Policy," pp. 6–9.
128. Human surgery, no less than economic surgery, operates on an organism of immense complexity. Viewed through the lenses of medieval, Enlightenment, or Victorian biology, that organism appeared far too complicated to permit regularly successful transplantation of organs or restoration of severed limbs. Today, however, many such operations succeed routinely.
129. An example of such evolution in human surgery is organ transplants. The problem with such operations lies not in attachment of organs to bodies but in prevention of organ rejection by the patient. To prevent such rejection, surgeons seek to fool the recipient's immune system by employing organs with characteristics similar to those of the organs they replace. This procedure (tissue matching) is both tedious and difficult. At best, it is accomplished tolerably rather than perfectly; so drugs must be developed to suppress immune responses engendered by imperfect matching. The less selective the drugs, the greater the recipient's difficulty in fighting genuine disease. (Early transplant patients tended to die from infection.) Over time, however, surgical techniques, including tissue matching, have improved to the point where some organs are transplanted frequently. Moreover, advances in pharmacology have resulted in drugs that suppress immune responses selectively, preserving the antibodies necessary to fight infections and other dangerous invasions of the patient's person.

terized by stable technologies and products, alleged asymmetries of information favoring market over government decisions shed much of their plausibility.[130] Blanket critiques of industrial policy, questioning how a bunch of government bureaucrats can know better than the market, are no more appropriate than queries as to how a few doctors can know better than nature. The issue is not who knows better, but whether and how intervention can cure properly diagnosed instances of market failure.

Successful surgery must ultimately be defined in terms of systemic performance, not systemic structure.[131] Government can create and kill particular enterprises, promote and discourage particular activities; but it cannot always guarantee that the resulting economic actors will behave as desired. Many of the national champions nurtured by French structural policies failed to win their shares of tournaments in domestic and world markets.

One reason why structural policy failed to achieve its goals was the perverse incentives created by government's initiatives.[132] But the mere fact that structural intervention can trigger perverse outcomes does not in itself call policy into question. As long as the microstructure of the system remains stable, government can accumulate the information required to adapt a policy preventively to its anticipated side effects.

In the economic world, unlike its biological counterpart, systemic relationships change continually. When change in such basic parameters of structural policy as technology is rapid, information may not accumulate quickly enough for government to develop a good understanding of the sources of and remedies for market failure. This is a

130. Overwhelming asymmetry of information can also be questioned where government is the principal buyer of output. Earlier in this chapter, I suggested that the government occupied just such a role in many of the activities favored by French industrial policy.

131. In the context of human surgery, consider the restoration of severed limbs. The surgeon reconnects arteries, veins, and nerves. In the case of veins and arteries, success depends largely on the quality of sutures; and, by the end of the Korean War, sutures had been developed that could join even small veins and arteries. In the case of nerves, however, mere reconnection does not guarantee return of function. Nerves transmit electrical impulses; since reconnection often creates scar tissue, and since scar tissue impedes transmission of electrical impulses, function does not always return after reconnection.

132. See Zysman, *Political Strategies for Industrial Order.*

plausible explanation of the French government's inability to develop triumphant national champions in electronics.[133] Industrial policy may be better suited to bringing a specific sector up to a known best-practice technique than it is to identifying best-practice technique in a rapidly changing industry. It may thus prove especially useful in reconstructions after wars and industrialization of developing countries. Even if France had kept the policy scalpels it lost when the EEC was formed, it might have maintained only with difficulty the success in structural policy that it had achieved while operating on mature industries. Still, one must not forget that pervasive technological change also jeopardizes the realization of long-run market equilibria; hence it may also dull the edge of market selection mechanisms. Coupled with the absence of perfect competition, perpetual disequilibrium may suffice to put government policy back in legitimate contention against the market in choices of new paths for industrial specialization.

POLITICAL THEORY: SUSTAINING WINNERS

The success of medical surgery depends not only on technique but also on hospital management—on the stockage of necessary supplies, the provision of a controlled environment, and the organization of patient flow. Similarly, many of the problems of industrial policy are political rather than economic. They result from the structure and function of government, not the structure and function of the economy.

Viewed economically, structural policy must be selective to be effective. If all activities are subsidized proportionately, then no activity is favored and economic structure is unaffected, except potentially by the manner in which subsidies are financed. In comparison with American government, the French system facilitates selective economic policy. To begin with, government discretion is constrained lightly if at all by notions of horizontal equity. France has no analogues to U.S. rules of administrative practice.[134] French individuals and companies enjoy few rights against government, even in the face of seemingly arbitrary policy. The government that wishes to intervene selectively will not be bridled by the courts.

---

133. Ibid.
134. Goux, "Parliament Should Play a Larger Role in Industrial Policy."

The internal organization of French government also permits effective use of its discretion. Any government is a collection of ministries, agencies, and ultimately people, each with a distinct agenda. The more broadly power is diffused among them, the less likely it is to be employed coherently. In the French system, many bodies participate in the formulation and implementation of structural policy. These include parliament; the planning commission; the spending ministries (industry, telecommunications, defense, transport, and international trade); the twin towers of the executive branch (president and prime minister); and the ministry of finance—not to speak of local governments and public enterprises. Most observers would agree, however, that power is effectively concentrated in the treasury.[135] American students of the French system tend to focus on the Commissariat Général du Plan as if it were the primary locus of economic policymaking. This focus may be attributed partly to interest in an institution that has no American counterpart and partly to the origins of the agency: to receive aid from the United States after World War II, the French had to convince their patrons that they were moving to stabilize their economy. Persuasion was especially important because France was perceived to have mismanaged its ration of lend-lease funds during the war.[136] How better to show control over the economy than to point to a freshly baked planning agency endowed with proclaimedly broad powers? Nevertheless, Jean Monnet, the father of planning, lost his battle with François Bloch-Lainé, head of the treasury; and Marshall money fell under control of the ministry of finance. The planning commission developed great moral authority and used it to considerable effect, but the planners enjoyed little power within government to induce the budgetary decisions they desired. Treasury's principal rivals were probably the two executives.[137]

135. See Zysman, *Governments, Markets, and Growth*; Saint-Geours, *Pouvoir et Finance*; and Bloch-Lainé, *Profession Fonctionnaire*. On the weakness of parliament, see Goux, "Parliament Should Play a Larger Role in Industrial Policy."

136. Kuisel, *Capitalism and the State in Modern France*, p. 231.

137. Soulage and Thiery, "Quelles Institutions pour une Nouvelle Politique Industrielle?" Presidents and prime ministers undoubtedly participate in major decisions involving aid to France's largest enterprises. To the extent, however, that

Armed with legal discretion, structured for the purpose, French governments did indeed act sustainedly to promote specific activities. Nuclear weapons, nuclear power, and petroleum were all subsidized to a great degree, and all developed robustly in comparison with corresponding activities in comparable countries. Nevertheless, the pattern of government intervention was not completely consistent with a strategy of accelerating economic change. Several major beneficiaries of subsidies—agriculture, coal, and rail transport—were declining in importance. Other major beneficiaries, especially housing and hospitals, reposed peacefully far from the battle for world markets in manufactures. Because, perhaps, of comparatively infrequent recourse to tax expenditures, French governments have concentrated their support on a few business activities to an extent greater than that usually found abroad; but French behavior cannot be characterized as single-minded promotion of pervasive structural change.

From a political perspective, however, government's devotion of resources to traditional activities need not be inconsistent with efforts to promote structural change.[138] Consider an economy capable of achieving static economic efficiency, say a competitive market economy in which government sets optimal rules for interactions between private parties and deals efficiently with externalities and public goods. As incomes, technologies, and comparative advantages evolve, preservation of efficiency will require structural change. The greater the changes indicated, however, the less likely they are to occur. Uncompensated losers from evaporation of the status quo might lobby government to intervene conservatively in market mechanisms. If successful, they will obstruct change.[139]

Suppose, however, that as it protects declining activities, government also promotes those destined for relative growth. In theory, it could fashion support to leave the evolution of output on exactly the path it would have followed in the absence of intervention. And yet, to the extent that those who fear structural evolution suffer from subsidy illusion, they will create no political obstacles to change.

---

day-to-day decisions exert a greater cumulative influence on the allocation of resources, the role of high-level civil servants in the treasury department deserves pride of place.

138. Zysman, *Governments, Markets, and Growth*.

139. Olson, *The Rise and Decline of Nations*.

Focused narrowly on the support they themselves receive, they will relax in the belief that government is catering to their interest, and the market will be left to do its work.

Once the political function of government intervention is understood, targeting support loses much of its significance. Even if the net economic effects of intervention work against change, government may be promoting evolution to the extent that it deflates political momentum toward even greater protection of the status quo. To the extent that political power varies in step with economic importance, subsidies can eventually be withdrawn from declining groups.

Since World War II the French government has been pressured to halt change.[140] Periodically, such pressure has proved explosive: the Poujade movement of the 1950s, the events of May 1968, the Nicoud movement of the late 1960s, and the Le Pen movement of the 1980s—catalyzed one and all by the desire to reverse modernization—left serious scars on the political landscape.[141] Government support of declining activities can be interpreted as an effort to dissipate the political strength of economic reaction, preserving the political system of the Fifth Republic and guaranteeing the continuation of structural change. Whether or not government subsidized declining activities in a manner designed to fail, one must appreciate the significance of the overt acceptance of modernization—of the market as arbiter of economic structure—exhibited by the governments of Laurent Fabius and, ultimately, Pierre Mauroy. Such a stance would have been unthinkable twenty-five years earlier, when small shopkeepers, farmers, and already declining segments of manufacturing played larger roles in political, social, and economic life.

Although persuasive in several respects, this political theory of government policy requires a plinth of strong assumptions. In the first place, it depends on the persistence of subsidy illusion. And yet, in time, declining groups will surely perceive that aid proffered by government has not sufficed to preserve established positions. Such perceptions are likely to inspire increased political intervention on

140. Caron, *An Economic History of Modern France*, p. 309, cites the 1954 report of the Commission des Comptes, which urges moderation in the target rate of economic growth lest there be "violent readaptation crises in many sectors that could unleash a serious social and economic crisis in the country as a whole."

141. See Hoffmann, *Le Mouvement Poujade*; and Roy, *Les Commerçants*.

behalf of the status quo. In the second place, the argument depends on a correlation between the numerical size and the political strength of interest groups. Otherwise, economic contraction need not entail political atrophy. And yet neither organizational theory nor historical experience supports such a correlation.[142] Finally, the argument presumes that government can establish the appropriate support and then vary it as the constellation of political forces evolves. Such a presumption may not be plausible.

ECONOMIC IMPACT

What, then, should one conclude about government's structural initiatives since the war? How did they affect the composition of economic activity, and what was government's intent?

Motives are clearer than effects. For centuries, France has been keenest to engage in structural policy when it has feared most for its national independence: both Colbert and de Gaulle promoted structural change for military purposes. But even when narrowly military objectives failed to shape policy, the most galling implication of market failure—the one justifying government intervention—was not loss of per capita income but emasculation of France's position in the international pecking order.[143] Neither Colbert nor de Gaulle believed even intuitively in the virtues of Pareto optimality or the intrinsic splendors of modernization. Neither thought of himself as heightening the intensity of market signals to compensate for inelastic responses in the private sector.

Turning from intent to effect, one faces nearly insuperable problems of inference. There is no one-to-one correspondence between expenditure and impact. Elasticities of company response to government support are critical and yet difficult to measure on a systematic basis. Much of government's support has been indirect in the economic sense. Its nominal recipients, such as SNCF, RATP, and the banks, were neither the intended nor the actual beneficiaries. Much of government's support, such as aid to agriculture and small business,

142. See Schattschneider, *Politics, Pressures, and the Tariff*; and Olson, *The Logic of Collective Action.*

143. It is often argued that under Georges Pompidou, French industrial policy began to focus on economic growth. See, for example, Gauron, *Histoire Economique et Sociale de la Cinquième République*, vol. 1: *Le Temps des Modernistes.*

has also been indirect in that it was designed to operate through the political, not the market, system. Finally, much of the support has been veiled in that the rhetoric of industrial policy has not always squared with its content. Such allegedly strategic industries as petroleum, aerospace, and nuclear power were indeed promoted intensively. Others, however, were not: by the measures employed in this study, government has impinged very little on electronics broadly defined, even though that sector has epitomized for the past quarter century government's preoccupation with industrial structure. In contrast, such industries as coal and rail transport continued to receive substantial aid well after they had lost their strategic appellation. And agriculture and housing were promoted intensively even though they had never enjoyed such a label. When measuring the impact of structural policy on the composition of economic activity, one must correlate performance not with government's stated concerns but rather with the impact of aid actually received. Trompe l'oeil complicates endemically the measurement of industrial policy's impact. So does the need to evaluate the net effect of an ensemble of policies as opposed to disjoint results of piecemeal initiatives.[144]

Despite these difficulties, it is possible to say something about impact. At the very least, one may safely reject the hypothesis that government initiatives failed to affect economic structure. Intervention was too substantial for its effects to have cancelled cleanly. Moreover, if one is prepared to specify a concept of performance, one can even say something about the kind of impact structural policies have had.

If performance is equated with rapid growth of targeted industries, then structural policy undoubtedly worked in some cases: nuclear weapons, nuclear power, aerospace, and housing absorb more of France's resources than would have been the case in the absence of government initiative. Note, however, that several of the industries that grew especially rapidly after World War II, including pharmaceuticals, manufactured gases, plastics products, organic chemicals, and scrap products (see table 3), did not receive much government support as measured by the variables employed here.

144. This point is stressed in Saxonhouse, "The Micro- and Macroeconomics of Foreign Sales to Japan."

If performance is defined more generally in terms of French convergence on the economic structure of Germany, the designated rival, then structural policy had mixed results. On the one hand, by 1982 many manufacturing industries accounted for shares of value added that differed little between the two countries (appendix table A-51); and the structure of value added in manufacturing differed less between France and Germany than between Germany and either Italy or the United Kingdom.[145] On the other hand, between 1960 and 1980 France did no better than Italy in approaching Germany's broad structure of economic activity (appendix table A-52); and in 1982, the industrial composition of French value added looked more like the British than like the German.

If performance is assigned a more conventional definition, such as movement of the economy toward *a* Pareto-optimal state or toward *the* Pareto-optimal state associated with the ideal distribution of income, then impact is much more difficult to judge. In the absence of government policy, markets would have functioned imperfectly, so the benchmark of a competitive economy devoid of public goods and externalities is inappropriate. Suffice it to say that some features of government policy, such as the introduction of marginal cost pricing to electricity, clearly promoted efficiency by virtually any standard; and some targets of promotion are now capable of competing without abnormal government support.

Finally, if performance means simply that government believed it got what it paid for, industrial policy probably failed to change the behavior of many target companies. So fragile was the observed relationship between subsidies accorded to a beneficiary and service rendered to government that embarrassed public officials decided to suppress the most important official evaluation of industrial policy.[146]

For the purposes of this study, the most important feature of structural policy's impact is its probable narrowness. At most, industrial policy impinged forcefully on just a few branches of the economy.

145. As measured by the sum (across two-digit manufacturing industries of the international standard industrial classification) of squared differences between the relevant two countries in shares of manufacturing value added.

146. The study is summarized in Mathieu, "Le 'Rapport Hannoun' Souligne la Forte Concentration et la Faible Efficacité des Aides Publiques à l'Industrie."

And yet the structural change of the postwar period has not been so limited. Unless one is prepared to believe that interventions in a small number of activities induced pervasive restructuring of the economy despite the absence of requisite input-output relationships, or that tightly focused interventions achieved broad economic results through their effects on politics, one must be skeptical of the impact of government initiative on the full structure of economic activity. Despite the number and diversity of its tools, despite the volume of resources devoted to the effort, government exerted less leverage on business enterprise than might be expected. Outside narrow compartments of intensive intervention, it exercised neither direct nor indirect influence sufficient to explain the structural changes documented in chapter 2. Still, even if dissection of government intervention fails to reveal direct impact at the level of particular policy levers, one cannot conclude that the system as a whole failed to impinge profoundly on economic structure. The evidence presented here should not be interpreted to imply that structural policy fails to affect business behavior; rather it seems to suggest that the role of policy might be overemphasized by friends and foes alike.

These findings justify the methodological choices made early in this chapter. The impact of structural policy on economic structure requires broad as well as deep understanding of relations between government and business. Focus on a few key policies or actors can help one understand how policy works, but it cannot by itself resolve the net effect of government on economic structure. This viewpoint bears some similarity to that of historians in the Annales school (sired by Marc Bloch and exemplified by Fernand Braudel), who argue for less attention to elite persons and institutions and more to the habits and environments of ordinary people. In the context of industrial economics, this view distills to a presumption that structural change depends less on the behavior of the top 500 enterprises than it does on the behavior of their anonymously small counterparts. In focusing on a narrow range of interaction between big business and government, one may blind oneself to major determinants of economic restructuring.

This interpretation is also consistent with two features of economic growth observed in chapter 1. First, by international standards the French economy grew especially rapidly between 1958 and 1973.

Second, during that period its rate of expansion was virtually identical to that of Italy. Pervasive, conscious, and effective structural policy does not explain either fact well. Most observers argue that French structural policy lost its potency when the EEC was formed.[147] And few would contend that industrial policy is a major feature of the Italian economic environment. What began around 1959 in Italy as well as in France was systematic and seemingly permanent exposure to foreign competition. Such exposure might have amplified the volume of signals emanating from the market. It is time, therefore, to explore the responses of private actors to those signals, to explore whether conservative economic behavior, the Malthusianism of the historical and sociological literatures, infected French society as virulently and durably as despairing observers have suggested.

147. See, for example, Balassa, "Whither French Planning?"

4 | A New International Environment

I HAVE explored two broad hypotheses as to why the French economy was able to sustain a high rate of growth after World War II despite its apparent rigidities. The first proposed that growth did not require behavioral flexibility because it failed to entail radical structural change, the second that government initiative induced the reallocations of resources required to achieve smooth and rapid growth. The evidence examined in chapters 2 and 3 does not appear to support these hypotheses sufficiently to make either alone or the two together a complete explanation of the postwar record: various forms of personal mobility occurred frequently, and well beyond the compartments of the economy receiving conscious government attention.

In this and the following chapters, I explore a third broad explanation of postwar growth and structural change. Government's structural initiatives did not account for all the changes people perceived in the economic environment. During the four decades that followed World War II, government dismantled many of the regulations it had introduced before and during the war. In such areas as product prices, securities markets, and bank credit the relaxation of controls did not proceed earnestly until the mid-1980s. In others, however, deregulation occurred much earlier. The impediments to international trade erected during the previous half century began to disappear within the decade following V-E day. So did the repression of large-scale retailing. Conceivably, changes of these sorts more than changes in individual tastes or in government's structural policies account for the seemingly heightened sensitivity to market signals after World War II.

This chapter discusses changes in the international environment, while chapter 5 examines their domestic counterparts. In each chapter the first few sections present the institutional changes, and succeeding sections explore the probable impact on market behavior. I argue that these environmental ruptures altered profoundly the opportunities and constraints encountered by business enterprises. Increasing exposure to foreign competition, diminishing reliance on sheltered foreign markets, and deregulation of domestic markets insulated naturally from international trade altered the relative desirability of three broad types of investment: political influence, oligopolistic cooperation, and new sources of competitive advantage.

The Psychology of 1945 Revisited

To understand the beginnings of deregulation requires further discussion of French attitudes in 1945. The humiliation of 1940 convinced the statesmen of the Liberation that France would have to break with the doctrines and elites that had prevailed before the war. One element of the new view, emphasized in chapter 3, was the perceived importance of government initiative in economic activity. Without such initiative, it was feared, the economy might fail to achieve the size and industrial structure of such designated rivals as Germany. But a domestic policy based on economic growth and structural change would not suffice. France would also need a foreign policy designed to deal with a rebuilt Germany. The strategy on which France had relied after World War I—political isolation and economic exploitation of an unforgiven enemy—had obviously failed. This time it seemed reasonable to take the opposite tack. Rather than set Germany apart, France would seek to keep it so intertwined with its neighbors that war in Europe would lose both its desirability and its feasibility. In the words of Luigi Barzini, "Three wars since 1870, all of them fought against Germany, cracked [France's] faith in its invincibility, and this is why France must now keep abreast of the Germans, keep them under surveillance, maintain the most intimate relations with them, and hold them in an embrace as close as a stranglehold. If France cannot dominate Europe alone, it hopes that maybe the two nations together might do so."[1]

1. Barzini, *The Europeans*, p. 154. Barzini also states, "The French were at first among the earliest and most determined champions of European unification. They

The best way to stay close to Germany was to steer both countries toward economic integration. Freedom of trade would reduce pressures to annex neighboring territories rich in raw materials. If, for example, Germany could acquire the iron ore of Lorraine on nondiscriminatory terms while France obtained comparable access to Ruhr coal, then Germany might feel less pressure to seize Lorraine and France might relinquish its claim to the Saar. Moreover, the international division of labor resulting from free trade would slice into the national economic autarky that had developed during the 1930s, severing the ability of any European country to fight its neighbors unilaterally. Finally, to the extent that integration proceeded beyond free trade, German nationalism could be restrained in more subtle ways. Economic union would vest a considerable part of each member's economic policy in a supranational authority, providing France and other European countries with a large and clear window on the German economy and an opportunity to ensure its synchrony with those of other member states.[2]

Thus despite its own predilection for self-sufficiency, France decided to surrender some of its economic sovereignty on political and military grounds. It did not choose economic integration to raise living standards through specialization in production.[3] Nor did it choose economic integration to expose domestic producers to competition.[4] Its primary goal was to achieve the greatest possible interdependence between Germany and its neighbors.

---

saw in it, among other advantages, a way to solve most of their national problems at one fell swoop. It helped keep the Soviets on their side of the fence, pacified the Germans' ferocious instincts, and ended the recurrent, bloody, costly, and senseless wars with the latter, which the French were not always sure they could win. At the same time, it would vastly widen the market for French industrial products . . . and with some sharp skill in negotiating, some polite blackmailing, and some government prodding and financing might give back to their country the economic and moral predominance, the great wealth, the radiance and the unquestioned prestige it had enjoyed before the First World War" (p. 117).

2. In this regard, it is interesting to note that French economists tended to advocate full economic union rather than mere formation of a customs union. See "L'Intégration Européenne," a special issue of *Revue Economique*, vol. 9 (March 1958), especially Marchal, "Marché Commun Européen et Zone de Libre-Echange," which identifies François Perroux and Pierre Uri as proponents of integration beyond the level of customs union.

3. Hoffmann, "Paradoxes of the French Political Community," p. 75.

4. I do not wish to argue that economists were unaware of the relationship between

The European Coal and Steel Community

On May 10, 1950, Robert Schuman, the French foreign minister, proposed that Europe create a common market in coal and steel. One year later, on April 18, 1951, Belgium, France, Germany, Italy, Luxembourg, and the Netherlands signed the Treaty of Paris establishing the European Coal and Steel Community (ECSC). The treaty was designed to prevent governments and enterprises alike from imposing national frontiers on pan-European markets.

The most symbolic power stripped from governments was the right to impose tariffs and quotas on movements of coal and steel between member countries. With minor exceptions, such obstacles to trade were dismantled in a single step—on February 10, 1953, for coal, iron ore, and steel scrap; on May 1, 1953, for ordinary steel; and on August 1, 1954, for special steel.[5]

In fact, however, the ECSC had very few tariffs and quotas to eliminate. When the common market took effect, the demands for coal, iron ore, and scrap were so strong in relation to domestic supplies that member countries actually encouraged imports. Italy alone collected duties on these products. Although the books of all six members contained tariffs on steel, France and Germany had suspended collections on ordinary steel before the common market had taken effect. Because Italy was allowed temporarily to keep its tariff, the only tariffs on ordinary steel actually eliminated on May 1, 1953, were those of the Benelux countries, which were the lowest in the community.

The most important tariffs to be eliminated were those on special steels. The height of these tariffs had differed among member countries—between 1 and 8 percent in the Benelux countries, between 7 and 25 percent in France, between 15 and 28 percent in Germany, and between 12 and 23 percent in Italy. Also eliminated were certain

---

international economic integration and the state of competition in national markets: see Scitovsky, *Economic Theory and Western European Integration*; and Houssiaux, *Concurrence et Marché Commun*. Rather, I wish to suggest that economic arguments, however prophetic, did not motivate French policymakers. See Bok, *The First Three Years of the Schuman Plan*, p. 3; Dillard, *Economic Development of the North Atlantic Community*, p. 654; and Caron, *An Economic History of Modern France*, p. 325.

5. Meade, Liesner, and Wells, *Case Studies in European Economic Union*, p. 197.

tarifflike compensatory taxes on imported coal, restraints on the export of iron ore and scrap, and French quotas on imports of ordinary steel.[6]

The disappearance of tariffs and quotas did not result in the disappearance of all impediments to trade. In more than one country, international trade still required a license. Granted automatically for trade with ECSC members, but not necessarily immediately, such licenses, together with examination of merchandise at national frontiers, "made international trade within the Community somewhat more burdensome, and to a small degree more costly, than internal trade within one of the member countries." Nevertheless, after studying the matter thoroughly, the High Authority concluded that these impediments were "of relatively minor importance."[7]

In addition to prohibiting tariffs or quotas on trade with other ECSC members, article 4 of the treaty prohibited governments from granting subsidies or imposing special charges "in any form whatsoever." Thus the treaty was designed to prevent them from distorting the pattern of trade by other means, although the convention on transition authorized several temporary departures from the general subsidy rule. The High Authority was given the power to allow Belgium and Italy to continue subsidizing their coal industries until two years after full implementation of the treaty. It was also empowered to levy a tax on the community's efficient mines, revenues from which would supplement national subsidies aimed at improving efficiency in mines whose long-term viability did not depend on continued receipt of transfers and helping workers laid off when less fortunate mines contracted or closed.

In practice, the High Authority usually interpreted subsidy narrowly to mean cash transfers from government to business. Coyly, it took the position that no government was subsidizing its producers of ordinary steel. For special steels the High Authority did find the French government to be subsidizing exports via tax rebates and forced it to stop insofar as it affected trade within the community.[8] For the most part, however, the High Authority concerned itself with cash subsidies from national governments to domestic coal industries.

6. Diebold, *The Schuman Plan*, pp. 142–48.

7. Ibid., p. 152.

8. Ibid., pp. 195–96. The recent experience with subsidies under the Davignon plan is discussed in Dominick, "Adjudicating European Steel Policy," pp. 591–616.

The French coal industry was neither inefficient enough to receive special assistance from the community during the transition period nor efficient enough to be taxed to provide assistance to others. At the time the common market in coal was opened, however, the French government was subsidizing its coal industry and distorting trade in a variety of ways. In general, the High Authority permitted the French to continue their subsidies, but only after attaching numerous conditions. According to William Diebold, "the Community's record in getting rid of the French coal subsidies is a good one."[9]

The High Authority also confronted price controls. In a genuine common market, differences in price among national markets would be limited to the costs of transportation. For prices to converge to that extent, the High Authority had to pursue two policies. It had to ensure relatively competitive pricing on the part of business enterprises, and it had to prevent national governments from regulating domestic prices. In principle, it accomplished the latter task immediately, for as soon as the Treaty of Paris took effect, the power to regulate prices passed from member governments to the High Authority. In coal the High Authority set maximum prices that were very close to those established earlier by member governments.[10] By April 1, 1956, however, it had removed the ceilings, except on the portion of Belgian coal that was subsidized by the community itself. In steel, from the beginning the High Authority chose not to regulate prices. Legally, steel prices were free from control by national and supranational government bodies alike.

In fact, however, concerned with inflation, the national governments did not want to relinquish control over prices of such heavily used intermediate products as coal and steel. They resorted to a number of indirect methods—regulating the prices of steel users, threatening to withhold tax advantages, threatening to withhold investment funds—if domestic enterprises failed to respect their

---

9. Diebold, *The Schuman Plan*, p. 199. It is important to note, however, that vigilance of the High Authority does not explain the decline of the French subsidy. The tremendous shortage of coal permitted French coal to compete in Germany, and the end to discriminatory coal pricing led to procurement of German coal at lower prices in France. For both reasons the need for subsidy declined after 1953.

10. Ibid., p. 244.

wishes. In France, "officials of the nationalized coal industry complained that the government would not let them raise prices as much as necessary," and French interference in steel prices was sufficiently egregious to provoke public reprimand from the High Authority in 1957.[11]

Articles 60 and 65 of the treaty covered company pricing. Under article 60, firms had to publish a schedule of list prices applicable at a basing point of their choice. Except when meeting the equally low price of a competitor (either inside or outside the common market) or using a price explicitly approved by the High Authority, the treaty required them to sell at those published prices. Article 60 also prohibited "discriminatory practices . . . especially on grounds of the nationality of the buyer." Article 65 limited the freedom of companies to collude when establishing list prices. Unless the High Authority determined that cooperation was necessary to achieve "substantial improvement" in production or distribution, agreements among companies would be illegal and void.

Although the pricing provisions of the treaty applied equally to coal and steel, the underlying conditions in the two industries differed appreciably. Coal was in short supply until the recession of 1958, but steel experienced a downturn after the Korean War boom as well. Moreover, seller concentration was even greater in coal than in steel, while the ratio of fixed to variable cost was much higher in steel than in coal. As a result, the steel industry faced stronger and more frequent downward pressures on price. During the recession after the Korean War, steel companies secretly and illegally offered discounts from list prices. During the recession of 1958 they aligned prices downward when necessary to retain their customers.

One especially interesting case of price cutting involved use of a public enterprise to achieve price competition. During November 1957 most German steelmakers raised prices against the wishes of their government. Ludwig Erhard made sure that Salzgitter, a small government producer, failed to match those increases. The relatively low price of Salzgitter permitted producers in other ECSC countries to undercut the Germans on their home turf, claiming they were merely aligning their prices on the equally low prices of a German

11. Ibid., pp. 247, 272.

competitor. Thus German companies in the private sector lobbied hard to get Salzgitter to raise its prices—not because they feared competition from Salzgitter but because they wanted to deter imports. Unsuccessful in that effort, they were obliged to lower prices to Salzgitter's level.[12]

Responding perhaps to the different circumstances in coal and steel, the High Authority established different pricing rules for the two industries. After initially setting ceiling prices for coal but not for steel, it allowed steel companies but not coal companies to align their prices downward to those of common market rivals at superior locations.[13] During the 1954 recession, however, when the right to align failed to alleviate downward pressure on steel prices, the High Authority allowed steel companies to change prices by 2.5 percent or less without modifying their published prices. Fearing, however, that introduction of secret discounts would result in increased imports, the French and Italian governments argued successfully before the court of justice that the High Authority had exceeded its powers under the treaty.

During the transition period as a whole, the High Authority imposed sixteen fines and issued sixteen warnings to steel companies violating the community's pricing rules. None of these related, however, to violations of the prohibition against cooperative pricing. In fact, the High Authority proceeded very cautiously against the cartels.[14] In coal, it accepted the notion of joint selling activities, even in the Ruhr, where it simply attempted to replace a single joint selling agency (GEORG) with many. In steel the High Authority disturbed private cooperation even less, and mergers among competitors were all but ignored.

Given the importance of transport cost in the prices of coal and steel, the High Authority also made extensive use of its right to regulate railroad rates on shipment of coal and steel between member

12. Ibid., p. 277.

13. Actually, the High Authority did allow certain coal firms, especially those with high production costs or poor locations to engage in "zone pricing," which amounted to their being able to meet the lower prices of rivals in designated markets. See Meade and others, *Case Studies in European Economic Union*, pp. 225–31.

14. Ludwig Erhard defended his attempts to cap the price of Ruhr coal by pointing out that "the coal price was still a cartel price." Diebold, *The Schuman Plan*, p. 248. See also Jeanneney, *Forces et Faiblesses de l'Economie Française, 1945–1959*, p. 50.

countries. During the transition period it reduced discrimination against shipments crossing national frontiers and, in its own view, by the end of 1953 the abolition of such discrimination was complete.[15] In April 1955 member countries took the additional step of establishing through rates on international shipments within the community.

The European Economic Community

On March 25, 1957, the six members of the European Coal and Steel Community agreed to extend the scope of their economic integration. The expression of their agreement, the Treaty of Rome creating the European Economic Community, took effect on January 1, 1958.[16] In several respects, the new treaty resembled the Treaty of Paris. Both prohibited tariffs, quotas, and subsidies that restricted or distorted international competition within the community. Both also regulated the exercise of market power by business enterprises. In other important respects, however, the treaties diverged. The EEC but not the ECSC had a common external tariff. The ECSC but not the EEC could regulate prices, production, and investment. Finally, the ECSC but not the EEC was designed to be implemented almost immediately. The ECSC transition lasted just five years and applied only to minor issues, but the Treaty of Rome prescribed a twelve-year transition, January 1, 1958, to December 31, 1969, for virtually all its liberalizations (the transition was accelerated, however, so that the treaty was implemented fully on July 1, 1968).

QUOTAS

Article 32 of the treaty declared that "quotas shall be abolished by the end of the transitional period at the latest" and specified the transition to a quota-free environment. Once the treaty took effect, no member could apply new quotas to trade with other members, nor could any country increase the restrictiveness of quotas in place.

15. Diebold, *The Schuman Plan*, p. 166.

16. The six also signed a treaty signalling a joint approach to atomic energy through creation of a European Atomic Energy Community (EURATOM). The French in particular demanded EURATOM as a quid pro quo for opening their markets to German competition. But EURATOM did not serve the grand purposes they had envisioned, and ultimately France proceeded independently on the nuclear front. See Vedel, "Euratom."

The process of eliminating existing quotas would begin on January 1, 1959, and consist of three procedures. First, article 33 declared that each member was to "convert any bilateral quotas open to any other Member States into global quotas open without discrimination to all other Member States." Second, each member was to "increase the aggregate of the global quotas so . . . as to bring about an increase of not less than 20 percent in their total value as compared with the preceding year. The global quota for each product, however, shall be increased by not less than 10 percent. The quotas shall be increased annually in accordance with the same rules and in the same proportions in relation to the preceding year." Third, "where, in the case of a product which has not been liberalised, the global quota does not amount to 3 percent of the national production of the State concerned, a quota equal to not less than 3 percent of such national production shall be introduced not later than one year after the entry into force of this Treaty. This quota shall be raised to 4 percent at the end of the second year, and to 5 percent at the end of the third. Thereafter, the Member State concerned shall increase the quota by not less than 15 percent annually. . . . At the end of the tenth year, each quota shall be equal to not less than 20 percent of the national production."

The intended effect of these procedures is best appreciated by example. Suppose that France produces three goods (A, B, and C), each in the amount of 100 a year. As of December 31, 1957, it maintained the following import quotas: Benelux, 0A, 5B, 2C; Germany, 0A, 10B, 5C; and Italy, 0A, 5B, 3C. Under the globalization provision of article 33, France had to substitute communitywide for country-specific quotas. In this example, globalization required France to establish communitywide quotas of 20 for B and 10 for C. Under the general relaxation provision of article 33, on January 1, 1959, France had to increase the total value of its intracommunity quotas by 20 percent. As of December 31, 1957, the total had been 30. The new total would thus have been 36. Moreover, in attaining the new aggregate ceiling, the quota on each individual product had to rise by at least 10 percent. Hence the new quotas on B and C had to be no less than 22 and 11. Finally, under the 3 percent rule, France could no longer prohibit all imports of A. With national production of 100, it had to establish a communitywide quota of at least 3. Taking account of the 3 percent rule, then, the sum of French quotas had to rise on January 1, 1959, from 30 to 39, in other words by 30 percent. The required rate of relaxation exceeded 20 percent because France's initial quota on A had been less than 3 percent of national production.

In practice, the elimination of quotas on intracommunity imports proceeded more rapidly than the Treaty of Rome required. On May 12, 1960, members decided to end all intracommunity quotas on industrial products by December 31, 1961. With few exceptions, this goal was achieved. By the beginning of 1965 virtually all quotas on imports of food had also been eradicated. At the end of the transition period, the quotas that remained applied to certain agricultural products and certain durables sold primarily to governments.[17]

For some members the common market's treatment of quotas had little significance. In 1949 the Organization for European Economic Cooperation (OEEC) had begun to dismantle quotas on trade among its members.[18] Using the 1948 structure of private trade among its eighteen members as a benchmark, the group agreed to eliminate quotas on imports of products accounting for first 50 percent, then 60 percent, then 75 percent, and finally 90 percent of all benchmark trade.[19] The 75 percent rule was to take effect in 1951, while the 90

17. Nême and Nême, *Economie Européenne*, pp. 41–42. Import quotas were not the only quantitative barriers to trade; safety regulations and fiscal monopolies fell in the same category.

18. Baum, *The French Economy and the State*, pp. 99–102. The original members of the OEEC were Austria, Belgium, Denmark, France, Germany, Greece, Iceland, Ireland, Italy, Luxembourg, the Netherlands, Norway, Portugal, Sweden, Switzerland, Turkey, and the United Kingdom. Spain was allowed to join in 1959. In 1961, the OEEC became the Organization for Economic Cooperation and Development (OECD). Canada and the United States, which had been associate members of the OEEC, became full charter members of the OECD. Joining the OECD after its formation were Japan (1964), Finland (1968), Australia (1971), and New Zealand (1973). Since 1961, Yugoslavia has enjoyed a special status within the organization. See Stein, Hay, and Waelbroeck, *European Community Law and Institutions in Perspective*, pp. 10–13.

19. "Private" trade meant trade not arranged by a national government. At the time, severe scarcities of raw materials, foodstuffs, and manufactures essential to reconstruction had prompted several governments to engage in procurement abroad on behalf of domestic producers and consumers. In certain countries the practice was important. Both Britain and France had arranged 25 percent of 1948 imports from OEEC countries. See Diebold, *Trade and Payments in Western Europe*, pp. 182–83. In most countries, however, including France, private trade and total trade were close to coincident in the manufacturing sector.

percent rule was adopted in 1955.[20] Since all members of the EEC belonged to the OEEC as well, the 90 percent rule seemed to render nugatory the quota policies of the former. In fact, however, the OEEC succeeded only partially in its effort to liberalize international trade. Two of the important failings involved France.[21]

The first concerned the timing of compliance. During most of the 1950s, under pressure from domestic producers, France failed to meet the OEEC timetable for loosening quotas.[22] Although it complied with the 75 percent standard just two months after the general deadline, it restored its quotas in 1952.[23] Between 1954 and 1957 it attempted gradually to return to compliance.[24] But in June 1957 it again invoked safeguard clauses and restored quotas that had been dismantled. Not until December 1958, after the Treaty of Rome had taken effect and just before the quota removals prescribed by the EEC, did it adhere definitively to OEEC rules. Among EEC countries France alone failed to apply in timely fashion the OEEC standards.[25]

The second limitation of the OEEC program concerned the incentive it created to maintain especially restrictive quotas. To understand this incentive, consider the following hypothetical example. Suppose that during the benchmark year of 1948 France had produced 100 each of A, B, and C while maintaining quotas of 0, 10, and 90 on internal imports of the three goods. If each quota had been binding, total imports during 1948 would have amounted to 100. France could have met the 90 percent standard merely by eliminating its least restrictive quota, that on imports of C. In particular, it could

20. Ibid., chap. 10. See also OEEC, *European Economic Cooperation*, pp. 14–20.

21. Others are described in Diebold, *Trade and Payments in Western Europe*, chap. 10. For example, although OEEC standards did apply to imports arriving from the colonies of member countries, they did not apply to imports of those colonies from the OEEC. Thus France was able to maintain sheltered markets for its exports within the franc zone.

22. Baum, *The French Economy and the State*, p. 102.

23. Diebold, *Trade and Payments in Western Europe*, p. 176.

24. Even so, "after 1953, as quotas were being abandoned, quantitative controls were replaced by tariffs; although labelled as 'temporary special taxes,' these tariffs were removed very slowly." Gruson, *Origine et Espoirs de la Planification Française*, pp. 91–92.

25. Ouin, "The Establishment of the Customs Union," in Stein and Nicholson, eds., *American Enterprise in the European Common Market*, vol. 2, p. 113.

have maintained the quota of 0 on A regardless of the quotas that had been applied to B and C. In fact, if France had produced 100 products, maintained 1948 quotas of 0 on 99 of them, and set a 1948 quota of 10 on the remaining one, it could have met the 90 percent standard merely by eliminating the quota of 10 on that last product. Every quota of 0 could have been maintained.

To the actual quota structure of four EEC countries, this hypothetical example has little relevance, at least in the context of manufacturing. To the quotas of France and Italy, however, the example is very relevant indeed. Even when the two countries adhered to OEEC standards, they retained very restrictive quotas on a large number of products. The importance of such quotas can be appraised by examining the degree to which the 3 percent rule of the Treaty of Rome obliged various countries to relax quotas by more than 20 percent in 1959. To the extent that an EEC country imposed no quotas on intracommunity imports in 1958 amounting to less than 3 percent of home production, and to the extent that it relaxed its quotas to the minimum required by the treaty, then the aggregate value of the country's quotas would have risen by exactly 20 percent on January 1, 1959. To the extent, however, that the country imposed quotas restricting intracommunity imports to less than 3 percent of domestic production, it would have been required to increase the aggregate value of these quotas by more than 20 percent.

According to Marc Ouin, application of the 3 percent rule "led two countries of the Community to increase by much more than 20 percent its aggregate quotas of 1958. France, whose 1958 quotas reached the sum total of one hundred billion francs, increased its quotas in 1959 to two hundred-fifteen billion francs, or by 115 percent. Italy increased them to twenty-eight billion lire in 1959, compared with the 8 billion lire in 1958, an increase of 250 percent."[26] Thus the stringency of French quotas did not really abate until the quota provisions of the Treaty of Rome took full effect at the end of 1961.

Articles 108 and 226 of the treaty permit exceptional and temporary quotas on intracommunity trade, and France has attempted to make use of them. In November 1967 it unsuccessfully requested authorization to impose quotas on imports of Italian refrigerators. After the

26. Ibid., p. 118.

events of May 1968 the EEC Commission allowed France to impose quotas on imports of automobiles, textiles, household electrical equipment, and steel. The quotas had to exceed by 1 percent the actual volume of imports during 1967, and none could last longer than six months.[27] In general the quotas authorized by the EEC Commission were removed on schedule, and even when in force, some barely affected market supply. So large, for example, was the inventory of new foreign automobiles at the beginning of 1968 that during the four-month quota inaugurated on July 1, the volume of new registrations of foreign automobiles exceeded by 75 percent the volume during the corresponding period of the previous year.[28]

Long-term quotas on industrial imports may have been eliminated by the end of the community's fourth year, but many quantitative barriers to trade remained. A good recent example involved French wine.[29] During August 1981 winemakers in southern France demonstrated forcefully against imports of cheap wine. In response, French customs began to refuse to release substantial amounts of Italian wine, claiming that the certificates of origin accompanying the wine failed to satisfy community regulations governing the description and presentation of wines. The French notified the Italian ministry of agriculture of the alleged irregularities and waited for rectification. They also began to analyze chemically all wine imported in bulk from Italy. As a result, Italian wines with alcoholic content below 13 percent remained bottled up in customs for four months. Following violent demonstrations in January 1982, France renewed its dilatory treatment of Italian wine. The commission intervened, and on appeal the court of justice ruled that France had failed to fulfill its obligations under the Rome treaty because it had engaged in measures equivalent to quantitative restriction of trade. This case suggests that quantitative obstacles to trade remained long after the elimination of quotas, but it also suggests that the commission and the court have worked diligently to identify and eradicate them. Insofar as trade among

27. The commission's decisions, taken under article 108(3) of the Treaty of Rome and article 37 of the Treaty of Paris, are reported in *Journal Officiel des Communautés Européennes*, L 178 (July 25, 1968).

28. Nême and Nême, *Economie Européenne*, p. 78.

29. *EC Commission* v. *France*, case 42/82, EC Court of Justice; [1984] 1 *CMLR* 160.

member countries is concerned, most examples involved agriculture rather than industry.

INTERNAL TARIFFS

Elimination of internal tariffs, those on goods arriving from other member countries, was governed by articles 12 through 17 of the Treaty of Rome. Effective January 1, 1958, no member country could create or increase any internal tariff. Between January 1, 1959, and the end of the transition period, benchmark tariffs, those applied on January 1, 1957, were to be reduced in steps specified (with exceptions) in the treaty itself. Thus on January 1, 1959, the benchmark tariff on each product had to be reduced by 10 percent. After that, at intervals of six, twelve, or eighteen months, the tariff on every product had to decline by at least 5 percent of the benchmark rate, tariffs still in excess of 30 percent ad valorem had to decline by at least 10 percent, and aggregate tariff receipts on internal imports had to decline by 10 percent of the benchmark amount.[30] In practice, the EEC abandoned internal tariffs even faster than the Treaty of Rome required; and many countries reduced their tariffs in advance of EEC requirements. For example, on April 1, 1961, France cut unilaterally its tariffs on automobiles, mechanical and electrical equipment, textiles, and chemicals by 10 percent; on most other industrial products, it reduced its tariffs by 5 percent.[31]

For the most part, members effected their 10 percent reductions in tariff receipts through across-the-board, or linear, tariff cuts of 10 percent. As a result, the average pace at which tariffs diminished applied also to the large majority of particular tariffs. By July 1, 1968, tiny was the number of tariffs affecting intracommunity trade; and virtually all applied to agricultural products not yet included in the common agricultural policy.

30. For details, see Nême and Nême, *Economie Européenne*, pp. 50–51. For each product, benchmark tariff receipts were determined by application of the benchmark tariff of January 1, 1957, to the value of internal imports during 1956. Benchmark tariff receipts comprised the sum of the receipts on each individual product.

31. Ibid., pp. 50–53. According to the authors (p. 55), France accepted acceleration in return for concessions on the common agricultural policy.

Comparable liberalization did not occur with respect to taxes that had the same effect as tariffs.[32] Although the intent was to follow the timetable established for tariffs themselves, quasi tariffs proved difficult to identify and to treat. As of January 1, 1969, the EEC Commission had identified 380 cases; of these, 279 had been modified or eliminated, 17 were being brought into conformity with the treaty, and 84 remained in effect.[33] Since 1969 the commission and the court of justice have both had to deal with quasi-tariff problems.[34]

SUBSIDIES

Though the distorting effects of domestic subsidies on international trade are recognized in articles 92–94 of the Treaty of Rome, the EEC has encountered great difficulty in regulating state aids.[35] So diverse are the means of subsidy and so eager are member states to preserve their authority to undertake apparently domestic policy that the commission has not been able to eliminate all transfers violating the treaty's spirit.[36] Nevertheless, it has taken steps toward that end. It has established general rules for region-specific or industry-specific subsidies granted by national and local governments, it monitors particular subsidy schemes, and occasionally it has forced their elimination.

The commission has established codes for regional subsidies and for subsidies to such specific industries as steel, ships, and textiles.[37]

32. These are discussed in Treaty of Rome, article 13(2). For example, in February 1986 the EEC Commission ruled that France's system for controlling the retail price of cigarettes discriminated against brands imported from the rest of the community; see *Economist*, "February in the EEC" (March 1, 1986), p. 50.

33. Nême and Nême, *Economie Européenne*, p. 56.

34. The leading case is *Sociaal Fonds voor de Diamantarbeiders* v. *Brachfeld & Sons & Chougol Diamond Co.*, joint cases 2/69 and 3/69, EC Court of Justice, 15 *REC* 211 (1969).

35. A recent discussion appears in Ross, "Challenging State Aids."

36. Considering the discussion of French industrial policy in chapter 3, this finding should not be surprising. Between 1959 and 1972, taxes paid by French companies net of subsidies received declined sharply. This may reflect a conscious government strategy to help French enterprises cope with exposure to European competition. See note 104.

37. For example, a code for aid to the steel industry was introduced in 1980 and "substantially reinforced in 1981"; Commission of the European Communities, *Twelfth Report on Competition Policy*, p. 115; see also the *Tenth Report on Competition Policy*, point 194; and *Eleventh Report on Competition Policy*, point 187. Similarly,

The strategy of the commission is to specify maximum rates of subsidy applicable to the ensemble of aids granted to particular enterprises. These rates depend not only on the severity of the alleged problem but also on the extent to which the subsidy promotes positive structural adjustment. Upon expiration, several codes have been renewed, sometimes after modification.

When aimed at reluctant governments, general rules usually require interpretation. As a result, the commission has continually asserted its authority to review particular subsidies. For example, on May 25, 1984, the French government implemented two systems of aid on behalf of textile and apparel firms.[38] The aids had not been notified to the commission. In a notice dated August 2, 1984, the commission informed "potential recipients that it considers the aid systems as illegal in relation to Community law from the time they came into operation. The Commission also informs potential recipients of the risk attaching to these aids, in that any recipient of an aid granted illegally, i.e., without the Commission having reached a final decision, may have to refund the aid."[39]

The commission has also deliberated on the substance of subsidy schemes and found many to be incompatible with the treaty. Such was the case when the Italian government attempted to subsidize a domestic manufacturer of engines and tractors. The company wished to invest in a flexible manufacturing system that would permit introduction of a new range of engines. The government wished to grant an interest subsidy of 8.4 percentage points on a loan covering half the amount of the investment. Relying partly on the argument that the scheme would serve to expand production capacity in an industry "suffering from excess capacity caused by weak demand," the commission declared the subsidy to be incompatible with the Treaty of Rome.[40]

The EC has acted less forcefully to curb regional and industrial subsidies than it has to restrict quotas, tariffs, and equivalent restraints

---

the fifth directive on aid to shipbuilding was adopted by the EC Council on April 28, 1981; see *Official Journal of the European Communities*, L 137 (May 23, 1982).

38. Details appear in *Journal Officiel de la République Française* (May 25, 1984).

39. [1984] 3 *CMLR* 191.

40. *Re Aid to an Italian Engine Manufacturer*, EC Commission (84/364/EEC);[1984] 3 *CMLR* 447.

of trade.[41] Nevertheless, neither the commission nor the court of justice has ignored its obligations to enforce article 92. Both branches of government have argued that virtually all subsidies affect community trade and hence fall within the article's presumptive ban, the principal exception being the lavender essence case, in which France contributed 95 percent of community output and exported virtually nothing to other member countries. Both branches have also sought to limit the opportunities afforded by article 92(2) to overcome the presumption against aid. For example, the court of justice has stated that exceptions to the presumptive ban "must be interpreted strictly when any national or regional measure is considered; in particular, an exemption may be granted only if the Commission is able to establish that the aid is necessary for the purpose of achieving one of the objectives laid down in [the provisions of article 92(3) of the EEC treaty]."[42]

The commission has not merely decided against the validity of subsidies but has also attempted to ensure compliance by member countries. For example, when it found that the Italian government had not complied satisfactorily with a commission decision barring certain national and regional subsidies to Sicilian wine, fruit, and vegetables, it succeeded in having the court of justice find the Italian government guilty of not fulfilling its treaty obligations.[43] Meanwhile, the court of justice instructed the commission to investigate subsidies in such a manner that all affected parties, including other member states and competing producers who do not qualify for subsidies,

41. The *Twelfth Report on Competition Policy*, p. 113, summarizes the commission's positions on particular subsidies from 1970 to 1982. It distinguishes subsidies to which the commission did not object from those that triggered procedures under article 93(2) of the Rome treaty or article 8(3) of decision 2320/81 ECSC. The "no objection" category includes schemes that were modified prior to approval. A final category lists the number of formal negative decisions published in the *Official Journal of the European Communities*. The number of commission actions doubled between 1970 and 1975 (from 21 to 45), between 1975 and 1977 (from 45 to 112), and between 1977 and 1982 (from 112 to 233). In 1982 the commission initiated 129 procedures under article 93(2) of the EEC treaty or article 8(3) of decision 2320/81 ECSC, and it published 13 formal negative decisions in the official journal. In 1970 the commission had initiated only 6 procedures and published just 1 negative decision.

42. *Italian Government* v. *EC Commission*, case 173/73, EC Court of Justice; [1974] *ECR* 709.

43. *EC Commission* v. *Italian Republic*, case 130/83, EC Court of Justice; [1984] *ECR* 2849.

would be heard.[44] In so doing, the court increased the likelihood that evidence damaging to the case for subsidies would come to light. Most important, perhaps, in attending to such politically sensitive and economically depressed industries as wine, shipbuilding, and textiles, the commission has revealed its willingness to tackle economically important examples of subsidies.

COMPETITION

The EEC regulates private as well as government restraints of trade.[45] It has used the rules of competition primarily as appendages to the rules of international trade to ensure that private cartels did not replace governments as obstacles to intracommunity trade.[46]

Thus the rebuttable prohibition of collusion has been used most aggressively to prevent discouragement of what in Europe is called "parallel imports." The leading case on the subject involved imports of German electronic equipment into France.[47] Grundig, a German manufacturer, decided to market its radios, televisions, and tape recorders in France through a single wholesaler. The agreement between Grundig and Consten provided that neither Grundig itself nor its wholesalers in other countries would supply French retailers with Grundig products. In return, Consten would supply only French retailers of electronics. To reinforce Consten's control over the sale of Grundig products in France, Grundig assigned all French rights on its trademark (Gint) to Consten, permitting the French wholesaler to attack legally any French retailer who obtained Grundig products from a different source. Following this agreement, French wholesale prices of Grundig products rose well above their German counterparts. On some products the gap between the two climbed to between 30 and 40 percent. At this point another French importer (UNEF)

44. *Federal Republic of Germany* v. *EC Commission*, case 84/82, EC Court of Justice; [1984] *ECR* 1451.

45. The rules of competition appear in articles 85 through 90 of the Treaty of Rome. State-owned enterprises, no less than their private counterparts, are subject to these rules; see Brothwood, "The Court of Justice on Article 90 of the EEC Treaty."

46. Compare the cynicism of "A People's Republic of Europe," *Economist*, February 22, 1986, p. 19: "True to its 1950s origins, the Brussels bureaucracy is happiest when it is running cartels (in farming, steel, against Japanese imports)."

47. *Etablissements Consten SA & Grundig-Verkaufs GmbH* v. *EEC Commission*, cases 56/64 and 58/64, EC Court of Justice; [1964] *CMLR* 418.

decided to attempt arbitrage. It persuaded certain German wholesalers to sell it Grundig products at prices well below those prevailing in France. It then sold these items to French retailers at prices below those charged by Consten. When Consten discovered the arbitrage, it sued UNEF for trademark infringement. Meanwhile, UNEF petitioned the Commission of the EEC to declare the agreement between Grundig and Consten in violation of the Treaty of Rome.

On September 23, 1964, the commission held that the agreement did indeed violate article 85 of the treaty. The commission's view was upheld by the court of justice. Ever since, both the commission and the court have rooted out and eliminated agreements that restrict the rights of intermediate buyers to resell to foreign customers. The court of justice has also held that agreements to limit parallel imports within the community serve to restrict competition even when the amount of commerce involved is very small. Efforts to limit parallel imports have become per se violations of article 85.[48]

Deployment of article 85 has not been limited to restrictions of parallel imports. Horizontal agreements limited to price fixing or market division have also been attacked persistently. But joint ventures and specialization agreements have often been allowed to stand. Hence the view that article 85 is a rule of reason while section 1 of the Sherman Act is a per se rule. Whatever the general accuracy of this appraisal, it should not lead one to underestimate the severity with which article 85 forbids limitations of international arbitrage.

Regarding abuse of dominant position, the court of justice has found a unilateral market share of 40 percent sufficient to establish a dominant position. It has then prohibited dominant firms from indulging in various forms of otherwise legal behavior. Among these is discrimination in price among the community's national markets. *United Brands* is a case in point.[49] United Brands dominated sale of bananas in several parts of the EEC. It shipped its bananas green to

48. The best recent example of community practice involves the automobile industry. See the discussion later in this chapter of price convergence in Europe; see also Lukoff, "European Competition Law and Distribution in the Motor Vehicle Sector," pp. 841–66.

49. See *United Brands Co.*, EC Commission, December 17, 1975, *Official Journal of the European Communities*, L 95 (April 9, 1976); and *United Brands Company and United Brands Continentaal BV* v. *EC Commission*, case 27/76, EC Court of Justice, *Official Journal of the European Communities*, C 76 (March 30, 1978), p. 3.

Rotterdam where it sold them to wholesalers for ripening. The wholesalers were obliged to hold the bananas until they matured. Although explained as a method of ensuring product quality, this obligation effectively prevented ripeners in low-price countries from supplying a perishable item to retailers in high-price countries. The court of justice ultimately held that such behavior constituted abuse of United's dominant position.

ENLARGEMENT OF THE EC

Advocates of European integration hoped to expand the ECSC in geographic as well as industrial terms. Among the seventeen countries that had formed the OEEC in 1948, only six became charter members of ECSC. The United Kingdom was clearly the most important of the European outsiders. (Like France, Britain was extremely reticent to surrender sovereign powers to a European organization; unlike France, however, it did not experience the humiliation of 1940. Accordingly, it felt no compulsion to embrace the risks of the cooperative venture.) Not until 1961 did it apply for membership in the three communities and not until 1971 did the EC and the UK agree on terms of accession. France was instrumental in blocking British accession during the 1960s, in part to maintain the bearhug on Germany. Nevertheless, British ambivalence, embodied in a tough bargaining position, increased the tenability of the French view in the eyes of other community members. Not until January 1, 1973, did the UK finally join, along with Denmark and Ireland. By July 1, 1977, customs union among the nine had been achieved.[50]

On the thirtieth anniversary of the Treaty of Rome, the EC comprised twelve countries. Greece had joined on January 1, 1981, and Spain and Portugal on January 1, 1986. Although the three had yet to become full members, the geographic extension of integration had proceeded considerably since Robert Schuman's speech in 1950.

Economic Relations with Other Rich Countries

France became a charter member of the General Agreement on Tariffs and Trade (GATT) in 1947 and a charter member of the Organization for European Economic Cooperation (OEEC) in 1948.

50. Morris and Boehm, *The European Community.*

As a result, even before creation of the ECSC France was constrained to endorse the principles of free trade among industrial countries. Nevertheless, it did not always implement those early endorsements. Not until the EEC was born did its economic relations change fundamentally with the rich countries outside little Europe.

THE EUROPEAN COAL AND STEEL COMMUNITY

Despite explicit authority to control international trade within the community, the ECSC exercised ambiguous authority over trade with outsiders. The Treaty of Paris did not ensure creation of a true customs union, for it did not mandate establishment of a common external tariff. Each member country retained the authority to set its own tariffs and quotas with respect to imports from third countries.[51] Article 72 of the treaty did express, however, the hope that member countries would establish jointly a range of tariffs for each product within which each member would set its own tariff. To increase the likelihood that a relatively narrow band could be established close to the lower end of the scale of protection prevailing at the opening of the common market, article 15 of the transition convention announced the willingness of free-trading Benelux to raise its duties on steel by up to 2 percentage points.

In practice, when the common market took effect, the tariffs prevailing in member countries did not always differ appreciably. For coal, iron ore, and scrap no country except Italy imposed a tariff. For special steels, France and Germany had harmonized their rates just before the common market opened. For ordinary steel, upon creation of the common market, the French and Germans resumed collection of the tariffs they had suspended earlier.[52]

During the transition period, tariffs on ordinary steels were harmonized. The Benelux countries did in fact raise most of their tariffs

51. Diebold, *The Schuman Plan*, pp. 472–73.
52. The average rate for special steels, roughly 11 percent, lay close to midway between the German average of 8 percent and the French average of 15 percent; ibid., p. 478. The tariffs on ordinary steel are reported in ibid., p. 145. To prevent tariff avoidance by outsiders wishing to sell in France, Germany, and Italy, article 15 of the transition convention required Benelux to establish tariff quotas. Only a specified volume of imports from third countries could enter Benelux at its normal tariff. The rest would be taxed at the next lowest tariff in the ECSC. As a further precaution, Benelux importers agreed not to reexport within the community any imports that had paid the normal Benelux tariff. Ibid., p. 474.

by 2 percentage points. The Germans reduced their tariffs to the new levels found in the Benelux. The French set their rates 1 percentage point above those in the Benelux, and the Italians fixed theirs 2 to 4 percentage points above those in the Benelux. For France, the decline in tariff protection was considerable: "French duties on steel products that had ranged between 10 and 22 per cent were now 6 to 9 per cent."[53]

THE EUROPEAN ECONOMIC COMMUNITY

The EEC was a customs union; hence the tariffs applied by France to imports from outside the community were ultimately identical to those prevailing in other member countries. The mechanics of harmonization were spelled out in articles 18 through 29 of the Treaty of Rome. The common external tariff was to take effect by the end of the transition period. For most products, the rate of duty would be the arithmetic average of four duties in force on January 1, 1957: the French, the German, the Italian, and the Benelux. However, some of the 1957 tariffs, especially those of Italy, were modified in specified ways before calculation of the average. Moreover, for several products the treaty specified the external tariff, established a maximum tariff, or left it to subsequent negotiation among member states.

The pace at which common external tariffs were to be established appeared in article 23 of the treaty. Where a member's 1957 tariff diverged by no more than 15 percent from the common external tariff, the member was to adopt the common tariff by January 1, 1962. Where a member's 1957 tariff diverged by more than 15 percent, the member was to reduce the gap by 30 percent on January 1, 1962, by another 30 percent at the end of the second stage of transition (set for January 1, 1966) and by the remaining 40 percent at the end of the third stage of transition (set for January 1, 1970).

The pace at which the common customs tariff was implemented exceeded that prescribed by the treaty. In the case of industrial products requiring the three-step adjustment process, the first reduction of 30 percent was taken one year early, on January 1, 1961. The second step was taken thirty months early, on July 1, 1963. The 40 percent step was taken eighteen months early on July 1, 1968.[54]

53. Ibid., p. 478.
54. Nême and Nême, *Economie Européenne*, p. 62.

Thus the common customs tariff was implemented fully at the same time as the common market itself.

MULTILATERAL AGREEMENTS WITHIN GATT

Under the Treaty of Rome, commercial negotiations with countries outside the community were to be conducted by the commission, and any resulting agreements were to be concluded by the council. Individual member countries were not to bargain for themselves.[55] Thus during the GATT session of October-November 1958, when C. Douglas Dillon proposed a 20 percent across-the-board reduction in tariffs, it was up to the community as a whole to develop a response. The community decided to agree to the 20 percent reduction on a wide range of products. As a result, although the Dillon round of negotiations did not begin formally until September 1960, the community began unilaterally to align the external tariffs of member countries not on the common customs tariff specified by the Treaty of Rome, but rather on 80 percent of that tariff. Even though it failed to achieve its 20 percent goal for GATT as a whole, the Dillon round did prompt members of the EEC to establish external tariffs well below those specified in the treaty.[56] The community's treatment of external imports was less discriminatory than might be expected from reading the treaty.

The Dillon round was followed almost immediately by the Kennedy round. Early in the negotiations the parties agreed to the principle of linearity. Only certain exceptional products, designated by each bargaining party, would be discussed individually. The EEC's list of exceptions contained goods accounting for roughly 20 percent of the community's industrial imports.[57] The principle of linearity was also modified in the case of products on which the tariffs of the major trading countries differed appreciably. Thus whenever the tariff in one country exceeded that in another by at least 10 percentage points and at least 100 percent, the low-tariff country was not obliged to

55. For a discussion of the community's success in asserting its authority to negotiate on behalf of member countries, see Jackson, Louis, and Matsushita, "Implementing the Tokyo Round," especially pp. 277–98.

56. According to Nême and Nême, *Economie Européenne*, p. 59, the average decline in tariffs, weighted according to the importance of trade under each tariff heading, was 7 percent.

57. Ibid., p. 380.

reduce its tariff at the linear rate. For some products the EEC would apply the linear reduction to the common customs tariff as specified in the treaty; for others it announced its willingness to apply the linear reduction to a benchmark equal to 80 percent of the treaty tariff.

On June 30, 1967, the negotiations were complete. On most industrial products the participants, including all members of the OECD, agreed to reduce most tariffs by 50 percent.[58] Taking account of the special cases in which tariffs fell by less than 50 percent, the mean reduction in the EEC's common customs tariffs, weighted according to the importance of each tariff heading in the volume of European imports, was 38 percent. The corresponding weighted means for the United Kingdom, Japan, and the United States ranged between 35 and 40 percent. The Kennedy round was implemented in five equal steps ending on January 1, 1972. For the large majority of tariffs that were to fall by 50 percent, each country was supposed to reduce its benchmark tariff by 10 percent on each January 1 starting in 1968 and ending in 1972. In fact, the EEC effected its first two cuts simultaneously on July 1, 1968.[59]

The Tokyo round of negotiations, launched in September 1973, achieved a series of agreements endorsed by the EC Council on November 20, 1979. Once again, the tariff negotiations proceeded on a linear basis. "The results have generally been estimated as approximately a thirty-five percent reduction in the industrial tariffs of the major industrial participants of the negotiations."[60] Unlike its predecessors, however, the Tokyo round also generated agreements on nontariff barriers to trade. It established codes for subsidies, countervailing duties, antidumping measures, government procurement, customs valuation procedures, import licensing procedures, and three specific industries (civil aircraft, beef, and dairy products).

---

58. Before the agreement, across all product categories the mean value of the common customs tariff was 12 percent. This compared with 17 percent in Japan and 18 percent in the United States and in the United Kingdom. Although low on average, particular tariffs could be stiff indeed. Almost 5 percent of EEC tariffs and close to 30 percent of U.S. and British tariffs exceeded 20 percent. Ibid., pp. 382–83.

59. Its behavior was matched by those of several other countries, including Japan, the United Kingdom, Sweden, Norway, and Denmark; ibid., pp. 380–85.

60. Jackson and others, "Implementing the Tokyo Round," pp. 272–73: "An Anti-

BILATERAL AGREEMENTS WITHIN EUROPE

Even before the EC's first enlargement, the insulation of French industry from producers outside Europe was on the wane. Not only did the original EC tariff lie well below its French counterpart for most products, but the Kennedy round reduced the EC duty substantially.

Once the United Kingdom agreed to join the EC, however, the community became willing to liberalize trade with members of the original OEEC that remained nonsigners of the Paris and Rome treaties. Thus seven months after the agreement on British entry, the EC agreed to free trade in industrial products with Austria, Iceland, Portugal, Sweden, and Switzerland. It subsequently signed similar agreements with Norway and Finland. All took effect during 1973, except that with Finland, which took effect January 1, 1974.

The impact of ECSC, EEC, and GATT on the exposure of French enterprises to foreign competition will be discussed in detail later. Suffice it to say now that despite the continued outcropping of public and private barriers to trade, Europe has achieved remarkable freedom of international movement in industrial products. With respect to trade within the original EEC, the key dates were 1962 (elimination of quotas) and 1968 (elimination of tariffs); with respect to external trade, the key dates were 1972 (full implementation of the Kennedy round) and 1973 (pan-European free trade in industrial products).

Decolonization

Creation and expansion of the European Communities, coupled with trade liberalization through GATT, tilted France's economic environment toward the rich countries of the world. So did the sometimes involuntary decolonizations that occurred after World War II.

France lost its first colonial empire during the Seven Years War (1756–63). In the 1830s it began to construct a second. Attempting to deflect his unpopularity at home and using a three-year-old insult from the Dey as a pretext, Charles X bombarded Algiers into

---

Dumping code was negotiated in the Kennedy Round (1967), but was not very successful."

submission. By 1848 the Second Republic had divided Algeria into three *départements*, integral parts of France rather than mere colonies. Before 1870 most of the French in Algeria were soldiers, and the ratio of Europeans to natives was small. Thereafter, the pace of European immigration quickened. With the loss of Alsace-Lorraine to Germany in 1870 came large numbers of Alsatians. With the French phylloxera epidemic of 1878 came large numbers of ruined farmers, especially from southern France. During the half century leading up to the First World War, French immigrants were joined in substantial numbers by Italians, Spaniards, and Maltese, "so much so that by 1917 only one in five of the non-Muslim population was said to be of French origin. As Anatole France muttered angrily: 'We have despoiled, pursued, and hunted down the Arabs in order to populate Algeria with Italians and Spaniards.'"[61]

Algeria was the first of many new colonies. During the second half of the nineteenth century, France vied with Italy for influence in Tunisia and with Spain, Germany, and Britain for influence in Morocco. Ultimately, France gained the upper hand in both. Meanwhile, French West Africa (1895) and French Equatorial Africa (1910) were created to consolidate spheres of influence in sub-Saharan Africa. Formal control of Madagascar was established in 1885, and the union of Indochina was created in 1887 (Laos joining in 1893). In nearly all these areas, France exercised de facto influence well before it established a formal colony.

In 1931, a century after its first expedition to Algeria, France could claim an empire of 12.4 million square kilometers and 64.3 million people; in comparison, metropolitan France comprised only 544 thousand square kilometers and 41.8 million people.[62] Sub-Saharan and North Africa accounted respectively for 60 percent and 22 percent of the territory. In population, although Indochina and sub-Saharan Africa were nearly identical and substantially larger than North Africa, the European settlers of the French empire were heavily concentrated in North Africa.

61. Horne, *A Savage War of Peace*, p. 32.
62. Yacono, *Les Etapes de la Décolonisation Française*, pp. 6, 15; and INSEE, *Annuaire Statistique de la France, 1986*, p. 8.

Before 1930 the empire accounted for modest shares of French exports, foreign investment, and imports.[63] To certain industries, however, especially cotton textiles and food, the empire constituted a major market. Already in 1906, a normal year, 86 percent of the bleached cotton fabrics, 85 percent of the unbleached cotton fabrics, 80 percent of the fabricated metal products, 74 percent of the locomotives and other mobile steam engines, 57 percent of the steel rails, 54 percent of the shoes, and 49 percent of the dyed cotton fabrics exported from France were destined for the empire. In 1913 the empire absorbed two-thirds of the refined sugar, two-thirds of the soap, and one-third of the cotton fabrics exported from France.

In the late 1920s and early 1930s, as the French franc rose sharply in value and the industrial countries of the world dismantled what remained of free trade, reliance on imperial markets diffused to a broad spectrum of manufacturing industries. In automobiles, for example, the ratio of imperial to total exports climbed from 16 percent in 1913 to 33 percent in 1929 to 46 percent in 1938.[64] More generally, at the beginning of World War II, declining and expanding industries alike relied heavily on imperial markets. Between 1927 and 1935 the fraction of aggregate exports that was destined for the empire rose from 15 percent to 32 percent. In 1928 the colonies overtook the United Kingdom at the summit of French trade relationships. By 1935 Algeria alone was France's largest trading partner.[65]

At the end of World War II the geographic composition of French exports returned to the pattern established during the 1930s. The high-water mark of colonial influence on French trade occurred in 1952.[66] Shortly thereafter, however, France fought major colonial

63. Between 1909 and 1913 it accounted for less than 13 percent of French exports. Yacono, *Les Etapes de la Décolonisation Française*, p. 29. More generally, see Hauser, "Colonies et Métropole"; and Marseille, *Empire Colonial et Capitalisme Français*, pp. 40–54.

64. Ibid., p. 54. As of 1938, 41 percent of motors and their parts, 42 percent of apparel, 44 percent of perfumes and soaps, 46 percent of automobiles, and 51 percent of fabricated metal products exported from France were destined for French colonies; ibid., pp. 29–30. See also Weiller, "Echanges Extérieurs"; and Franko, *The European Multinationals*, pp. 110–11.

65. Marseille, *Empire Colonial et Capitalisme Français*, p. 41; and Yacono, *Les Etapes de la Décolonisation Française*, pp. 29–30.

66. Marseille, *Empire Colonial et Capitalisme Français*, p. 35.

wars in Indochina and Algeria. With less bloodshed but still incomplete amity, it granted independence to Tunisia and Morocco in 1956. Most of its other African holdings became independent a few years later. In the eight years between 1954 and 1962, the formal content of French colonialism had all but disappeared.[67]

The end of political sovereignty does not necessarily entail the end of economic influence. Had France surrendered the trappings of empire preemptively, the colonial tropisms of the French economy might have persisted. But the bitterness of the wars in Indochina and Algeria precluded such an outcome. The countries of Indochina withdrew from the French union as soon as they received their independence. Algeria made dead letters of provisions in the Evian agreements safeguarding French economic interests, especially access to crude oil. Although the French government had estimated that only 10 percent of the 1 million European settlers would leave Algeria during its first year of independence, 350,000 left during June 1962, alone. Before the flow had abated, all but 30,000 had departed. Of those who left, roughly 50,000 went to Spain, 12,000 to Canada, 10,000 to Israel, and 1,500 to Argentina. The rest, including many of Italian, Spanish, and Maltese origin, as well as some Muslim refugees— 1,380,000 people in all—went to France.[68]

Measuring Impact

The international environment of French business changed radically after World War II. Did the revolution alter the opportunities or

67. Since 1962 France has also granted independence to Comoro Islands (1975) and New Hebrides (1980). For a complete calendar, see Yacono, *Les Etapes de la Décolonisation Française*, pp. 118–23. Among remaining French possessions, the Antilles produced tropical foodstuffs, Guiana launched French space vehicles, Polynesia hosted French nuclear tests, and New Caledonia produced minerals; *Economist*, August 25, 1984, pp. 42–43.

68. Horne, *A Savage War of Peace*, pp. 528–34. As of March 1, 1968, 1,358,940 people of French citizenship and 933,220 foreigners were living in France who had been living abroad on January 1, 1962; the number living in France who had been living in Algeria (excluding Algerians and Muslims of French citizenship) was 899,940; INSEE, *Annuaire Statistique de la France*, 1972, p. 45. Information on the number of passengers arriving in France from Algeria during 1962 (by month) appears in INSEE, *Annuaire Statistique de la France*, 1963, p. 41. Immigration of Algerian colonists by occupational category is reported in Elie, "Structure de la Population Totale au Recensement de 1968," table 1.

goals of business enterprises? In particular, did it tilt many companies away from the behavioral conservatism discussed in chapter 1?

The impact of environmental change on company behavior and market performance depends critically on the states of competition prevailing before and after the change occurs. The potential importance of the state of competition is readily apparent in two hypothetical examples.

First, suppose that French enterprises bought and sold in competitive markets before and after they became exposed to foreign rivals. Suppose further that all companies enjoyed complete information at all times about technological, organizational, and product opportunities. In this setting the institutional changes described earlier in this chapter would alter the international division of labor, reallocate national resources among uses, and change standards of living.[69] Although increased international exposure would augment efficiency in the allocation of global resources, productive and allocative efficiency at the national level would obtain before as well as after changed foreign exposure. Companies would modify their choices in response to movements in prices, but no enterprise would change its goals or pursue market power to a different degree. For this reason, companies could be said to alter their behavior without modifying fundamentally their approaches to business conduct.

Now suppose that French firms enjoyed market power before their exposure to foreign rivals but that the exposure eliminated most of the power. Suppose further that the firms initially possessed imperfect information about technological, organizational, and product opportunities and that the market power they enjoyed required them to invest in directly unproductive collusion or political influence. Finally, suppose that the competition prevailing after exposure was Schumpeterian in nature, such that rivalry included pursuit of new products or technologies designed to confer at least temporary competitive advantage. In this setting, far more than in its predecessor, the institutional changes described earlier could be expected to impinge profoundly on market performance and conduct.[70]

---

69. In keeping with traditional theories of international economics. See Caves, *Trade and Economic Structure*.

70. Such a setting should be analyzed using the tools of industrial economics. See

In terms of performance, before exposure the domestic economy realized neither allocative nor productive efficiency. The existence of market power precluded the first (unless market power resulted in perfect price discrimination and labor supply was insensitive to the opportunity cost of leisure), and the pursuit of market power precluded the second. As a result, foreign exposure could be expected to improve national as well as global efficiency. In terms of conduct, the prevalence of market power before exposure to foreign competition facilitated pursuit of goals other than profit. If the quiet life was among those goals, company knowledge of technological, organizational, and product opportunities might have been inefficiently imperfect. Exposure to competition could be expected to move companies in the direction of profit maximization. Observation of foreign rivals could be expected to stimulate learning about production, organization, and products. Reduction of barriers to international trade and investment could be expected to narrow the ability of domestic government to protect established advantages. Hence it could be expected to reduce the attractiveness of investments in directly unproductive political influence.

In this second setting, then, exposure to foreign rivals might have resulted in behavioral adjustment not simply in the sense of response to changes in market prices but also in the sense that enterprises appeared to increase their sensitivity to market signals. Rising fractions of the surviving business population might have exhibited profit-maximizing behavior, and rising fractions of the profit-maximizers might have substituted the innovative for the defensive path to rents.

A priori, it is plausible to assume that the environmental changes described earlier in this chapter diminished the prevalence of monopoly and oligopoly and extended the domain of competition. Through direct investment and personal migration, as well as through trade, economic integration of rich countries tends to increase the numbers of competitors and strategic groups serving each market. Nevertheless, reduction of public barriers to interpenetration does not lead necessarily to rising exposure to foreigners, and rising

---

Caves, *American Industry*; Scherer, *Industrial Market Structure and Economic Performance*; and Jacquemin, *The New Industrial Organization*.

exposure to foreigners does not lead necessarily to rising competition.[71] The second of these assertions requires elaboration.

FOREIGN EXPOSURE AND THE STATE OF COMPETITION

Increased exposure to international trade and investment is often and plausibly presumed to generate increased exposure to competition. But exposure of the first variety does not imply exposure of the second: for a variety of reasons, trade and investment are both logically compatible with sustained imperfections in competition; under certain circumstances they might even promote market power. Several objections clog the a priori path from foreign exposure to competition.

The vigor of competition in a market can often be predicted from its structure.[72] Therefore, a natural way to explore the competitive impact of international exposure is to measure exposure's effects on the major elements of market structure. In this section, I consider the potential linkages between international exposure and two established features of market structure: seller concentration as conventionally defined (that is, at the enterprise level) and concentration at the level of strategic groups.[73] Since the positive effects of exposure on competition are well understood, I shall dwell here on their neutral and negative counterparts.[74] I then explain why incomplete and imperfect information precludes a uniquely structural approach to empirical analysis of the relationship.

Increases in import exposure do not necessarily reduce domestic seller concentration. Included in international trade are goods traveling from one part of a multinational enterprise to another. If leading domestic producers import large quantities from foreign affiliates,

71. See Encaoua, "Pouvoir de Monopole et Groupes Industriels," p. 188.

72. Market structure must be distinguished from industrial structure. The latter refers to the distribution of output among economic activities, the former to the relatively immutable traits of well-defined markets that determine the likelihood of collusive or exclusionary practices or both on the part of market participants. Market structure is discussed comprehensively in Caves, *American Industry.*

73. The concept of strategic group is discussed in Newman, "Strategic Groups and the Structure-Performance Relationship."

74. See Caves, *International Trade, International Investment, and Imperfect Markets.*

intrafirm trade can easily increase seller concentration. Even if imports nudge seller concentration downward, the change might not suffice to invigorate competition. Competition does not vary linearly with concentration. If the pool of foreign suppliers is sufficiently small, oligopolistic behavior might be preserved. If the pool of foreign suppliers is large but each foreign supplier is small in relation to domestic rivals, then foreigners might align their conduct on that of a domestic oligopoly group. Such alignment is especially likely when foreigners believe that aggressive behavior on their part will provoke the home government to shelter its market from outside competition.

As for exports, not all need travel to competitive world markets. Some might find their way to markets dominated by a small number of suppliers. Some might even find their way to markets dominated by exactly the same enterprises that control the home market. Exports to such markets are unlikely to expose the home industry to increased competition.

Dependent export markets appear especially frequently in present or former colonies. Such countries contain few if any indigenous suppliers, and producers in third countries are often excluded artificially from the market. As a result, colonial markets tend to be no less concentrated than their domestic counterparts. Given the likelihood in the parent country of a positive correlation between company size and propensity to export, seller concentration might well be greater in the colonial than in the parent market.

Direct foreign investment can increase or decrease seller concentration. In the short run, the effect depends largely on the method of investment (acquisition versus construction) and on the importance of the multinational's exports to the host country before and after the investment. In the longer term, the effect depends on the ability of the multinational to increase its market share at the expense of other sellers, coupled with its relative market share at the time of the foreign investment.

In France, as in many countries where French goods are sold, government publishes data on concentration of production at the industry level. Unfortunately, this information measures true seller concentration rather poorly.

In the first place, it measures the concentration of domestic production rather than the concentration of domestic sales. In other words, it ignores imports and exports. The correspondence between producer and seller concentration cannot be achieved merely by substituting apparent home consumption for domestic production in the denominator of the concentration ratio.[75] Where international trade impinges heavily on the domestic industry, and especially where international trade occurs between companies belonging to the same enterprise, producer concentration fails not only to measure seller concentration accurately but also to provide an upper or lower bound on the meaningful ratio.

The second major problem with French and most other European data on concentration is the manner in which enterprise boundaries are established. Seller concentration should be a measure of the extent to which a few independent decisionmakers control most sales in a particular market. To the extent that decisions in some companies are ultimately made by executives in other companies—as, for example, when one company is a subsidiary of another—companies under common control should be grouped together and considered a single enterprise. The French data, however, treat each legally distinct company as a separate decisionmaking entity.[76] As a result, companies like Peugeot, Citroën, and Talbot are considered three distinct sellers of automobiles even though Peugeot controls the others. Given the propensity of European enterprises to be structured in terms of subsidiaries as opposed to operating divisions of a single company, this problem is serious in the French context.

Given the level of seller concentration, sellers are more likely to behave competitively the greater their heterogeneity. Sellers who produce the same mix of products in the same locations with the same mix of factors, and who sell in the same markets using the same distribution channels, can agree relatively easily on how best to profit from particular market situations. They are likely to constitute a strategic group.[77] The smaller the number of such groups operating in a market, the greater the likelihood of oligopolistic behavior.

75. Adams, "Producer-Concentration as a Proxy for Seller-Concentration."

76. A few studies have attempted to overcome this problem. See Encaoua and Franck, "Performances Sectorielles et Groupes de Sociétés"; and Encaoua and Jacquemin, "Organizational Efficiency and Monopoly Power." See also INSEE E71. Unfortunately, no benchmarks exist for the early postwar years.

77. Newman, "Strategic Groups and the Structure-Performance Relationship."

Nationality is likely to be an important determinant of strategic group affiliation. Foreign and domestic producers can be expected to differ regarding the geographic distributions of production and sales. They might also differ regarding methods of production and versions of the product. If the foreign firms differ with respect to their geographic patterns of activity, they also might disagree about how to exploit the domestic market.

But not all direct investment reinforces diversity among sellers. If leading sellers in each of several countries begin to supply each foreign market via local production, and if such parallel investments replace sporadic exports from the home country, then direct investment might cement cooperative behavior at the international level by harmonizing the market-specific goals and constraints faced by each seller.[78]

No government reports systematic information on strategic groups. Although such information would not be difficult to assemble for a small number of industries, systematic measurement of heterogeneity for the full population of domestic markets would require substantial effort indeed.

IMPLICATIONS

In the remaining sections of this chapter, I examine the empirical evidence supporting linkages between change in the international environment and change in the vigor of competition. The absence of systematic information on the two forms of concentration just discussed will complicate this endeavor. Nevertheless, abundant evidence will demonstrate clearly that international trade and investment now affect greatly most categories of French enterprise. It will also suggest that foreign trade and investment have frequently, if not ineluctably, vivified the competition experienced by French manufacturing enterprises.[79]

78. Such harmonization would end the dumping that might occur under conditions of sporadic trade and might destabilize local oligopolistic agreements fatally. See Casson, *The Firm and the Market,* pp. 50–52. A thorough analysis of the competitive consequences of direct foreign investment appears in Caves, *Multinational Enterprise and Economic Analysis,* pp. 94–130. The market power consequences of parallel integration are discussed in Adams, "Market Structure and Corporate Power."

79. I defer to another study the question of whether increased competition

Exposure to Foreign Trade

Abandonment of tariffs and quotas does not guarantee increased trade. Not only do governments possess more subtle means of hindering international movements of goods and services, but private parties, bent on preserving national cartels, might themselves attempt to neutralize the effects of altered institutional arrangements. On both accounts, it has been argued, the European Communities have failed to create a genuine common market and have avoided full participation in competitive world markets.[80]

This section documents the evolution of French exposure to international trade. It shows that goods produced abroad now account for considerable fractions of domestic consumption and that considerable fractions of domestic output are now sold abroad. These are the most important changes experienced by French industries since World War II.

EXPOSURE TO IMPORTS

As of 1959 few French industries were exposed heavily to imports.[81] In manufacturing, imports accounted on average for 8 percent of domestic consumption (table 19). Half of all manufacturing industries showed exposures of less than 5 percent (appendix table A-53). Only four of forty-six exhibited exposures of 20 percent or more, and all of these were near the raw materials ends of their vertical streams of production: unfinished nonferrous metals (27 percent), edible oils and fats (33 percent), sugar (34 percent), and bulk organic chemicals (36 percent). Outside manufacturing the mean exposure to imports was

---

improved economic performance, as measured by productive and allocative efficiency at the national level. The relationship between market structure and productivity is analyzed in Davies and Caves, *Britain's Productivity Gap.* For an attempt to measure the EEC's impact on French allocative efficiency, see Auquier, *French Industry's Reaction to the European Common Market.*

80. Europessimism, the lament that members of the European Communities are coming to rely less heavily on each other, is discussed in Stein, "The European Community in 1983." See also Commission of the European Communities, *Completing the Internal Market.*

81. Exposure to imports (IM) is measured as $100\ (M + T)/(\ Q - X + M + T)$, where M is imports c.i.f., T is tariff paid, Q is domestic output, and X is exports f.o.b.

Table 19. *Mean Ratio of Imports to Consumption, 1959–80*[a]
Percent

Year	Manufacturing	Non-manufacturing	Year	Manufacturing	Non-manufacturing
1959	8	13	1970	17	16
1960	9	13	1971	17	17
1961	9	13	1972	18	17
1962	10	13	1973	19	18
1963	11	14	1974	21	19
1964	11	14	1975	20	18
1965	12	14	1976	22	19
1966	12	15	1977	23	19
1967	13	15	1978	23	19
1968	14	15	1979	25	19
1969	16	15	1980	25	20

Source: INSEE input-output tables in current prices, level S (unpublished).

a. Mean values for forty-six manufacturing and thirty-two nonmanufacturing industries. Ratio of imports to consumption (exposure to imports) is $100 (M+T)/(Q+M+T-X)$, where M is imports c.i.f., T is tariff collected, Q is output (*production distribuée*), and X is exports f.o.b. Industries defined according to NAP-S79 (see appendix C). Industry S56 omitted.

greater (table 19), but the median exposure was only 2 percent. Thus in a few nonmanufacturing industries, import exposure attained very high levels, accounting for more than two-thirds of domestic consumption in air and sea transport (68 percent), nonferrous metallic minerals (88 percent), and crude petroleum (95 percent). In most, however, imports accounted for small fractions of domestic consumption. In twenty of thirty-two, exposure was less than 5 percent (table A-53); in thirteen, imports were nil. Together, these twenty industries accounted for 71 percent of nonmanufacturing consumption.

Between 1959 and 1980, import exposure changed fundamentally. Mean exposure increased by 17 percentage points in manufacturing and by 7 percentage points in nonmanufacturing (appendix table A-54). Outside manufacturing the rise in exposure was confined to coal (up 27 percentage points), fish (up 38), ferrous minerals (up 59) and natural gas (up 71). Leaving aside these exceptional cases, the ratio of imports to domestic consumption failed to rise appreciably. In fact, eight of thirty-two nonmanufacturing industries experienced less exposure: in all but air and sea transport the decline was slight— between 3.2 and 0.6 percentage points. In air and sea transport, exposure fell by 9 percentage points. Another eleven of the thirty-two experienced no imports at any time between 1959 and 1980.

Altogether, in twenty-five of the thirty-two, import exposure rose less than 5 percentage points (appendix table A-55). In manufacturing, import exposure increased appreciably and pervasively—more than 10 percentage points in thirty-one of forty-six industries. In five it increased by at least 30 points: shoes (up 30 points), knitwear (up 35), woven textiles (up 36), household electronics (up 52), and manmade fibers (up 56). At the other end of the spectrum, exposure to imports declined only for sugar.

Many of the industries experiencing large increases in exposure had received substantial tariff protection in 1959. In the textiles sector, for example, high rates of duty had applied to manmade fibers (19 percent), shoes (23 percent), and knitwear (30 percent).[82] Associated with the high tariffs were meager imports. In manmade fibers, shoes, and knitwear, imports accounted for less than 5 percent of domestic consumption in 1959. By 1980 the rate of duty had fallen below 5 percent in each case, and import exposure had increased by more than 30 percentage points. More generally, among all manufacturing industries, tariff level in 1959 correlates positively with change in import exposure between 1959 and 1980.[83] Appendix table A-56 identifies the manufacturing industries in which exposure increased less than 10 percentage points between 1959 and 1980. The list includes perishables, difficult-to-transport products, and goods rarely produced abroad in substitutable form. In these cases it is hardly surprising that domestic production satisfied most internal consumption even after the economy opened. In other cases, however, the failure of exposure to increase cannot be attributed to "natural" protection of domestic producers. For example, government buys a large share of output or regulates the sale of petroleum products, ships, railway vehicles, and drugs. Moreover, drugs and petroleum products are produced by companies known to have engaged in cartel activities at the international level.[84] In these cases at least, the failure of exposure to rise appreciably is plausibly unnatural.

82. The rate (t) is measured as $100 (T/M)$, where T is duty collected and M is imports c.i.f. Data are from INSEE input-output tables in current prices, level S (unpublished).

83. At the .001 level of significance in a one-tail t-test ($r = 0.49$, $N = 46$).

84. Stocking and Watkins, *Cartels in Action*, pp. 363–429; and Blair, *The Control of Oil*.

Given the widespread belief that the EC has come untracked, that early efforts to deregulate trade have been halted and perhaps eroded by revived protectionism, it is interesting to examine the timing of these changes in import exposure. Toward this end I compared the changes in import exposure during 1959–69 with those during 1970–80. I also compared changes in import exposure during 1959–66 with those during 1973–80: the earlier period covers the first two stages of transition toward full achievement of the EEC; the later covers years of substantial macroeconomic shock. In effect, this second comparison juxtaposes the period when tariffs within the common market were declining most substantially with the period when member countries were allegedly restricting imports most energetically.

Outside manufacturing, import exposure proceeded at a fairly steady pace, tending to rise to the same degree during 1970–80 as during 1959–69, during 1973–80 as during 1959–66 (table A-54). For manufacturing, import exposure also failed to decline. Changes in exposure tended to the same levels during 1959–69 as during 1970–80; changes in exposure during 1973–80 actually tended to exceed those during 1959–66.

By 1980, manufacturing was heavily exposed to imports, with a mean exposure value of 25 percent (table 19). In virtually all forty-six industries, imports accounted for major fractions of domestic consumption (table A-53). Only four industries in 1980 (compared with twenty-three in 1959) displayed exposures of less than 5 percent; twenty-eight industries in 1980 (compared with four in 1959) displayed exposures of at least 20 percent. In sixteen product categories accounting for more than one-quarter of French consumption of manufactures in 1980, exposure exceeded 30 percent. In such major industries as bulk organic chemicals, crude steel, unfinished nonferrous metals, mechanical equipment, automobiles, household electrical equipment, and professional electronic and office equipment—each of which accounted for more than Fr 50 billion of domestic consumption in 1980—imports contributed more than one-quarter of domestic sales.

One way to appreciate this transformation is to examine exposure in 1980 for industries in which imports accounted for less than 5 percent of domestic consumption in 1959. In seven of twenty-three cases exposure remained below 10 percent in 1980 (appendix table

Table 20. *Mean Ratio of Exports to Output, 1959–80*[a]
Percent

Year	Manufacturing	Non-manufacturing	Year	Manufacturing	Non-manufacturing
1959	14	9	1970	19	8
1960	14	9	1971	19	8
1961	14	9	1972	20	8
1962	13	9	1973	21	8
1963	13	8	1974	23	9
1964	14	8	1975	23	8
1965	15	8	1976	24	8
1966	14	8	1977	25	9
1967	15	8	1978	26	9
1968	15	8	1979	27	8
1969	16	8	1980	27	8

Source: INSEE input-output tables in current prices, level S (unpublished).
a. Mean values for forty-six manufacturing and thirty-two nonmanufacturing industries. Ratio of exports to output (propensity to export) is 100 (X/Q), where X is exports f.o.b. and Q is output (*production distribuée*). Industries defined according to NAP-S79 (see appendix C). Industry S56 omitted.

A-57). In another six cases, imports came to account for between 10 percent and 20 percent of domestic consumption. In ten of twenty-three cases, however, imports ultimately accounted for over 20 percent of domestic consumption. Half of the ten involved textiles broadly defined. The other five included two major industries—road vehicles, in which exposure rose from 4 percent in 1959 to 27 percent in 1980, and electrical equipment, in which it rose from 4 percent in 1959 to 21 percent in 1980.

Outside manufacturing, mean exposure to imports was 20 percent in 1980 (table 19). At the industry level, exposure varied greatly. For fish, natural gas, ferrous minerals, nonferrous metallic minerals, crude petroleum, and air and sea transport, more than half of domestic consumption was satisfied by imports. In other cases, however, including twelve categories of services, imports were nil. Agricultural imports accounted for 13 percent of domestic consumption, a share almost identical to that obtaining in 1959.

PROPENSITY TO EXPORT

In 1959 manufacturing industries displayed a mean propensity to export (exports f.o.b. divided by output) of 14 percent (table 20). Most manufacturing industries exported small fractions of their output: one-half of manufacturing output was attributable to industries exporting less than 10 percent of production (appendix table A-58). Nearly two-thirds of manufacturing output was attributable to industries exporting less than 15 percent of production. Only semifinished steel and sugar displayed ratios of exports to output of 30 percent or more. No manufacturing industry exported a majority of its output. Outside manufacturing the mean propensity to export in 1959 was 9 percent. The corresponding median, however, was less than 1 percent. Thirteen of the thirty-two industries exported nothing; another eleven had export propensities between 0 and 5 percent. Together, these industries accounted for 91 percent of nonmanufacturing output (table A-58). Meanwhile, five industries exported at least 20 percent of production: transport related services (21 percent), nonmetallic minerals (27 percent), nonferrous metallic minerals (41 percent), ferrous minerals (54 percent), and air and sea transport (94 percent).

Between 1959 and 1980, in manufacturing the mean propensity to export doubled, increasing by 13 percentage points (table 20). Export propensity tended strongly to increase (appendix table A-59): only in miscellaneous manufactures and wood did it decrease; and in both it fell by less than 5 percentage points. In ten of the forty-six export propensity increased by more than 20 percentage points (appendix table A-60). Among the ten were electrical equipment (up 20 percentage points), business electronics and office equipment (up 23), unfinished nonferrous metals (up 25), bulk organic chemicals (up 30), and aerospace equipment (up 37). Each accounted for over Fr 35 billion of output in 1980. Outside manufacturing, the mean ratio of exports to output fell by half a percentage point between 1959 and 1980 (table A-59). Statistically speaking, however, export propensity tended not to change. At the industry level it declined in ten of thirty-two industries, sometimes substantially, as for air and sea transport (down 13 percentage points), nonferrous metallic minerals (down 16), and ferrous minerals (down 27). In no nonmanufacturing industries did export propensity rise by as much as 20 percentage points, and only in land and freshwater transport, agriculture, and fish did it increase by as much as 10 points.

Export propensities did not increase steadily in manufacturing between 1959 and 1980. The mean propensity did not begin to rise until the late 1960s (table 20). Between 1959 and 1966 the ratio of exports to output did not tend to grow (table A-59), and in 1969 the mean propensity to export exceeded its 1959 counterpart by less than 3 percentage points. Following the devaluation in 1969, however, export intensity tended to increase markedly. The timing of this jump reminds one that increases in the propensity of French manufacturers to export cannot be attributed solely to governmental deregulation of international trade. Nevertheless, one must also remember that imports as well as exports were increasing rapidly and across the board during this period, suggesting the importance of trade liberalization in this context. The mean ratio of exports to output increased significantly between 1970 and 1980 as well as between 1973 and 1980. The surge of export propensity during the second half of the period lends credence to the belief that resurgent protectionism within and beyond the common market has not come to prevent French companies from competing outside their home markets.

By 1980 manufacturing industries on average sent one-quarter of their output abroad. Some nineteen manufacturing industries, accounting for 40 percent of manufacturing output, exported at least 30 percent of their output. (In 1959 only two industries, accounting for 2 percent of manufacturing output, could claim the same.) Five industries—manmade fibers, aerospace equipment, military products, sugar, and bulk organic chemicals—exported over half their output. Manufacturing industries producing at least Fr 50 billion of output in 1980 and exporting at least 30 percent of that output were crude steel (35 percent), road vehicles (38 percent), business electronics and office equipment (38 percent), mechanical equipment (38 percent), and unfinished nonferrous metals (41 percent). By 1980 only the exceptional French manufacturing industry could be said not to rely substantially (and, over the business cycle, consistently) on foreign markets.

Exposure to Foreign Investment

The treaties of Rome and Paris and the General Agreement on Tariffs and Trade reduced barriers to international trade more than barriers to international investment. Nevertheless, French business also became heavily exposed to direct foreign investment. In the first part of this section, I describe the control of French output by foreign

Table 21. *Number of French Manufacturing Subsidiaries of Foreign Parent Companies, 1900–70*

First link to parent	Parent home		First link to parent	Parent home	
	United States	Other		United States	Other
1900–13	12	23	1964	27	25
1914–18	1	0	1965	8	23
1919–29	23	21	1966	23	29
1930–38	20	10	1967	25	26
1939–45	4	4	1968	31	82
1946–50	6	13	1969	24	38
1951–57	28	28	1970	30	124
			Total	397	500
1958	11	6			
1959	19	5	*Mean*		
1960	32	16	1919–38	2	2
1961	27	15	1946–57	3	3
1962	25	6	1958–70	23	31
1963	21	6			

Source: Unpublished data bases USEMY and FOREMY in the care of Louis T. Wells, Harvard Business School, gathered for Vaupel and Curhan, *The World's Multinational Enterprises.*

multinational companies (IDFI); in the second part, I consider the importance of French direct investment abroad (ODFI).[85]

INWARD DIRECT FOREIGN INVESTMENT

Raymond Vernon's data on manufacturing subsidiaries of foreign parent companies suggest that France's exposure to inward direct investment is a recent phenomenon (table 21). Of the 500 French subsidiaries of foreign companies based outside the United States, 80 percent entered their parent's entourage after 1958. In fact, 244 of the 500 were created or acquired during the last three years of Vernon's observation (1968–70). As for the 397 French subsidiaries of American companies, only 26 percent had established their parental links before 1959.[86]

85. Appendix G describes French data on direct foreign investment. Those who skip the appendix should note that IDFI and ODFI are defined slightly differently in the several data sets employed in this section.

86. Balance of payments statistics confirm the influx of private long-term investment at the end of the 1950s. See International Monetary Fund, *Balance of Payments Yearbook,* vols. 8, 12; and Bertin, *L'Investissement des Firmes Etrangères en France (1945–1962),* pp. 292–93.

The exposure of French markets to foreign investment can be measured in terms of industry-level ratios of foreign-controlled to total domestic output. Gilles Bertin and Jacques Gervais used information from the business press to construct such ratios for the early 1960s.[87] Their studies indicate that some narrowly defined commodities, including carbon black, synthetic rubber, and margarine, were produced almost exclusively by companies under foreign control. Even in more broadly defined industries, such as agricultural or telecommunications equipment, companies controlled by foreigners accounted for over half of national output. Unfortunately, it is difficult to draw general conclusions from these studies. Obliged to construct their data from scratch, Bertin and Gervais focused on a small number of products. Given their interest in multinational corporations, they chose to emphasize activities presumed to be heavily controlled by foreigners. As a result, their findings can be taken to show that foreigners sometimes dominated certain French industries even before creation of the EEC, but they cannot be used to establish the frequency of such dominance. Neither Bertin nor Gervais considered inward foreign investment to be a critical element of French market structure during the fifteen years following World War II.

The first systematic evidence regarding foreign control of the French economy derives from a 1962 government census. Among all manufacturing industries the mean value of the inward direct foreign investment variable (IDFI) was 9 percent. In thirty-one of the forty-three industries, foreigners controlled less than 10 percent of industry sales (appendix table A-61). In only five did foreign-controlled companies account for as much as 20 percent of sales: precision goods; products of edible oils and fats, including soap, cosmetics, and perfumes; petroleum; musical instruments, including record players and records; and rubber. The maximum value of IDFI was 46 percent. Thus as of 1962, foreigners controlled very small shares of most manufacturing industries. This conclusion is equally applicable to the nonmanufacturing sectors of the economy. Among the forty-seven industries outside manufacturing, the mean value of IDFI was 4 percent. Thirty-four of the industries registered values of IDFI less

87. Ibid.; and Gervais, *La France Face aux Investissements Etrangers*. A compact summary of both sets of results appears in Gervais, pp. 63–65.

than 5 percent. Only radio and television broadcasting, at 46 percent, exhibited a value of IDFI above 20 percent.

Two decades later, foreigners tended to control much larger fractions of manufacturing. Among the thirty-seven such industries for which information is available, the mean value of IDFI was 25 percent in 1980, nearly three times its magnitude in 1962. In twelve of the thirty-seven, foreigners controlled at least 30 percent of value added. In three of these—agricultural equipment, chemical products, and office equipment—they controlled over half of value added. More than 50 percent of total value added for the thirty-seven was generated in industries in which foreigners controlled at least one-fifth of value added. In only one, aerospace equipment, accounting for less than 1 percent of combined value added, was IDFI less than 5 percent. Systematic information is unavailable for IDFI outside manufacturing in 1980. The only such data published by the ministry of industry relate to three mining activities: nonmetallic minerals (IDFI of 17 percent), ferrous minerals (23 percent), and nonferrous metallic minerals (27 percent).[88]

Changes in industry definition prevent industry-level comparisons between 1962 and 1980. With industries defined as in 1980, the earliest year for comparison is 1974. Among the thirty-two manufacturing industries for which information is available, the mean value of IDFI changed from 19 percent in 1974 to 20 percent in 1980. Even at the .30 level of statistical significance, it is impossible to reject the hypothesis that incidence of foreign control tended to the same level in 1980 as it had in 1974.[89] In twelve of the thirty-two the importance of foreign influence declined. In one of these, rubber products, it declined by more than 10 percentage points. In one mining industry, ferrous minerals, IDFI also declined by more than 10 percentage points. In no industries did the index of foreign influence increase by more than 10 points, and in only two, precision goods and shoes, did it increase by as much as 8 points.

Sparse as they are, the data on inward investment support two conclusions. First, France's exposure to inward direct investment increased markedly and pervasively after formation of the EEC.

88. Ministère de l'Industrie et de la Recherche, *9 Ans d'Implanatation Etrangère dans l'Industrie, 1er Janvier 1973–1er Janvier 1981*, pp. 103–27.

89. In a one-tail *t*-test ($t = 1.04$, $N = 32$). The data source is ibid., table 9.

Foreigners controlled paltry shares of output in most manufacturing industries in 1962 but substantial shares of several in 1980. Thus international trade was not the only corridor in which French companies came to brush against foreign rivals. By 1980, within the manufacturing sector the share of domestic output controlled by foreign parent companies tended to be just as large as the share of domestic consumption attributable to imports.[90] Second, exposure to inward direct investment started later and abated earlier than did exposure to imports. Four years after creation of the EEC, IDFI but not import exposure tended to be small in value; between 1974 and 1980, IDFI but again not import exposure tended to remain steady.[91]

PROPENSITY TO INVEST ABROAD

According to Raymond Vernon's data, which included 21 parent companies, French manufacturers did not control many foreign subsidiaries until the late 1960s.[92] At one time or another the 21 had controlled 448 manufacturing companies abroad, 49 percent of which were created or acquired between 1968 and 1970.[93] Another 32 percent entered their parent company's orbit between 1959 and 1967. Less than 20 percent predated the EEC. Charles-Albert Michalet and Michel Delapierre found a similar temporal pattern to French direct investment. Of the 72 multinationals in their sample, 56 did not produce abroad until after World War II; in fact, 30 did not own a foreign subsidiary until after 1961. Even the foreign investments in

90. Across all available manufacturing industries defined according to NAP-100, the mean difference between import exposure and IDFI (3.63) failed to differ from 0 at the .20 level of significance in a one-tail t-test ($t = 1.26$, $N = 37$).

91. Across all manufacturing industries defined according to NAP-S79, the mean increase in import exposure between 1974 and 1980 (4.54) differed positively from 0 at the .001 level of significance in a one-tail t-test ($t = 4.83$, $N = 46$). Further evidence on inward direct investment is presented in Auquier, *French Industry's Reaction to the European Common Market*, pp. 451–548. Auquier found that between 1962 and 1972 inward direct investment increased greatly. Moreover, the shares of such investment originating in European and in small parent companies rose.

92. For a different perspective emphasizing the importance of French foreign investment before World War II, see Lévy-Leboyer, *La Position Internationale de la France, XIXe–XXe Siècles*; and Marseille, *Empire Colonial et Capitalisme Français*, pp. 93–158.

93. As of January 1, 1971, these 21 controlled 427 manufacturing companies abroad; Vaupel and Curhan, *The World's Multinational Enterprises*, pp. 424–25, 485.

France's overseas union tended to occur after World War II. Only 9 of the 72 produced before the war in poor or developing countries.[94]

Perhaps the best single measure of French propensity to outward foreign investment is the ratio of foreign to total investment by domestic enterprises (ODFI). The greater the ratio, the more foreign environment and behavior can be expected to affect domestic producers. Unfortunately, information of this sort appears neither in government documents nor in private studies. The best one can do with available data is to examine the distribution of outward investment among industries. Using the Vernon data, one discovers that foreign subsidiaries of French companies were distributed unevenly among manufacturing industries: 357 were assigned to one of 54 categories.[95] Of the 54 industries, 14 had no foreign subsidiaries of French parent companies, and another 16 accounted for only 8 percent of the foreign subsidiaries. In contrast, 7 industries accounted for 52 percent of the foreign subsidiaries: glass products; industrial chemicals; motor vehicles and equipment; other petroleum products; stone, clay, and concrete; drugs; and iron and steel. Within those broad categories, the subsidiaries tended to be located upstream—in industrial chemicals rather than in soap, cosmetics, or paints; in iron and steel rather than metal cans or structural metal products; in electronic components rather than office machines and computers.

In the study by Delapierre and Michalet, ten of the fifty companies producing abroad belonged to the petroleum or chemical industries; eight specialized in nonindustrial activities; seven produced nonelectrical machinery; and another seven engaged in metallurgy.[96] Just three produced textiles or wood-based products, four built electrical equipment, and five processed food. The remaining six specialized in construction.

In sum, the number of French investments abroad, like the propensity of France's manufacturers to export, began to rise sharply at the end of the 1950s. Unlike the propensity to export, however,

94. Michalet and Delapierre, *La Multinationalisation des Entreprises Françaises*, table 230. The sample was selected from the 500 largest industrials in France during 1970.

95. Vaupel and Curhan, *The World's Multinational Enterprises*, cross-tabulation 6.21.1. The industries are two- or three-digit categories of the U.S. standard industrial classification.

96. Delapierre and Michalet, *Les Implantations Etrangères en France*, table 8.

the number of foreign investments appeared by the 1970s to vary appreciably among industries; and unlike their American counterparts, French foreign investments did not appear concentrated in industries heavily engaged in research or advertising.[97]

Import Discipline

Imports are especially likely to increase competition when the domestic industry does not function competitively, when the domestic buyer and the foreign seller do not belong to the same parent company, and when foreign sellers do not align their conduct on that of domestic rivals. To what extent do these conditions obtain in French markets?

FREQUENCY OF INTRAFIRM TRADE

It is not difficult to cite European examples of intrafirm trade. In the automobile industry, Ford's English subsidiary imports right-hand-drive vehicles from Ford's German subsidiary. The trade accounts "for a substantial proportion of Ford Germany's total production and exports."[98] Where direct evidence is lacking, it is sometimes possible to infer captive trade from a combination of industry-level data on trade and company-level data on foreign investment. For example, France imports bauxite, alumina, and aluminum from French Guiana, New Caledonia, and Greece. Pechiney, France's major producer of aluminum, operates subsidiaries in all three countries. The imports in question probably travel within the Pechiney family of companies.[99]

Although illustration is easy, systematic information on captive trade does not exist. The best one can do is to argue that captive imports will be unimportant to a domestic industry as long as domestic

97. On the differences between American and European patterns of direct investment, see Auquier, *French Industry's Reaction to the European Common Market*, pp. 451–508; and Franko, *The European Multinationals*.

98. *Re the Agreement of Ford Werke AG* (No. 2), EC Commission (83/560/EEC); [1984] 1 *CMLR* 596, 599.

99. Pechiney began manufacturing alumina and aluminum in Greece in 1966. As of 1971 some 80 percent of its output was exported to Europe; half of these exports went to France. Beaud, Danjou, and David, *Une Multinationale Française*, p. 50.

companies have engaged in little foreign investment and the industry contains few subsidiaries of foreign companies.

FREQUENCY OF PRICE ALIGNMENT

In large measure the increased exposure of French companies to international trade is attributable to increased trade within the EC. And yet even at the EC level, production can be sufficiently concentrated in a few companies to warrant suspicion of oligopolistic behavior. Under such circumstances the competitive consequences of imports and exports are far from obvious. For a variety of reasons, leading producers may conspire to allow international trade, but only on terms unlikely to disturb national price levels. Several antitrust cases brought by the EC Commission reveal that oligopolistic cooperation does occur at the EC level. One in particular, the sugar case, illustrates clearly how increased exposure to international trade need not entail increased exposure to competition.[100] For this reason, the case merits discussion in some detail.

Within the common market Italy, the Netherlands, Luxembourg, and Western West Germany consume more sugar than they produce; France, Belgium, and the rest of Germany produce more than they consume. At the time of the commission's investigation, in each region of the community, a small number of refiners accounted for most production of white sugar. In Belgium one company controlled 85 percent of production; in the Netherlands, two accounted for all production; in Italy, three groups of companies controlled 90 percent; in France, five companies accounted for 75 percent; and in Germany production was most concentrated in the south, where one company accounted for 70 percent. Not only were the individual production areas characterized by high concentration, but joint ventures served to link producers from different areas. For example, four leading producers (one Belgian, one French, one Italian, and one German) exercised collective control over another leading producer in France.

100. *Re the European Sugar Cartel*, EC Commission; [1973] *CMLR* D65. Also *Cooperatieve Vereniging 'Suiker Unie' UA and Others* v. *EC Commission*, cases 40-48/73, 50/73, 54-56/73, 111/73, and 113-114/73, EC Court of Justice; [1976] 1 *CMLR* 295.

On July 1, 1968, the EEC replaced its member states as regulator of raw and refined sugar. In organizing these product markets, member states had generally relied on regulation and subsidy rather than on competitive supply and demand. Although the EEC preserved many features of the national systems, including price supports for raw and refined sugar, it also wished to establish free trade within the community as a whole. While regulated by their national governments, refiners in exporting regions had usually sent their surpluses outside the EEC.

During its first year of regulatory authority, the EEC Commission noted the paucity of intracommunity trade despite price differentials that exceeded transport costs. After the first year intracommunity trade increased, but in most cases it took the form of refiners in surplus areas selling refined and raw sugar to refiners in deficit areas. The latter would sell the sugar under their own labels and at their own prices. Only with the explicit approval of refiners in deficit areas would refiners in surplus areas export to buyers who were not themselves refiners. When they did sell to nonrefiners, their prices were higher than those charged to refiners. To the extent that refiners in surplus areas distributed their sugar through independent wholesalers, they warned those wholesalers not to export to deficit areas without the approval of local refiners. Meanwhile, refiners in deficit areas warned their wholesalers not to buy sugar in surplus areas, or at least not to sell such sugar without prior refiner approval of the terms. Both importing and exporting wholesalers were told that failure to comply with these arrangements would entail refusal by the refiners to supply them with sugar. Given the dominant positions, unilateral or collective, of the refiners, the wholesalers had reason to take such threats seriously, and they did.

Until the commission took action against this system, community markets for refined sugar exhibited substantial amounts of trade but precious little competition. For example, between 1968 and 1972 Belgium exported 88,800 tons of white sugar to Germany. Of that amount, 68,100 tons, or 77 percent, was designated by the EC Commission as "controlled"—unlikely to affect market prices in Germany—because it was sold to a German refiner, sold to a German user but with the prior approval of a German refiner, sold to a German user at a price higher than that charged to German refiners, or sold to customers vowing either to denature the sugar or to reexport it outside the EC.[101]

Small wonder then that refiners in deficit areas maintained their control over local prices despite the arrival of imports or that certain countries could import substantial amounts of sugar without experiencing greater competition in domestic sugar markets. For the companies themselves, the purpose of the system was to preserve the authority of each group of refiners in its home area.

How typical is the situation in sugar? Has increased exposure to international trade failed across the board to increase the intensity of competition in European markets? To answer these questions, it is useful to return to the French evidence on trade exposure between 1959 and 1980. In 1959, imports accounted for 34 percent of French consumption of sugar and sugar products (NAP-S402). Only one manufacturing industry, bulk organic chemicals, could claim greater exposure to imports at that time. Between 1959 and 1980 the incidence of imports on domestic sugar consumption declined by 17 percentage points. In fact, sugar was the only manufacturing industry to register a decline in import exposure. As of 1980, however, imported sugar still accounted for 16 percent of domestic consumption.

The very fact that sugar was the only manufacturing industry to register a decline in import exposure between 1959 and 1980 suggests that the experience of the industry was hardly typical. To paint a more general picture, I shall employ a palette of studies linking prices to imports at the industry level. Specifically, these studies correlate exposure to imports with price-cost margins, price movements, elasticities of price with respect to cost and demand, and international price convergence.

IMPORTS AND PRICE-COST MARGINS

In competitive markets, prices tend to approximate marginal costs; in monopolistic and oligopolistic markets they tend to exceed marginal costs. If exposure to imports intensifies competition, one would expect

---

101. [1976] 1 *CMLR* 295, 435. Deliveries to German refiners accounted for only 4,500 tons, or 7 percent of the total amount of controlled trade. Of the 20,700 tons of uncontrolled exports to Germany, small Belgian refineries outside the orbit of the dominant producer accounted for 11,300 tons (55 percent).

price-cost margins and profitability to correlate negatively with exposure to imports. Negative correlations of these sorts have been observed in cross-sections of French manufacturing industries.[102]

At the industry level, time-series analysis of the relationship between price-cost margins and import exposure has not been conducted frequently.[103] In the French setting the major intertemporal study of profitability during the period surrounding birth of the EEC was undertaken at a more aggregate level. Using his preferred measure of profitability, Christian Sautter discovered that competition appeared to increase after formation of the EEC: between 1954 and 1960 profitability rose moderately; between 1960 and 1974 it declined fairly steadily and very sharply. In 1960 the return to the aggregate of French productive assets was roughly 29 percent; by 1974 it had declined to 20 percent.[104]

IMPORTS AND PRICE CHANGES AT THE INDUSTRY LEVEL

Exposure to imports should affect changes of prices as well as levels. To the extent that import exposure increases elasticities of supply at existing prices, upward shifts of market demand are not as likely to result in upward movements of price. Over time, therefore, one might expect to observe a negative correlation at the industry level between import exposure and increase in price.

---

102. Auquier, *French Industry's Reaction to the European Common Market*, chap. 3. See also Jenny and Weber, *Concentration et Politique des Structures Industrielles*; and Adams, "International Differences in Corporate Profitability."

103. In the American setting, this may be attributed to failure of import exposure to vary sufficiently over time. Although cross-section in design, the study by Krause, "Import Discipline," focuses on price changes rather than price-cost margins.

104. Sautter, "L'Efficacité et la Rentabilité de l'Economie Française de 1954 à 1974." The author's preferred measure of profitability is $(VA - W)/K$, where VA is value added and W is remuneration of labor, each valued at constant prices. The alternative is $(Y - T + I)/K$, where Y is income, T is taxes on income, I is interest paid, and K is fixed investment, each valued at constant prices. By this second measure the average return to capital remained roughly constant between 1954 and 1974.

Of the four reasons Sautter offers to explain why his two measures of profitability differed so markedly, one is especially interesting in the present context. Between 1959 and 1972, taxes paid by companies, net of subsidies received, declined sharply, maintaining after-tax profitability in the face of falling before-tax profitability. One naturally wonders whether this was a conscious strategy on the part of government to deal with exposure of French companies to EEC competition.

During the five years following creation of the EEC, in twelve industries accounting for 25 percent of output, domestic prices rose at least 30 percent (appendix table A-62). In eleven industries, accounting for 5 percent of output, prices actually declined. These movements in prices can be linked to changes in exposure to imports. Among all seventy-nine activities the correlation between change in price and change in import exposure differed negatively from zero.[105] Such evidence is consistent with the view that rising exposure to imports did indeed promote competition.

IMPORTS AND THE SENSITIVITY OF PRICE
TO COST AND DEMAND

In competitive markets with imperfectly elastic supply curves, prices should change each time cost or demand curves shift. For a variety of reasons, however, markets supplied by powerful sellers can be expected to exhibit some price inertia.[106] David Encaoua and Philippe Michel have studied the elasticities of French prices with respect to costs and demand and have found that exposure to imports correlated positively with such elasticities.[107] Their findings are consistent with the view that exposure to imports did promote competition in domestic markets.

IMPORTS AND THE INTERNATIONAL CONVERGENCE
OF PRICES

Elimination of artificial barriers to international trade can extend market boundaries beyond national frontiers. If the resulting market functions competitively, prices within it should differ by no more than transport costs and should converge toward the minimum of the levels prevailing before creation of the multinational market.

In the coal and steel industries, prices did not converge in durable fashion. True, during the early years of the European Coal and Steel Community, price inequalities in both industries did abate. In steel, for example, the United Nations Economic Commission for Europe

105. At the .001 level of significance during 1959–64 ($r = -.38$), and at the .01 level during 1959–69 ($r = -.36$) in one-tail t-tests.

106. Domberger, *Industrial Structure, Pricing and Inflation.*

107. Encaoua and Michel, *Dynamique des Prix Industriels en France*, pp. 148–58, 164–76, 187–88.

asserted that as of 1954 the "approach to uniformity of prices is more striking than the continuing differences." By the late 1950s, however, the High Authority itself lamented the disparities in list prices among member countries, acknowledging that in "a great number of cases, the difference between the published prices of different groups of producers is much greater than the cost of transportation between the corresponding basing points."[108] Nevertheless, informed observers do believe that the ECSC reduced considerably the prevalence of double pricing: individual producers filled the gaps between their domestic and export prices.[109]

In recent years, the EC Commission has studied price convergence in a wide variety of manufacturing industries. Its most interesting investigation focused on automobiles. This investigation warrants exegesis because it illustrates very clearly how trade does not always result in price convergence. The commission found that model-specific prices tended to differ systematically among member countries. In 1975, prices were lowest in Denmark and highest in Italy, the difference amounting on average to 16 percent. Seven years later, prices were still lowest in Denmark but highest in Britain. British prices exceeded those in Denmark by 45 percent and those in Italy by 22 percent.[110]

This pattern of prices could not be explained in terms of transport costs. Cars produced in England were sold for less abroad than at home. For example, in a 1983 survey of model-specific pretax prices, the European federation of consumers groups (BEUC) found that the price of an Austin Metro 1000 L was 49 percent greater in Britain

---

108. Diebold, *The Schuman Plan*, pp. 279–82; see also Meade, Liesner, and Wells, *Case Studies in European Economic Union*, p. 266. Two features of coal and steel signal the need for caution when interpreting the evidence on price convergence. First, most evidence pertains to list prices; despite the community's requirement of open pricing, discrepancies between list and transactions prices did exist and may have varied in magnitude among member countries. Second, both industries are structured oligopolistically, even at the community level. Price convergence does not imply convergence on a competitive price.

109. Between the two world wars, when demand was slack, export prices were lower than domestic prices. After World War II, when production capacity was fully utilized and national governments regulated domestic prices, export prices were greater than domestic prices. On the general importance of double pricing in European oligopolies see Auquier, *French Industry's Reaction to the European Common Market*.

110. "Cheaper Cars and Drugs?" *Economist*, April 16, 1983, p. 50.

than in Belgium. The British price also exceeded those in France and Germany.[111] Nor, in the view of the commission, could international differences in prices be explained by corresponding differences in government price control.[112] According to London's Institute of Fiscal Studies, if Britons had been able to purchase the cars they actually acquired in 1981 at Belgian rather than British prices, they would have saved 1.3 billion pounds—0.6 percent of GDP.[113]

The commission's investigation revealed how the automobile companies succeeded in maintaining such price differentials, especially those between Britain and other parts of the EC.[114] Because the cost of producing automobiles was higher in England than on the Continent, companies with production facilities in both places had an incentive to produce cars on the Continent for sale in the British market. Such a strategy required Continental production of cars with right-hand drive. Ford's German subsidiary produced a large number of these. Nominally they were destined for English military and diplomatic personnel residing in Germany, but Ford Germany exported a considerable percentage of its production to Britain, and its English subsidiary distributed the cars in its home market at prices related to the English cost of production.[115]

Although Ford's contracts with its distributors permitted them to acquire Ford automobiles from Ford wholesalers and retailers in other EC countries, English retailers of Fords did not avail themselves of this opportunity. As a result, international trade exerted no direct downward pressure on the prices of Fords in England. Aware of international differences in prices, many English customers sought to buy their cars abroad. Under Ford Germany's standard agreement

111. "Cars: Autosuggestion," *Economist*, October 29, 1983, p. 52.

112. "Cheaper Cars and Drugs?" p. 50. The position of the manufacturers appears in Perrin-Pelletier, "Industrial Policy and the Automobile Industry," in Adams and Stoffaës, eds., *French Industrial Policy*, pp. 74–81.

113. "Car Prices: Another Billion," *Economist*, October 2, 1982, p. 52.

114. *Re the Agreement of Ford Werke AG* (No. 2), EC Commission (83/560/EEC); [1984] 1 *CMLR* 596.

115. *Ford of Europe Inc. and Ford Werke AG* v. *EC Commission*, cases 228–229/82, EC Court of Justice; [1984] 1 *CMLR* 649, 652. Whether this strategy maximized profit depended partly on governmentally imposed constraints on reduction of Ford employment in Britain.

with its German distributors, the manufacturer undertook to provide its distributors with any model Ford produced. This included, of course, right-hand-drive cars that Ford Germany was exporting to Ford England. The German distributors were all too willing to sell them to British nationals. On April 27, 1982, however, Ford AG informed its principal dealers that it would cease four days later to supply them with right-hand drives. Even Britons residing in Germany would have to purchase such vehicles from a British subsidiary. In other words, Ford AG moved to stop the arbitrage.

The actions of Ford were unusual only to the extent that they resulted from production of right-hand-drive vehicles on the Continent. Other manufacturers employed different tactics to discourage the purchase of automobiles in Belgium by customers residing elsewhere in the EC. Some delayed delivery to Belgium of cars meeting the technical specifications of other countries; some established wholesale prices for such cars that exceeded the prices of corresponding vehicles with Belgian specifications; and some established warranties that discriminated against after-sales service outside the country of purchase. When the EC Commission intervened, several companies abandoned these practices.[116]

Unlike its European rivals, however, Ford chose to fight the commission before the court of justice. Early in the combat the court supported Ford on a procedural matter, but ultimately it accepted the commission's view that Ford's system of selective distribution violated article 85(1) of the EEC treaty and failed to qualify for exemption under article 85(3). The court argued simply that Ford's refusal to supply English-type cars to German dealers impeded parallel imports and hence contravened the public interest.[117]

In keeping with its position in the Ford case, the commission has announced a general strategy for dealing with geographic differentials in auto prices. Companies setting list prices for a given vehicle that

116. *Re Fiat Auto SpA*, EC Commission; [1984] 2 *CMLR* 497. See also *Re Alfa Romeo Cars*, EC Commission; [1985] 1 *CMLR* 480.

117. *Ford Werke AG and Ford of Europe Inc.* v. *EC Commission*, cases 25/84 and 26/84, EC Court of Justice; [1985] 3 *CMLR* 528. Rather than sacrifice its system of selective distribution, Ford agreed to supply right-hand drives to its German dealers.

differed among member countries by more than 12 percent for a year or more, or 18 percent for less than a year, would lose their presumptive right to employ selective networks of dealers.[118]

Convergence of prices within the EC is especially likely to signal competition if the level upon which they converge corresponds to the level in competitive world markets. Such correspondences have not been studied systematically.[119] There is reason to believe, however, that French prices sometimes repose well above those prevailing outside the EC.

The French government has signalled clearly its willingness and ability to exclude aggressive, non-EC competitors from its domestic markets. Its treatment of video tape recorders during the first half of the 1980s provides a case in point. Alarmed by the success of Japanese manufacturers in supplying French markets for consumer electronics, the French government applied dubious customs procedures to delay imports of VCRs from Japan: all such imports had to clear customs in Poitiers, a remote and lightly staffed customs house. France abandoned the tactic only after it induced the EC to develop a communitywide policy on VCR imports.[120] The Japanese concluded that the best way to supply the European VCR market involved formation of joint ventures with European firms and assembly in Europe of components

118. See Lukoff, "European Competition Law and Distribution in the Motor Vehicle Sector," pp. 841–66. The regulation itself and an explanatory note sent to manufacturers appear in *Official Journal of the European Communities,* L 15 (January 18, 1985), and C 17 (January 18, 1985). Note the expected importance to the manufacturers of selective distribution. The commission clearly believed that they would reduce their price discrimination just enough to keep it, perhaps from a desire to force Japanese producers to create their own distribution networks in Europe.

119. It would be interesting to correlate these indicators of price behavior (price-cost margins, elasticities of price with respect to cost, and changes in price over time) not only with exposure to all imports but also with a geographic breakdown of such exposure. In particular, it would be interesting to distinguish the impact of exposure to EC rivals from the impact of exposure to rivals outside the community. Unfortunately, French input-output data, the best source of information on trade in relation to production and consumption, does not separate intra- from extracommunity trade. In his study of French exposure to international competition, Auquier did distinguish EEC from other imports. He observed that imports from the EEC exerted the stronger positive effect on competition, as measured (negatively) by price cost margins. See *French Industry's Reaction to the European Common Market,* pp. 224–329.

120. The policy consisted of persuading MITI to impose minimum export prices on Japanese producers, effective March 18, 1983. See *Bulletin of the European Communities,* vol. 16, no. 3 (1983), point 2.2.22.

produced in Asia. At the components level, then, European exposure to imports remained, but the degree of competition in VCR markets was hardly the greater therefor. (Joint ventures of this type have caused new problems for EC commercial policy. Components travel from Asia to Europe at low prices, permitting products assembled by the joint ventures to be sold at commensurately low prices. The EC takes the position that such pricing of components is tantamount to dumping of final products, and it has threatened in such cases to impose antidumping levies on goods assembled within its borders if value added within the EC fails to exceed a specified share of total product value.)

The VCR episode is not the only case in which France has protected itself from suppliers outside the community. In fact, many times the French have protected themselves to a greater extent than has the community as a whole. France's quota on Japanese automobiles, for example, was far more restrictive than those of most EC countries.[121] It is important, however, to recognize the limits of such behavior. France may be able to restrict imports from Japan, just as it once restricted inward investment from the United States; but it cannot always oblige other EC countries to follow suit. If the foreigners then export to or produce in other EC countries, and if companies in those member countries respond to the competition by improving their own products and technology, then the French do not escape the competitive effects of foreign enterprise. The competitive advantages of non-EC rivals become embodied in EC rivals, who enjoy relatively free access to the French market. In other words, French companies may be obliged indirectly to meet the standards of competitive world markets as long as other EC countries adopt a liberal stance toward imports and investment originating outside the community.

Systematic evidence, then, suggests that exposure to imports is associated with quasi-competitive pricing behavior. Such evidence is consistent with the hypothesis that imports did stimulate competition. If it is important not to exaggerate the positive effects of trade on competition, it is also important not to exaggerate the compatibility of pervasive arbitrage with substantial market power.

121. Italy also shielded itself relatively completely from Japanese vehicles. See Wells, "Automobiles."

Table 22. *Share of French Exports, by Destination, 1952–84*
Percent

Year	French Overseas Union[a]	French North Africa[b]	Other French Africa[c]	Indo-china[d]	Algeria	OECD	Europe	Original EEC	West Germany
1952	42.2	22.4	9.9	8.2	12.6	43.2	38.0	15.9	5.6
1953	37.0	20.1	8.7	6.6	11.3	46.9	40.5	18.6	7.0
1954	37.2	19.9	10.3	5.5	11.8	45.6	40.5	21.9	8.4
1955	31.8	19.1	8.7	2.5	11.9	51.7	45.8	24.4	10.5
1956	32.8	20.8	8.9	1.5	13.6	51.8	45.2	25.3	10.5
1957	35.0	21.9	9.4	1.8	16.0	49.9	43.6	25.1	10.8
1958	37.5	24.8	9.6	1.3	19.2	46.6	39.1	22.2	10.5
1959	31.8	21.6	7.1	0.6	17.0	53.5	43.4	27.2	13.1
1960	30.0	20.6	6.9	0.9	15.9	55.0	47.5	29.8	13.7
1961	26.1	16.4	7.5	0.7	12.3	59.6	52.2	33.5	15.2
1962	20.8	11.2	7.3	0.6	7.6	64.7	57.3	36.8	17.3
1963	19.6	10.3	7.2	0.5	6.9	66.3	59.4	38.3	16.6
1964	18.0	8.8	7.0	0.3	5.5	67.9	60.8	38.8	17.4
1965	16.2	7.7	6.1	0.3	5.1	69.9	62.1	40.9	19.3
1966	14.6	6.5	5.7	0.4	4.0	70.9	62.5	42.3	19.3
1967	14.3	6.0	6.0	0.3	3.6	70.3	61.8	41.3	17.3
1968	13.5	5.7	5.5	0.4	3.7	70.0	61.5	43.0	18.6
1969	12.1	4.9	4.8	0.5	3.1	73.1	65.4	47.8	20.6
1970	11.8	5.0	4.6	0.3	3.2	73.7	66.1	48.8	20.8
1971	10.3	4.2	4.3	0.3	2.5	74.7	67.1	49.4	21.5
1972	9.3	3.5	4.2	0.2	1.8	76.5	68.9	49.9	21.3
1973	9.2	3.9	3.9	0.1	2.1	76.1	69.0	48.6	19.6
1974	9.8	4.8	3.7	0.1	2.9	74.1	66.8	46.1	17.5
1975	11.5	6.0	4.2	0.1	3.6	66.8	61.0	41.0	16.3
1976	10.4	4.9	4.3	0.1	2.6	67.6	61.4	42.5	16.9
1977	10.7	5.1	4.4	0.1	2.8	67.8	60.9	41.7	16.7
1978	9.5	4.1	4.1	0.1	1.9	68.6	61.3	42.5	16.8
1979	9.5	4.1	4.1	0.1	1.9	69.6	62.9	42.6	16.8
1980	9.4	4.1	4.1	0.1	2.3	67.2	61.1	41.0	15.4
1981	9.3	4.3	3.8	0.1	2.2	64.4	57.0	37.2	14.2
1982	9.8	4.3	4.1	*	2.2	65.3	57.5	37.7	14.2
1983	9.5	4.3	3.7	0.1	2.6	66.7	58.1	38.0	15.0
1984	9.3	4.4	3.3	*	2.8	68.0	57.7	37.3	14.1

Sources: 1952–74: INSEE, *Annuaire Statistique de la France.* 1975–84: International Monetary Fund, *Direction of Trade Statistics Yearbook*, 1980 and 1986 editions.
  * Less than 0.05 percent.
  a. See appendix G.
  b. Algeria, Morocco, and Tunisia.
  c. Cameroon, Comoro Islands, French Equatorial Africa, French West Africa, Madagascar, Réunion, and Togo.
  d. Cambodia, Laos, and Vietnam.

Export Discipline

I suggested above that increased reliance on export markets is especially likely to signal increased competition when foreign markets are not colonial in nature. In this section, I demonstrate that most French exporters have ceased to rely on colonial markets. Usually, they must compete if they wish to succeed in the markets they now supply.

AGGREGATE EVIDENCE

Since World War II the distribution of French exports by destination has changed remarkably. Early in the postwar period France relied heavily on the French Overseas Union for export markets (table 22). In 1952, 42 percent of all French exports went to FOU—half to North Africa, one-quarter to the rest of French Africa, and one-fifth to Indochina. The remainder flowed to French territories in the Americas (principally French Guiana, Guadeloupe, Martinique, and St. Pierre and Miquelon) and in Oceania (principally French Polynesia, New Caledonia, New Hebrides, and Wallis and Futuna). Algeria alone accounted for 13 percent of French exports in 1952.

After 1952 FOU declined in importance as a destination, its share shrinking by 50 percent between 1952 and 1962 and by another 50 percent between 1962 and 1972. In just two decades its share thus plummeted from 42 percent to 9 percent, so that in 1972 the whole of FOU absorbed a smaller share of French exports than had Algeria alone in 1952. Since then its share has stabilized between 9 and 12 percent.

Typically, the importance of a colony as a recipient of French exports began to decline about the time it received its independence. Indochina was the first FOU market to constrict. Accounting for 8 percent of French exports in 1952, it never absorbed as much as 1 percent after 1958. The next markets to shrink were Tunisia and Morocco, which achieved independence in 1956. Between 1952 and 1957, their importance in French exports declined from 10 percent to 6 percent. Since Algeria's independence in 1962, they have accounted for less than 4 percent. The next colonies to receive their independence were located in sub-Saharan Africa. Most of them achieved independence peacefully in 1960, and their French imports reflected the form and substance of these political events.

Algeria illustrates dramatically the evaporation of France's colonial markets. Between 1955 and 1958 its share of French exports escalated along with its war for independence, and by 1958 it accounted for 19 percent of all French exports. Thereafter its role declined precipitously. By 1962 Algeria's share was 8 percent, by 1966, 4 percent, and since then has remained below 4 percent, dipping occasionally under 2 percent.

As colonial markets declined, competitive world markets took over. In 1952 France exported almost as much to FOU as it did to countries now comprising the OECD (table 22). North Africa's three members of FOU imported 140 percent as much from France as did the five countries joining France that year to form the ECSC. Germany bought less than half as much from France as did Algeria. After 1961, however, France exported more to charter members of the common market than it did to charter members of FOU. It also sent more to Germany than to Algeria. European members of today's OECD buy twice as much from France as do past and present members of FOU. The OECD accounts for 60 percent of French exports.

In 1972 the importance of the OECD, of the original common market, and of Germany as destinations for French goods reached a peak, the OECD accounting for 77 percent of French exports, the common market for 50 percent, and Germany for 21 percent. Thus in 1972 Germany alone bought more French goods than did the entire overseas union (as it had been defined in 1950). After 1972 the destinations of French exports changed again. The importance of Germany declined by one-third and the importance of the original common market by one-quarter. In part these changes reflected the EC enlargements of 1973 and 1981 (although this was not the whole story, since the importance of both OECD Europe and the entire OECD also declined). By 1984 the OECD took two-thirds of French exports as compared with 43 percent in 1952.

INDUSTRY-LEVEL EVIDENCE

To what extent, however, did France come to rely on competitive world markets for all types of exports? Has it become (as some predicted it would) the breadbasket of the common market, supplying food to the "real" industrial countries of the community while dispatching manufactures to its colonies past and present? Should one stop short of concluding from the aggregate figures that most French manufacturers now export to competitive world markets, subjecting themselves thereby to export discipline?

To examine the uniformity across industries in the propensity to direct exports toward competitive world markets, I calculated for each French industry (each one-digit section and two-digit division of the standard international trade classification) the share of exports destined for the OECD. During 1983, in the aggregate, 69 percent of French exports went to the OECD (appendix table A-63). Among the four manufacturing sections of the SITC (sections 5–8), only machinery and transport equipment sent less than 70 percent of exports to the OECD, and even there the ratio exceeded 60 percent. Each of the other manufacturing sections sent a larger fraction of its exports to the OECD than did the section covering food. At this level of industrial detail, it would be difficult to argue that French agriculture catered to rich countries while French manufacturing supplied the third world.

Between 1952 and 1973 the share of exports headed to the OECD increased in every industry (appendix table A-64). With one small exception the relative importance of this group of countries rose substantially. Especially noteworthy was the evolution of exports of machinery and transport equipment. In 1952 one-quarter were absorbed by the OECD, but by 1973, 65 percent went that way. After 1973 the organization's importance declined for most French industries, but in all manufacturing sections its importance remained substantially greater than it had been in 1952.

When industries are defined at the two-digit level of the SITC, the OECD no longer bought uniformly great and rising shares of French exports (appendix table A-65). Among the thirty-five manufacturing industries, seven sent less than half their exports to the OECD. One-third of French manufacturing exports were attributable to eleven industries sending less than 60 percent of their exports to the OECD. In such cases, a large propensity to export did not necessarily entail exposure to competitive world markets. On the other hand, seventeen industries sent more than 70 percent of their exports to the OECD. Especially reliant were office machines and automatic data processing equipment (86 percent of exports), nonferrous metals (85 percent), organic chemicals (85 percent), photographic, optical, and timing equipment (82 percent), paper (81 percent), textiles (81 percent), and inorganic chemicals (80 percent). Given the number and importance of the industries exporting heavily to the OECD, one must conclude that only some manufacturing industries still fail to rely on rich market economies to absorb the bulk of their exports.

Appendix table A-66 shows the seven manufacturing industries that sent less than half their exports to the OECD in 1983, together with their reliance on the original FOU. In a few cases the habits of the old economic regime persisted. Manufacturers of metal products sent one-fifth and manufacturers of drugs sent more than one-third of their exports to FOU. But in each of the machinery industries FOU bought less than 20 percent of French exports. In fact, manufacturers of transport equipment other than road vehicles sent a smaller proportion of their exports to FOU than did French exporters as a group. If these four machinery industries did not send most of their exports to the OECD, neither did they continue to rely on the once-sheltered markets of the overseas union.

RELIANCE OF FRANCE'S CLIENTS ON FRENCH EXPORTS

I employ the OECD as a proxy for competitive world markets on the presumption that member countries are supplied by producers of many nationalities. In effect, I have assumed that even at the level of particular products, no small group of exporters could claim to dominate trade with an OECD country.

As colonies, members of FOU had purchased most of their imports from France, so French exporters had faced little foreign competition in their markets. As imperial alumni, however, FOU countries have diversified; French exporters now face serious competition from rivals in other OECD countries.

Algeria provides the most important example of economic decolonization. In 1958 France accounted for 84 percent of all Algerian imports and 91 percent of Algerian imports from the OECD.[122] Imports from

---

122. International Monetary Fund, *Direction of Trade Annual, 1958–1962*; and International Monetary Fund, *Direction of Trade Statistics Yearbook, 1986*.

FOU, controlled no doubt by French companies, accounted for another 5 percent. For each franc of imports from the Netherlands, its second largest source of foreign supply, Algeria received 132 francs of imports from France. It is difficult to imagine a developing country more dependent on an economic overlord. In 1983 the French share of Algerian imports had declined to 23 percent and imports from the old FOU dropped to less than 1 percent. In round numbers, then, Algerian imports from areas under French influence dropped from 90 percent in 1958 to 25 percent in 1983. The French share of Algeria's imports from the OECD declined from more than 90 percent to less than 30 percent. Germany had replaced the Netherlands as Algeria's second largest source of imports, accounting for almost half the value of imports attributable to France. If France remained the leading source of Algerian imports, French producers could no longer consider the Algerian market safe from foreign competition.

Algeria is an extreme case, generated by the terms on which France surrendered sovereignty there. But some members of the old FOU, along with some clients of current importance who had not belonged to the union, do rely substantially on France, at least for certain goods. Such is the case, for example, in telecommunications and audio equipment, the SITC manufacturing division in which French exporters relied least heavily on OECD markets as of 1983. Dividing the countries of the world into three groups—OECD, FOU, and all others—one finds that OECD countries tended to buy just 5 percent of their imported telecommunications and audio products from French exporters, while members of the old FOU tended to purchase 55 percent of such imports from France. The corresponding mean for the rest of the world was 22 percent. Thus, on average, FOU remained the preserve of French exporters, the OECD remained the opposite, and the rest of the world formed intermediate ground.[123]

The three sets of countries also differed with respect to intragroup variation in dependence on France. Among OECD clients, the French share of exports always fell within the limited range of 0 to 8 percent (Spain depended most and Canada least on French exports of tele-

123. Author's calculations based on data from OECD, *Foreign Trade by Commodities, 1983*, series C, vol. 1: *Exports*. The ratio calculated for each destination is $100 \ (XF_j/XOECD_j)$, where XF_j is French exports to country j of goods in SITC 76, and $XOECD_j$ is OECD exports to country j of goods in SITC 76.

communications and audio equipment). In contrast, six FOU countries—Kampuchea, Vanuatu, Vietnam, Algeria, Mauritania, and
Guinea—relied on France for less than one-quarter of imports, while
another five depended on it for more than four-fifths of imports.
Three of the six with low dependence used force to obtain their
political autonomy, and another, Guinea, left France's entourage on
strained terms; but Martinique and French Guiana, two of the three
countries relying on France for more than 90 percent of imports,
remain under French sovereignty while the third, Comoro Islands,
received its independence only in the 1970s. For countries belonging
neither to the OECD nor to FOU, dependence on France varied. Of
the 130 countries in this group, 18 imported no telecommunications
and audio equipment from France. For another 33 the ratio of French
to OECD exports was less than 1 percent. At the other end of the
spectrum, for Yemen, Iraq, and Sierra Leone, the French share of
exports exceeded 40 percent. For Yemen and Iraq the ratio was 44
percent; for Sierra Leone it was 61 percent.

Although I have not performed similar analyses for other divisions
of the SITC, these figures should allow several conclusions about the
impact of exports on competition. First, exports to the OECD are
exports to competitive world markets. French sellers do not dominate
exports of most products to rich market economies. Second, some
members of the old FOU—Algeria and Indochina in particular—no
longer rely heavily on France to satisfy their import needs. Third,
other members of FOU, especially those that remain legally linked
to France, continue to rely heavily on France for imports. Finally,
countries belonging neither to the OECD nor to the original FOU
exhibit a degree of dependence on France that lies between those
displayed by the other two groups. The dependence of some of these
countries is as pronounced as that to be found in the overseas union,
but most fall well below that level.[124]

124. France continues to be the principal source of inward direct investment for
its former colonies, however. According to the Vernon data, on January 1, 1971, it
still accounted for 61 percent of the Algerian, Moroccan, and Tunisian subsidiaries of
multinationals based outside the United States. It also accounted for 58 percent of
such subsidiaries in the rest of French Africa. See Vaupel and Curhan, *The World's
Multinational Enterprises*, cross-tabulation 21.1.1.

EXPORTS AND THE SENSITIVITY OF PRICES TO COST
AND DEMAND

If attention to export markets erodes oligopolistic cooperation at home, then, in a cross-section of industries one would expect sensitivity of domestic price to shifts in domestic cost or demand to correlate positively with propensity to export. David Encaoua and Philippe Michel have observed just such a correlation since formation of the EEC.[125]

CONCLUSION

The declining importance of colonial and quasi-colonial markets, the opening of former colonies to imports from other rich countries, and the rising importance of competitive world markets have all served to increase the vigor of competition experienced by French companies. The timing of these changes is worth juxtaposing with the timing of the increased propensity to export. The propensity to export did not rise until the late 1960s, but it was precisely between 1959 and 1966 that the destination of French exports changed so radically. Thus changes in French export behavior, first in terms of destinations and then in terms of incidence on production, served throughout the period since 1959 to increase the intensity of competition experienced by French sellers.

Foreign Investment and Competition

To what extent did proximate exposure to foreign rivals, through inward and outward direct investment, create competition in markets supplied by French companies?

INWARD INVESTMENT

In the short term the impact of inward foreign investment on competition depends on the method by which it is effected. Creation of a new local company is the method most likely to reduce producer

---

125. Encaoua and Michel, *Dynamique des Prix Industriels en France*, pp. 148–58, 164–76, and 187–88. Moreover, Auquier, *French Industry's Reaction to the European Common Market*, p. 318, found a negative correlation between price-cost margin and propensity to export in a cross-section of manufacturing industries.

concentration. In the Vernon data bank on multinational enterprises, foreign companies tended to establish French subsidiaries by acquiring already existing firms. Although true of American and non-American parents alike, the former were nearly twice as likely to build their French subsidiaries from scratch.[126]

Inward investment is especially conducive to competition when it occurs in industries exhibiting high producer concentration and low import exposure. As of 1980, across all available manufacturing industries, the simple correlation between four-firm producer concentration (PC4) and foreign control of domestic value added (IDFI) did differ positively from zero.[127] Thus foreign investment did tend to impinge relatively strongly on concentrated industries; but so did the ratio of imports to domestic consumption (IM).[128] Across the same thirty-seven industries, the simple correlation between PC4 and IM also differed positively from zero.[129]

Appendix table A-67 presents industry-level data on IM and IDFI where PC4 exceeded 50 percent. In all but one of the fourteen industries, inward investors controlled at least 15 percent of domestic value added. In both of the fourteen in which imports impinged lightly on domestic consumption, IDFI exceeded 15 percent. In one of the two (grain mill products), foreigners controlled 44 percent of domestic value added.

Inward foreign investment can also promote competition by increasing the number of strategic groups operating in particular markets. Since nationality is a plausible element of strategic group

126. Vaupel and Curhan, *The World's Multinational Enterprises*, cross-tabulations 13.1.1 and 13.1.2. I shall not attempt to explain this divergence. To the extent that the same pattern obtains in other host countries, company strategy is the plausible factor. To the extent that the French pattern is not replicated in other host countries, the explanation may lie in discrimination by the host government against American companies seeking authorization to acquire established companies.

127. At the .05 level of significance in a one-tail t-test ($r = 0.40$, $N = 37$). Industries are defined according to NAP-100. The ministry of industry data exclude military products, tobacco products, and five food industries.

128. Such had not been the case in 1962. Among all available manufacturing industries defined according to NAE-2, the correlation between IDFI in 1962 and PC4 in 1963 failed to differ from 0 at standard levels of significance ($r = 0.16$, $N = 43$). For data sources see table A-61 and note 139.

129. At the .05 level of significance in a one-tail t-test ($r = .35$). IM and IDFI correlated positively at the .01 level in a one-tail t-test ($r = .44$, $N = 37$).

identity, the number of nationalities cohabiting a country's production community might correlate positively with the intensity of competition in its markets.

As of 1980 virtually all foreign companies with direct investments in French mining and manufacturing were based in Europe or North America.[130] American investors controlled more than one-third of the sales attributed to companies under foreign influence; Dutch, German, and British multinationals controlled 10 to 15 percent each; most of the remaining investors were Belgian or Swiss.[131]

At the level of individual manufacturing industries, in thirty-two of thirty-seven at least five different nationalities were represented among the foreign investors.[132] Nevertheless, in ten of the twenty-seven for which the information was available, the leading source country accounted for over half the value added controlled from abroad (the United States was the leading source in eight of the ten). For example, although companies from six different countries invested in the French glass industry, American-owned companies accounted for 87 percent of all value added in companies under foreign control. The number of nationality-based strategic groups in this industry was two, not seven.

In twelve of the fourteen concentrated industries identified in table A-67, direct investors were based in at least three countries. In five they were based in at least five countries. Once again, however, in most a small number of source countries accounted for most of the direct investment. In office equipment, for example, although 91

130. Ministère de l'Industrie et de la Recherche, *9 Ans d'Implantation Etrangère dans l'Industrie*, table 10–2.

131. Between 1965 and 1978 the United States accounted for 26.5 percent of the foreign investment inflow (net of withdrawals) from nine rich countries. Meanwhile, Switzerland accounted for 16.1 percent, Germany 15.4 percent, the United Kingdom 13.9 percent, the Netherlands 13.3 percent, Belgium-Luxembourg 9.2 percent, Italy 4.4 percent, and Canada 0.4 percent. See Arnaud-Ammeler and Marnata, *Les Flux d'Investissement Direct entre la France et l'Extérieur, 1965–1978*, table 10. The Vernon data bank, based on numbers of foreign subsidiaries, also suggests concentration of control in a few source countries. Among 441 French subsidiaries of non-American parents, 51 percent were owned by British or German companies. Only 14 percent had parents based outside Europe, and none were controlled from Japan. See Vaupel and Curhan, *The World's Multinational Enterprises*, cross-tabulation 21.1.1.

132. The information in this and the following paragraphs is taken from Ministère de l'Industrie et de la Recherche, *9 Ans d'Implantation Etrangère dans l'Industrie*, table 20. Manufacturing excludes NAP-100 industries 09, 12, and 14.

percent of domestic value added was influenced by foreign investors, 98 percent of that 91 percent was attributable to companies based in the United States.

Perhaps the best way to appraise the impact of inward investment on strategic groups is to examine the national identities of leading producers in highly concentrated industries. Toward this end, I attempted to identify the ultimate parents in 1985 of each of the four largest sellers in all narrowly defined (NAP-600) manufacturing industries satisfying two criteria in 1975: PC4 exceeded 70 percent and the value of shipments exceeded Fr 1 billion.[133] Thirty-six industries satisfied both criteria. For eighteen it was possible to identify the ultimate parents of each of the four leading producers. For another seven it was possible to identify the ultimate parents of three leading producers. In this set of twenty-five industries, only five—hollow glass, automobiles, airframes, outer space equipment, and bottled water—revealed no foreign control of a leading seller. In contrast, in five others—soaps and detergents, agricultural tractors, elevators, semiconductors, and bearings—at least three of the leading producers were controlled from abroad. In eleven of the twenty-five, companies based in the United States controlled at least one of France's leading producers. In none of the twenty-five was a foreign parent based anywhere but in Western Europe or North America. It is useful to examine some specific cases:

—Computers (NAP 2701). Two of the four leading producers were controlled by a single French company (Bull). A third (Logabax) was affiliated with, but not controlled by, Italy's Olivetti. The final leader was IBM. Neither Bull nor Logabax was a major competitor of IBM outside France, hence the French market was unlikely to play cog in a scheme of multinational oligopolistic collusion. Given the paucity of domestically based potential entrants, inward investment may have offered the best hope for competition in this market.

—Soap and detergents (NAP 1805). All of the leading producers— Procter and Gamble, Colgate Palmolive, Unilever, and Henkel— were based outside France. Two had American parents, the other two European parents. The four competed against each other in many

133. The identities of the four largest producers, as well as the concentration ratios, were taken from INSEE E64, pp. 131–61. The information on parentage was taken from *Who Owns Whom: Continental Europe.*

lines of business and many parts of the world. Foreign investment is unlikely to have spurred competition in this market.

—Semiconductors (NAP 2916). Of the leading sellers, Motorola and IBM were American, Philips was Dutch, and Thomson was French. The French company was large by French standards but medium by global standards. Given the paucity of domestically based potential entrants, Thomson was unlikely to have faced serious competition without inward investment. Unlike Bull, however, it did hold important shares of several foreign markets, although typically in products other than semiconductors. As a result, oligopolistic cooperation with foreign rivals cannot be excluded.

—Tires (NAP 5201). A single French multinational, Michelin, controlled two of the leading French producers (Kléber-Colombes and itself). Unlike Bull in computers or even Thomson in semiconductors, Michelin was a powerful force in the world tire business, meeting the parents of its two leading domestic rivals in many markets. As a result, cooperative behavior among the three would hardly have been surprising, but France was definitely Michelin's home base, giving it an attitude about the market that the foreigners may not have shared. Without inward investment, however, the domestic industry would almost certainly have remained dominated by Michelin.

Some foreign investments are joint ventures of several parent companies. Such ventures, like mutual interpenetrations of national markets, might facilitate cooperation at the supranational level among oligopolists who have previously succeeded in colluding only at the national level. In other words, under certain circumstances, foreign investment might promote convergence of perspective among enterprises of different nationalities, reducing the number of strategic groups operating in the market.

Vernon's data suggest that many French manufacturers have more than one parent, at least one of which is foreign. Among the 380 French manufacturers controlled by non-American multinationals, only 42 percent were owned at least 95 percent by the parent company responding to the survey (appendix table A-68). American multinationals were more likely to own at least 95 percent of their French subsidiaries, but even so, in 22 percent of the sample they owned no more than 50 percent of their offspring.

For a few French subsidiaries of foreign parents, Vernon obtained detailed information on the composition of ownership (table A-68).[134] The non-American investors tended to engage in joint ventures with French enterprises. In only 8 percent of the companies they influenced was the remaining equity capital distributed widely among outside shareholders. American investors also tended to take on French partners, but the Americans were nearly three times as likely not to be involved in a joint venture as were the other foreign investors. On this criterion, multinationals based in the United States were especially likely to enhance competition in French markets.

Much of the evidence considered to this point suggests that foreign investments by U.S. companies were especially likely to improve competition in French markets. U.S. multinationals were especially likely to create rather than acquire subsidiaries, to own completely the companies they influenced, and, when they failed to retain sole ownership, to avoid joint ventures. Adding the likelihood that parallel foreign investment occurred less between France and the United States than between France and the countries of Europe, it becomes probable that U.S. multinationals were relatively unlikely to have used foreign investment to promote international collusion.[135]

134. The data in table A-68 imply that foreign multinationals based outside the U.S. exerted less than complete ownership influence on 220 French manufacturing companies. (This figure is obtained by multiplying 380, the number of French companies influenced by foreigners based outside the United States, by 58 percent, the fraction in which the foreign investor held less than 95 percent of the French company's equity.) The corresponding figure for U.S.-based multinationals was 90 (43 percent of 209). And yet, information on residual shareholding is available for only 67 French companies controlled by non-U.S. foreigners and for only 53 French companies under U.S. control. As a result, the data employed in this paragraph are too sparse to support strong conclusions.

135. Relevant, if imperfect, information on intraindustry investment can be gleaned from comparing the industrial composition of direct investment by country A in country B with the composition of investment by B in A. I have performed such comparisons between France, on the one hand, and Germany, the United Kingdom, and the United States, on the other, using the data of Arnaud-Ameller and Marnata for 1965–78. Intraindustry investment appeared most pronounced between France and Germany, least pronounced between France and the United Kingdom. See Arnaud-Ameller and Marnata, *Les Flux d'Investissement Direct entre la France et l'Extérieur, 1965–1978*, tables 4, 10; see also Mucchielli and Thuillier, *Multinationales Européennes et Investissements Croisés*, pt. 2.

This point of view is certainly consistent with distinctions drawn by French government and business between U.S. and European inward investment: the former was frequently condemned, while the latter was occasionally encouraged.[136] To some extent this reflected a genuine fear that American companies would use their substantial financial resources to entrench themselves in French markets, increasing seller concentration, raising barriers to entry, and reducing competition. Given the pervasive imperfections of French capital markets, which handicapped French firms that were not favored by government policy and were seeking funds with which to compete, this fear was not unfounded. Nevertheless, I suspect that hostility toward the Americans was fanned by fear that they might not behave as responsible members of local oligopoly groups—that they might jeopardize the control of domestic markets by French companies and government agencies alike.

Given the possibility that U.S. multinationals were relatively likely to promote competition in French markets, the role of the Americans warrants closer scrutiny. The U.S. Department of Commerce has collected data on the nominal stock of U.S. direct investment in various countries since 1950. The relevant data for France appear in table 23. U.S. investment in French manufacturing increased by at least 10 percent during twenty-three of thirty-four years between 1951 and 1984. During fourteen of these years it increased by at least 15 percent, and in seven by more than 20 percent. Only during the first half of the 1980s, as the dollar rose against the franc, did the stock decline in dollar value. Before the 1980s the periods of especially rapid increase, 1958–65 and 1970–75, corresponded to the launching of the EEC and to its expansion from six to nine members. The periods of slow growth corresponded to macroeconomic disturbance, coupled occasionally with political uncertainty, as in 1968, or else to periods of announced government animosity toward the presence of foreign firms, as in 1966 and 1967. In general, however, these data confirm that U.S. investment in French manufacturing grew substantially after World War II.

136. See, for example, Servan-Schreiber, *Le Défi Américain*; and Torem and Craig, "Control of Foreign Investment in France."

Table 23. *Nominal Stock of U.S. Direct Investment in France, 1950–84*

	All		Manufacturing	
Year	Millions of dollars	Percent change from previous year	Millions of dollars	Percent change from previous year
1950	217	. . .	114	. . .
1951	249	14.7	137	20.2
1952	275	10.4	158	15.3
1953	302	9.8	175	10.8
1954	330	9.3	192	9.7
1955	373	13.0	213	10.9
1956	425	13.9	239	12.2
1957	464	9.2	243	1.7
1958	546	17.7	279	14.8
1959	640	17.2	342	22.6
1960	741	15.8	402	17.5
1961	860	16.1	484	20.4
1962	1,030	19.8	603	24.6
1963	1,240	20.4	764	26.7
1964	1,446	16.6	909	19.0
1965	1,609	11.3	1,076	18.4
1966	1,790	11.2	1,162	8.0
1967	1,942	8.5	1,260	8.4
1968	1,965	1.2	1,303	3.4
1969	2,170	10.4	1,464	12.4
1970	2,643	21.8	1,812	23.8
1971	3,059	15.7	2,107	16.3
1972	3,492	14.2	2,441	15.9
1973	4,295	23.0	2,943	20.6
1974	4,902	14.1	3,428	16.5
1975	5,743	17.2	3,844	12.1
1976	5,954	3.7	3,968	3.2
1977	6,093	2.3	4,138	4.3
1978	6,806	11.7	4,686	13.2
1979	7,651	12.4	5,229	11.6
1980	9,348	22.2	5,916	13.1
1981	9,102	−2.6	5,501	−7.0
1982	7,807	−14.2	4,774	−13.2
1983	6,911	−11.5	4,228	−11.4
1984	6,478	−6.3	4,187	−1.0

Sources: 1950–75: U.S. Department of Commerce, Bureau of Economic Analysis, *Selected Data on U.S. Direct Investment Abroad, 1950–76.* 1976–84: *Survey of Current Business* (various August issues).

The expanding presence of U.S. companies was reflected in the rising shares of French industries subject to American control. As of 1962, among twenty-eight manufacturing industries, the mean percentage of equity capital under U.S. control (U.S. IDFI) was 4 percent. Among these industries the corresponding mean for the fraction of share capital under foreign influence from any source was 15 percent, 3 percentage points higher than the mean among all forty-three manufacturing industries. In only five did the American share exceed 10 percent (appendix table A-69): automobiles (11 percent), certain nonelectrical machinery, including agricultural machinery (13 percent), rubber (17 percent), petroleum (20 percent), and precision goods (24 percent). By 1980, among twenty-nine manufacturing industries, the mean share of value added contributed by U.S.-controlled companies had risen to 11 percent.[137] Although this figure is not strictly comparable to the 4 percent figure for 1962, it does suggest that the average incidence of American investment on French industries may have risen sharply between 1962 and 1980. At the industry level the importance of American control varied substantially in 1980 (appendix table A-70). In twenty industries, U.S. companies controlled less than 10 percent of French value added; in four others—petroleum, miscellaneous chemical products, agricultural equipment, and office equipment—however, U.S. parents controlled at least 20 percent of value added. But only in office equipment, where American companies controlled 89 percent of French value added, did the American share exceed 33 percent.

European direct investment also increased between 1962 and 1980.[138] The most important difference between the American- and the European-based investment was in the relation to French levels of producer concentration. In 1962 neither U.S. IDFI nor other IDFI

137. The twenty-nine accounted for 90 percent of the combined value added of the thirty-seven manufacturing industries for which foreign investment information is published by the ministry of industry. Recall that NAP distinguishes forty-four manufacturing industries at the two-digit level. For seven of these the ministry of industry publishes no information whatsoever regarding inward direct investment; for eight more it did not reveal the exact importance of American investment in 1980. In five of these eight, however, it is possible to establish an upper bound on American involvement that puts American control of industry value added at less than 5 percent.

138. According to Auquier, *French Industry's Reaction to the European Common Market*, chap. 5, it increased more rapidly than did U.S. investment.

was correlated with PC4.[139] Among the six industries where PC4 exceeded 50 percent, only one, petroleum at 20 percent, exhibited a value of U.S. IDFI in excess of 5 percent. In tobacco products and nonferrous metals, where producer concentration was greatest, no American enterprise owned any manufacturing facilities in France. In 1980 other IDFI remained uncorrelated with PC4, but U.S. IDFI and PC4 now varied positively with each other.[140] In other words, in 1980 American companies controlled especially large fractions of value added in French industries exhibiting high producer concentration; such had not been the case in the early 1960s.[141]

This change in the relationship between U.S. IDFI and PC4 is consistent with a variety of hypotheses. Of these, the two most interesting are: U.S. companies came to invest more heavily in industries characterized by high concentration of production, or else producer concentration rose in those industries in which U.S. companies had invested heavily. The former is compatible with the view that U.S. direct investment helped to mitigate the anticompetitive effects of concentrated production. The latter is more in keeping with the view that U.S. investment increased the concentration of French production in a few enterprises.[142]

Inward direct investment may sometimes increase and sometimes reduce domestic competition, depending on the remaining structural configuration of the industry. With this in mind, it is useful to consider the behavioral evidence supplied by Encaoua and Michel regarding variations among French industries in the sensitivity of prices to changes in cost and demand. With import exposure, export exposure, and producer concentration controlled, they found a negative relationship between sensitivity of prices to costs and demand on the one

139. Other IDFI is IDFI less U.S. IDFI. The correlation between U.S. IDFI in 1962 and PC4 in 1963 was .07, insignificantly different from 0 at the .50 level in a one-tail t-test ($N = 28$). The corresponding correlation between other IDFI and PC4 was .02 ($N = 28$). The concentration data are taken from Jenny and Weber, *Concentration et Politique des Structures Industrielles*.

140. Other IDFI uncorrelated at the .2 level of significance in a one-tail t-test ($r = .17$, $N = 29$); U.S. IDFI positively correlated at the .05 level in a one-tail t-test ($r = .37$; $N = 29$).

141. According to Auquier, *French Industry's Reaction to the European Common Market*, p. 515, with size of firm controlled, PC4 and IDFI were negatively correlated.

142. The determinants of inward foreign investment are explored in ibid., chap. 5.

hand and foreign control of domestic production on the other.[143] This is consistent with the hypothesis that direct foreign investment has not generally dissipated oligopolistic behavior in French markets.

OUTWARD INVESTMENT

Vernon's data bank offers several clues regarding competition in the markets supplied by foreign subsidiaries of French multinationals. In the first place, French-owned companies abroad tended to sell in the countries in which they produced, and they tended to sell primarily to customers unaffiliated with their parents.[144] As a result, the relevant markets to consider are those where the subsidiaries are located. Although France was the principal foreign investor in its former colonies (among subsidiaries of non-American multinationals, 61 percent of those in North Africa and 58 percent of those in sub-Saharan Africa had French parents), FOU absorbed little of its foreign investment.[145] Only 14 percent of the foreign subsidiaries of French multinationals were located in French Africa (appendix table A-71); more than half were located in Europe.[146]

The degree of competition experienced by European subsidiaries of French multinationals is difficult to resolve. On the side of vigorous

143. Encaoua and Michel, *Dynamique des Prix Industriels en France,* pp. 172–76.

144. See Vaupel and Curhan, *The World's Multinational Enterprises,* cross-tabulations 15.2.1, 16.21.1. Among 153 foreign subsidiaries of French parents, 90 percent stated that they produced primarily for the local market rather than for export. Among 160 subsidiaries of French parents, 79 percent stated that their principal customers lay outside the entourage of their parent company.

145. Vernon gathered his information through surveys of existing enterprises. Since many of France's colonial companies had died before his study, the data may understate the importance of colonial investment earlier in the century. According to Jacques Marseille, as of 1914 the French empire ranked third behind Russia and Latin America (and ahead of Austria-Hungary, Spain, and the Ottoman empire) as a destination for French foreign investment. But Marseille's data appear to include all (as opposed to just direct) foreign investment. See *Empire Colonial et Capitalisme Français,* pp. 100–01.

146. Half the African subsidiaries were in Algeria, Morocco, and Tunisia and half were in sub-Saharan Africa; see Vaupel and Curhan, *The World's Multinational Enterprises,* cross-tabulation 1.21.1. Note, however, that in comparison with other European multinationals, French multinationals tended not to invest in countries with high standards of living (ibid., cross-tabulation 3.21.1). According to Marseille, *Empire Colonial et Capitalisme Français,* chap. 5, the emphasis on Western Europe developed after World War II.

competition, one could cite the universally heavy and broadly sourced exposure of European markets to imports and inward investment. One could also cite the tendency of French multinationals to create rather than acquire their foreign subsidiaries (51 percent of the 297 examined by Vernon were creations). By foregoing acquisition of local companies, the French may also have foregone participation in already established cooperative relationships with local rivals. On the side of anemic competition, however, in about half of Vernon's cases, French multinationals owned no more than 50 percent of their foreign subsidiaries.[147] French parents also tended to share control of their subsidiaries with other enterprises. Among subsidiaries in which companies other than the reporting parent held at least 5 percent of the equity capital, 37 percent had a local private partner and another 37 percent had a private partner based outside the host country.[148] The prevalence of joint ventures facilitated cooperation among rivals and hence reduced the likelihood of foreign-based competition. Finally, one could cite the possibility that French multinationals were engaged in cooperative interpenetration of markets, perhaps with the intent of curbing mutually inconvenient dumping.[149]

The foreign investments most likely to increase the competition experienced by French companies were those in North America and Japan. There, as in Europe, French investors faced powerful, locally based rivals. There, but not in Europe, economic and cultural distance impeded recognition and exploitation of mutual interdependence. As table A-71 shows, however, North America and Japan accounted for just 7 percent and 1 percent of France's foreign subsidiaries in Vernon's sample, and most French subsidiaries in North America were created only very recently.[150]

147. Vaupel and Curhan, *The World's Multinational Enterprises*, cross-tabulation 10.21.1.

148. Ibid., cross-tabulation 12.21.1.

149. See note 135.

150. From 1965 to 1978 the United States hosted 22 percent of French direct investments net of withdrawals; Arnaud-Ameller and Marnata, *Les Flux d'Investissement Direct entre la France et l'Extérieur, 1965–1978*, table 4. Of the seventy-two French multinationals studied by Michalet and Delapierre in *La Multinationalisation des Entreprises Françaises*, table 22, only three began to produce in the United States before 1960, while eleven began to do so between 1961 and 1971.

Without good evidence on parallel foreign investment in Europe, it is difficult to assess the impact of outward investment on the competitive environment of French multinationals. Nevertheless, the geographic composition of France's direct investment portfolio cannot be characterized as quasi-colonial. At the very least, French investments permitted French companies to observe at close range the products and production methods of major participants in competitive world markets.

Conclusion

To this day, France deploys quotas, fastidious customs procedures, and discriminatory public procurement to repel unwanted imports. Moreover, the EC has yet to create a unified internal market. Public and private barriers continue to impede trade and investment, sheltering the community as a whole from the outside world and one EC country from another.[151] Nevertheless, fundamental changes in French foreign policy occasioned fundamental changes in French business exposure to foreign competition. Foreign goods came to account for major shares of French consumption, French producers came to export major fractions of domestic output, and international investments came to migrate copiously in both directions across French borders. Virtually all manufacturing enterprises are now exposed to foreign rivals, enough so to give pause to those in the United States who argue that France remains a protectionist country despite its EC membership.

IMPACT ON BUSINESS STRATEGY

From the perspective of French business, change in the international environment signalled change in the relative desirability of the several basic strategies discussed in chapter 1.[152] In the old international environment, France could attempt to protect some industries

151. See Shutt, *The Myth of Free Trade*; Taylor, *The Limits of European Integration*; and Petersmann, "International and European Foreign Trade Law," pp. 441–87.

152. In the rest of this chapter, I employ the term "strategy" in the sense of Porter, *Competitive Advantage*. Support for the substance of my conclusions appears in Caron, *An Economic History of Modern France*, p. 310.

without attempting to protect others; and it could switch between free trade and protection at moments it considered opportune.[153] The feasibility of fine-tuning prompted policymakers to focus on the national economic interests affected by protection, and to do so separately for each commodity. In the new international environment, France enjoys much less discretion in commercial policy. Despite the existence of a franc zone, France's economic influence on the most important of its former colonies, in Indochina and in North Africa, has declined appreciably. In its relations with rich countries, it has delegated much commercial authority to a supranational organization. Unless it can persuade the European Communities to adopt pan-European protection against nonmembers or to neglect benignly French protection against members, and thus indirectly against their outside trading partners, the price of protectionism, even temporary or localized in version, is continued membership in the EC. Commercial policy has become difficult to target.[154]

To individual companies and industries, transformation of the international environment has raised the cost of political influence sought for protection of established positions. Demanders of protection must now convince two layers of government rather than one. Neither is likely to be receptive. At the national level France did not join the EC to increase the profits of its firms or the utilities of its consumers. It joined to avoid further military confrontation with Germany. Faced with the choice between leaving the EC and protecting industry, France could be expected to remain in the community, even if it

153. French commercial policy during the nineteenth century is discussed in Dunham, *The Anglo-French Treaty of Commerce of 1860 and the Progress of the Industrial Revolution in France*; Golob, *The Méline Tariff*; and Smith, *Tariff Reform in France, 1860–1900*.

154. I do not wish to underestimate the ability of a member country to induce the EC to violate the spirit of the Paris and Rome treaties. France in particular has rolled many a log within the EC Council. Consider, for example, the sequel to Poitiers, the French effort to impede imports of Japanese video tape recorders, discussed earlier in this chapter. Shortly after France agreed to lift its restraints in 1982, European producers of video tape recorders filed an antidumping complaint against their Japanese rivals. In February 1983, MITI agreed to administer a system of minimum export prices, effective March 18, 1983. *Bulletin of the European Communities*, vol. 16 (issue 3, 1983), point 2.22.2. The episode suggests the EC was prepared to accept the substance of France's position in return for French willingness to concede the procedural point of EC jurisdiction.

accepted the socioeconomic merits of protectionism. A good example of how the new environment constrains the French government occurred in March 1983. During the previous eighteen months the new Socialist government had engaged in sharply expansionary macroeconomic policy. Imports rose faster than exports, and the budgetary deficit ballooned. Rather than abandon the pursuit of full employment through macroeconomic stimulation, many elements of the ruling coalition advocated reduction of economic interdependence to ensure that domestic stimulation resulted in domestic jobs. Recognizing that this implied withdrawal from the European Monetary System and possibly from the European Communities, the government decided, if only by a whisker, to endorse economic austerity and to reaffirm France's commitment to the EC.

Membership in the EC also proved useful when France opposed insulation of the home industry. The French government could now fend off the protectionists by claiming that treaty obligations render it powerless to protect particular industries or companies. As Thomas Schelling noted long ago, the ability to bind oneself in advance to a particular course of conduct—in this case, sustaining an open economy—may permit one to survive subsequent pressures to modify that position. Certain types of weakness are strength in disguise.[155] As for the EC, the identity of which is based on economic integration, protection of particular industries in particular countries would create potentially haunting precedents. Although the EC has not expunged all forms of protection, it has certainly increased the cost to national governments of devising protection consistent with the Treaties of Paris and Rome. Aiding the EC in its effort to keep markets open are rival companies in other member countries: they have a natural incentive to share with the EC Commission their knowledge of restrictive practices elsewhere in the community. And the commission's procedures guarantee that such companies will be heard.

In short, military weakness during World War II, coupled with involuntary decolonization, served to refocus French international policy from the third world to the first. Since 1957 important elements of French commercial policy have been bundled together with the decision to remain in the European Communities. The credible

155. Schelling, *The Strategy of Conflict*, chap. 2.

permanence of France's commitment to the EC, coupled with the credible permanence of the EC's commitment to internal free trade, has served to increase sharply the cost to individual companies and industries of protecting established positions through the political process.[156]

In the new international environment, the cost of oligopolistic cooperation has also risen sharply. Domestic cartels had to be transformed into communitywide ventures. Any new cartels had to embrace more companies and more strategic groups. On both counts, explicit or implicit cooperation designed to protect and exploit established advantages became more difficult to achieve; and successful cooperation merely invited action from the EC Commission to invalidate the cartel and fine its members.

The new international environment also increased the advantages of innovation. Relaxation of foreign-exchange rules permitted companies to finance desired projects without access to government-controlled sources of funds.[157] More important, the cost to a company of conceiving and implementing an innovative course of conduct declined as the company became directly exposed to dynamic foreign firms in its lines of business.[158] It also declined as individuals who had achieved such innovation in North Africa and Indochina, environments rich in certain resources and creative of mentalities similar to those engendered by the American frontier, migrated to France upon decolonization. Many retained their innovative ethic, establishing enterprises in a variety of industries, especially agriculture.[159] Exposure to innovators also increased the benefits of innovation. In an environment permeated with innovators, failure to develop sources of competitive advantage results at best in decline.[160] Moreover, investments in such advantage could now be recouped more effec-

156. Gruson, *Origine et Espoirs de la Planification Française*, pp. 125–26.

157. See chapter 3, as well as INSEE, *Le Mouvement Economique en France, 1949–1979*, pp. 359–63.

158. Exposure to best-practice technique should not be construed narrowly. It applies to organizational as well as technological method. For this reason, inward direct investment from outside the EC provided especially important role models. On the benefits to be expected from international exposure, see Scitovsky, *Economic Theory and Western European Integration*.

159. Kramer, *Unsettling Europe*.

160. Compare Richardson, *Information and Investment*.

tively. French companies were selling in much broader markets, and domestic cartels found it more difficult to punish expansive rivals.

COMPARISONS

The exposure of French firms to foreign competition, in French and foreign markets alike, served to change the parameters used to select among the three basic forms of investment. Innovation became relatively advantageous; and French firms became more innovative.[161]

This is not the first French example of such a sequence of events. In 1860 when Napoleon III agreed to free trade with England, French firms were considered backward and unlikely to compete effectively with their cross-channel rivals. When trade liberalization occurred, however, many acquitted themselves well. As the rules of the game changed, French firms no less than firms from other countries learned how to compete.

The major difference between free trade after World War II and free trade in the nineteenth century was the ease with which government could reverse policy. Because the political cost of reversal has been far greater since World War II, actual reversal has been less likely. As a result, the logic of innovative behavior is stronger and more durable than it was a century ago.

The salutory effects of international exposure, and of the credibility of its permanence, may be examined in the context of other countries as well.[162] Italy also experienced credibly permanent exposure to world market forces only after World War II. That the Italian and French economies grew at remarkably similar rates after formation of the EEC, and faster even than their German counterpart, is certainly consistent with the view that sheltered economies gain vitality from

161. Marseille, *Empire Colonial et Capitalisme Français*, especially pp. 60, 150–56, and 367–73, reaches the same conclusion in the specific context of decolonization. In his view imperial preference conferred unnatural longevity on declining French industries, postponing the structural change required by restoration of liberalism to the world economy. Similarly, French imperial investments, public as well as private, reduced the resources available to the domestic industrial policies designed to facilitate structural adjustment. As Charles de Gaulle put it in 1961, "Decolonization is in our interest, and therefore it shall be our policy." (Quoted in ibid., p. 373.)

162. Bairoch, *Commerce Extérieur et Développement Economique de l'Europe au XIXe Siècle.*

such exposure.[163] Moreover, given the lack of Italian renown in the domain of industrial policy, this similarity in growth performance reinforces the suspicion, stated at the end of chapter 3, that the structural initiatives of the French government do not explain fully the growth and structural change experienced by the French economy after World War II.

International exposure explains less well the performance of the British economy. Before World War II and during the 1950s, the United Kingdom displayed a degree of exposure that France and Italy would not match even after European economic integration. During the early 1950s the British ratios of imports and exports to GDP were nearly twice as large as those in France or Italy; before 1974 neither Continental country ever matched the British exposure to international trade. Between 1974 and 1985 Britain always exported a larger fraction of GDP than either France or Italy. Only during the second oil shock did France and Italy have ratios of imports to GDP in excess of their British counterpart.[164] If international exposure promotes microeconomic innovation and macroeconomic growth, the British economy should have performed very well during the first decades after World War II. Such was not the case.[165] Although British growth looked good by prewar British standards, it failed to match the contemporary French record, which in turn failed even to approximate the German miracle. Even in the late 1960s when Britain appeared close to EC membership, large segments of British business did not appear game for innovative behavior.

Britain deserves and has received attention in its own right, so I will simply mention some potential clues in the puzzle of why international exposure failed to impinge more tonically on its economic performance.[166] The first clue may lie in the geographic composition

163. The basic growth data appear in table 1. On the Italian experience, see Stern, *Foreign Trade and Economic Growth in Italy*.

164. See Marseille, *Empire Colonial et Capitalisme Français*, p. 61; and OECD, *Historical Statistics, 1960–1985*, tables 6.12, 6.13.

165. For a complete economic portrait of the United Kingdom during this period, see Caves, *Britain's Economic Prospects*; and Caves and Krause, *Britain's Economic Performance*.

166. On the period before World War I, see Aldcroft, *The Development of British Industry and Foreign Competition, 1875–1914*. See also Bairoch, *Commerce Extérieur et Développement Economique de l'Europe au XIXe Siècle*, chap. 10.

of British exports. Perhaps Britain relied relatively persistently on quasi-colonial markets. In 1930, before the Ottawa agreements had established imperial preference, Britain sent 44 percent of its exports to the empire; in 1938 the fraction was 50 percent.[167] In 1952, despite the early liberalizations undertaken within the OEEC, it still sent 46 percent of its exports to the sterling area.[168] Although the rich countries came to absorb larger fractions of British exports, the reliance on empire crumbled less rapidly than it did in France. In 1965 the OECD accounted for 55 percent of British exports but 69 percent of French exports; in each of the three SITC divisions accounting for the largest amounts of British exports, less than half of the merchandise sold abroad was absorbed by OECD countries.[169]

The second clue may lie in the British pattern of direct foreign investment. Even after World War II, British multinationals were investing heavily in the former empire. Admittedly, by 1970 they seemed as focused as were their French counterparts on the rich countries of the world. Both the British and the French parents in Raymond Vernon's data set held exactly 61.3 percent of their foreign

167. See Glickmann, "The British Imperial Preference System"; and Aldcroft, *The Inter-War Economy*, p. 294. Even before World War I, many British industries showed a tendency toward "concentration on Imperial markets" because the competition of other rich countries, notably Germany and the United States, was less intense there. Aldcroft, *The Development of British Industry and Foreign Competition, 1875–1914*, pp. 21, 30, 35.

168. In comparison, FOU took 45 percent of French exports in 1952. See OEEC, *OEEC Statistical Bulletins, Foreign Trade*, Series II, no. 4 (1952), p. 14. The sterling area is defined as British overseas territories plus countries outside the OEEC but inside the sterling area. At the industry level, among the five SITC product groups accounting for the largest amounts of British exports, the mean fraction of exports destined for the sterling area was 52.1 percent; among the ten largest exporting groups, the mean was 46.3 percent. See OEEC, *OEEC Statistical Bulletins, Foreign Trade*, Series IV, *Member Countries Combined*, 1952 (1953).

Marchal, "Marché Commun Européen et Zone de Libre-Echange," p. 263, notes, however, that members of the commonwealth traded with nonsterling countries to a much greater extent than did members of FOU with nonfranc countries. Nevertheless, he concludes that "England, like France in Indochina, will sooner or later pay the price for failing to promote economic development in its territories. . . . The strategy of sheltered markets will retard growth in the territories and the home country alike" (p. 263).

169. In France the top three exporting divisions sent 62 percent, 63 percent, and 73 percent of their exports to the OECD. See OECD, *Foreign Trade*, series B, *Commodity Trade Analysis by Main Regions, January–December 1965*. The OECD includes the original OEEC, Spain, the United States, Canada, and Japan.

manufacturing subsidiaries in the countries of the OECD.[170] For the French, however, 83 percent of the OECD-based subsidiaries were located in Europe; for the British, 32 percent of them were located in Australia and New Zealand and only 46 percent in Europe. Many of Britain's imperial subsidiaries produced mature products, such as cotton textiles, with mature technologies.[171] This helped British enterprises maintain control over production of goods in which Britain itself was losing comparative advantage. As a result, it may also have retarded redeployment of British initiative and expertise from mature to rapidly growing industries, jeopardizing Britain's ability to participate in the competitive foreign markets of the world.

A third clue may lie in the manner in which Britain decided to join mainstream Europe. The British debate on participation in European integration was usually framed in economic terms—whether income per capita would rise more with special ties to Europe than it would with special ties to the Commonwealth. In such a frame, it was by no means obvious to British business that participation in the European Communities, if it ever occurred, would last. Britain's failure to participate in the European monetary system merely accentuated the potential for belief that Britain was only partially committed to Europe. In such an environment, industrialists could reasonably continue to believe that investments in political influence, designed to secure protection of established positions, remained profitable. Like France, then, Britain may have joined the European Communities and retreated from its colonial empire; but it did so on very different terms, terms that failed to confer credible permanence on the associated economic arrangements. As a result, British enterprises may not have felt the same compulsion to shift their investment strategies away from preservation of established positions toward the creation of new ones. Perhaps the recent improvement in British performance relative to the rest of Europe stems partly from the gradual disappearance of EC exit as a realistic political option.

170. Vaupel and Curhan, *The World's Multinational Enterprises*, cross-tabulations 1.17.3, 1.21.1. I have used an unpublished version of the latter cross-tabulation in the files of Raymond Vernon. In one respect, the British were even more focused on rich countries than were the French: 44 percent of Britain's foreign subsidiaries, but only 31 percent of their French counterparts, were in countries with 1970 per capita incomes in excess of $2,500 (cross-tabulation 3.21.1).

171. Marseille, *Empire Colonial et Capitalisme Français*, p. 190.

Whatever the ultimate verdict on the sources of British and Italian performance, the French postwar record is consistent with the view that exposure to competitive world markets through international trade and investment does stimulate economic growth and structural change.

5 | A New Domestic Environment

AFTER WORLD War II, major changes occurred in the domestic as well as the international environment of French business. Many of these fortified competition in French markets. From today's perspective the clearest manifestations of change were government decisions to deregulate business behavior. In product markets, regulation began to lose its grip in 1978, when Raymond Barre decontrolled first producer prices, then bakers' prices (prices of some breads had been controlled since before 1789), and finally retail prices of several other goods.[1] After a few zigzags under the Socialists, Barre's policy was confirmed when Jacques Chirac rescinded the 1945 ordinance authorizing government to regulate prices whenever and however it pleased.[2] Chirac also announced his intention to limit future price control to industries deficient in competition.[3]

In financial markets, deregulation began as early as the late 1950s. As government shed fears of its own inability to borrow at acceptable rates of interest, it allowed increasing numbers of private enterprises

1. The impact of deregulation on prices and competition is described in Conseil Economique et Social, "L'Analyse des Circuits et des Coûts de Transformation et de Distribution de Produits Agro-Alimentaires et Leur Eventuel Aménagement." On private efforts to maintain collusive pricing of freshly baked goods, see Commission de la Concurrence, *Rapport au Ministre pour l'Année 1981*, pp. 79–84, 156–65, 184–87.

2. Socialist Pierre Mauroy imposed general controls in June 1982; many of these were relaxed by Socialist Laurent Fabius toward the end of 1985. See Encaoua and Michel, *Dynamique des Prix Industriels en France*, p. 77. Ordinance 86-1243 of December 1, 1986, rescinded ordinance 45-1483 of June 30, 1945; see *Journal Officiel de la République Française* (December 8, 1987), pp. 14773–78.

3. To minimize the number of such industries, Chirac strengthened the antitrust laws at the same time he deregulated prices; see Ministère de l'Economie, des Finances et de la Privatisation, "Liberté des Prix et Nouveau Droit de la Concurrence."

to float securities on the French market. Moreover, on several occasions it temporarily removed quantitative controls on the expansion of bank credit.[4] Still, the markets remained tightly corseted. In February 1986, during its last days in power, the government of Laurent Fabius published a white paper on the French financial system, which broadly speaking urged the creation of a unified market for investible funds and the reduction of regulation to a minimum. For example, it advocated changes designed to facilitate introduction of new types of financial instruments (certificates of deposit, options, and futures), to amplify competition among investment banks and among securities brokers, to eliminate quantitative controls on loans of individual banks, and to facilitate the international migration of saving. The report also favored curtailment of interest subsidies.[5] During the parliamentary elections of March 1986, Jacques Chirac's financial platform differed little from that in the Socialist white paper, and once in office, Chirac implemented several of its proposals. As in the case of price controls, however, the longevity of these reforms may depend more on the degree to which economic conditions remain favorable than on the declared political philosophy of the prime minister.

Government's enthusiasm for deregulation cannot explain the growth and structural change that occurred after World War II. These flourishes of liberalism occurred too recently to shape events decades old. As a result, I shall focus on two areas where changes did occur early enough to influence business behavior during the past quarter century: sector-specific regulation and taxation, and domestic antitrust law. Although they pale in comparison with their international counterparts, these changes of domestic regime are important. First, they introduced substantial competition into some of the markets touched only lightly by alterations in the international environment. I shall illustrate this phenomenon by describing developments in retail trade, a prototypical sheltered industry despite its partial exposure to import competition and its potentially complete exposure

4. Bloch-Lainé and de Vogüé, *Le Trésor Public et le Mouvement Général des Fonds*.

5. Ministère de l'Economie, des Finances et du Budget, *Livre Blanc sur la Réforme du Financement de l'Economie*. An extended description of financial deregulation since 1986 appears in OECD, *France*, chap. 3 and annex B.

to inward foreign investment. Second, although the new domestic environment affected few industries directly, it may have affected many indirectly. In particular, the proliferation of large-scale retailers as alternatives to single-shop family enterprises may have helped foreign manufacturers penetrate French markets.[6]

Changes in Government Policy

Among the most important changes in government policy were those affecting the regulation and taxation of retail trade. The department store appeared in France as early as 1826, but small shopkeepers induced government to curb the competitive consequences of the innovation.[7] Before and immediately after World War II, taxation and regulation prevented the emergence of aggressive rivalry in retailing. By law a moratorium existed on creation of new variety stores; and the tax code discriminated against retailers with multiple outlets or large amounts of selling space per store.[8] During the following three decades, however, the newer forms of retailing came to suffer less discrimination at the hands of government. In 1951 the moratorium on new variety stores was terminated, and until 1957 the number of such stores increased rapidly.[9] Thereafter, the locus of rapid development shifted to self-service supermarkets and the even larger hypermarkets. Until the end of 1973, government did little if anything to impede establishment of large-scale retailing.

A number of changes in the tax laws also served to reduce the fiscal advantages of traditional shopkeepers. For example:

—In 1959 the income tax was modified to include a surtax (*taxe complémentaire*) on income not reported by the payer. This measure, designed to compensate for the widespread underreporting of such

6. The relationship between large retailers and foreign merchandise is discussed in OECD, *Japan*, pp. 40–43.

7. See Défossé, *Le Commerce Intérieur*, p. 85; and Nord, *Paris Shopkeepers and the Politics of Resentment*. The social impact of the department store is described in Zola, *Au Bonheur des Dames*.

8. Retailing between the world wars is described in Picard, "Structure Commerciale."

9. Under the law of May 24, 1951, the national government's representative in each *département* (the *préfet*) was empowered to authorize new construction. Such authorization quickly became routine. See Krier and Jallais, *Le Commerce Intérieur*, pp. 74–75.

income, affected self-employed shopkeepers more than large retail corporations.

—In 1954 the value-added tax began to replace the sales tax. In retail trade the transition was not compulsory until 1968; however, between 1954 and 1968 the new system could be adopted voluntarily. For the large retailer the VAT offered two big advantages. First, levied only on that portion of merchandise value that is added by the retailer, it was more favorable than a sales tax to sellers with low markups. Second, it entitled firms to deduct from VAT owed on their own sales the VAT included in their purchases of capital goods. Since the capital intensity of retailing tends to rise with retailer size, this opportunity tended to favor the large retailers.[10]

—For salaried employees, France's current system of social security, covering health and maternity as well as old age, survivorship, and unemployment, dates from 1945.[11] In 1961 the system was extended to self-employed farmers. Under the law of July 11, 1966, the health and maternity parts of the system were extended to self-employed shopkeepers on January 1, 1969. The fund created by this legislation was kept separate from those for other workers. Because shopkeepers tended to be old and declining in numbers, the social security taxes they could expect to pay were steeper than those paid by the large corporate retailers on behalf of their employees.

—In 1975 the government replaced the *patente* with the *taxe professionnelle*. Although the two had many points in common, the rate of the taxe professionnelle rose less steeply as the sizes and numbers of outlets owned by the taxpayer increased.[12]

These changes in regulation and taxation, considered individually, were certainly of modest import. Moreover, several advantages withdrawn from the small shops were replaced by new ones. For example, in a series of steps culminating in the loi Royer, the freedom to establish large retail stores was restricted.[13] The loi Royer required

10. Roy, *Les Commerçants,* p. 77.

11. Direction de la Sécurité Sociale, *La Sécurité Sociale en France,* p. 5.

12. Not all large retailers fared better under the taxe professionnelle than under the patente. According to Uri, *Changer l'Impôt (pour Changer la France),* pp. 189–90, the taxe professionnelle was introduced to reduce the burden of small enterprises; others found their taxes rising by as much as 700 percent.

13. Messerlin, *La Révolution Commerciale,* pp. 240–63. See also Roy, *Les*

anyone wishing to establish a retail outlet with selling area in excess of 1,500 square meters (1,000 square meters for towns of fewer than 40,000 people) to obtain the approval of a local planning commission. Each *département* would have its own commission, made up of nine local public officials, nine local merchants, and two representatives of consumers. If the commission failed to approve the project, its decision could be appealed to the minister of commerce, who, upon recommendation of a national commission could overturn the original decision. Only with the ultimate approval of the planning commission, local or national, could someone wishing to build a large store apply for a building permit.

The loi Royer also mandated harmonization of taxation as between self-employed merchants and salaried employees. In the context of income taxes this meant that the 20 percent exemption on salaried income would be extended to earnings from self-employment. In the context of social security contributions, it meant that the contributions paid by the self-employed would be no higher than those paid by the salaried.

DOMESTIC ANTITRUST LAW

On paper, at least, France's rules of competition underwent major changes after World War II. At midcentury, French antitrust law consisted primarily of article 419 of the criminal code. Although it appeared to prohibit pursuit or enjoyment of artificial profit (profit "other than that which would be derived from the natural operation of the law of supply and demand") in terms as sweeping as those of the Sherman Act, article 419 had not been enforced consistently.[14] Over the next four decades, on several occasions the French government strengthened its antitrust laws.[15]

Commerçants, pp. 120–21; and the circular published in *Journal Officiel de la République Française* (August 27, 1970), urging that retailers be allowed to play larger roles in urban planning. The loi Royer (no. 73-1193 of December 27, 1973) bears the name of the incumbent minister of commerce.

14. Plaisant, "France," vol. B3, p. FRA 1-2. The spirit of article 419 first appeared in legislation of 1791; its current form dates to 1926.

15. Throughout this chapter, unless otherwise noted, I shall refer to the version of legislation in effect on February 12, 1986, as published in Commission de la Concurrence, *Rapport au Ministre pour l'Année 1985*, pp. 133–40. This version includes the revisions contained in law 85-1408 of December 30, 1985. It does not reflect the major reforms in ordinance 86-1243 of December 1, 1986, which appears

As of 1985

—collective restraint of trade was potentially void, illegal, and subject to punishment;

—abuse of dominant market position was potentially illegal and subject to punishment;

—merger was subject to prevention or modification by the minister of economic affairs;

—certain unilateral restraints of trade, including resale price maintenance, refusal to sell, and discrimination among buyers, were potentially illegal and subject to punishment.

The first three rules were designed such that the legality of business behavior was determined by comparing losses of competition with gains of other sorts. Thus those who restrained trade collectively or abused dominant positions were exonerated if they could show that they simply obeyed relevant laws and regulations or that they contributed to economic progress while allowing consumers a fair share of the resulting gains.[16] Similarly, mergers that promoted economic progress sufficiently to compensate for their deleterious impact on competition were immune from modification or prevention by government.[17] In contrast, the rules limiting unilateral trade restraints did not entail balancing procedures.[18]

The administration of French antitrust law was complicated. Cases involving collective restraint or dominant position were studied by the specialized Commission de la Concurrence. The commission could launch an inquiry on its own initiative; it could also be activated by

---

in *Journal Officiel de la République Française* (December 8, 1987), pp. 14773–78; see appendix D.

16. The most often claimed source of economic progress was increased productivity. See Plaisant, "France," pp. FRA 2-42–FRA 2-44. The current version of this balancing formula is ordinance 86-1243, article 10, which resembles closely article 85(3) of the Treaty of Rome.

17. Law 77-806 of July 19, 1977, article 4. By statute, the measurement of competition must be conducted in an international framework. The current language on merger exemptions, ordinance 86-1243, article 41, differs little from that in law 77-806.

18. Under current rules, embodied in ordinance 86-1243, article 8, these practises are illegal only if they constitute abuse of a dominant market position or a dominant position vis-à-vis particular suppliers or customers. In this respect the French system has converged on the EC prototype. See, for example, *Istituto Chemioterapico Italiano SpA and Commercial Solvents Corp.* v. *EC Commission* [1974] 1 *CMLR* 309 (refusal to sell); and *United Brands Co. and United Brands Continentaal BV* v. *EC Commission*, [1978] *ECR* 207 (discrimination).

the minister of economic affairs, by regional governments, or by designated associations of consumers, producers, or workers.[19] However activated, the commission relied heavily on the ministry of economic affairs to supply it with evidence. Upon completion of its study the commission recommended a course of action to the minister of economic affairs.[20] The minister could hand the case to the public prosecutor for judicial proceedings, or, if the commission had so recommended, he could impose administrative fines.[21] Mergers were treated much like collective restraints and dominant positions. The main differences were that no one other than the minister of economic affairs could launch a merger inquiry by the commission and that companies engaged in merger could be punished only for violating a ministerial order, not for merger itself.

Before the reforms of 1986, unilateral restraints of trade (resale price maintenance, tying, discrimination, and refusal to sell) were treated less as antitrust issues than as problems associated with inflation control. As a result, ministerial decisions to attack such restraints did not result in deliberations of the Commission de la Concurrence. The staff of the ministry of economic affairs investigated potential violations of the law, and the ministry then decided whether to allow those accused of illegal restraints to pay a settlement fee (and

19. Until 1967, only the minister of economic affairs had the power to launch an inquiry. The commission received such authority in ordinance 67-835 of September 28, 1967; the other groups acquired it in law 77-806 of July 19, 1977, article 15.

20. Under ordinance 86-1243, article 11, the powers described in the next sentence now belong to the commission (renamed the Conseil de la Concurrence), not the minister.

21. Judicial proceedings could be based either on article 419 of the criminal code or on ordinance 45-1484 of June 30, 1945; see ordinance 45-1483 of June 30, 1945, article 52. Both types of cases entailed ordinary rules of criminal procedure (see ordinance 45-1484, article 38; and Plaisant, "France," pp. FRA 1-4, FRA 4-13). In most situations, the maximum penalties were two years in prison and Fr 360,000 in fine (*amende*) under article 419(2); and four years in prison and Fr 400,000 in fines (*sanction pécuniaire*) under ordinance 45-1484, article 41; see *Concurrence et Prix*. Today, the corresponding penalties, applicable to physical persons, are four years in prison and Fr 500,000.

The maximum administrative fine was 5 percent of the firm's domestic sales, calculated net of value-added tax. The minister could not choose a fine in excess of that recommended by the commission. Under circumstances specified in article 55 of ordinance 45-1483, the minister could impose fines of up to Fr 500,000 without a prior recommendation from the commission.

escape prosecution thereby) or to forward the case to a prosecutor for judicial action.[22] The prosecutor could return the case for settlement or launch judicial proceedings governed by substantially the same rules as those applied to collective restraint or abuse of dominant position.

The initial version of the 1945 antitrust ordinance did not allow private parties to sue for damages.[23] Nevertheless, French courts "eventually upheld the right of aggrieved parties to receive compensation as a result of violations of French antitrust law."[24] In 1973 both individuals and designated consumer groups acquired the explicit right to sue for damages.[25] Private parties may also sue for damages resulting from violation of article 419 of the criminal code.[26]

Despite their impressive development after World War II, most French rules of competition bear little relevance to the hypotheses under investigation here. In the first place, as with deregulation of product prices and financial markets, some of the legislation is too recent to have influenced French growth and structural change over the postwar period as a whole. For example, only since 1977 has the minister of economic affairs been able to control mergers or impose administrative fines on colluders and abusers of dominant positions. Even the public prosecutor was powerless to attack dominant positions until 1963. In the second place (and more important), until the late 1970s, infractions within the purview of the Commission de la

22. The settlement fee is known in French as a *transaction*. Initially, administrative settlements were also possible in cases involving article 50 of ordinance 45-1483, but this option had disappeared even before that ordinance had been repealed. See de Roux and Voillemot, *Le Droit Français de la Concurrence et de la Consommation*, p. 340, note 1.

23. The right to recover private damages was considered incompatible with the doctrine that economic legislation protects general, not individual, interests and also with the practice of administrative settlements (ibid., p. 353). If the latter interpretation is correct, one is led to ponder the possibility that government's revealed preference for *transactions* was caused less by a concern for competition than by a desire to have in hand one of those cards (described in chapter 3) that conferred general-purpose leverage over business enterprises.

24. Plaisant, "France," p. FRA 4-17.

25. Law 73-1193, article 45. Unlike American consent decrees and nolo contendere pleas, French settlement fees created presumptions of guilt in damage suits. In cases involving article 50, private parties could sue for damages as soon as the ministry of economic affairs handed over the matter to the prosecutor.

26. Plaisant, "France," p. FRA 4-18.

Concurrence were rarely enforced with relish. As long as the commission was activated solely by the minister of economic affairs, it investigated few collective restraints and even fewer dominant positions. During its first twenty years, from 1954 to 1973, the commission examined 105 cases, an average of 5 a year. Of the total, 99 involved collective restraint and only 6 pertained exclusively to dominant position. More recently, the pace of the commission's activity has quickened. From 1978 through 1986, it was activated on 294 occasions (139 times by the minister, 77 times by private organizations, 43 times by the judiciary, 27 times on its own motion, and 8 times by parliament); and it filed 179 reports. Some of the activations, however, merely requested the commission's point of view on prospective legislation.[27]

Not only was the number of investigations small but the number of exemptions was large. Between 1966 and 1973 the commission delivered forty-four reports in which it argued that firms had violated one or both of the presumptions against collective restraint and abuse of dominance. In nine of these, however, it also argued that the accused deserved an exemption.[28] Those unable to secure an exemption were rarely prosecuted. Not until 1966, more than a decade after the commission's birth, did one of its investigations result in a ministerial decision to pursue court action.[29] Of the thirty-five reports during 1966–73 in which the commission suspected illegal collective restraint or abused dominance, only eight were taken to court. Although the minister of economic affairs could declare particular restraints and abuses illegal, his "decisions" lacked legal force. Perhaps for that reason, as Clément notes, "cartels have never openly disagreed with them. How far they were followed is another question."

Whether or not they were prosecuted, few companies were punished severely. Until 1977 the minister of economic affairs lacked the authority to exact settlement fees from those engaged in collective trade restraint or abuse of dominant position. And the maximum

27. See Jenny and Weber, "French Antitrust Legislation," pp. 625, 638; and Commission de la Concurrence, *Rapport au Ministre pour l'Année 1986*, pp. 5–11.

28. Jenny and Weber, "French Antitrust Legislation," p. 625.

29. The first case was not litigated until 1968, the second not until 1971. Clément, "An Appraisal of French Antitrust Policy," p. 592.

penalty available to the courts was "much too low."[30] Nearly all companies that felt the bite of the law exercised their power in markets of minor economic consequence. No wonder such authorities as Frédéric Jenny and André-Paul Weber intimated that the pre-1977 version of French policy was an exercise in futility.

At one level, these failures of French antitrust policy can be imputed to the poverty of resources devoted to it. During the early 1970s the commission employed only six full-time investigators. Until the reforms of 1977 the commissioners occupied simultaneously "important positions either in government or in the business community."[31] Even today, only the chairman is expected to work full time on commission business. Under French enforcement procedures, the infrequency of commission reports constricted sharply the number of cases that could be brought to court for punishment. Given the rarity of punishment, the system had little deterrent value.

Ultimately, regulation of collective restraints, dominant positions, and mergers failed to impinge forcefully on France's major industrial markets because government did not want it to. Convinced that productive inefficiency in the industrial sector could and should be remedied by increases in the sizes of plants and companies as well as by specialization and technological cooperation among companies, government first tolerated and then encouraged activities incompatible with a vigorous antitrust policy. Even as the antitrust law of July 19, 1977, was being debated in parliament, the prime minister assured interested parties that the law would not be used "to call into question the policy of industrial concentration that has been pursued for many years by successive French governments."[32] Under the circumstances it is hardly surprising that government allocated few resources to antitrust enforcement during the bulk of the period examined in this volume. Nor is it surprising that few of the investigations mounted by the commission touched the central nervous system of the economy.

30. Ibid., p. 593. Initially, the maximum penalty for violation of ordinance 45-1483 was Fr 100,000 (new francs). Currently, it is Fr 200,000 and two years in jail. Criminal prosecutions under article 419 of the criminal code entail a maximum fine of Fr 360,000.

31. Jenny and Weber, "French Antitrust Legislation," p. 638.

32. Aujac, "An Introduction to French Industrial Policy," p. 28.

Although government failed to move vigorously against collective restraints, dominant positions, and major mergers, it did intervene actively against certain unilateral restraints of trade. The oldest, strongest, and most distinctive of these regulations covered refusals to sell. In June 1945, confronted by the inflationary legacy of wartime scarcity, France's provisional government established a pervasive system of price control. Recognizing that mere regulation of prices might simply induce hoarding, the government included in its ordinance a provision whereby refusals to sell to bona fide buyers would, under most circumstances, be considered tantamount to illegal pricing (see appendix D).

In both administrative guidelines and judicial opinions, refusal to sell was interpreted broadly. It was held to occur when sellers charged abnormally high prices, offered credit on abnormally restrictive terms, or offered unrequested versions of differentiated products.[33] Although the ordinance offered several defenses to those who had refused to sell, only three were important in practice.[34] The first was based on exclusive dealing. During the 1950s French courts supported manufacturers with networks of exclusive dealers who argued that their inventories should be legally unavailable to merchants outside the network. As a result, virtually any seller could establish a dealer network and avoid the presumption against refusal to sell. During its first fifteen years, the presumption against refusal to sell signified little indeed.[35]

In 1960 the government issued guidelines designed to limit the use of exclusive dealing to negate the presumption against refusal to

33. On the last point, for example, see *Barjolle*, Cour de Cassation, chambre criminelle, July 13, 1961, in which a manufacturer of cookies and crackers was convicted of refusal to sell when he sought to package cookies ordered by a particular wholesaler (known for his discounting) in a manner different from that used for other clients (and hence known to ultimate customers).

34. The defenses based on state action and on physical availability of merchandise were interpreted extremely narrowly. If a seller wished to invoke laws or regulations to justify his reluctance to deal, he had to show that they prohibited the sale in explicit and specific terms. As for availability, although the seller was entitled to maintain a reasonable inventory, he had to handle orders on a first-in, first–met basis. Unless output was unavoidably limited over a longish period of time, the seller could not even give preference to customers of long standing.

35. Azéma, *Le Droit Français de la Concurrence*.

sell. Two years later the guidelines were endorsed by France's highest appellate court.[36] Since 1962 exclusive dealing arrangements must satisfy many conditions before they can be used to justify refusal to sell. In particular, the exclusive dealing must be reciprocal: within the relevant geographic territory, neither buyer nor seller can deal with a third party.[37] Moreover, neither the aim nor the effect of the exclusivity can be to maintain resale prices.[38] Finally, the exclusivity must benefit consumers. In relatively few industries did exclusive dealing meet these and other requirements. As a result, the presumption against refusal to sell suddenly acquired practical significance.

Shortly after the *Brandt* decision, certain lower courts began to accept a second defense of refusal to sell known as selective selling. In selective selling as in exclusive dealing, the manufacturer establishes a network of dealers; unlike exclusive dealing, however, selective selling requires neither the buyer nor the seller to refrain from transactions with third parties. In the eyes of the favorable courts, selective selling justifies refusal to sell as long as the seller's distribution network is constructed objectively, provides desirable services to consumers, does not restrict intrabrand competition unduly, and does not buttress resale price maintenance. These views have been upheld by the Cour de Cassation.[39] In practice, however, the legality of

36. *Nicolas et Société Brandt,* Cour de Cassation, chambre criminelle, July 11, 1962 (*Jurisclasseur Périodique,* 62, II.12799). The guidelines had appeared in the Fontanet Circular of March 31, 1960.

37. See *Brunel,* Cour de Cassation, chambre criminelle, October 22, 1964 (refusal to supply third parties is not justified by an agreement whereby the seller agrees to deal exclusively with a group of retail pharmacies, but the pharmacies fail to agree to deal exclusively with the manufacturer).

38. In the *Brandt* case, upon remand, the Cour d'Appel d'Amiens ultimately found (May 9, 1963) that the manufacturer designed his dealer network primarily to exclude price competition at the retail level. See also *Sénéclauze et Thurin,* Cour de Cassation, chambre criminelle, March 21, 1972 (a seller may require a buyer not to solicit sales outside his territory, but he may not require a buyer to ensure that those who buy from him do not resell the merchandise outside that territory).

39. *Lanvin,* Cour de Cassation, chambre criminelle, November 2, 1984; and *Biscottes Clément,* Cour de Cassation, chambre criminelle, November 15, 1984. To choose one's dealers objectively means to choose them on the basis of their ability to provide the kinds of services customers are likely to want in respect of the goods in

selective selling has been confined to a few types of products, such as perfumes and beauty aids.

The third important defense against a charge of refusal to sell involves the nature of the buyer's request. If the buyer intends to denigrate the seller's merchandise—for example, by comparing it adversely with that of another manufacturer—or if the seller lacks the facilities necessary to sell the good, such as refrigeration for perishable foods, then the seller is justified in refusing to deal. Between 1970 and 1980 a buyer's request was sometimes considered abnormal if he intended to resell at discount prices. Under a 1963 law sellers were entitled to refuse buyers who sold their goods at unusually low markups. Between the circular of May 30, 1970, and its replacement in 1980, "abnormally low" was sometimes interpreted to mean "below the norm in retail trade as a whole." Since 1980, however, "abnormally low" has meant "below the markup on competing brands sold in the same retail outlet." After three decades of interpretation, the definition of abnormal request to purchase remains incompletely settled. On one point, however, the courts have been consistent. To demonstrate the abnormality of a buyer's request, it is necessary (but not sufficient) for the unwilling seller to show that he applies the same criteria to all buyers.

Resale price maintenance, establishment by a seller of the minimum price at which buyers can resell the product, is the other unilateral restraint of trade to receive major attention under French law. Although a general presumption against RPM was established in 1952, it initially lacked force.[40] The ministry of economic affairs exempted many differentiated products, including electrical appliances and perfumes, from the ban.[41] Moreover, those lacking such an exemption could still recommend resale prices with impunity. Over time,

---

question. See Cour d'Appel de Paris, May 26, 1965 (*Gazette du Palais*, 1965, 2, p. 76). See also *Estée Lauder*, Tribunal de Grande Instance de Paris, February 1, 1978.

40. Law 52-835 of July 18, 1952. Before ordinance 86-1243 of December 1, 1986, the relevant text was ordinance 45-1483 of June 30, 1945, article 37(4); see appendix D.

41. Guyénot, *Le Droit des Ententes Industrielles*, p. 19; compare Clément, "An Appraisal of French Antitrust Policy," pp. 595–96, who asserts that "very few exemptions are granted, so that the rule of prohibition, rightly deemed fundamental in 1953, can be said to have been maintained with the same spirit throughout these twenty years."

however, "it has become increasingly difficult to secure exemptions," and under the terms of a 1967 ordinance the minister of economic affairs acquired the right to ban by regulation the suggestion of resale prices.[42] During the late 1970s the minister made frequent use of this authority.[43]

Unfortunately, it is impossible to quantify government's effort to curb unilateral vertical restraints. Enforcement was handled by the ministry of economic affairs, not the Commission de la Concurrence, and many of the ministry's investigations ended in administrative settlement rather than legal prosecution. In keeping with French administrative practice, such settlements were rarely publicized. Even judicial decisions could escape full reporting.[44]

In sum, the teeth in French antitrust policy were developed to masticate inflation, which, if less intense than it was shortly after World War II, continued to afflict and constrain French governments. Hence the sustained desire of public officials to curb vertical restraints. If horizontal restraints and dominant positions were regulated weakly until government tempered its partiality for industrial concentration, refusal to sell and RPM have been treated harshly since 1960 at least.

Impact on Market Structure

Changes in the regulation and taxation of large commercial enterprises, coupled with changes in domestic antitrust policy, led to increased competition in retail trade. The change is discernible in market structure and market conduct alike.

I suggested in chapter 4 that concentration measured both at the level of individual sellers and at the level of strategic groups is the

42. Plaisant, "France," p. FRA 2-29, note 9. The 1967 ordinance was 67-835 of September 28, 1967.

43. Azéma, *Le Droit Français de la Concurrence*, p. 237, note 8.

44. According to a former director of antitrust activity in the ministry of finance, "ninety-nine percent of the cases relating to refusal to sell, resale price maintenance, price discrimination, loss-leader selling, and so on, are settled without anything at all being published. Such a practice leads inevitably to an underestimation of the work really done." See Clément, "An Appraisal of French Antitrust Policy," p. 590. Since implementation of ordinance 86-1243 of December 1, 1986, refusal to sell and RPM are both handled by the Conseil de la Concurrence. Apart from any substantive merits of the change, the new system should open policymaking in these areas to greater public scrutiny.

single most important element of market structure. In the context of retail trade, however, seller concentration does not always correlate well with market power. Even in local markets, retailing of particular commodities is often handled by a large number of similarly sized enterprises, and yet behavior and performance often diverge sharply from the predictions of the competitive model.

In retailing, it is concentration at the strategic group level that provides the better understanding of market behavior. As long as most sellers share the same view of the world because of similarities in production methods, patterns of integration, and patterns of control, cooperation tends to be pursued relatively easily. Accordingly, I shall focus my attention here on the postwar evolution of concentration at the level of strategic groups.

Starting in the early 1960s, retail sales became much less concentrated in a few strategic groups of sellers. The decline was especially apparent in food. At the beginning of this period, food was sold primarily in small, individually owned stores (appendix table A-72). Chains of small general stores split most of the rest of the business with enterprises outside retailing (bakeries, for example, are classified in manufacturing rather than in retail trade). In most important respects—procurement of goods, scale of operations, role of the shopkeeper in selection of the client's merchandise—the three types of store differed little one from another.[45]

The first French supermarket opened its doors in 1957. At the time, no chain store exceeded 100 square meters in floorspace.[46] Since then the number of such outlets has grown rapidly. Starting in 1962, the number of supermarkets increased by at least 100 a year. Expansion was especially pronounced during 1969-70, when the number of supermarkets increased by 783 (appendix table A-73). In 1962 supermarkets sold 1 percent of food purchased by French households; by 1984 their share had risen to 18 percent.

---

45. Self-service first appeared in 1948; see Nicolas and Bury, "Les Grands Groupes Commerciaux Français de 1972 à 1979," p. 18. Messerlin, *La Révolution Commerciale*, p. 30, argues that the practice did not assume practical significance until the late 1950s.

46. Nicolas and Bury, "Les Grands Groupes Commerciaux Français de 1972 à 1979," p. 18.

In some respects the supermarkets seemed to constitute a new strategic group. Their scale and their use of self-service conferred levels and structures of cost that diverged sharply from those of their rivals. As a result, the supermarkets were unlikely to share the price opinions of their wizened colleagues. On the other hand, supermarkets and small shops were often controlled by the same parent company. Just as most of the variety stores had been launched by companies originally specialized in the operation of department stores, so the supermarkets were frequently opened by companies with chains of small general stores. For example, in 1979, Casino operated 2,025 small shops and 74 supermarkets; Radar operated 1,718 small shops and 144 supermarkets, Comptoirs Modernes operated 1,174 small shops and 153 supermarkets, and Docks de France operated 256 small shops and 50 supermarkets.[47] As a result, many of the supermarkets, like many of the variety stores before them, could be expected to exercise restraint in their rivalry with traditional outlets.[48]

The first of France's giant discount stores was opened by Carrefour in 1963. Unlike the early supermarkets, the first hypermarkets (stores with more than 2,500 square meters of selling space and a large parking lot, most of which emphasize food but also stock home furnishings, apparel, and home and personal care products) were launched by enterprises not yet well established in retailing.[49] As a result, the early hypermarkets differed from other food outlets not only in level and structure of cost but also in ownership. The appearance of the hypermarkets clearly signaled the creation of a new strategic group. The growth of the hypermarkets paralleled the growth of the supermarkets. The growth was especially pronounced between 1968 and 1973, so that by 1972 hypermarkets accounted for more than 5 percent of household expenditure on food (table A-72). By 1975 the hypermarkets sold almost as much food to households as the

47. Marenco and Quin, *Structures et Tendances de la Distribution Française,* pp. 42–43 (cited hereafter as Marenco and Quin, *Tableau de Bord, 1980–1981*).

48. Over time, however, the share of the chain stores in supermarket sales declined. As of 1984 chain stores accounted for 33 percent of supermarket sales, and cooperatives contributed another 7 percent; but the remaining 60 percent was attributable to independents (see INSEE C128, p. 153). Today it may be reasonable to consider supermarkets a nontraditional strategic group.

49. Krier and Jallais, *Le Commerce Intérieur,* p. 100.

supermarkets did, and by 1984 they accounted for 17 percent of household food expenditure.

By 1967 the traditional chain store companies recognized the importance of hypermarkets and began to create their own. Meanwhile, some of the early hypermarket specialists acquired chains of supermarkets and small shops. As a result, by the late 1970s the distinction between hypermarkets and other strategic groups had blurred.[50] Nevertheless, in 1979 Carrefour, the largest hypermarket chain, continued to realize 100 percent of its food sales in giant discount stores; the corresponding figure for the fifth largest hypermarket chain was 93 percent.[51] As late as 1984 the traditional chains, involved in supermarkets and small shops as well as in hypermarkets, accounted for just 24 percent of all hypermarket sales.[52]

The hypermarkets tended to locate in suburbs of major metropolitan areas, and each such area tended to contain more than one. Thus, in a study of forty-nine hypermarkets in the Carrefour chain, six faced one local competitor, twenty-four faced two, and seventeen faced three.[53] Food markets with structural competition across strategic groups also displayed some structural competition within the hypermarket category.[54]

In sum, the number of food retailers has been declining. Among the largest chains, several mergers have occurred.[55] Nevertheless, when retail establishments are divided by scale, by type of ownership, or by both, the number and size distribution of strategic groups reveal unmistakable evolution toward competitive market structure.

50. Thus in 1979 the number of hypermarkets per chain was as follows: Casino, fifteen; Docks de France, thirty-five; Radar, nineteen; and Comptoirs Modernes, twelve. See Marenco and Quin, *Tableau de Bord, 1980–1981*, pp. 42–43.

51. The chain in question, Auchan, was another early independent; see ibid., pp. 50, 66.

52. INSEE C128, p. 153. Recent information on the importance of hypermarkets appears in "La Croissance du Commerce en 1987."

53. Messerlin, *La Révolution Commerciale*, p. 146.

54. According to Nicolas and Bury, "Les Grands Groupes Commerciaux Français de 1972 à 1979," pp. 7–9, few of the chain store corporations operate nationwide. As a result, within geographically meaningful markets the strategic group labeled supermarkets probably contained fewer sellers than one might expect from the aggregate number of French chain store corporations.

55. Marenco and Quin, *Tableau de Bord, 1980–1981*, pp. 58–64.

It is difficult to pronounce generally on the evolution of strategic groups in the rest of retailing. If conventional classifications are used, other branches of retail trade have undergone little change (appendix table A-74). The traditional representatives of large-scale distribution, the variety stores and the department stores, failed to increase their share of nonfood sales. In fact, between 1962 and 1984, the share of nonfood sales to households decreased for department stores as well as for small food stores. During the same period, hypermarkets came to account for 7 percent of such sales, while nonfood specialty stores, which accounted for two-thirds of relevant sales in 1962, lost 8 percentage points of market share.

These figures give the impression of little movement, but they may underestimate the amount of change that actually occurred. During this period a number of discount houses, some of them chains, were launched. In terms of selling area, however, few differed perceptibly from their established rivals. As a result, changes in the roles of two strategic groups—independents on the one hand and discount chains on the other—are difficult to detect (table A-74 also does not distinguish among specialty stores of different scales). Fortunately, it will be possible to examine evidence of competitive behavior, and that evidence accords with the hypothesis that structural change did occur.

The Story of Edouard Leclerc

The emergence of large discount stores does not guarantee the emergence of genuinely competitive behavior. In some lines of business such stores have yet to establish market shares sufficient to shape market outcomes.[56] In other lines of business the opposite is true, opening the possibility that the large stores would exercise market power after driving smaller ones out of business. Finally, regardless of market share, fearful that government might intervene

56. For example, as recently as 1981, the Commission de la Concurrence stated that "industrial bakeries do not yet constitute a substantial factor in markets for freshly baked products." Quoted in Conseil Economique et Social, "L'Analyse des Circuits et des Coûts de Transformation et de Distribution de Produits Agro-Alimentaires et Leur Eventuel Aménagement," p. 17.

to protect small business, the large stores might have discounted only a few prices, just enough to gain a reputation for low prices, aligning the rest on those of the traditional shops and realizing hefty profit margins.[57]

It is certainly possible to observe anticompetitive behavior in major merchandisers. One important example involved Darty, a large retailer of household appliances.[58] Darty advertised prominently that the chain would match the price of any competitor. When furnished by a customer with specific evidence of a rival's low price, Darty would urge the appropriate manufacturer to orchestrate mutual price increases at the retail level. The Commission de la Concurrence concluded that this amounted to illegal cooperation and recommended a heavy administrative fine (Fr 5 million). The minister of economic affairs opted for Fr 2.5 million.

The Darty case may not be exceptional, but it certainly fails to convey an accurate picture of the impact of the new forms of distribution on competition in retailing. The competitive behavior of discounters is more readily apparent in the story of Edouard Leclerc, which merits sustained attention because Leclerc is widely perceived to be the leading French practitioner of competition since World War II.

ACT I

In 1949 Leclerc opened a general food store in his hometown of Landerneau (population 15,000) in western Brittany. Similar in scale to traditional food stores but austere in construction and decoration, Leclerc's shop sold a slim selection of products at discount prices.

---

57. Later in this chapter, gasoline shall appear as a major arena for discounting; and yet in 1984 gasoline, lubricants, and tires accounted for only 8.6 percent of hypermarket sales; see INSEE C128, pp. 148–49.

Edouard Leclerc has argued that many hypermarkets, like the variety stores and department stores before them, are content to price their merchandise just below the levels established in small shops, even though the big stores buy their goods for far less. In Leclerc's view, big stores of this type need the small stores to justify the height of their prices; see *Ma Vie pour un Combat*, p. 84.

58. Commission de la Concurrence, *Avis sur des Pratiques Concertées entre Fournisseurs et Distributeurs dans le Secteur des Appareils Electroménagers et Electro-Acoustiques*; and Minister of Economic Affairs, *Décision no. 80-01/DC Concernant le Secteur des Appareils Electroménagers et Electro-Acoustiques*. Both appear in Commission de la Concurrence, *Rapport au Ministre pour l'Année 1980*, app. 3.

The strategy succeeded. Not only did the store rapidly outgrow its quarters, but by 1953 several other stores had appeared under the Leclerc name. These were owned not by Leclerc himself but by independent merchants prepared to limit gross margins to the relevant wholesale margin or 11 percent, whichever was smaller. In return, they could use both the Leclerc name and (after its formation a few years later) the Leclerc subsidiary specializing in purchase of goods from manufacturers. Leclerc's strategy provoked first derision and then discomfort among established retailers, and they were soon plotting to force him out of the market.

A few years after Leclerc began business, a local representative of the treasury department came to visit him. Claiming that Leclerc could only afford to charge such low prices if he cheated on his taxes, the civil servant threatened to accuse him of tax fraud. In particular, he demanded that Leclerc pay a tax on empty bottles. When Leclerc offered to contact the ministry of finance to determine whether he was obliged to pay such a tax, the official urged him to forget the whole matter. Apparently, he had been put up to the task by Leclerc's competitors.[59]

Next, the retailers threatened to boycott any wholesalers or manufacturers who continued to supply the discounter with mer-chandise, and by 1953 several major manufacturers did attempt to withhold supplies.[60] Among these was Lesieur, one of France's leading suppliers of edible oils. When a meeting with Paul Lesieur failed to restore deliveries, Leclerc took his case directly to the ministry of finance. His timing was propitious. The government of the day was preoccupied with rising prices and decided that support of Leclerc's efforts to reduce gross margins in retailing would signal commitment to a serious attack on inflation. The ministry's triumvirate in charge of fighting inflation told the discounter that renewed shipments from

59. Leclerc, *Ma Vie pour un Combat*, pp. 44–45. This is the principal source for much of the following narrative.

60. Even if they had not been pressured by their traditional clients, manufacturers and wholesalers had reason to view Leclerc with alarm. If aggressive discounters became major forces in food retailing, they might succeed in forcing their suppliers to reduce profit margins upstream, much as John Kenneth Galbraith predicted (at just this time) in *American Capitalism*. In particular, as large numbers of retailers began to pressure their suppliers, oligopolistic arrangements at the manufacturing and wholesaling levels might be jeopardized.

Lesieur would be arranged. Shortly thereafter, Lesieur's oil did flow anew.

Within a matter of months, however, a leading manufacturer of chocolate notified Leclerc of his intention to stop supplies. Once again, Leclerc complained directly to the ministry of finance, and although the composition of the government had changed, the ministry once again supported him. It immediately launched an investigation of the chocolate company's taxes, which revealed that the company's accountant was trafficking illegally in foreign exchange. After negotiations between ministry and manufacturer, shipments to Leclerc resumed. In no small measure, government's decision to build a new weapon against vertical restraints (the decree of August 9, 1953, prohibiting RPM under most circumstances) was a response to Leclerc's request for help.

Viewing government's early and public support of Leclerc, many manufacturers and wholesalers resumed their dealings with him. Had government not intervened, the discounter probably would have expired. And if he had failed, other innovators, from André Eyssel to Marcel Fournier, might not have followed his lead.[61] In the event, one year after the new rules limiting vertical restraints of trade, Leclerc had formed an association of twenty-five stores, most of which were independently owned.

Despite the signals indicating government's lack of tolerance for vertical restraints of trade, conservative retailers continued to pressure manufacturers to withhold supplies from discounters. As a result, traditional manufacturers, wholesalers, and retailers fought the government's effort to prohibit RPM. In 1958 their efforts seemed to succeed when France's highest administrative court, the Conseil d'Etat, declared that certain parts of the 1953 decree were void on technical grounds.[62] While the government remained committed in

61. In 1954 André Eyssel and his Fédération Nationale des Achats des Cadres (FNAC) opened a tiny discount store specialized in photographic equipment. Today, the FNAC operates a chain of stores, some quite large, selling a wide variety of nonfood products at discount prices. Marcel Fournier, together with Denis Defforey, founded Carrefour, the first and largest operator of hypermarkets, and has openly acknowledged his debt to Leclerc; see Roy, *Les Commerçants*, p. 47.

62. *Syndicat des Grossistes en Matériel Electrique de la Région de Provence et Autres; Recueil des Arrêts du Conseil d'Etat*, 1958, pp. 358–59. According to the Conseil d'Etat, the law of July 11, 1953, did not extend to the establishment of

principle to the modernization of retailing, restoring within a matter of days the substance of the 1953 decree, it did not leap to prosecute those refusing to sell to discounters.

Leclerc immediately felt the effects of these developments. Because a disproportionate number of the stores belonging to his association were located in Brittany, the large chain store companies, which operated in many regions, began to sell at cost in Leclerc's home region. In addition, several large manufacturers, among them SOPAD (the French subsidiary of Nestlé), Fromageries Bel, Biscuiterie Alsacienne, Biscuiterie Brun, and Liebig, sought to cut him off. Apart from bald refusals to sell, they engaged in such discriminatory tactics as requiring him to pay in advance, refusing customary rebates for fidelity and quantity, and even sabotaging shipments. They also withdrew their advertising from newspapers that endorsed his philosophy of retailing.

Leclerc reacted quickly. He diversified the geographic distribution of Leclerc stores. In particular, at the urging of several labor unions, he entered the Grenoble market in 1958. Using union money to open the store, he himself took charge of operations. To retaliate against those lowering margins selectively in Brittany, he set his Grenoble margins at 7 percent, well below the 11 percent practiced in other Leclerc stores. When manufacturers refused to supply his new store, Leclerc trucked to Grenoble merchandise ordered for the purpose and delivered to his Breton outlets. After inciting the chain stores to surround his Grenoble store with a bevy of shops, he suddenly withdrew from the market.

In October 1959 Leclerc turned to political action. Writing to Michel Debré, president of the council of ministers, he requested enforcement of the law and argued that his decision to open new stores in areas not yet benefiting from his approach, including Paris and Marseille, would depend on the government's willingness to intervene. Debré quickly promised action from public prosecutors. But when Leclerc stores began to open in the retailing of apparel, they encountered resistance from such manufacturers as Eminence, Le Bourget, Poron, and Seligman. As a result, on March 8, 1960, the

---

criminal penalties for certain types of behavior. As a result, the conseil declared *ultra vires* articles 2 and 3 of the decree of August 9, 1953.

discounter wrote anew to the prime minister. This time, according to Leclerc, Charles de Gaulle intervened. In response to de Gaulle's instructions, the minister of commerce, Joseph Fontanet, issued a circular warning the traditionalists that government meant to enforce the presumptions against refusal to sell and RPM.

Observing the determination of government to prosecute, the traditionalists sought a judicial interpretation of the rules that would exonerate de facto their refusals to sell to discounters. In particular, they claimed it was abnormal for discount stores with spartan interiors and unskilled salespeople to want to sell such fancy items as perfumes and such technically complex items as radios.

With both sides eager to establish the meaning of the rules against vertical trade restraints, extensive litigation ensued. When the smoke had cleared, the Cour de Cassation had interpreted the rules in favor of the discount stores.[63] In 1954 there had been 25 stores using the Leclerc name. In 1958 there were 15 such stores in Brittany alone. By 1974 the association numbered 350 stores, including 30 in the Paris area.[64]

By the mid 1960s, then, government seemed to have demonstrated firmly its commitment to modernize retailing. It is no accident that discount retailing began to proliferate when it did. Whatever its effect on the state of competition in general, France's regulation of refusal to sell certainly helped to force reluctant manufacturers to supply discount retailers. In the words of a former director of antitrust activity at the ministry of economic affairs: "Many changes [in the field of distribution] may be imputed to external causes, such as the growing part of the population living in towns. It may also be observed that somewhat similar changes have taken place in countries . . . with milder legal provisions. But I am quite sure that the changes in France would not have been so rapid and important as they have been and still continue to be, without our rules and their vigilant and vigorous administrative enforcement."[65] In persistently expanding his association of stores while cajoling government to ensure his supplies,

63. *Nicolas et Société Brandt*, Cour de Cassation, chambre criminelle, July 11, 1962.

64. As of 1983 there were 450 Leclerc stores, including 58 hypermarkets; Krier and Jallais, *Le Commerce Intérieur*, p. 96.

65. Clément, "An Appraisal of French Antitrust Policy," p. 602.

Edouard Leclerc deserves much of the credit for rooting discount retailing in France.

ACT II

After losing the battle on the judicial front, the traditionalists turned to legislative and administrative tactics. In 1963, just one year after the *Brandt* decision, it became illegal under most circumstances for merchants to set selling prices below purchase prices.[66] The measure was not as bland as it sounded. Purchase prices were to be measured on the basis of invoices, even though French manufacturers customarily granted rebates that did not appear there. Tied to the quantity purchased, the rebates were paid monthly, quarterly, and annually, amounting, according to Leclerc, to as much as 25 percent of the purchase price appearing on an invoice.[67] Since the rebates went primarily to large retailers, the new rule discouraged more than selling at a loss. It impeded large retailers from selling at low margins. When the bureaucracy proceeded to enforce this law desultorily, the traditional merchants pressured the fledgling government of Georges Pompidou into writing a circular warning discounters that rebates not appearing on the invoice could not be subtracted from the purchase price.[68]

The tightening of the rule against selling below acquisition cost was accompanied by inauguration of a rule against promotional pricing. With promotional pricing defined as sale of a brand of merchandise at abnormally low markups (abnormal being defined as low in comparison either with the past or with markups on competing brands), the measure was designed to curb price competition in retailing. As an incentive to comply, the circular announced that merchants engaged in promotional pricing would forfeit their protection from refusal by manufacturers or wholesalers to supply them. Although the government replaced the 1970 text with the circular of September 22, 1980, reaffirming the right to sell at systematically low markups, it remained the case that manufacturers and wholesalers could legally refuse to supply those guilty of promotional pricing.

66. Law 63-628 of July 2, 1963, article 1.
67. Leclerc, *Ma Vie pour un Combat*, p. 85.
68. Circular and communiqué of May 30, 1970, *Relative à Certaines Mesures d'Assainissement de la Concurrence.*

In 1985 the government again weakened the presumption against refusal to sell.[69] Manufacturers and wholesalers could now refuse to sell as long as their distribution contracts met criteria established in ordinance 45-1483, article 50, which accepted vertical restraints more readily than had article 37. However laudable the attempt to unify domestic antitrust law within the framework of article 50, this reform weakened the behavioral obligation of manufacturers to supply maverick retailers. In their biggest legislative coup the traditionalists won enactment of new restrictions on the creation of large retail outlets. As discussed above, under the loi Royer of 1973, subject ultimately to appeals heard by the minister of commerce, local boards could block construction of new large stores.

Leclerc did not greet these changes in the government's position passively. He deliberately defied the law against selling below purchase price by taking account of future rebates. He challenged the loi Royer, which he considered unconstitutional, in much the same manner. Despite physical attempts by a small business group to prevent it, he proceeded with construction of a Leclerc store in Rochefort, a small town on the Atlantic Coast, without awaiting the approval of the regional zoning commission.

In recent years, various members of Leclerc's association have persisted in their efforts to obtain authorization to build large stores. When the local commissions have denied requests, they have appealed with mixed results to higher authority. In 1981 Leclerc himself obtained approval from the minister of commerce to build a large store in his home town of Landerneau, an approval the local merchants fought in administrative court but lost. Then in 1982 the préfet of Morbihan, the département in which Landerneau is located, refused to grant Leclerc a building permit on the grounds that his project was incompatible with the land-use plan developed for the area. The Conseil d'Etat upheld an administrative court's decision that the préfet's behavior was justified.[70] In contrast, another member of the Leclerc association, the Société Thouars Distribution, received authorization from the minister of commerce to build a shopping center in the small town of Parthenay. Although the minister failed to approve

69. Law 85-1408 of December 30, 1985.
70. *L'Hénaff*, Conseil d'Etat, December 4, 1985; *Recueil des Décisions du Conseil d'Etat*, 1985, pp. 350–51.

the project according to the timetable set out in law, the Conseil d'Etat did not side with the Parthenay merchants seeking to block it.[71] The conclusion to be drawn from these cases is the unwillingness of Leclerc to allow the loi Royer to block all new construction of large stores.[72]

ACT III

If Leclerc spent the 1950s fighting private efforts to limit his ability to charge low prices, he devoted the early 1980s to challenging government's efforts to control his behavior. Books and gasoline formed the terrain of battle.

When the Barre government of the late 1970s deregulated industrial prices, the ministry of finance prohibited publishers from suggesting retail prices for books.[73] This led to substantial expansion of such discount booksellers as the FNAC. For that very reason, perhaps, on August 10, 1981, parliament enacted a bill establishing RPM for books.[74] With respect to books published in France, it required French retailers to charge no less than 95 percent of the manufacturer's suggested retail price. Greater discounts could be offered on books published more than two years earlier and held by the store for more than six months. Sales to libraries, government bodies, and educational institutions were exempt. Books published abroad were treated in much the same way, except the task of establishing a suggested retail price fell to the importer. In the case of books published in France, exported, and then reimported, the importer could not set a price below that established by the French publisher.

The Société Thouars Distribution, a member of Leclerc's association located in Thouars, a small town near Poitiers, challenged the law by

71. *Union des Commerçants Artisans et Industriels de Parthenay,* Conseil d'Etat, February 25, 1983; *Recueil des Décisions du Conseil d'Etat,* 1983, pp. 80–81.

72. Even the Chirac government, committed in principle to increased competition, gave instructions, through Minister of Commerce Georges Chavanes, that the loi Royer should be strictly enforced. See Delavennat, "Qui A Peur de la Concurrence?" p. 29.

73. Arrêté 79/07P of February 23, 1979; Azéma, *Le Droit Français de la Concurrence,* p. 237, note 8. Article 37(4) of ordinance 45-1483 created a presumption against RPM but permitted suggestion of resale prices in all industries where it was not explicitly prohibited by regulation.

74. It became known as the loi Lang, after Minister of Culture Jack Lang. See Messerlin, *La Révolution Commerciale,* pp. 264–82.

selling books published in France at prices more than 5 percent below those established by the publishers. On the initiative of several competing bookshops and the trade association of French bookstores, a trial court ordered the discounter to stop violating the 1981 act; otherwise, he and the Leclerc group would both be subject to fines.[75] On appeal, the discounter and the Leclerc group argued that the French law was void because it violated the Treaty of Rome. In their view the treaty prevented the French government from regulating the price at which books imported into France, even those that had been published in France, could be sold. The French appellate court asked the EC Court of Justice to appraise the merits of this allegation.[76]

The EC Court of Justice struck down two features of the French law. It held that retail prices of books published outside France could not be set by the importer because such a requirement is tantamount to a quantitative restriction of trade and violates article 30 of the Treaty of Rome. It also held that retail prices of books published in France, exported, and then reimported for sale in France could be set in practice by the publisher under only one circumstance: when it could be established that the books "were exported for the sole purpose of re-importation in order to circumvent the legislation in question."[77]

Although the court's judgment supported him incompletely, Leclerc continued to discount his books by 20 percent, and as a result the Leclerc stores became the second largest bookseller in France.[78] To some extent, Leclerc's boldness may stem from the expectation that the EC Commission will preempt national policymaking on RPM in books. The significance of this round of legal skirmishing is not only the continued efforts of Leclerc to erode private and public impediments to competition in retailing but also the potential constraints faced by the French government when it seeks to weaken the forces of competition in particular retail markets.

75. Tribunal de Grande Instance, Bressuire, order of March 11, 1982.

76. *Association des Centres Distributeurs Edouard Leclerc* v. *Thouars Distribution SA and Others,* Cour d'Appel de Poitiers, September 28, 1983; [1984] 1 *CMLR* 273.

77. *Association des Centres Distributeurs Edouard Leclerc and Others* v. *"Au Blé Vert" Sarl and Others,* case 229/83, EC Court of Justice, January 10, 1985; [1985] 2 *CMLR* 286, 315.

78. Santini, "Livre: La Solution Douce," p. 29.

From a legal standpoint the situation in gasoline differed little from that in books. In both cases, government established minimum prices for retail sale, and Leclerc claimed its actions violated the Treaty of Rome. In terms of economic significance, however, the two differed substantially.

Ever since 1928, ostensibly for national security, the government had regulated the industry to ensure that domestically owned petroleum companies would enjoy world-class expertise and market power in all phases of the petroleum business. The retail market for gasoline was regulated with that objective in mind.[79] At the time of Leclerc's challenge the government had set minimum and maximum retail prices for gasoline. The maximum was determined for each retailer on the basis of the price at which the gasoline was purchased (the ex-refinery price) and the maximum markup allowed by the regulators. The minimum price was the same for all retailers in a given area and was set by subtracting a fixed amount (9 centimes per liter for regular, 10 centimes for premium) from the average of the maximum prices applicable to area retailers.

Government also regulated the wholesale price of gasoline. Unlike the retail price, the wholesale price was subject to a ceiling but not a floor. The value of the ceiling depended on the cost of refining in France and the wholesale price prevailing in the European Communities. If the French cost of refining gasoline lay within 8 percent of the EC wholesale price, then the French ceiling was set to the European market price. If, however, the French cost of refining diverged more than 8 percent from community prices, then the ceiling was set equal to the French cost of refining.

In practice the wholesale price rarely differed from the ceiling price. Moreover, the EC wholesale price tended to lie more than 8 percent below the French unit cost of refining. Hence the ceiling price at wholesale, which determined the minimum price at retail, was based on the unit cost of producing gasoline in France.

In 1983 several Leclerc stores deliberately priced their gasoline below government's floor. A rival in the Toulouse area, Henri Cullet, brought suit, claiming harm from their infringement of the regulations.

79. An early study of petroleum policy is Faure, *La Politique Française du Pétrole*; a more recent study is Chevalier, "L'Energie."

In the commercial court of Toulouse, Leclerc argued that the French regulations violated the Treaty of Rome because they hindered imports from the rest of the community. Although France maintained no quotas or tariffs on such imports, and although importers were free to price as low as they pleased, the inability of retailers to lower their prices below a floor based on French production cost meant that retailers lacked full incentive to procure foreign gasoline.

The commercial court of Toulouse referred the issue to the EC Court of Justice. In 1985 the court held that French regulations did indeed violate article 30 of the treaty because their method of establishing minimum prices did deter imports.[80] Evidence presented by the French government that imports had been rising over time was not considered adequate to demonstrate that trade had not been distorted. Once again, Leclerc had injected a dose of price competition into French retailing.

Generalizing from the Leclerc Experience

Of what general significance is the story of Edouard Leclerc? Have the discount houses, together perhaps with other new types of sellers, increased competition in retailing? Several pieces of evidence suggest they have indeed.

EVIDENCE ON MARKUPS

If the new retailers aligned their prices on those of conservative rivals, despite having purchased their merchandise on favorable terms, then retail markups should vary directly with retailer size. The greater the rebates received and the smaller the discounts offered by large retailers, the greater the predicted effect of size on markup.

Among retailers specializing in food, just before passage of the loi Royer, the largest sellers did indeed tend to set the greatest markups (appendix table A-75). Thereafter, however, the markups of the small retailers began to rise, while those of their large counterparts did not. During each of the years between 1974 and 1976, sellers with

---

80. *Henri Cullet and Chambre Syndicale des Réparateurs Automobiles et Détaillants de Produits Pétroliers (C.S.N.C.R.A.)* v. *Centre Leclerc, Toulouse (SA Sodinord) and Centre Leclerc, Saint-Orens de Gameville (SA Sodirev)*, case 231/83, EC Court of Justice, January 29, 1985; [1985] 2 *CMLR* 524.

one to nine employees tended to set markups above the large-seller average. Three years after passage of the law, sellers with more than nine employees exhibited below-average markup tendencies, while sellers with zero to nine employees exhibited the opposite. On the reasonable assumption that relatively large retailers procured merchandise at relatively low prices, this is hardly evidence of price alignment.

In nonfood retailing, size of markup tended to rise with size of retailer throughout the first half of the 1970s (table A-75). These data are consistent with the proposition that large nonfood retailers bought their merchandise at low prices, sold that merchandise at prices close to those of smaller sellers, and realized comfortable profit margins in the process.[81]

EVIDENCE ON PRICES

The best way to investigate price alignment is to examine direct evidence on prices. Fortunately, price dispersion in retailing has received considerable attention. Most studies confirm the impression left by markup data that large food retailers compete actively on price.

The evidence of Jean-Michel Rempp shows clearly that hypermarkets charged the lowest prices (appendix table A-76). It also suggests that hypermarket chains charged less than did other types of hypermarkets.[82] Supermarkets tended to price between the hypermarkets and the small-scale shops. Among the supermarkets, independently owned stores tended to price below outlets belonging to department stores, cooperatives, or chain store corporations.

81. These data must be interpreted with caution. Because the unit of observation is the company, not the store, the larger size classes apply both to chains of hypermarkets and to chains of small stores. Worse yet, the large firms may be engaged in a variety of activities simultaneously, including wholesaling as well as retailing, distribution of foods and nonfoods, and selling in hypermarkets as well as in small shops. For such firms the evidence on margins might reveal more about the mix of activities than about the markup in any particular activity. In addition, all of the firms used as observations in tables A-75 to A-77 are taxed on the basis of their actual profits. Excluded in effect are myriad small firms that pay either no tax or a lump sum negotiated with tax officials. Such firms are likely to be among the least progressive of the small retailers. Finally, earlier and later experience need not dovetail with that of 1971–76.

82. Rempp, "Les Différences de Prix entre le Petit et le Grand Commerce," table 1. Rempp used two surveys from 1976, one conducted by INSEE, the other by SECODIP.

In the study conducted for the European Communities, during every period of observation, the same six stores displayed the lowest prices.[83] The six included all four hypermarkets and two of the fourteen supermarkets. One of the low-price supermarkets was an independent, a Centre Leclerc, the other was owned by Casino, the large chain store corporation. The six shops with the highest prices changed from year to year. In 1977 one high-price store was a supermarket belonging to the Economats du Centre chain; and in every year but 1979 one high-price store was a supermarket belonging to the consumers' cooperative (the prices of cooperatives are overstated, however, insofar as such organizations grant periodic rebates to members). Most of the high-price stores were small outlets of the chain store corporations.

In sum, hypermarkets tended to charge the lowest prices for food. As a group, supermarkets tended to charge more than the hypermarkets, but independent supermarkets tended to charge less than the rest. These are precisely the patterns one would expect to observe if the new retailers failed to align their prices on those of the old order. (Note that the first finding is also consistent with the hypothesis of increasing returns to scale at the store level, but the second is inconsistent with the hypothesis of increasing returns to scale at the company level.)

Unfortunately, variations in retail prices by type of store have been studied primarily in the context of food. In the absence of systematic evidence of this sort regarding a wide variety of nonfood products in many parts of the country, it is useful to recall the plethora of antitrust cases in which traditional retailers have pressured manufacturers to constrict deliveries to discount sellers.

In its report for 1985 the Commission de la Concurrence described such a case.[84] Chapelle, a small independent retailer, sold audio equipment and large household appliances at discount prices from two otherwise traditional stores, one in Valence, the other in Grenoble.

83. Ghersi, Allaya, and Allaya, *Etude sur la Concentration, les Prix et les Marges dans la Distribution des Produits Alimentaires*. This study examined the prices of thirty foods in twenty-four stores near Montpellier during 1976–79.

84. "Avis Relatif aux Relations de la S.A. Semavem avec Différents Fournisseurs d'Appareils Electroménagers et Electro-Acoustiques," Commission de la Concurrence, *Rapport au Ministre pour l'Année 1985*, pp. 45–49.

Despite his low prices Chapelle earned a substantial return on investment. At the end of the 1970s he established a cash-and-carry type outlet on the outskirts of each city he already served. Citing pressure from Chapelle's rivals, several manufacturers balked at supplying him with merchandise, leading to a number of suits in a variety of jurisdictions. Meanwhile, Chapelle attempted to open a new cash-and-carry outlet near Paris. Toward this end, he sought membership in a joint purchasing organization composed of twenty-three retailers. He even signed an agreement with various members of the group, allowing them to participate in his suburban Paris outlet. Initially, he was accepted in the joint venture and received supplies from manufacturers on the group's terms. But when the manufacturers discovered Chapelle's plans for the store outside Paris, they urged certain members of the purchasing group to reject his membership unless he agreed to desist from his commercial strategy. Chapelle was in fact ousted, and shortly thereafter he went bankrupt. (Interestingly, it was the court-appointed head of the bankruptcy proceedings who asked the commission for its opinion as to whether bankruptcy had been caused by illegal concerted practices.) The Commission de la Concurrence concluded that the manufacturers had definitely operated to force Chapelle to desist from discounting. Unable, however, to reject the hypothesis that they had acted independently of one another, it found them innocent of violating the antitrust laws.[85]

The evidence contained in these vertical restraint cases dovetails with evidence culled from their horizontal counterparts. Frequently, associations of retailers have pressured their members not to cut

85. A similar legal conclusion was drawn by the commission in *Ménard-Discount*. Until 1975 Ménard sold a full range of agricultural equipment in the traditional manner. Thereafter, he specialized in small agricultural equipment sold at discount prices. After his conversion to discounting, several manufacturers impeded his efforts to buy their merchandise. Ménard sued for refusal to deal, and at least one manufacturer agreed to pay a fine in lieu of prosecution. During this period the trade association of conventional retailers met with the trade association of manufacturers and urged it to discourage discounting at the retail level. After the meeting, the manufacturers continued their harassment of Ménard. Arguing that parallel behavior does not suffice to establish concerted practice, the commission concluded that the manufacturers had not violated article 50 of ordinance 45-1483. See "Avis Relatif à des Difficultés d'Approvisionnement de la Société Ménard-Discount en Petit Matériel Agricole," Commission de la Concurrence, *Rapport au Ministre pour l'Année 1985*, pp. 79–82.

prices. For example, the association of pharmacists in Rennes urged the regional umbrella organization to remind all members that discounting of nonpharmaceutical products and of over-the-counter drugs would not be tolerated. The regional association dispatched letters to that effect, forced a known discounter off its regional board, and threatened discounters with punishment under its authority, delegated by government, to enforce "conduct befitting a pharmacist" on its members. Following the recommendation of the commission, the minister of economic affairs fined the regional association Fr 50,000 for illegal concerted practices.[86]

The evidence on price behavior to be gleaned from antitrust proceedings can be interpreted in two ways. On the one hand, small discounters ran serious risks as they battled with traditional retailers of nonfood merchandise. On the other hand, discounting clearly did exist: retailers did diverge on how best to exploit their markets. Whatever their views on its desirability, most sellers would agree that price competition has come to nonfood retailing.

EVIDENCE ON PROFITABILITY

If the large retailers competed actively on price, then what was to prevent them from driving out the smaller sellers and oligopolizing their lines of business? One brake on predation is the expectation that enough large retailers would remain to preclude effective collusion. As long as big enterprises can be expected to fight among themselves, their smaller brethren are inessential to preservation of competition—whatever their virtues on other grounds. The profitability of the large retailers provides one measure of the competition they felt. If they realized consistently high rates of return, perhaps the competition among them was too spotty to be considered vigorous.

During the first half of the 1970s the highest rates of return in food retailing were earned by the smallest enterprises (appendix table A-77). Conceivably, this occurred because small entrepreneurs took

---

86. "Avis Relatif à des Interventions du Syndicat des Pharmaciens d'Ille-et-Vilaine et du Conseil Régional de l'Ordre des Pharmaciens de Bretagne Concernant des Ventes à Prix Réduits d'Articles Délivrés en Pharmacie," Commission de la Concurrence, *Rapport au Ministre pour l'Année 1985*, pp. 118–22.

their managerial salaries in profit rather than in wages.[87] Nevertheless, even retailers with 10–99 employees were more profitable than certain larger rivals. Only in comparison with firms of 10–999 employees did those with 1,000 or more tend to achieve high rates of return. In nonfood retailing the largest sellers tended to earn negative premiums in relation to their smaller counterparts. Profitability tended to decline with size of firm.

The data on profitability have two implications. First, the low margins and low prices of large retailers do not appear to have had predatory effect; if they had, small retailers would have exhibited relatively low, not relatively high, profitability. Second, the large retailers appear to have competed among themselves, hence their relatively low rates of return.[88] On both counts, one might conclude that the new retailers stimulated competition in markets they supplied. (Note, however, that these rates of return fail to adjust for risk. On a risk-adjusted basis, large retailers may be more profitable than small retailers. Note also that large food retailers exhibited rates of return that on average were close to double those found in nonfinancial enterprises drawn from all lines of business.)

EVIDENCE ON EXIT

Perhaps the ultimate indicator of competition is the extent to which inefficient firms are forced to exit from the market. The evidence presented in chapter 2 indicates clearly that small retail shops declined. This evidence must be interpreted cautiously, but it certainly is consistent with the view that competition in retailing has increased.[89]

---

87. According to Stigler, *Capital and Rates of Return in Manufacturing Industries*, the opposite holds true in the United States: to avoid double taxation of profit, owners of small American businesses tend to take their profit in wages. However, French and American methods of minimizing taxes might diverge.

88. According to Messerlin, *La Révolution Commerciale*, p. 149, "the conditions leading to sustained and even increased competition among large retailers are likely to be permanent."

89. Caution is required because the decline of small retailers began before the emergence of the giant discounters and because much of it can be attributed to urbanization of the French population. A recent assessment of competition in retailing is "Commerce: Concurrence Accrue en 1984."

Conclusion

When economic enterprises choose among potential business strategies, they must occasionally decide whether to protect existing advantages or to develop new ones. Either basic strategy can be pursued unilaterally or cooperatively, and either might entail political as well as market behavior. The relative advantages of the two depend on the environment in which the enterprise operates.

Postwar changes in the domestic environment modified the relative profitability of conservative and innovative behavior in several lines of business, but especially in retailing. At the behest of traditional retailers, until the Liberation, government discriminated onerously against those most likely to upset the established order. Fearing the political repercussions of inflation even more than it feared small retailers, however, early postwar government tended to favor competition, reinforcing the relative profitability of innovation.

Domestic institutional change, like international institutional change, has promoted competition in France. In magnitude, however, the impact of domestic change must be relegated to second place: the changes in question were too easy to undo. In the international arena, economic integration, coupled with involuntary decolonization, stripped French governments of many policy levers.[90] But in the domestic arena, French governments enjoyed substantial freedom to restore a protectionist order. Enterprises could maintain the hope that voice would still induce a return to the status quo. The relative profitability of innovation was still open to challenge.

The very manner in which government supported innovative retailers signaled a lack of commitment to the new policy. In 1953 it attacked resale price maintenance by decree rather than by law, permitting it to avoid parliament, the home court of the traditional shopkeepers. In 1958, after its initial measure was overturned on technical grounds and it had to reaffirm its desire for innovative retailing, government again chose to proceed by decree. Fearing lack of public support, it published no account whatsoever of its antitrust activities until August 1959—after the Treaty of Rome took effect.[91]

---

90. Balassa, "Whither French Planning?"
91. The Commission de la Concurrence now publishes all its reports. Unfortunately,

The tentative nature of government initiative is certainly under-standable when placed in political context. In the parliamentary elections of January 2, 1956, the Union de Défense des Commerçants et Artisans led by Pierre Poujade, owner of a small stationery shop in the Lot and champion of civil disobedience against tax assessors investigating small businesses, received more than 9 percent of the vote.[92] Following the social and political turbulence of May 1968, under Gérard Nicoud the traditional shopkeepers again forced their way onto the national agenda, securing passage of the loi Royer in the process. As recently as the presidential election of 1988, Jean-Marie Le Pen captured 14 percent of the first-round vote by rallying "an embittered coalition that feels threatened in a France that they feel has modernized too quickly."[93] As long as conservative merchants retain their political strength at the national level, government's commitment to competition in retailing cannot be taken for granted.

French retailers did not face much competition from imports when artificial barriers to international trade were dismantled. Nevertheless, they have been exposed to substantial increases in competition since World War II. This surge would not have occurred without changes in domestic economic policy, especially the creation of strong pre-sumptions against refusal to sell and resale price maintenance. However ineffectual in areas emphasized by American antitrust authorities, the French rules of competition encouraged aggressive rivalry in retailing.

Although competition in retailing and other sheltered activities was shaped primarily by domestic economic policy, one should not be blind to its interconnections with the international developments described in chapter 4.

In the first place, international economic integration promoted foreign investment as well as foreign trade. Several multinational retailers have set up shop in France. Between 1965 and 1978 wholesale and retail trade accounted for 21 percent of the net inflow of direct investment originating in France's most important investment part-

---

until December 1986 its activities represented "only part of the work done to foster competition." Clément, "An Appraisal of French Antitrust Policy," p. 589, note 5. And the rest remained largely hidden from public view.

92. Roy, *Les Commerçants*, p. 8; also see Hoffmann, *Le Mouvement Poujade*.
93. Markham, "France at Crossroads."

ners. Dutch investors devoted an especially large fraction (33 percent) of their flow to wholesale and retail trade.[94]

In the second place, the rise of large-scale retailing might have increased the ease with which foreign manufacturers could penetrate French markets. It is sometimes argued that domestic manufacturers employ exclusive and selective networks of dealers in a manner that forecloses foreigners from local retail outlets. Once the new forms of distribution took root, such foreclosure became very difficult to achieve. In comparison with small shops, large establishments enjoy sufficient leverage vis-à-vis manufacturers to avoid reluctant agreement not to stock the goods of other producers. Moreover, since the incentive to search for the best merchandise at the best prices rises with the expected volume of purchase, the large retailers were especially likely to explore foreign sources of supply. (To the extent that small retailers were supplied by large wholesalers free of dependence on domestic manufacturers, however, the small retailers would not ignore foreign goods on this account.) Most important, perhaps, the new retailers competed more on the basis of price than on the basis of merchandise quality and retailer service. In apparel and household durables, at least, this probably dictated recourse to goods produced outside the EC.[95] It is conceivable, therefore, that the rise of discount retailing served to facilitate introduction of foreign manufactures to French markets.

Finally, involuntary decolonization generated a discrete influx of new entrepreneurs. Although many of the innovaters chose agriculture, and many of the conservatives opened traditional shops, others

94. See Arnaud-Ameller and Marnata, *Les Flux d'Investissement Direct entre la France et l'Extérieur*, table 10.

95. Défossé, *Le Commerce Intérieur*, mentions that large stores were frequently accused of stocking foreign goods. He cites evidence to rebut the charge, but such evidence is largely irrelevant to the current situation. Not only was the French market closed for other reasons during the 1930s, but the large stores of the period, the *grands magasins*, were not discounters. Current evidence against the link between size of retailer and propensity to stock foreign merchandise appears in Jenny, "Rapport sur la Relation Pouvant Exister entre les Pratiques de Certains Types de Distributeurs et la Pénétration Croissante de Notre Marché par les Produits Etrangers." Studying three products in detail, Jenny found that large stores were not especially likely to stock imported merchandise. The study is summarized in Commission de la Concurrence, *Rapport au Ministre pour l'Année 1984*, app. 2, pp. 38–39.

did pursue discount retailing. I wonder how many of Leclerc's adherents had spent time in Algeria.

Beset by *Poujadisme* and *Nicoudisme,* French domestic policy did not embrace competition unwaveringly.[96] On occasion, it felt compelled to retard development of discount stores. This in turn must have led small retailers to entertain the belief that political protest could be profitable.[97] Some probably considered it more profitable than adaptation. Many of these perished.

96. According to Caron, *An Economic History of Modern France,* p. 309, fear of social reaction "forced the politicians, even those most anxious to see France develop rapidly, to moderate their ambitions."

97. Especially under the Fourth Republic. According to Gauron, *Histoire Economique et Sociale de la Cinquième République,* vol. 1: *Le Temps des Modernistes,* p. 60, "The new political institutions [of the Fifth Republic], and especially the reinforcement of administrative power, conferred on government the means to conduct economic policy free from the constraints of party politics and pressure groups." Farmers and shopkeepers exerted more influence on parliament than they did on the executive branch.

6 | Implications

BETWEEN THE mid-1950s and the mid-1970s, French living standards improved pervasively and substantially. In no small measure these improvements stemmed from public policies that resulted in or were disciplined by market competition. During the mid-1980s, as governments of left and right advocated modernization and implemented deregulation, the commitment to competition seemed credibly permanent—serenely independent of electoral politics.

Over the past few years, however, the French economy has performed disappointingly. Between 1983 and 1986 French gross domestic product grew at the lethargic annual pace of 1.5 percent; it grew more than 50 percent again as fast in Germany and Italy, and two to three times as fast in the United Kingdom, Japan, and the United States.[1] Worse than slow growth itself was the failure to generate enough jobs. Between 1983 and 1986 the unemployment rate rose every year (appendix table A-78). Meanwhile, unemployment rates elsewhere in Europe either fell or rose less rapidly than did those in France. In December 1988 the French rate remained over 10 percent.[2] Similarly unfavorable performance occurred with respect to prices and exports.[3] "The immediate outlook for France's economy is mixed at best."[4]

1. OECD, *National Accounts, 1960–1986*, vol. 1: *Main Aggregates*, pt. 5.
2. *Economist*, February 4, 1989, p. 101.
3. Between 1983 and 1986 consumer prices grew at average annual rates of 10.1 percent in Italy, 6.4 percent in France, 4.8 percent in the United Kingdom, 3.3 percent in the United States, 1.9 percent in Germany, and 1.7 percent in Japan; see *OECD Economic Outlook*, no. 41 (June 1987), table R10. Between 1981 and 1986 the ratio of French to world exports decreased at an average annual rate of 3.3 percent; meanwhile, the share of world exports that was contributed by eight large OECD exporters declined at an average annual rate of only 1.8 percent; see "La Croissance

Although some people argue that recent lackluster performance should be imputed to the Socialist economic policies of 1981–83, the decline predates left-wing arrivals in the corridors of power.[5] GDP grew less rapidly than the big-seven average in 1973, 1977, and 1978; steady increase in the unemployment rate began in 1974.[6] Both capital's share of value added and corporate profitability declined during most of the 1970s.[7]

Poor economic performance since the 1970s catalyzed an explosive political movement protesting the arrogance of antiseptic civil servants, the ravages of modernization, and the shame of decolonization— hardly surprising, since economic success had been attributed to the munificence of modernization and the skills of the technocratic elite. When 14.4 percent of the electorate voted for the radical rightist Jean-Marie Le Pen in round one of the 1988 presidential election, it was venting its spleen against market forces and structural change. Ironically, the protest occurred well after slow growth had moderated the pace of structural evolution along many if not all of its dimensions.[8]

What does the future hold for the French economy? Continued inability to replicate the achievements studied here? Prolonged decline in relation to the OECD? Quick disappearance of current adversity? The answers to these questions depend, of course, on myriad factors, many of which lie beyond the scope of this book.[9] Arguably, the most

---

Confisquée," *Observations et Diagnostics Economiques: Revue de l'Observatoire Français de Conjoncture Economique*, no 19 (April 1987), p. 71.

4. "A Survey of France," *Economist*, March 12, 1988, p. 15.

5. Critical evaluations of Socialist economic policy appear in Balassa, "Selective versus General Economic Policy in Postwar France," pp. 100–01; and Balassa, "La Politique Economique Socialiste," pp. 13–22. On the decline, see Dubois, "La Rupture de 1974."

6. Ibid.; and *OECD Economic Outlook*, no. 41 (June 1987), table R1. The big seven are the United States, Japan, Germany, France, the United Kingdom, Italy, and Canada. The unemployment rate began to exceed the big-seven average in 1978; ibid., table R12.

7. Caffet and others, "L'Economie Française à l'Horizon 1991," p. 25.

8. See Boudoul and Faur, "Depuis 1975, les Migrations Interrégionales Sont Moins Nombreuses"; and Cézard and Rault, "La Crise A Freiné la Mobilité Sectorielle." See also, however, Cunéo, Dupont, and Mabile, "1980–1985: Des Mutations Sectorielles Plus Profondes Que Prévu."

9. For example, Maddison, *Phases of Capitalist Development*, might emphasize the exhaustion of opportunities created by France's initial backwardness. Many French enterprises entered the postwar period with technologies and products inferior to

important of these involve the extent to which international exposure constrains France's ability to pursue domestically desirable macroeconomic policies.[10] In any event, evaluation of the various hypotheses requires evidence of a comparative nature: French achievements cannot be fathomed fully without parallel investigations of economic structure and conduct in other rich countries.[11] No matter how much in need of supplement, however, the microeconomic issues and evidence discussed in this book bear directly on France's economic future.[12]

In the 1930s and 1940s, initiative for economic development appeared to lodge with private enterprise. As a result, those who argued that French attitudes and institutions failed to mesh with the requirements of sustained growth dwelled on the culture of business enterprise. More recently, after a period of government initiative, cultural and institutional hypotheses have been addressed to government's side of the street.[13] The allegation that strong government of

---

those abroad. More than many, they stood to learn from exposure to foreign competition; and the reallocation of resources toward more productive uses that followed the learning-cum-competition might have spurred relatively rapid growth. Now that the gap between French and best-practice technique has narrowed, France cannot continue to outperform its OECD rivals. The benefits of learning, like the benefits of traditional comparative advantage, are one-shot in nature, and France has taken its shot. However, this argument fails to explain why the *absolute* rate of growth failed to revive as global technological change drove wedges in all countries between actual and optimal technique.

10. See especially Boyer, "Industrial Policy in Macroeconomic Perspective"; "The Current Economic Crisis"; "Is France Declining Relative to the OECD?"; and, with Ralle, "Croissances Nationales et Contrainte Extérieure avant et après 1973."

11. Two fine examples of comparative analysis, the first macroscopic, the second microscopic in focus, are Hall, *Governing the Economy*; and Maurice, Sellier, and Silvestre, *Politique d'Education et Organisation Industrielle en France et an Allemagne.*

12. The position that French problems are structural rather than cyclical is expressed in Mistral, "125 Ans de Contrainte Extérieure"; and Stoffaës, *Fins de Mondes.* Stoffaës argues that hard times since the early 1970s should be attributed to the world's position in a Kondratieff cycle. On the one hand, a cluster of revolutionary technologies has coalesced sufficiently to make the established institutional order undesirable. On the other hand, the new technologies have not matured enough to clarify the institutional modifications required to restore prosperity. This argument addresses the intertemporal, not the international, deterioration of French performance.

13. The shift in question is one of degree. The Armand-Rueff report, describing the 1950s, devotes attention to public as well as private restraints of competition. See *Rapport sur les Obstacles à l'Expansion Economique.*

the sort that has existed in France for centuries serves to handicap French enterprise in world markets represents a reincarnation of the quasi-cultural style of argument manifested earlier in the doctrine of economic Malthusianism.

One version of the argument is advanced by John Zysman.[14] After World War II, government sought actively to influence the relative profitability of various activities. As a result, individual enterprises found it advantageous to structure themselves in ways that facilitated capture of government's largesse. Operationally speaking, this meant concentrating industry-level production in a few enterprises and preserving hierarchy within enterprises. Since the industrial policies of the reconstruction period were aimed at activities in which minimum efficient scale was large and technology seemed maturely stable, this effect of government activism was initially market-compatible: it did not prompt firms to organize themselves in a manner that inhibited their ability to compete with foreign rivals.

After reconstruction, industrial policy shifted to activities in which technology was changing rapidly and failing to confer obvious advantages on large-scale operations. As a result, pursuit of competitive advantage required deconcentration of target industries and decentralization of target enterprises; but the persistence of government initiative encouraged the opposite. Government's industrial policy had become dysfunctional.

During the late 1960s, government was still the principal buyer of many high-technology products. As a result, competitive advantage was not critical to commercial success. Increasingly, however, profitability came to require attraction of private as well as public customers. Having relied for so long on government, French enterprises and industries lacked the organizational forms needed to respond to the challenge. In export markets, as at home, they depended on sales arranged by the French government. These tended to involve military products, factories, and infrastructure purchased by governments of developing countries. As a result, France found itself with a pattern of trade in high-technology products that emphasized intraindustry exchange: it exported its most advanced goods to

14. Largely with the electronics industry in mind; Zysman, *Political Strategies for Industrial Order.*

developing countries, while it imported products of the same category from the richest countries.[15] Sophisticated French exports could not compete in the world's most competitive markets.

Emphasizing different features of the French environment, Michael Piore and Charles Sabel extend the implications of Zysman's argument beyond the high-technology arena. In their view postwar microeconomic policy aimed primarily to achieve American-style methods of production throughout the economy. This meant adoption of inflexible mass production based on a combination of unskilled and supervisory labor. Through the productivity missions of the Marshall Plan and through the technostructure's absorption of a quantitative production ethic, government's policy succeeded to the point where France, more than any of its major European rivals, had matched the American system.[16] Unfortunately, when technological change crowned flexible production of customized goods as the new best-practice technique, government's success in closing earlier technological gaps proved counterproductive. The very source of its early success—government compensation for poor private performance—was now the chief obstacle to France's adaptation.

To the extent that Zysman and Piore and Sabel are correct, the French government must develop new forms of intervention in the microeconomy, avoiding policies with dysfunctional incentives. In the context of policies aimed at business, it must appreciate the basic message of this book: to an important degree, successful economic performance during the period of rapid growth is attributable to credibly permanent exposure of many French enterprises to competition. The new industrial policy must facilitate structural adjustment while promoting and protecting competition.

15. Boyer, "The Current Economic Crisis," p. 43. See also Lassudrie-Duchêne and Mucchielli, "Les Echanges Intra-Branche et la Hiérarchisation des Avantages Comparés dans le Commerce International."

16. Piore and Sabel, *The Second Industrial Divide*. See also Mistral, "La Diffusion Internationale de l'Accumulation Intensive et sa Crise." In some respects, Piore and Sabel argue, the French outdid the Americans in their own game. For example, more than their American counterparts, French firms sharply distinguished conception from execution of tasks, resulting in the proliferation of bureaucracy. In general, "bureaucratization—along with features of economic organization that are more directly borrowed from the United States—may prove to be liabilities in the changed competitive environment of the 1980s" (p. 142).

Such a feat will certainly be difficult. Not only does slow growth provoke shrill demand for protection, but the stability of French institutions since 1958, coupled with the stability of French elites since 1945, facilitates capture of the policy process by protectionist coalitions.[17] So does the electoral success of a Jean-Marie Le Pen.[18] Three features of the French environment—domestic deregulation, the role of the European Communities, and French economic structure—will help determine the speed with which France regains the path of stable prosperity.

The postwar period is not the first in French history when government has relied on market forces to solve major economic problems. Although foreign observers tend to focus on France's interventionist tradition from Colbert through Saint Simon to Chevènement, France also possesses a less distinctive but no less impressive tradition of economic liberalism. Like its interventionist counterpart, this tradition dates back to the monarchy.

During much of the eighteenth century, France's foremost economic problem was famine. Accordingly, the ministers of Louis XV and Louis XVI pondered carefully the production and distribution of food. Given its importance in contemporary diets as well as its relative suitability for transport, grain received special attention.

Since the Middle Ages, local markets for grain had been regulated tightly.[19] Early in the reign of Louis XV, grain could not be exported or sent from one region to another without royal approval. Farmers had to bring their output to market shortly after the harvest and had to sell their entire stock, giving preference to households over bakers and traders. With markets compartmentalized in this fashion, local shortages developed frequently. To deal with them, several of the king's advisers, faithful to Colbert's legacy, advocated government initiative. In their view, when the national harvest failed to match

17. Such is the implicit prediction of Olson, *The Rise and Decline of Nations.*

18. Like George Wallace in the presidential primaries of 1976, Le Pen adopted the rhetoric of racism. At a deeper level, however, he played on "the anxieties and anger of a number of Frenchmen who feel threatened by modernity, alienated by the maneuverings of the 'political class' and neglected, or abandoned, as the majority of the nation has prospered." Markham, "Outsiders' Candidate."

19. The following account relies heavily on Faure, *La Disgrâce de Turgot*; and the preface of Bernard Cazes to Turgot, *Ecrits Economiques.* See also Brewer, "Turgot: Founder of Classical Economics."

domestic consumption needs, government had to purchase and distribute foreign grain. Regardless of aggregate production, it also had to buy grain in regions of relative plenty and sell or stock it in regions of relative shortage. Finally, it had to complement its trading activities by milling grain into flour, ensuring thereby the supply of cereal in readily consumable form.

In 1746 Louis XV accepted these interventionist prescriptions. Without publicity, his administration authorized a loosely regulated private party to buy and sell grain to ensure its availability at reasonable prices in all parts of the country. Shortly thereafter, again without publicity, royal officials took over the bulk of these activities. Using an account at the royal treasury created specially for the purpose, public officials traded, stored, and milled grain, a policy similar in form to that of today's FDES.

But local shortages of food did not abate. Neither did rumors of corruption among the lesser officials implementing government's trading activities. As a result, several of the king's agents, including Anne-Robert Jacques Turgot, *intendant* of Limousin, expressed disenchantment with interventionism. In their opinion, regional segmentation of grain markets, coupled with ineffective public arbitrage, discouraged both agricultural production and socially desirable speculation by private parties. According to Turgot, "there is only one way to prevent people from dying when food is scarce, and that is to take grain to places where there isn't any and to save grain for times when it is short. . . . But that is a job for traders, a job that will be performed at least cost only when trade is free; every other method will perform the task poorly, slowly, and expensively."[20]

In 1764 Louis XV reduced regulation of the grain trade. He ended the requirement of prior approval before grain could be sent out of a region or out of the country and also eased restrictions on farmers and traders in local markets. He did not, however, curtail the activities of the royal traders. After a few poor harvests, Louis chose in 1770 to restore the regulatory régime that had been curtailed six years earlier. Although grain could still be shipped between provinces

20. "Septième Lettre au Contrôleur Général sur le Commerce des Grains," in Turgot, *Ecrits Economiques*, p. 350. The argument that deregulation will increase the profitability of farming and hence expand the supply of grain is contained in the sixth letter, reprinted in ibid., pp. 321–31.

without prior approval, commerce in local markets became subject to a host of rules; and government continued its direct involvement in grain.

When Turgot became minister of finance under Louis XVI, he ignored those skeptical of private initiative and moved immediately to reinvigorate market forces. In 1774, a year before publication of *The Wealth of Nations,* and seventy years before the Corn Laws were abolished in England, Turgot eliminated the remaining constraints on private trade in food and ended the trading activities of government. In other words, he attempted to deregulate and privatize the most important economic activity of his day. Just as Colbert believed that the most important dimensions of economic life required government intervention to ensure high levels of social welfare, Turgot believed that market forces unencumbered by government intervention offered the best hope of achieving the same end.

Turgot's ministry demonstrates that belief in the virtues of competition can be detected in French economic thought well before the American economic juggernaut of World War II left the postwar French elite in awe. Just as Colbert's policies inspired French planners in every succeeding generation of policymakers, so Turgot's policies found subsequent expression in commercial treaties with England, in the economic theories of Jean-Baptiste Say, and in the political economy of Frédéric Bastiat.[21] Those in France who wish to preserve today's inclination to remove regulatory barriers to competition have a well-developed, home-grown tradition on which to draw. Such a tradition may reduce the fragility of current commitments to this course of government action.

Turgot's approach to the food problem also demonstrates, however, that French liberalism rarely flourishes enduringly. Within a year of his famous edict, he was forced to resign, and his policies did not survive his ministry. Does this augur ill for the current round of deregulation? Would the return of inflation prompt restoration of controls on prices, wages, and interest rates, just as a few bad harvests prompted restoration of controls on the grain trade?

21. See Dunham, *The Anglo-French Treaty of Commerce of 1860 and the Progress of the Industrial Revolution in France;* and Bastiat, *Economic Sophisms,* and *Selected Essays on Political Economy.*

Many of the remaining obstacles to structural change are rooted in activities sheltered naturally from foreign competition. To weed them from the environment will require commitment from government to continue the current process of deregulation.[22] Despite the vote for Le Pen in April 1988, there is reason to believe that the process will endure.

The political consensus favoring competition covers a very broad spectrum of opinion. The business community has heard government after government proclaim loyalty to modernization and competition. This was true in the Gaullist era, when all successive governments were nominally center-right but differed considerably in economic rhetoric, and it remains true in the period of alternation, when governments represent a fuller range of the political spectrum.[23] Without denying the importance of and reasons for his support, one can believe wholly plausibly that Jean-Marie Le Pen will never come close to winning a national election. His showing may moderate the ritualistic praise veneered to structural change, but after the Mitterrand landslide in round two of the 1988 presidential election, it is unlikely to retard the actual promotion of that change.

Consensus in support of competition demonstrates the flexibility of French political thinking. As recently as the late 1960s, many groups to the right of center and most groups to the left of center expressed little faith in competitive markets; by the mid-1980s, however, most had come to embrace competition. The path of the Socialists is especially interesting.[24] In some respects it resembles the philosophical route of Franklin D. Roosevelt during the 1930s. Roosevelt did not begin his administration as a Keynesian; he

22. Recent developments are described in Balladur, *Une France Plus Forte*, especially pp. 26–32, 46–51.

23. The Socialist decisions of March 1983 constituted powerful tests of future behavior because the government and hence the party faced strong pressure to abrogate temporarily or permanently the French commitment to free trade within the European Communities; see Hall, "The Evolution of Economic Policy under Mitterrand," p. 56. The Socialist position may have been motivated by fear that even a modest welfare state for individuals cannot survive if the welfare state for enterprises is allowed to thrive; and the Socialists had learned by then that an active industrial policy of the traditional sort implied a generous welfare state for business enterprise.

24. Stanley Hoffmann also detects pragmatism, albeit in different contexts. See his conclusion in Ross and others, eds., *The Mitterrand Experiment*, especially p. 343.

experimented with corporatism and competition before resorting to macroeconomic stimulation. In retrospect he is remembered as a pragmatist, willing to try different approaches until the economic crisis was tamed. Similarly, the French Socialists have revealed their willingness to abandon preconceived solutions to serious economic problems. Just as the French business community showed during the 1960s that it could respond elastically to changes in its environment, so the Socialist period of governance demonstrates that the political community is also more adaptable than culturalists believe.

In product and financial markets, the best predictors of government's future support of competition will be the forms that deregulation and denationalization take. Government disengagements of these kinds do not necessarily promote market competition. Where economic rivalry fails to thrive naturally, government must intervene actively with antitrust and other policies. If deregulation becomes tantamount to laissez-faire and tolerates private efforts to maintain established positions, public policy will lie not in the Turgot tradition but rather in the line of François Guizot, who incited the bourgeoisie in 1843 with "Enrichissez-vous!"

In several fundamental respects, market competition is nourished by economic and political decentralization. During the 1980s national government surrendered several powers to its local counterparts and required business enterprises to create new channels of dialogue with their workers. These policies have received far less attention than have the reflation and the nationalizations of the early 1980s. It is too soon to gauge their impact, but their effects on market conduct and competition may be profound—even if, or perhaps because, they were designed for other purposes.[25]

While awaiting the verdict on these larger reforms, one might look to the labor market for gauges of government's intentions regarding deregulation. The rate of unemployment is high. Politically speaking, further deregulation of the labor market entails far more risk than does further deregulation or privatization of product and financial

---

25. Note the similarity in this respect between decentralization on the one hand and European integration and decolonization on the other. The potential importance of decentralization is expressed in Mistral, "125 Ans de Contrainte Extérieure." The policies of the 1980s are described in Gremion, "Decentralization in France"; and Mény, "The Socialist Decentralization."

markets. Emphasis on positive adjustment through a labor-market-centered industrial policy would reveal a strong commitment to market forces.

France's postwar experience with liberalism also differs from its historical antecedents through its international dimensions.[26] In theory, continued participation in the European Communities is predicated on continued adherence to the principle of international economic integration. Since withdrawal from the EC is credibly unthinkable, national policy is bound to accept the course established jointly with the other major powers of the Communities, most of which tend to embrace liberalism at least as eagerly as does France. The tighter the Communities' constraints on national policy, the more easily the French government can reject the claims of those who seek protection from competition.

In practice, of course, the European Communities have not always served the interests of competition. Individual member countries enjoy more power than is commonly thought to protect their markets from foreigners based outside the EC:

The Treaty of Rome gives the Commission considerable authority on trade questions. . . . But, a fact others have to accept is that the member states have, in practice, kept considerable power in trade matters to themselves. In times past, considerable international friction has resulted from this and it seems likely to continue. Deals made and understandings reached, in good faith, between a Commission official on the one hand and officials of a third government on the other have come unstuck because one or another member state found them unacceptable, or, in its view, went beyond the Commission's authority. . . . For a sector like steel in which most of the Ten have not too dissimilar interests, the Commission can be the locus of negotiation and decision. But, as the Japanese have found, when the EC wants something done to restrain imports on electronic products, or automobiles, where EC member states' interests vary greatly, the talks have been not only between national governments, but also between represen-

26. Mistral, "125 Ans de Contrainte Extérieure," p. 14, prefers to emphasize the skilled use of devaluation since World War II.

tatives of the Japanese industry and those from one, two, or three of the national industries in Europe as well as the Commission.[27]

Even within the EC, many nonmanufacturing activities remain heavily regulated by governments, and in certain manufacturing activities the influence of private cartels is tolerated or even endorsed. As a result, far from helping France to fend off protectionists, the European Communities may be providing them with the opening they need. It is important, therefore, to know whether the EC will protect France from its own protectionist impulses. There are two reasons to believe that it will.

The first is the energy now being devoted to relaunching the European Communities. Fully aware of the backsliding that can follow the initial integration of markets, the European Communities have declared their intention of creating a genuinely unified internal market by 1992.[28] On the one hand this involves elimination of remaining nontariff barriers to trade in manufacturing. These include regulations that entail examination of imports at national borders, that prevent goods considered safe and effective in one country from receiving similar billing in other countries, that handicap foreigners in the competition for public contracts, that explicitly ban the sale of the foreign products in the domestic market, and that use the tax system to favor domestic over foreign suppliers. On the other hand it involves extension of integration to activities such as financial and transport services that remain governed by national regulations. Although 1992 may be an unrealistic target, no one doubts the intentions of the commission, the parliament, or the court of justice.[29] Currently, the EC Commission is working obstinately to bring international competition to such industries as airlines and banking.[30]

27. Patterson, "The European Community as a Threat to the System," pp. 226–27.

28. The Single European Act took effect in July 1987; see Commission of the European Communities, *XXIst General Report on the Activities of the European Communities,* pp. 24–26. For a fuller description of the issues, see Commission of the European Communities, *Completing the Internal Market.*

29. One must be careful, however, not to ignore the hidden agenda of some adherents of this movement. Along with the desire to perfect the internal market may come a desire to expand control of exposure to competition from the outside world. Such a desire would express itself in creation of a "fortress Europe."

30. The principal problem is the council of ministers, as evidenced by footdragging

The second reason for optimism comes from opportunities associated with the admission of Greece, Portugal, and Spain to the European Communities. During its first three decades of operation, the European Economic Community reserved most of its protectionist instincts for agriculture. Devised supposedly as France's quid pro quo for exposing its industrial sector to German competition, the common agricultural policy has been supported energetically on both sides of the Rhine. Because the policy was designed at a time when conservatives ruled comfortably in both Germany and France, its subsidies flow primarily to those agricultural commodities (dairy products and grain) that are produced in politically conservative parts of each country. As of 1978, French and German producers captured 54 percent of the benefits associated with the common agricultural policy.[31]

The emergence of the French Socialist party, coupled with enlargement of the EC, may help to change agricultural politics in the community. Socialist agriculture produces Mediterranean products. It benefits little from the current pattern of European subsidies. Enlargement of the community affects the situation in two ways. On the one hand, it strengthens the hand of Mediterranean agriculture at the expense of its northern counterpart. This reduces the appeal to Germany and to conservative elements in France of continued agricultural protection. On the other hand, enlargement implies that subsidizing Mediterranean products would reduce the share of European subsidies captured by French farmers. As a result, it reduces the French Socialist interest in continued agricultural protection. It is not surprising, therefore, that the Germans have replaced the French as the most vigorous defenders of such protection.[32] Given

---

on application of the Treaty of Rome, article 85, to air transport and to mergers. See Adams, "Should Merger Policy Be Changed?"

31. The shares received by producers in other member countries were: Italy, 16 percent; the Netherlands, 10 percent; the United Kingdom, 8 percent; Denmark, 5 percent; Belgium-Luxembourg, 5 percent; and Ireland, 3 percent. See Davenport, "The Economic Impact of the EEC," table 8.6. According to the figures reported by Davenport, France, Denmark, Ireland, and the Netherlands are the only members of the community where consumers lost less than producers gained from operation of the common agricultural policy.

32. "Though French and West German finance ministers seem to agree on reforming the EEC's farm policy, the West German farm minister is behaving like

the severity of the community's budget deficit, caused primarily by its agricultural policy, and given the importance to Europe as well as the United States of a solution to the American trade deficit, France's diminished appetite for the common agricultural policy may suffice to tilt European subsidies in the direction of positive adjustment. In any event, the French government appears to recognize that in the common market as currently constituted, France stands to gain less from defense of agriculture than from comparable promotion of electronics and biotechnology.

The third feature of the French environment that will help to determine the speed with which France regains stable prosperity is French economic structure.

Rich countries will remain rich by developing comparative advantage in the production of differentiated products, which are insulated somewhat from price competition and thus cost competition. They can develop this advantage through product customization or else through product quality. France has long enjoyed success in producing differentiated products, and continues to enjoy it in a wide variety of mature products, including foods and textiles.[33] According to many observers, however, France must extend these advantages to adolescent products, especially those resulting from the revolutionary developments in electronics and biotechnology.[34] Such extension will not come easily if slow growth continues at the OECD level. And slow growth abroad is not the only problem. Robert Boyer argues that development of new comparative advantages may also be jeopardized by deregulation of domestic prices, which has caused prices

French ones of old in defending indefensible farm subsidies." "France Peers into the German Soul, and into Its Own," *Economist*, October 24, 1987, p. 55.

33. On the historical evidence, see Nef, *Industry and Government in France and England, 1540–1640*. On the contemporary period, the work of Bernard Lassudrie-Duchêne suggests that French industries, more than those of most rich countries, display a strong negative correlation between the ratio of exports to output and the ratio of exports to imports plus exports. To the extent that intraindustry trade signals trade in differentiated products, this piece of trade evidence supports the view that France enjoys competitive advantage in differentiated products.

34. Stoffaës, *La Grande Menace Industrielle*, pp. 624–29, 643–50. A critique of French export structure that emphasizes the need to develop comparative advantage in a few broad sectors, as opposed to many narrow niches spread throughout manufacturing, appears in Orléan, "L'Insertion dans les Echanges Internationaux," pp. 25–39.

to rise more rapidly in the sheltered sector (services) than in the exposed (manufacturing), encouraging investment in sheltered activities.[35] Further and major doses of structural adjustment may be required before high-technology expertise develops outside the pale of military products.[36] Nevertheless, the evidence accumulated in chapter 4 suggests that France has changed profoundly the geographic composition of its exports.[37] However much remains to be accomplished, France appears capable of changing its specific sources of comparative advantage, and arguably, now that France is rich, the product cycle should reinforce its ability to compete in the domain of differentiated products.

The felicity of national economic structure depends not only on the composition of output but also on the methods of production. In this connection many authorities believe that flexible production is the wave of the future; they differ, however, as to what flexibility entails.[38] To Piore and Sabel it implies shifting coalitions of artisans applying prodigious human capital to simple and cheap machinery. To others it implies mass production using complicated and expensive machinery.

Historically, the French industrial landscape has been relatively densely populated with small-scale plants.[39] In virtually all industries, tiny plants have posted dramatic gains since 1972. Whatever the goals of the planners, France has participated fully in the wave of decen-

35. Linkages between domestic prices, domestic profits, and domestic investment are also discussed in Mistral, "125 Ans de Contrainte Extérieure," pp. 6–10, which argues that protection from imports facilitated French economic development before 1929 because it afforded the dynamic elements of French business a margin for maneuver.

36. Stoffaës, *La Grande Menace Industrielle*, pp. 690–702.

37. Compare Delattre, "1979–1984: Une Nouvelle Donne pour les Branches de l'Industrie," p. 13, which shows that six industries (drugs, foundry products, electrical equipment, railway vehicles, aerospace, and ships) still send more than half their exports to developing countries. It also shows that France still accounts for relatively large shares of world exports to Algeria, Morocco, and Tunisia (22 percent) and sub-Saharan Africa (24 percent), but relatively low shares of world exports to the newly industrializing and rapidly growing countries (2 percent).

38. A useful discussion of the many meanings of flexible production appears in Aggarwal, "MRP, JIT, OPT, FMS? Making Sense of Production Operations Systems"; see also Jaikumar, "Postindustrial Manufacturing."

39. A careful study of the subject appears in INSEE E1; see also Pryor, "The Size of Production Establishments in Manufacturing."

tralization now sweeping the OECD. As flattered as they might be by the suggestion, civil servants in the ministry of industry and in the planning commission would be surprised to learn that France is the promised land of mass production.[40] Arguably, French industrial structure is well suited to a future in which rich countries must modify production methods frequently and pervasively and in which product differentiation requires artisanal methods of production. The more correct Piore and Sabel are about the direction of the world economy, the less warranted may be their pessimism about French economic prospects.

Culture affects economic behavior, and culture is durable; but the evidence reported in this book suggests an adaptability of French economic structure that preceded and exceeded today's political pragmatism. Structural handicaps can be overestimated.

French policymakers tend studiously to ignore similarities between the French and Italian economies. Not only do they fail to note the parallel in actual performance, but they fail to consider the possibility that if each attempted to occupy that niche of the world economy that offered the best standard of living for its citizens, the two countries would be occupying similar positions—specializations defined largely in terms of the Italian ideal type.

But no rich economy corresponds perfectly or even mostly to its caricature in academic discussions, so it is unlikely that France should mimic a single model. In fact, the most important handicap France might face as it attempts to restore good economic performance is a continuing obsession with Germany, a continuing need to treat the performance and structure of the economy across the Rhine as the benchmark for its own success.[41] The real issue is not which model

40. Note the implication for the argument, discussed above, that government initiatives in the microeconomy resulted in the systematic concentration of production. The evidence is consistent with the hypothesis, advanced in chapter 3, that government impinged on business less forcefully than one might believe from examining government behavior alone. To the extent that enterprises recognized the limits of government's ability to contravene market forces durably and appreciably in a broad spectrum of industries, most may not have organized themselves with government favors foremost in mind. Serious evaluation of the hypothesis requires evidence on enterprises as well as on establishments.

41. Germany is "an almost unconscious and not always accurate yardstick many French people use when thinking about their own country." "France Peers into the

for France but rather whether France has come to terms with World War II sufficiently to dispense with the need to treat Germany as its designated rival. The major cultural disability France has to fear is continued economic awe of Germany.

Long in convalescence, French self-esteem is mostly healthy once again.[42] The new self-confidence appears clearly in the diplomatic and military arenas, where petulance and development of separate strength are both on the wane: "France is multiplying defence initiatives with its European neighbours. French and West German politicians have told their military staffs to look into setting up a French-German brigade and to establish a defence council to promote co-operation. Operationally, neither idea has got beyond the head-scratching stage. Symbolically, they could be important."[43] Fewer and fewer government officials denounce the cultural imperialism and military hegemony of the United States. Several segments of society have finally confronted the ignominious aspects of the Vichy period. Perhaps the humiliations of 1870 and 1940 have finally been exorcised. If so, perhaps France will shed the German norm as it seeks to fashion a new set of goals for industrial policy.

Whatever its current economic prospects, France has avoided so far the cruel dilemma it seemed to face at the end of World War II. Writing in 1951 David Landes presented the French predicament in stark terms: "To change and, in changing, die; or not to change, and risk a swifter death."[44] In fact, France preserved its cultural identity and vitality while exposing itself to global market forces: however incompletely, it restructured its economy successfully.

* * *

This is a book about France. Its relevance to the United States cannot be established without further research. Nevertheless, its

---

German Soul, and into Its Own," *Economist*, October 24, 1987, p. 56. The dangers in such an obsession are that France will attempt to copy a model unsuited to its natural advantages or that replication will be achieved only after the model has lost its desirability.

42. Ibid. Also "A Survey of France," *Economist*, March 12, 1988, especially p. 22. The nadir in national self-satisfaction is described in Luethy, *France against Herself*.

43. "France Peers into the German Soul, and into Its Own," pp. 55–56.

44. Landes, "French Business and the Businessman," p. 353.

contents do justify certain observations on American perceptions of foreign protectionism and the suitability of French-style industrial policies to the United States.

During the past two decades foreign competition has forced several large American industries to contemplate, and a few to effect, major restructuring. For the first time since industrialization the United States is now hard pressed to export as much as it imports. Although some observers attribute negative trade balances to an overvalued dollar, others impute both the restructuring and the trade deficits to the behavior of governments abroad. Allegedly the foreigners restrict access to their home markets and subsidize their domestic industries. On both accounts they sever the natural links between national comparative advantage and the international division of labor. Unless the American government matches their behavior and flattens the field of international competition, the United States will continue to bear disproportionately the global burden of structural economic adjustment. The history of the Omnibus Trade and Competitiveness Act of 1988 suggests that the legislative and executive branches of government both embrace this view.[45]

As the sins of the foreigners are tallied up, the Europeans are often considered the prime offenders—worse even than the Japanese. For example, it has been argued that the United States was obliged to restrain automobile imports from Japan because protectionism in Europe was diverting Japanese cars artificially to the American market. More generally, when asked by an American think tank to describe "US trade practices that create problems for the trade policymakers of other countries," the Canadian ambassador to the Tokyo round of trade talks quickly imputed much of the blame for American protectionism to the European Communities:

> I do not attach the major share of the blame for the strains and contradictions in the trade relations system to actions by the United States. The European interest in creating a preference system around the European heartland . . . has done more damage to the system than any policy misconceptions, misunderstandings,

45. Presidential veto of an earlier trade bill had little to do with the measure's protectionist provisions. Kilborn, "U.S. Rearranging Its Top Priorities for Trade Policy."

and miscalculations in Washington. Moreover, it is not from Europe that we are likely to get the intellectual initiatives and inventiveness, or the necessary recognition of value in a system of order that will be necessary to rebuild the system."[46]

Some Europeans accept that blame: as one German put it, the tendencies of the EC "are clearly protectionist. Even internal free trade within the European Community is eroding. . . . The second enlargement of the EC will lead to more protection to secure Spain and Portugal against competition from the newly industrialized countries."[47]

The protectionist arguments now emanating from Washington are not devoid of irony. Early in the postwar period, it was the foreigners, including many French, who doubted the proposition that comparative advantage determines patterns of trade.[48] Although the foreigners believed private as well as public power impedes the workings of pure trade theory, the implications they drew for policy—protection plus promotion—are not unrelated to their current American counterparts.[49] Today's American arguments for protectionism are even less compelling than were their foreign predecessors'. They have already been criticized effectively on several counts. First, the United States engages in its share of protectionism, not all of which can be justified as reluctant efforts to neutralize restrictive practices abroad. As Robert Heilbroner commented, "there is the embarrassing fact that it is not only our rivals who tilt the playing field. The European Community has cited more than thirty such discriminatory practices on the part of the United States, such as the provision that the Pentagon purchase only American machine tools; and the General Agreement on Tariffs and Trade . . . has also found United States violations of its free-trade charter."[50] Second, other countries do not

46. Grey, "A Note on US Trade Practices," p. 257.

47. Donges, "Comment," p. 320.

48. This is hardly surprising: "As might have been expected, Ricardo's doctrine was always more enthusiastically endorsed by nations that produced machinery than by those that produced handicrafts." Heilbroner, "Reflections: Hard Times," p. 97.

49. A recent French expression of this view is Jeanneney, *Pour un Nouveau Protectionnisme*.

50. Heilbroner, "Reflections," p. 103.

protect their domestic markets hermetically.[51] If the field on which national economies compete does slope, it does not obviously disadvantage American enterprises. Even if American business does look uphill, its handicap is far too slight to account for the U.S. commercial deficit.[52]

The evidence in this study confirms the view that countries like France, pigeonholed as protectionist, are exposed to much more foreign competition than American protectionists would like to believe. It also suggests that France has undertaken considerable structural change entailing considerable absolute contraction of employment in declining industries and considerable unemployment in depressed industrial regions. It contradicts the belief that American enterprise has suffered disproportionately from structural adjustment. Growing acceptance of a quasi-liberal trading order by countries like France makes it difficult to justify the stampede of American politicians in the opposite direction.

During the first half of the 1980s many Americans called persuasively for a national industrial policy. But when growth accelerated, the dollar dropped, and unemployment fell, industrial policy disappeared from the agendas of many politicians. Nevertheless, the persistence of structural problems, coupled with a change of political administration, may summon the concept back to policy's major league. In several respects the evidence examined here might inform an American debate.

51. Exaggerations of Japanese protectionism are deflated convincingly in Saxonhouse, "The Micro- and Macroeconomics of Foreign Sales to Japan," pp. 259–304. As for Europe: "The actual data, as opposed to theory or a priori judgments, indicate that EC imports . . . of manufactured goods exceed those of the United States and Japan and grew faster between 1968 and 1980. . . . The EC is now more open than its main partners." Berthelot, "Comment," p. 310. Berthelot goes on to show that ratios of manufacturing imports to population and to GNP were higher in the EC than in the United States or Japan, even when intracommunity trade is excluded from the calculation. He also shows that per capita imports (similarly defined) of textile products—frequent objects of managed trade—were higher in the EC than in the United States or Japan.

52. "Gary Hufbauer . . . has calculated that if all European and Japanese barriers to trade were eliminated our trade gap would be reduced by only about twenty per cent." Heilbroner, "Reflections," pp. 102–03.

First, French industrial policies tended to work best when they promoted specific technologies and products, mostly for military uses. They tended to work less well when they aimed to facilitate general adaptation to global market competition. In the military arena the United States already engages in industrial policy. It now employs most of the techniques found in France to promote and protect domestic producers.[53] For better or worse, in this sector of the economy the United States has little to learn from French policy.

Second, by American and Japanese standards the French economy is modest in size; so, therefore, is government's budget. Budget constraint forced France periodically to curb its appetite for industrial policy. This in turn forced it to confront the issues of appropriate targets and methods of intervention. Needless to say, government did not establish a schedule labeled "marginal efficiency of subsidy" and then move along that schedule in accordance with the severity of its budget constraint. Nevertheless, industries that received substantial and sustained support often achieved at least some of the goals that government set for them; and industries that received temporary support during periods of extensive intervention rarely improved their performance in any sense of the term.

The weaker the budget constraint, the weaker the pressure to identify specific sources of market failure that industrial policy can remedy—and the harder the task of resisting Mancur-Olson-type coalitions demanding protection.[54]

Over the past several years, American government has behaved as if it faced nary a spending constraint. Whatever the macroeconomic virtues of the resulting budget deficits, the potential for microeconomic perversity is clear: the deeper the government's pocket, the longer its ability to feed the illusion, shared by target enterprises and civil servants alike, that fundamental market forces can be contravened. As long as the American budget remains unbridled, an American

53. The U.S. military-industrial complex nourishes much of the Gallic belief that France helps its industries in practice no more than does the United States. See Vernier-Palliez, "Preface," p. 1.

54. "French microeconomic policy erred during the 1950's, and restrained the otherwise powerful forces acting for growth, by a stubbornly misdirected reliance on universal application of the selective techniques which worked well in concentrated industrial structures." Sheahan, *Promotion and Control of Industry in Postwar France*, p. 276.

industrial policy runs the risk of insufficient selectivity and insufficient emphasis of positive adjustment.

Third, French industrial policies were implemented contemporaneously with exposure of the French economy to foreign competition. Opening the economy to such rivalry appeared to weaken government's ability to influence the microeconomy.[55] Even for microeconomic policy, however, exposure may have been a blessing in disguise. The greater the vigor of foreign competition, the greater the cost to government of protecting existing sources of rent. (The cost to government of protectionism also increased because it had to be converted from regulations, which do not require expenditure of government monies, to subsidies, which do.) The combination of parameters faced by France's postwar governments—budget constraints and uncontrollable competition—instilled an appreciation for positive structural adjustment. Although such appreciation developed slowly, it is now broadly diffused among top-level civil servants.

The American economy is not an open economy—not by the standards of Europe since formation of the European Economic Community. Its relative autarky follows largely but incompletely from its historical embarrassment of natural resources and its distance from rich trading partners. Such autarky dulls the incentive for government to employ industrial policy in the service of positive structural adjustment. The French experience suggests that those who favor industrial policies for the United States should think twice before building their program on protectionist foundations. The complementarity of government and market mechanisms was essential to French success.[56] Competition in the marketplace disciplined government intervention no less than it disciplined business; and government enforced competition more effectively than did the market itself. This, perhaps, is the most important lesson of the French experience.

55. Balassa, "Whither French Planning?" pp. 537–54.

56. "It is as much a mistake in France as in the United States to consider issues of alternative market organization primarily in terms of a conflict between government intervention and private business choice. The true opposition is between the complex forces favorable to initiative and progress, which may come from either government or private enterprise, and the obstacles to progress which may equally well come from either side." Sheahan, *Promotion and Control of Industry in Postwar France*, p. 282.

After the United States imbibes its measure of deregulation, ample residues of market imperfection will remain. Antitrust, the policy on which the United States has relied since before World War I, is unlikely to remedy all maladies attributable to market power.[57] If industrial policy is just a label for the process of identifying specific sources of market failure and prescribing remedies appropriate to both the illness and the patient industry, then industrial policy may be a good thing for the United States. If so, it will require substantial pragmatism. Although competition may be desirable in all industries, its ideal sources and forms may vary among them on the basis of their underlying characteristics.[58] Fundamentally, competition means nothing more than the existence of genuine alternatives; and the French experience suggests that government can indeed generate such alternatives in many ways.[59]

If the United States is to adopt industrial policies, it must find a way to commit itself to competition as credibly as did France when it promoted European economic integration and accepted economic decolonization. As long as protectionist coalitions can exploit vulnerabilities in any of the many corridors of American government, threatened enterprises will continue to invest defensively rather than

57. In fact, under the Reagan administration the vigor of American antitrust has declined perilously. The recent supreme court decision on discount retailing, *Business Electronic Corp.* v. *Sharp Electronics* (*U.S. Law Week*, vol. 56 [May 3, 1988], pp. 4387–98), may be of minor significance in the American context, but it certainly provides interesting comparison for the Leclerc experience discussed in chapter 5. According to Stuart Taylor, Jr., "High Court Backs Discounter Curbs by Manufacturers," *New York Times*, May 3, 1988, "Though the full impact of the decision remains to be determined, corporate lawyers and antitrust experts said the ruling would almost certainly cause some retailers to limit discounts, particularly in the electronics and clothing industries."

58. Piore and Sabel would emphasize instead the importance of cooperation, "the need for collaboration in which all the parties share a goal—so that they all profit from complementary innovations," but they also recognize that collaborators should not become "so tightly integrated as to lose the competitive spirit to innovate." Piore and Sabel, *The Second Industrial Divide*, p. 284.

59. "An outside force, be it new entry, new management in one of the existing firms, import competition, or direct promotion of change by government, may . . . alter the pressures and cause enterprise choices to change in directions favorable for more rapid aggregate progress. . . . In the postwar French economy, the government independently created such forces in several important cases." Sheahan, *Promotion and Control of Industry in Postwar France*, p. 269.

innovatively. Nor will periodic adjustments of exchange rates lead American enterprises necessarily to the path of positive adjustment.

The Uruguay round of GATT negotiations offers the United States an opportunity to commit itself to fuller and more durable exposure to foreign competition; so does implementation of free trade with Canada.[60] Strenuous promotion of binding arbitration in trade disputes, which would diminish the size of Washington's trade policy bureaucracy, might help the American economy far more than would any currently feasible liberalization of trade in services or agriculture.

During its period of rapid growth the United States possessed an abundance of natural resources. As a result it adopted a pattern of economic development that emphasized exploitation and depletion of raw materials. Its exports embodied unusually large doses of primary products, providing rare evidence in support of the Heckscher-Ohlin model of international trade.[61] As the United States confronts exhaustion of its comparative advantage in natural resources, it must contemplate a new basis for growth. It must reorient itself from a culture based on extraction and depletion toward a culture based on modification and then reallocation of durable resources.

Other nations, including France, have been coping with relatively poor endowments of natural resources since the nineteenth century. Initially, therefore, the United States may face a cultural disadvantage in its search for a reallocative mode of growth. An important message of this book, however, is that cultural traditions adjust to competitive pressures, and they can do so surprisingly quickly in countries that are already rich. Just as economic Malthusianism disappeared in one generation from most lists of France's pressing problems, so the United States can be expected to experience the diffusion of a modify-and-redeploy mentality in its economic agents, provided that they are exposed to foreign competition.

60. Vernon and Spar, *Beyond Globalism.*
61. Wright, "American Industrial Leadership, 1879–1940." In his abstract, Wright says his results "suggest that the competitive advantage of American manufacturing was not rooted in capital-intensity, nor in labor skills, nor in across-the-board technological superiority. Instead, the single most robust finding is that American exports were characterized by intensity in natural resources. In fact, their relative resource-intensity was *increasing* over the half-century prior to the Great Depression."

In an earlier economic era, when economies of scale and scope dictated concentration of many an industry's production in large and complex enterprises, those dissatisfied with microeconomic performance understandably looked especially carefully at business organization and behavior, and hence at traditional industrial policies. In the present era, however, most industries are experiencing a decentralizing wave of technological change, prompting dramatic increases in the employment and employment share of small plants. In such an environment, natural barriers to births and deaths of enterprises have waned, shifting attention to the quality and flexibility of the labor force. In no small measure, structural policy should migrate from the industrial to the labor arena.

France, too, may be recognizing the importance of replacing conventional industrial policies with attention to labor markets.[62] It will be interesting, therefore, to see who learns what from whom. I would like to believe that the American traditions of decentralization, self-reliance, and individualism—what Michael Piore and Charles Sabel call yeoman democracy—will help the United States to overcome the scleroses that France attacked earlier in this half-century with remarkable success.

62. Salais and Thévenot, eds., *Le Travail*; Maurice, Sellier, and Silvestre, *Politique d'Education et Organisation Industrielle en France et en Allemagne*; and Petit, "Full-Employment Policies in Stagnation," p. 404.

Appendix A
Tables

Table A-1. *Growth of GDP per Capita, by Country, Selected Periods, 1950–85*

Percent increase in volume of GDP per capita

Period	France	Germany	Italy	Japan	United Kingdom	United States
1950–58	33	65	47	n.a.	15	13
1960–73	77	56	79	184	39	39
1973–85	21	26	22	40	16	15
1960–85	115	97	118	299	62	61

Sources: OECD, *Statistics of National Accounts, 1950–1961*, pt.1, table 3; and OECD, *National Accounts, 1960–1985*, vol. 1: *Main Aggregates*, pts. 2, 4.
n.a. Not available.

Table A-2. *Relative Standards of Living, by Country and Data Source, Selected Years, 1950–85*

France = 100

Source and Period	France	Germany	Italy	Japan	United Kingdom	United States
World Bank[a]						
1950	100	85	57	35	123	207
1955	100	107	63	42	119	200
1960	100	115	65	50	108	169
1965	100	111	66	62	100	160
1970	100	106	67	81	87	139
1975	100	101	66	84	78	122
1980	100	105	65	89	79	120
Organization for Economic Cooperation and Development[b]						
1970	100	107	95	88	102	154
1975	100	99	88	86	96	139
1980	100	102	91	91	90	135
1985	100	106	95	103	95	144

Sources: Kravis, Heston, and Summers, *World Product and Income*, table 8-3; and OECD, *National Accounts, 1970–1985*, supplement to vol. 1: *Purchasing Power Parities*, table 13.
a. Real gross domestic income per capita; purchasing power parity exchange rates.
b. GDP per capita at current prices; current purchasing power parities.

Table A-3. *Coefficients of Variation in Annual Rates of Growth, by Country, Selected Periods, 1953–85*[a]
Percent

Period	France	Germany	Italy	Japan	United Kingdom	United States
1953–57	0.31	0.29	0.28	0.14	0.42	1.26
1958–73	0.23	0.47	0.33	0.30	0.58	0.57
1974–85	0.73	1.11	1.31	0.48	1.63	1.24

Sources: OECD, *National Accounts of OECD Countries, 1950–1979*, vol. 1: *Main Aggregates;* and OECD, *National Accounts, 1960–1985*, vol. 1: *Main Aggregates*.
a. Variation in growth of GDP volume.

Table A-4. *Mean Growth of Output at the Industry Level, 1959–80*[a]
Production distribuée in millions of 1970 francs unless otherwise specified

Industries	Number	Mean output		Mean increase 1959–80	Standard deviation	t-ratio[b]
		1959	1980			
All	79	8,774	23,493	14,719[c]	18,543	7.06
Manufacturing	46	5,889	15,877	9,988[c]	9,275	7.30

Source: INSEE input-output tables in 1970 prices, level S (unpublished).
a. Industries defined according to NAP-S79 (see appendix C).
b. Relates to hypothesis that mean in column 4 is 0.
c. Differs from 0 at the .001 level of significance in a one-tail test.

Table A-5. *Growth of Employment at the Industry Level, 1954–75*[a]

Industries	Employment		Change 1954–75	Percent change 1954–75
	1954	1975		
Manufacturing	4,432,100	5,398,550	966,450	21.8
All	18,946,300	20,943,900	1,997,600	10.5

Sources: Praderie and Carré, "La Population Active par Secteur d'Etablissement," pp. 9–17; and INSEE D67, p. 188.
a. Industries defined according to MCBCND (see appendix C).

Table A-6. *Distribution of Industries by Growth of Employment, 1954–75*[a]

Percent growth 1954–75	Number of industries	Share of total employment 1954	Share of total employment 1975	Change 1954–75	Percent change 1954–75
Less than 0	8	41.1	18.0	−4,024,910	−51.6
0–49	10	21.8	24.8	1,063,380	25.8
50 or more	14	37.1	57.2	4,959,130	70.6
All industries	32	100.0	100.0	1,997,600	10.5

Sources: Praderie and Carré, "La Population Active par Secteur d'Etablissement," pp. 9–17; and INSEE D67, p. 188.
a. Industries defined according to MCBCND (see appendix C).

Table A-7. *Mean Growth of Employment at the Industry Level, 1954–75*[a]

Industries	Number	Mean employment 1954	Mean employment 1975	Mean increase 1954–75	Standard deviation	t-ratio[b]
Manufacturing	18	246,228	299,919	53,692	149,050	1.53
All	32	592,072	654,497	62,425	669,740	0.53

Sources: Praderie and Carré, "La Population Active par Secteur d'Etablissement," pp. 9–17; and INSEE D67, p. 188.
a. Industries defined according to MCBCND (see appendix C).
b. Relates to hypothesis that mean in column 4 is 0. In neither row could the hypothesis be rejected at the .05 level of significance in a one-tail test.

Table A-8. *Labor Mobility, by Sex, Selected Declining Occupations, 1959–77*
Percent

Occupation in year t	Different occupation in t + 5[a]		
	t = 1959	t = 1965	t = 1972
Farm owner			
Male	9.9	8.4	5.4
Female	5.5	8.9	5.5
Agricultural laborer			
Male	27.2	30.4	31.3
Female	50.0	45.7	42.5
Small shopkeeper			
Male	9.8	14.6	17.8
Female	5.9	10.1	11.7
Miner			
Male	14.4	13.9	18.8
Female	. . .	100.0	. . .
Household servant			
Male	25.0	55.0	25.6
Female	29.7	27.9	25.7

Sources: Praderie and Passagez, "La Mobilité Professionnelle en France entre 1959 et 1964," appendix 4; and INSEE D91, tables 57, 60.
a. Observation confined to people employed at both ends of the period.

Table A-9. *Change in Salaried and Unsalaried Employment at the Industry Level, 1954–75, 1975–82*[a]

Industries	Number	Salaried employment as percent of total		Change 1954–75	Percent change 1954–75	Change in unsalaried employment 1954–75	Percent change in unsalaried employ-ment 1954–75
		1954	1975				
Manufacturing	18	90.6	96.3	1,184,705	30	−218,255	−52
Other	14	57.3	77.0	3,660,365	44	−2,629,215	−42
All	32	65.0	82.0	4,845,070	39	−2,847,470	−43

Industries	Number	Salaried employment as percent of total		Change 1975–82	Percent change 1975–82	Change in unsalaried employment 1975–82	Percent change in unsalaried employ-ment 1975–82
		1975	1982				
Manufacturing	20	95.2	94.6	−591,240	−10.5	1,470	0.5
Other	18	76.8	79.2	1,244,730	10.8	−132,900	−3.8
All	38	82.0	83.0	653,490	3.8	−131,430	−3.5

Sources: Praderie and Carré, "La Population Active par Secteur d'Etablissement," pp. 9–17; INSEE D67, pp. 101, 188; and INSEE D100, table 03.
a. Industries defined according to MCBCND (1954–75) or NAP-T (1975–82); see appendix C.

Table A-10. *Change in Share of Salaried Employment at the Industry Level, 1954–75*[a]

Industries	Number	Mean ratio of salaried to total employment		Mean percentage point change 1954–75	Standard deviation	t-ratio[b]
		1954	1975			
Manufacturing	18	91.8	95.9	4.1[c]	5.7	3.05
All	32	88.1	92.0	3.9[c]	6.8	3.27

Sources: Praderie and Carré, "La Population Active par Secteur d'Etablissement," pp. 9–17; and INSEE D67, p. 188.
a. Industries defined according to MCBCND (see appendix C).
b. Relates to hypothesis that mean in column 4 is 0.
c. Differs from 0 at the .01 level of significance in a one-tail test.

Table A-11. *Change in Salaried and Unsalaried Employment, Selected Industries, 1954–75*[a]

Code	Industry	Ratio of salaried to total employment 1954	Ratio of salaried to total employment 1975	Change in salaried employment 1954–75	Percent change in salaried employment 1954–75	Change in unsalaried employment 1954–75	Percent change in unsalaried employment 1954–75
01	Agriculture	21.7	18.0	− 732,600	− 67	− 2,312,905	− 59
29	Wholesale / retail trade	53.1	75.3	886,715	97	− 218,840	− 27
28	Miscellaneous services	54.2	75.1	1,270,700	130	− 80,675	− 10
19	Leather	70.9	89.2	− 33,305	− 20	− 51,310	− 77
02	Food	73.4	81.8	82,730	18	− 44,595	− 27
18	Apparel	75.2	90.6	− 61,505	− 17	− 87,080	− 74
20	Wood / furniture	78.6	87.4	3,850	2	− 31,185	− 46

Sources: Praderie and Carré, "La Population Active par Secteur d'Etablissement," pp. 9–17; and INSEE D67, p. 188.
a. Industries in which salaried employment was less than 80 percent of total employment in 1954. Industries defined according to MCBCND (see appendix C).

Table A-12. *Mobility from Unsalaried to Salaried Work, 1959–77*[a]
Percent

Position in year t	Salaried in t + 5		
	t = 1959	t = 1965	t = 1972
Self-employed			
No employees			
Male	6.1	8.1	6.7
Female	5.9	8.6	9.3
Employed others			
Male	3.8	6.8	8.2
Female	2.7	7.2	4.1
Family helper			
Male	23.7	27.0	19.4
Female	5.5	9.3	7.4

Sources: Praderie and Passagez, "La Mobilité Professionnelle en France entre 1959 et 1964," table 19; INSEE D32, tables 2.1, 2.2; and INSEE D91, table 53.
a. Observation confined to people employed in unsalaried positions in *t* and employed in some position in *t* + 5.

273

Table A-13. *Change in Employment Shares of Plants of Different Sizes, Manufacturing Industries, Selected Periods, 1954–82[a]*

Number of salaried employees	Period	Classification code[b]	Number of industries in which size-class share of industry employment	
			Decreases	Increases
10–19	1954–62	NAE-2	33	7
	1962–72	NAE-2	35	5
	1962–72	NAP-100	38	2
	1972–82	NAP-100	3	37
20–49	1954–62	NAE-2	31	9
	1962–72	NAE-2	31	9
	1962–72	NAP-100	31	9
	1972–82	NAP-100	5	35
50–99	1954–62	NAE-2	16	24
	1962–72	NAE-2	26	14
	1962–72	NAP-100	27	13
	1972–82	NAP-100	23	17
100–199	1954–62	NAE-2	16	24
	1962–72	NAE-2	23	17
	1962–72	NAP-100	25	15
	1972–82	NAP-100	21	19
200–499	1954–62	NAE-2	15	25
	1962–72	NAE-2	13	27
	1962–72	NAP-100	13	27
	1972–82	NAP-100	22	18
500–999	1954–62	NAE-2	18	20
	1962–72	NAE-2	15	24
	1962–72	NAP-100	11	29
	1974–80	NAP-100[c]	24	13
1,000 or more	1954–62	NAE-2	12	19
	1962–72	NAE-2	12	23
	1962–72	NAP-100	12	27
	1974–80	NAP-100[c]	24	11
500 or more	1972–82	NAP-100	28	12

Sources: INSEE, *Les Etablissements Industriels et Commerciaux en France en 1954*, table I-S; INSEE, *Les Etablissements Industriels et Commerciaux en France en 1962*, table II; INSEE, *Les Entreprises et Leurs Etablissements au 1er Janvier 1983*, p. 73; Ministère de l'Industrie et de la Recherche, *La Concentration dans l'Industrie de 1974 à 1980*; and INSEE E43, pp. 79–94, 103–202.

a. Although industry definitions vary, unless otherwise noted the number of industries represented in each row is forty.

b. Codes described in appendix C.

c. Thirty-seven industries.

Table A-14. *Change in Distribution of Salaried Employment by Size of Plant, Mean Values among Manufacturing Industries, 1954–62[a]*

Number of employees	Mean salaried employment 1954	Mean salaried employment 1962	Mean change 1954–62	Standard deviation	t-ratio[b]	Mean share[c] 1954	Mean share[c] 1962	Mean percentage point change 1954–62	Standard deviation	t-ratio[d]
11–20	7,143	6,871	−273	1,871	−0.92	9.5	8.3	−1.29[e]	1.64	−4.97
21–50	14,155	14,815	660	4,029	1.04	17.7	16.5	−1.21[f]	2.56	−2.99
51–100	10,547	12,454	1,907[f]	3,859	3.13	12.5	13.1	0.58	2.51	1.47
101–200	12,740	14,637	1,897[f]	4,348	2.76	13.1	14.1	1.00[g]	2.97	2.13
201–500	17,367	20,459	3,092[g]	8,232	2.38	18.8	19.4	0.63	3.82	1.05
501–1,000	11,444	12,810	1,366	6,893	1.25	11.6	12.0	0.37	4.83	0.49
1,000 or more	19,926	23,704	3,778[g]	9,610	2.49	16.8	16.7	−0.10	4.69	−0.13
11 or more	93,322	105,750	12,427[f]	28,649	2.74	100.0	100.0	. . .	. . .	. . .

Sources: INSEE, *Les Etablissements Industriels et Commerciaux en France en 1954*, table I-S; and INSEE, *Les Etablissements Industriels et Commerciaux en France en 1962*, table II.

a. Forty industries defined according to NAE-2 (see appendix C). Sources include industries 10, 16–32, 35–59. Sources combine industries 23 and 24, 35 and 36, 17 and 185, and 16 and rest of 18. Changes in definition over time result in omission of industries 61 and 62.

b. Relates to hypothesis that mean change in salaried employment is 0.

c. Share is salaried employment in plants of the given size class in a given industry divided by all salaried employment in the industry (percent).

d. Relates to hypothesis that mean percentage point change in share is 0.

e. Differs from 0 at .001 level of significance in a one-tail test.

f. Differs from 0 at .01 level of significance in a one-tail test.

g. Differs from 0 at .05 level of significance in a one-tail test.

Table A-15. *Change in Employment Share of Plants with 10–99 Salaried Workers, Selected Industries, 1962–72[a]*

Code	Industry	Employment in small plants as percent of employment in all plants 1962	Employment in small plants as percent of employment in all plants 1972	Percentage point change 1962–72	Change in employment 1962–72 (thousands)	Percent change in employment 1962–72
46	Ice/related products	90.6	61.6	−29.0	−1.43	−44
43	Dairy products	54.3	34.3	−20.0	−8.69	−25
53	Wood/furniture	68.4	49.7	−18.7	−24.96	−24
58	Audio/musical instruments	44.1	28.3	−15.8	−1.31	−43
44	Preserved foods	48.1	33.2	−14.9	−4.94	−32
61	Plastics products	49.4	35.1	−14.3	9.15	40
32	Building materials	55.6	41.6	−13.9	−0.30	−1
40	Grain mill products	56.6	44.2	−12.4	−6.15	−42
22	General mechanical engineering	48.9	37.8	−11.1	−4.69	−10
59	Ornaments	53.9	43.7	−10.2	−1.89	−20

Source: INSEE E43, pp. 103–202.

a. Industries defined according to NAE-2 (see appendix C). Industries are those in which employment in small plants as a percentage of employment in all plants changed at least 10 percentage points.

Table A-16. *Change in Distribution of Salaried Employment by Size of Plant, Mean Values among Manufacturing Industries, 1962–72*[a]

Number of employees	Mean salaried employment		Mean change 1962–72	Standard deviation	t-ratio[b]	Mean share[c]		Mean percentage point change 1962–72	Standard deviation	t-ratio[d]
	1962	1972				1962	1972			
10–19	5,880	3,316	−2,564[e]	3,746	−4.33	7.4	4.7	−2.78[e]	3.06	−5.74
20–49	13,178	12,542	−636	3,315	−1.21	15.7	13.3	−2.46[e]	4.08	−3.81
50–99	12,259	12,991	732	3,390	1.37	13.5	12.3	−1.15[f]	3.35	−2.17
100–199	14,730	16,496	1,766	6,086	1.84	14.5	15.2	0.74	4.29	1.09
200–499	20,161	24,807	4,646[g]	8,845	3.32	18.5	21.4	2.94[g]	5.72	3.25
500–999	13,944	16,950	3,006[f]	7,712	2.46	12.1	14.4	2.26[f]	6.93	2.06
1,000 or more	25,972	31,388	5,416	22,881	1.50	18.3	18.8	0.45	6.65	0.42
10 or more	106,124	118,490	12,366[f]	38,067	2.05	100.0	100.0	. . .	. . .	. . .

Source: INSEE E43, pp. 103–202.
a. Forty industries defined according to NAE-2 (see appendix C). Source combines industries 23 and 24, 35 and 36, 17 and 185, 16 and rest of 18. Source omits industries 38 and 60.
b. Relates to hypothesis that mean change in salaried employment is 0.
c. Share is salaried employment in plants of the given size class in a given industry divided by all salaried employment in the industry (percent).
d. Relates to hypothesis that mean percentage point change is 0.
e. Differs from 0 at .001 level of significance in a one-tail test.
f. Differs from 0 at .05 level of significance in a one-tail test.
g. Differs from 0 at .01 level of significance in a one-tail test.

Table A-17. *Change in Distribution of Salaried Employment by Size of Plant, Mean Values among Manufacturing Industries, 1972–82*[a]

Number of employees	Mean salaried employment		Mean change 1972–82	Standard deviation	t-ratio[b]	Mean share[c]		Mean percentage point change 1972–82	Standard deviation	t-ratio[d]
	1972	1982				1972	1982			
10–19	3,380	6,934	3,554[e]	6,715	3.35	3.1	5.4	2.23[f]	2.61	5.40
20–49	12,880	16,429	3,549[e]	6,449	3.48	10.7	12.9	2.22[f]	2.42	5.82
50–99	13,244	13,534	290	2,952	0.62	11.3	11.2	−0.04	1.72	−0.16
100–199	16,890	16,241	−650	5,993	−0.69	13.6	13.6	−0.03	2.82	−0.07
200–499	25,303	24,159	−1,144	8,942	−0.81	21.5	21.3	−0.21	5.99	−0.22
500 or more	49,025	43,823	−5,203[g]	13,044	−2.52	39.8	35.6	−4.18[e]	7.74	−3.42
10 or more	120,722	121,119	397	26,035	0.10	100.0	100.0	. . .	. . .	. . .

Sources: INSEE E43, pp. 79–94; and INSEE, *Les Entreprises et Leurs Etablissements au 1er Janvier 1983*, p. 73.
a. Forty industries defined according to NAP-100 (see appendix C). First source includes industries 5, 10, 11, 13, 15–25, 27–34, 36–37, 39–41, 43–54.
b. Relates to hypothesis that mean change in salaried employment is 0.
c. Share is salaried employment in plants of the given size class in a given industry divided by all salaried employment in the industry (percent).
d. Relates to hypothesis that mean percentage point change is 0.
e. Differs from 0 at .01 level of significance in a one-tail test.
f. Differs from 0 at .001 level of significance in a one-tail test.
g. Differs from 0 at .05 level of significance in a one-tail test.

Table A-18. *Change in Distribution of Salaried Employment by Size of Plant, Mean Values among Manufacturing Industries, 1962–82*[a]

Number of employees	Mean share[b]		Mean percentage point change 1962–82	Standard deviation	t-ratio[c]
	1962	1982			
10–19	5.8	5.4	−0.47	2.14	−1.38
20–49	13.0	13.0	−0.00	3.47	−0.01
50–99	12.0	11.2	−0.76	3.08	−1.55
100–199	14.2	13.6	−0.58	3.61	−1.02
200–499	18.9	21.3	2.38[d]	4.96	3.03
500 or more	36.2	35.6	−0.57	9.00	−0.40

Sources: INSEE E43, pp. 79–94; and INSEE, *Les Entreprises et Leurs Etablissements au 1er Janvier 1983*, p. 73.

a. Forty industries defined according to NAP-100 (see appendix C). First source includes industries 5, 10, 11, 13, 15–25, 27–34, 36–37, 39–41, 43–54.

b. Salaried employment in plants of the given size class in a given industry divided by all salaried employment in the industry (percent).

c. Relates to hypothesis that mean percentage point change is 0.

d. Differs from 0 at the .01 level of significance in a one-tail test.

Table A-19. *Manufacturing Industries in Which Small-Plant Share of Salaried Employment Declined at Least 5 Percentage Points, 1962–72*[a]

Code	Industry	Small-plant share of industry employment		Percentage point change 1962–72
		1962	1972	
17	Bulk chemicals	13.2	7.8	−5.4
19	Drugs	14.4	9.0	−5.5
18	Chemical products n.e.c.	18.6	12.5	−6.1
25	Mechanical equipment II	16.3	9.5	−6.8
47	Apparel	32.0	24.3	−7.7
16	Glass	12.6	4.1	−8.5
41	Beverages	26.7	17.9	−8.8
54	Miscellaneous manufactures	40.3	31.1	−9.1
37	Preserved foods	24.8	13.2	−11.6
21	Metallic products	29.4	17.4	−12.0
53	Plastics products	28.6	15.8	−12.8
15	Building materials	35.5	21.8	−13.7
36	Dairy products	33.4	19.6	−13.7
48	Wood	46.9	29.9	−17.0
49	Furniture	51.1	29.8	−21.3

Source: INSEE E43, pp. 79–94.

a. Small plants are those with 10–49 salaried workers. Industries defined according to NAP-100 (see appendix C).

Table A-20. *Change in Share of Salaried Employment by Size of Plant, Mean Values among Manufacturing Industries, 1962–72*[a]

Number of employees	Mean share[b]		Mean percentage point change 1962–72	Standard deviation	t-ratio[c]
	1962	1972			
10–19	5.8	3.1	−2.70[d]	3.05	−5.60
20–49	13.0	10.7	−2.23[d]	3.01	−4.68
50–99	12.0	11.3	−0.71[e]	2.20	−2.05
100–199	14.2	13.6	−0.55	3.75	−0.93
200–499	18.9	21.5	2.58[e]	6.22	2.63
500–999	13.4	15.2	1.81[e]	4.75	2.41
1,000 or more	22.7	24.5	1.79	7.72	1.47

Source: INSEE E43, pp. 79–94.

a. Forty industries defined according to NAP-100 (see appendix C). Source includes industries 5, 10, 11, 13, 15–25, 27–34, 36–37, 39–41, 43–54.

b. Share is salaried employment in plants of the given size class in a given industry divided by all salaried employment in the industry (percent).

c. Relates to hypothesis that mean percentage point change is 0.

d. Differs from 0 at the .001 level of significance in a one-tail test.

e. Differs from 0 at the .05 level of significance in a one-tail test.

Table A-21. *Change in Distribution of Salaried Employment by Size of Plant, Mean Values among Manufacturing Industries, 1974–80*[a]

Number of employees	Mean salaried employment		Mean change 1974–80	Standard deviation	t-ratio[b]	Mean share[c]		Mean percentage point change 1974–80	Standard deviation	t-ratio[d]
	1974	1980				1974	1980			
500–999	17,802	14,485	−3,317[e]	5,108	−3.95	17.2	15.7	−1.48	5.14	−1.75
1,000 or more	33,708	27,584	−6,124[f]	12,761	−2.92	26.8	25.3	−1.47	5.05	−1.77
500 or more	51,510	42,069	−9,441[e]	13,877	−4.14	43.9	41.0	−2.94[f]	6.33	−2.83
10 or more	119,162	107,858	−11,304[e]	18,527	−3.71	100.0	100.0	. . .	. . .	. . .

Source: Ministère de l'Industrie et de la Recherche, *La Concentration dans l'Industrie de 1974 à 1980*, pp. 30–39.

a. Thirty-seven industries defined according to NAP-100 (see appendix C). Includes industries 5, 10, 11, 13, 27–34, 39, 43–54.

b. Relates to hypothesis that mean change in salaried employment is 0.

c. Share is salaried employment in plants of the given size class in a given industry divided by all salaried employment in the industry (percent).

d. Relates to hypothesis that mean percentage point change is 0.

e. Differs from 0 at the .001 level of significance in a one-tail test.

f. Differs from 0 at the .01 level of significance in a one-tail test.

Table A-22. *Percentage Change in Population by Region, 1954–82*

Code	Region	Population change 1954–82	Percent rural 1954[a]	Percent urban 1954[b]	Code	Region	Population change 1954–82	Percent rural 1954[a]	Percent urban 1954[b]
94	Corse	−3	61	0	22	Picardie	26	62	11
74	Limousin	−0	67	14	52	Pays de la Loire	26	61	19
83	Auvergne	7	63	9	43	Franche-Comté	27	59	9
54	Poitou-Charentes	13	68	8	42	Alsace	29	44	29
53	Bretagne	16	67	10	24	Centre	29	63	12
25	Basse-Normandie	16	69	6	23	Haute-Normandie	30	42	20
26	Bourgogne	16	63	8	91	Languedoc-Roussillon	33	47	22
31	Nord-Pas de Calais	16	25	13	11	Ile de France	38	9	54
73	Midi-Pyrénées	18	59	14	82	Rhône-Alpes	38	46	23
41	Lorraine	19	43	11	93	Provence-Alpes-			
21	Champagne-Ardenne	19	54	16		Côte d'Azur	64	22	50
72	Aquitaine	20	58	12		France	27	44	23

Sources: INSEE, *Recensement Général de la Population de 1982: Population de la France (Métropole et Départements d'Outre-Mer), Régions, Départements, Arrondissements, et Cantons,* table C; and INSEE, *Recensement Général de la Population de Mai 1954: Population Légale (Résultats Statistiques),* table PL10.

a. Rural population of a region is population of its rural *communes.* A *commune* is rural if fewer than 2,000 people inhabit the communal seat.

b. Urban population of a region is population of its *communes* with 50,000 or more inhabitants.

Table A-23. *Geographic Mobility of Population between Census Years, by Type of Change in Location, 1954–82*
Percent

Location type	Different location at end of period[a]			
	1954–62	1962–68	1968–75	1975–82
Dwelling unit	n.a.	n.a.	48.8	47.5
Commune	27.0	24.2	30.3	29.5
Département	11.1	11.3	14.5	13.3
Region	7.4	6.8	9.0	8.3
Country	n.a.	4.6	3.2	2.4

Sources: INSEE, *Annuaire Statistique de la France 1967,* p. 70; INSEE, *Annuaire Statistique de la France 1970/71,* p. 54; INSEE D52, table P5; and INSEE D97, table D11 (corrected).

n.a. Not available.

a. In columns 1-3 relevant population is people residing in France at both ends of period. In column 4 relevant population is people residing in France at end of period.

Table A-24. *Relationship at Regional Level between Labor Mobility and Population Density, Census Intervals, 1954–82*
Pearson correlation coefficients (N = 22)

Population density in 1954	Migration of the labor force[a]			
	1954–62	1962–68	1968–75	1975–82
Rural[b]	.61[c]	.61[c]	.45[d]	.22
Urban[e]	−.57[c]	−.49[d]	−.48[d]	−.21

Sources: INSEE, *Annuaire Statistique de la France 1967*, table II; INSEE D97, tables 4–6 and erratum pp. 4–5; and INSEE, *Recensement Général de la Population de 1982: Population de la France (Métropole et Départements d'Outre-Mer), Régions, Départements, Arrondissements, et Cantons*, table C.

a. Percentage of region's residents at beginning of period that inhabited a different region at end of period. Observation confined to members of the labor force at end of period.

b. Percentage of the region's population living in rural *communes* in 1954. A *commune* is rural if fewer than 2,000 people inhabit the communal seat.

c. Differs from 0 at the .01 level of significance in a one-tail *t*-test.

d. Differs from 0 at the .05 level of significance in a one-tail *t*-test.

e. Percentage of the region's population living in *communes* of at least 50,000 people in 1954.

Table A-25. *Share of State-Owned Enterprises in Value Added, by Nonfinancial Industry, 1959, 1969*[a]
Percent

		SOE share	
Code	Industry	1959	1969
09B	Telecommunications	100	100
03A	Coal	99	99
03B	Electricity/water	92	90
09A	Transport services	54	41
10A	Real estate	51	50
05E	Ships/planes/weapons	42	44
05D	Road vehicles	22	21
02	Food/tobacco	19	17
10C	Miscellaneous services	10	12
06B	Chemicals/rubber	8	10
03C	Petroleum[b]	3	4
07F	Printing/publishing	1	1
	All industries	12	11

Sources: INSEE C4, pp. 182–205, 230–42, 272; and INSEE C20, pp. 228, 230, 232.

a. Industries defined according to ENF (see appendix C). State-owned enterprises identified in appendix tables F-5, F-6. SOE share is less than 0.5 percent in both years in the following industries: agriculture (01), ferrous minerals/metals (04A), nonferrous minerals/metals (04B), fabricated metals (05A), mechanical equipment (05B), electrical equipment (05C), glass (06A), textiles (07A), apparel (07B), leather/shoes (07C), wood (07D), paper (07E), miscellaneous manufactures (07G), building materials (08A), construction (08B), hotels/restaurants (10B), and wholesale/retail trade (11).

b. Importance of SOEs is understated.

Table A-26. *Share of State-Owned Enterprises in Sales, by Industry, 1982*

Code	Industry	1980 sales (millions of francs)	Percent attributable to SOEs, ownership pattern of		Code	Industry	1980 sales (millions of francs)	Percent attributable to SOEs, ownership pattern of	
			January 1, 1982	December 31, 1982				January 1, 1982	December 31, 1982
07	Gas (excluding natural)	24,624	97.2	97.2	10	Crude steel	65,593	*	73.5
04	Coal	9,334	97.0	97.0	09	Ferrous minerals	1,066	*	64.4
06	Electricity	69,418	96.2	97.1	30	Home appliances	19,993	*	37.5
33	Aerospace equipment	40,498	48.9	85.7	16	Glass	17,677	*	33.2
05	Petroleum	250,847	29.2	29.2	11	Semifinished steel	18,203	*	15.5
17	Bulk chemicals	99,220	15.2	42.3	28	Electrical equipment	47,851	*	15.0
13	Nonferrous metals	44,368	11.4	57.4	27	Office equipment	21,481	*	10.0
19	Drugs	32,096	8.9	21.2	48	Wood	20,033	*	2.6
34	Precision goods	14,896	8.1	10.8	44	Textiles	64,306	*	0.8
18	Chemical products n.e.c.	49,431	4.3	8.9	51	Publishing	56,218	*	0.5
23	Machine tools	13,622	3.5	4.9	49	Furniture	20,369	*	0.1
21	Metallic products	79,953	2.6	7.8	54	Miscellaneous manufactures	18,643	*	0.1
53	Plastics products	30,535	2.3	10.5	45	Leather	8,010	*	*
24	Mechanical equipment I	76,009	1.4	20.5	46	Shoes	14,129	*	*
25	Mechanical equipment II	24,154	0.8	1.8	47	Apparel	33,130	*	*
29	Electronic equipment	66,707	0.1	43.3	12	Nonferrous metals/minerals	229	*	*
50	Paper	41,538	0.1	7.9	43	Manmade fibers	3,427	*	*
15	Building material	46,674	0.1	5.3	14	Nonmetallic minerals	4,128	*	39.2
08	Water/steam	13,370	0.1	4.4	31	Ground transport equipment	181,603	*	37.0
22	Agricultural equipment	12,802	0.1	0.1	20	Foundry products	16,287	*	26.1
32	Ships	6,781	0.1	0.1	52	Rubber products	26,809	*	2.7

Source: François and Grosbois, *Le Secteur Public dans l'Industrie avant et après les Nationalisations*, table 3.

n.a. Not available.

* Less than 0.05 percent.

a. Industries defined according to NAP-100 (see appendix C). Source omits industries 26 and 35–42.

Table A-27. SOE-Controlled Inputs as Percent of Total Intermediate Consumption, by Consuming Industry, 1981[a]

Input	Code	Consuming industry	Input share of total intermediate consumption
Coal and coke[b]	042	Coke	93.5
	041	Coal	45.4
	06	Electricity	22.8
	10	Crude steel	15.5
	15	Building materials	3.3
	09	Ferrous minerals	2.3
	14	Nonmetallic minerals	2.0
Gas[c]	07	Gas, except natural	84.0
	08	Water/steam	10.8
	16	Glass	9.0
	43	Manmade fibers	6.5
	52	Rubber products	5.6
	19	Drugs	5.5
	21	Metallic products	4.2
	06	Electricity	4.0
	171	Bulk inorganic chemicals	3.8
	172	Bulk organic chemicals	2.9
	18	Chemical products n.e.c.	2.9
	11	Semifinished steel	2.8
	14	Nonmetallic minerals	2.6
	15	Building materials	2.3
	20	Foundry products	2.3
	10	Crude steel	2.0
Rail transport[d]	56	Scrap products	6.6
	73-4	Transport-related services	6.5
	09	Ferrous minerals	4.8
	57-4	Wholesale/retail trade	4.0
	89	Finance	3.1
	10	Crude steel	2.5
	20	Foundry products	2.2
	75	Telecommunications	2.2

Input	Code	Consuming industry	Input share of total intermediate consumption
Electricity[e]	09	Ferrous minerals	22.7
	14	Nonmetallic minerals	15.0
	041	Coal	14.4
	171	Bulk inorganic chemicals	14.1
	68	Rail transport	14.0
	12	Nonferrous metallic minerals	12.9
	06	Electricity	12.5
	13	Nonferrous metals, unfinished	11.7
	812	Building rental, nonhousing	10.3
	052	Natural gas	10.1
	08	Water/steam	8.7
	16	Glass	6.3
	811	Building rental, housing	6.1
	57-4	Wholesale/retail trade	5.5
	20	Foundry products	5.4
	15	Building materials	5.2
	10	Crude steel	5.1
	50	Paper	4.4
	90-8	Government	3.8
	42	Tobacco products	3.3
	52	Rubber products	3.3
	11	Semifinished steel	3.2
	67	Hotels/restaurants	3.2
	53	Plastics products	3.1
	43	Manmade fibers	3.0
	18	Chemical products n.e.c.	2.6
	65	Auto sales/service	2.6
	54	Miscellaneous manufactures	2.5
	19	Drugs	2.2

Aerospace equipment[f]				(Petroleum continued)		
33	Aerospace equipment	36.2		55	Construction	6.7
72	Air transport	19.6		09	Ferrous minerals	6.3
26	Military products	12.0		75	Telecommunications	6.0
90-8	Government	6.4		53	Plastics products	6.0
32	Ships	2.1		82-3	Education/R&D, private	5.9
				90-8	Government	5.9
Petroleum[g]				041	Coal	5.7
053	Petroleum products	90.8		38	Freshly baked goods	5.5
692	Road transport n.e.c.	57.5		19	Drugs	5.3
70	Freshwater transport	49.9		08	Water/steam	5.1
71	Maritime transport	38.8				
02	Forest products	38.5		Telecommunications[h]		
12	Nonferrous metallic minerals	35.0		75	Telecommunications	36.7
72	Air transport	26.8		89	Finance	11.9
691	Intercity trucking	26.6		56	Scrap products	10.0
03	Fish	23.1		76-9	Miscellaneous business services	8.7
812	Building rental, nonhousing	19.9		80	Rental of equipment	7.4
06	Electricity	17.6		66	Repair services, miscellaneous	6.2
56	Scrap products	16.9		82-3	Education/R&D, private	6.1
172	Bulk organic chemicals	16.9		85-7	Miscellaneous services	5.5
16	Glass	16.2		57-4	Wholesale/retail trade	5.0
84	Health care, private	14.0		88	Insurance	4.2
051	Petroleum, crude	13.6		90-8	Government	4.2
15	Building materials	13.5		65	Auto sales/service	3.8
68	Rail transport	10.9		27	Office equipment	3.2
42	Tobacco products	10.7		30	Home appliances	2.9
57-4	Wholesale/retail trade	8.4		51	Printing/publishing	2.8
76-9	Business services	8.2		20	Foundry products	2.5
171	Bulk inorganic chemicals	8.0		812	Building rental, nonhousing	2.5
14	Nonmetallic minerals	7.8		26	Military products	2.2
18	Chemical products n.e.c.	7.0		49	Furniture	2.2
052	Natural gas	6.7		68	Rail transport	2.2
				84	Health care, private	2.2

Source: INSEE input-output tables in current prices, level S (unpublished).

a. Industries are those for which stated input represents at least 2 percent of total direct intermediate consumption, except as noted. Industries defined according to NAP-S89 (see appendix C).

b. NAP S041 and S042.

c. NAP S052 and S07.

d. NAP S68.

e. NAP S06.

f. NAP S33. Industries are those with positive direct intermediate consumption of aerospace equipment.

g. NAP S051 and S053. Industries are those for which petroleum represents at least 5 percent of total direct intermediate consumption.

h. NAP S75.

Table A-28. *Nonfinancial Enterprises' Sources of Finance, 1953–72*
Percent

Year	Internally generated equity	Credit	Bonds	Externally generated equity	Adjustment[a]	All
1953	68.4	20.9	2.6	3.2	0.8	95.9
1954	66.9	20.8	3.4	5.6	1.0	97.7
1955	67.5	21.9	5.2	5.7	−0.7	99.6
1956	60.0	28.4	4.9	4.9	−0.3	97.9
1957	59.0	23.6	7.7	5.2	0.2	95.7
1958	61.0	20.0	5.1	5.5	4.7	96.3
1959[b]	58.7	28.1	7.5	4.9	−0.2	99.0
1959[c]	60.7	30.0	4.2	6.1	0.1	101.1
1960	60.6	29.5	3.6	4.1	2.2	100.0
1961	62.7	33.2	4.0	5.2	−5.1	100.0
1962	60.0	26.8	3.3	5.7	4.4	100.2
1963	62.4	23.2	3.0	12.3	−0.9	100.0
1964	63.1	27.6	2.5	5.0	2.0	100.2
1965	65.8	24.8	3.1	6.4	−0.1	100.0
1966	64.6	27.3	2.5	5.5	0.1	100.0
1967	62.4	28.0	3.3	3.9	2.4	100.0
1968	62.6	29.8	1.6	3.7	2.3	100.0
1969	62.9	23.0	1.8	5.0	7.3	100.0
1970	58.0	31.8	2.8	4.6	2.8	100.0
1971	60.9	30.2	5.2	3.3	0.4	100.0
1972	59.8	30.1	3.4	5.4	1.3	100.0
Mean	62.3	26.6	3.8	5.3	1.2	99.2

Source: INSEE E31–32, vol. 2, p. 119.
a. Includes errors of measurement and funds from abroad.
b. 1956 System of National Accounts (SNA) for 1953–59. INSEE does not identify sources of funds omitted.
c. 1962 SNA for 1959–72.

Table A-29. *Sources of Finance, by Industry, 1951*
Percent

Code	Industry	Internal	Banks	FME[a]	Bonds	Stock
04	Gas	29.3	*	70.7	*	*
03	Electricity	36.2	10.9	46.4	6.5	*
32	Air transport	37.6	12.8	32.0	16.0	1.6
35	Wholesale/retail trade	38.9	57.8	1.2	0.2	1.9
07	Coal	42.4	*	57.6	*	*
19	Rubber	50.0	46.4	*	3.2	0.5
10	Metallurgy	58.8	27.2	11.8	1.3	0.9
24	Leather	59.6	39.7	*	*	0.7
18	Construction	62.9	32.1	*	3.6	1.5
22	Textiles	64.1	33.2	2.1	0.1	0.5
21	Food	64.3	34.8	*	*	0.9
34	Telecommunications	66.5	*	9.0	24.5	*
15	Electrical equipment	66.6	30.3	*	0.5	2.6
09	Chemicals	71.8	18.3	2.0	1.1	6.8
06	Petroleum	73.5	15.0	9.3	1.2	1.1
30	Freshwater transport	73.5	14.3	*	10.2	2.0
33	Transport-related services	74.3	22.9	*	1.9	1.0
25	Wood	75.9	18.4	*	3.8	1.9
11	Mechanical equipment	77.1	19.4	*	0.3	3.3
08	Metallic minerals	77.2	19.0	1.3	*	2.5
26	Paper	77.9	20.9	*	0.2	1.0
14	Aircraft	78.2	21.1	*	*	0.8
13	Automobiles	79.0	18.5	*	1.3	1.2
37	Banking/insurance	79.2	9.0	*	9.0	2.8
16	Handcrafted machines	81.7	18.3	*	*	*
01	Fish	82.6	17.4	*	*	*
27	Miscellaneous manufactures	82.8	17.2	*	*	*
17	Building materials	82.9	14.5	*	1.5	1.1
02	Agriculture	83.1	7.1	9.8	*	*
12	Ships	85.3	14.7	*	*	*
31	Maritime transport	86.1	5.5	4.7	3.0	0.7
23	Apparel	87.6	11.5	0.8	0.2	*
36	Services n.e.c.	89.3	9.3	*	*	1.4
28	Road transport	90.0	7.0	*	2.2	0.9
29	Rail transport	90.7	1.1	*	8.1	*
05	Water/steam	94.4	4.2	*	*	1.4
20	Tobacco	100.0	*	*	*	*

Source: Ministère des Affaires Economiques et Financières, *Tableau Economique de l'Année 1951*, comptes relatifs aux entreprises.

* Less than 0.05 percent.

a. Fonds de Modernisation et d'Equipement (forerunner of FDES).

Table A-30. *Credit Institutions' Sources of New Finance, 1970–80*[a]
Percent

Source[b]	Credit institutions		Source[b]	Credit institutions	
	Monetary (S41)	Other (S42)		Monetary (S41)	Other (S42)
Subsidies (R30 + R71)	2.1	1.0	Bills (F30)	0.2	0.9
Capital transfers (R79)	*	1.1	Bonds (F40)	5.2	11.9
Other internal (N4 − R30 − R71)	3.5	5.7	External equity (F50)	1.3	6.6
Foreign currency (F00)	0.3	0.1	Financial credit,		
Domestic currency (F10)	26.7	4.2	short-term (F60)	−0.8	12.3
Deposits (F20)	59.7	39.7	Financial credit,		
			medium- and long-term (F70)	1.6	16.5

Source: INSEE, *Rapport sur les Comptes de la Nation* (annual), comptes détaillés des secteurs institutionnels.
* Less than 0.05 percent.
a. Mean values for the period.
b. Variable tags (in parentheses) correspond to the nomenclature of transaction in the 1971 SNA.

Table A-31. *New External Equity as Percent of Total Finance, by Nonfinancial State-Owned Enterprise, 1959–68*[a]

Code	State-owned enterprise	New external equity as percent of total finance[b]	Code	State-owned enterprise	New external equity as percent of total finance[b]
02	Alcools	*	09A	CGT	*
02	SEITA	*	09A	MM	*
03A	CDF	*	09B	PTT	*
03B	CNR	*	10C	Havas	*
05E	ONERA	*	05E	NORD	0.7
06B	SCC[c]	*	03C	SNPA	1.8
06B	CEA	*	05E	SNECMA	6.5
06B	MDPA	*	09A	AF	7.4
06B	SNPE	*	05E	SUD	7.6
07F	IN	*	03C	TRAPIL	9.6
09A	SNCF	*	06B	ONIA[d]	10.3
09A	RATP	*	03B	GDF	15.6
09A	AP	*	03B	EDF	22.1

Source: INSEE E11.
* Less than 0.05 percent.
a. 1962 SNA. Abbreviations explained in appendix B. Principal activities defined according to ENF (see appendix C). Mean values for the period.
b. Total finance is sum of gross saving, indemnities received for damage to capital, new external equity, new bond issues net of reimbursements, net new financial credit, and miscellaneous sources of finance.
c. 1968 only.
d. 1959–67.

Table A-32. New External Equity as Percent of Total Finance, by Grande Entreprise Nationale, 1959–76[a]

Industry code[b]	Enterprise	New external equity as percent of total finance[c]	Industry code[b]	Enterprise	New external equity as percent of total finance[c]
T31	RATP	*	T04	CDF	6.8
T32	PTT[d]	*	T31	AF	9.7
T31	SNCF	0.8	T06	EDF	16.6
T31	AI[e]	3.5	T06	GDF	22.1

Source: INSEE E57.

* Less than 0.05 percent.

a. 1971 SNA. Abbreviations explained in appendix B. Mean values for the period.

b. Industries defined according to NAP-T (see appendix C).

c. Total finance is sum of gross saving (NB4), capital subsidy received (R71), other capital transfers received (R79), new external equity (F50), new bond issues net of repayments (F40), net new financial credit (F60 and F70), and new nonmonetary deposits (F20). Variable tags in parentheses correspond to the nomenclature of transactions in the 1971 SNA.

d. 1970–76.

e. 1963–76.

Table A-33. Government Shares of Aggregate Intermediate Consumption and Gross Fixed Capital Formation, by Division of Government, 1959–80[a]

Code	Division	Percent of aggregate intermediate consumption			Percent of aggregate gross fixed capital formation		
		Mean	Minimum	Maximum	Mean	Minimum	Maximum
S11	Grandes entreprises nationales	3.4	2.9	4.6	10.5	7.0	15.8
S61	National government	5.2	4.4	6.0	4.8	2.9	7.2
S62	Local government	2.0	1.8	2.1	9.7	7.4	11.1
S63	Social security system	0.3	0.1	0.4	0.3	0.2	0.4
	All	10.9	9.9	11.4	25.2	20.5	29.0

Sources: INSEE C67–68; INSEE E57, pp. 70–71; and INSEE, Rapport sur les Comptes de la Nation (annual), tableaux économiques d'ensemble and comptes détaillés des secteurs institutionnels.

a. 1971 SNA.

Table A-34. Government Purchases as Percent of Sales, by Industry and Size of Company, 1974[a]
Percent

Code	Industry	Number of employees in company			
		20–199	200–499	500–1,999	2,000 or more
3301	Aircraft fuselages	24.3	25.4	18.2	60.7
2911	Telephone/telegraph equipment	9.8	19.8	30.8	58.2
3302	Aircraft engines	14.7	28.9	7.3	50.8
2914	Professional electronic equipment	17.0	35.0	29.1	56.7
3303	Special equipment for planes	37.4	41.5	36.1	29.1
2811	High-voltage electrical equipment	7.5	60.7	29.5	45.5
1803	Explosives	18.7	19.0	0.1	60.7
3121	Railway vehicles	1.8	1.8	2.2	59.0
2406	Pumps/compressors	6.4	1.6	36.2	0
	All manufacturing	2.2	2.4	3.2	6.7

Source: Mathieu and Suberchicot, Marchés Publics et Structures Industrielles, table 9.

a. Industries from which government purchased at least 25 percent of shipments. Industries defined according to NAP-600. Source excludes NAP-100 industries 8, 26, and 35–42. See chap. 3, note 63.

Table A-35. *Importance of Public and Private R&D Expenditure, by Industry, 1975*[a]

Code	Industry	Total R&D expenditures as percent of sales	Government-financed R&D as percent of all R&D	Code	Industry	Total R&D expenditures as percent of sales	Government-financed R&D as percent of all R&D
45,46	Leather/shoes	*	*	23	Machine tools	0.6	7.4
48,49	Wood/furniture	*	1.9	24	Mechanical equipment I	0.7	6.0
20	Foundry products	0.1	3.5	12,13,14	Nonferrous minerals/metals	0.9	3.1
50,51	Paper/printing	0.1	1.9	06	Electricity	1.2	0.2
54	Miscellaneous manufactures	0.1	7.1	34	Precision goods	1.2	8.6
11	Semifinished steel	0.2	*	16	Glass	1.6	1.9
21	Metallic products	0.2	3.3	18	Chemical products n.e.c.	1.7	27.9
43,44,47	Textiles/apparel	0.2	1.8	31	Ground transport equipment	2.0	1.1
32	Ships	0.2	*	04	Coal	2.2	15.2
05	Petroleum	0.3	4.0	28	Electrical equipment	2.4	11.7
15	Building materials	0.3	2.5	17	Bulk chemicals	2.6	3.9
53	Plastics products	0.3	8.3	52	Rubber products	3.5	0.2
30	Home appliances	0.3	*	19	Drugs	3.7	0.1
07	Gas	0.4	*	27	Office equipment	7.4	32.0
09,10	Ferrous minerals/metals	0.4	9.8	29	Electronic equipment	7.6	32.2
25	Mechanical equipment II	0.5	0.5	33	Aerospace	20.9	77.5
22	Agricultural equipment	0.5	*		Weighted average	1.7	30.3

Source: Ministère de l'Industrie, *La Recherche Développement dans les Entreprises Industrielles en 1975*, tables 2, 6.
* Less than 0.05 percent.
a. Industries defined according to NAP-100 (see appendix C). Source excludes industries 08, 26, and 35–42.

Table A-36. *Share of Measured Subsidies to Nonfinancial Enterprises, by Type of Enterprise, 1959–69*[a]

Percent unless otherwise specified

Year	Enterprises State-owned	Private	Total (millions of francs)	Year	Enterprises State-owned	Private	Total (millions of francs)
1959	66	34	6,509	1965	73	27	18,024
1960	66	34	7,402	1966	75	25	19,969
1961	66	34	9,745	1967	74	26	21,234
1962	67	33	11,982	1968	73	27	27,395
1963	72	28	13,821	1969	70	30	27,577
1964	74	26	15,882	Mean	71	29	. . .

Sources: INSEE C4; and INSEE C20.

a. Private enterprises defined in 1962 SNA; SOEs identified in appendix table F-5. Measured subsidy defined in appendix F.

Table A-37. *Share of Measured Subsidies to Nonfinancial Enterprises, by Industry and Type of Enterprise, 1959–69*[a]

Code	Industry	Percent of all measured subsidies	Percent of subsidies to SOEs	Percent of subsidies to private enterprises
07B	Apparel	*	. . .	0.01
08A	Building materials	*	. . .	0.01
06A	Glass	0.01	. . .	0.02
07G	Miscellaneous manufactures	0.01	. . .	0.02
07D	Wood	0.01	. . .	0.04
07C	Leather	0.02	. . .	0.07
05A	Fabricated metals	0.04	. . .	0.16
05D	Road vehicles	0.04	*	0.15
04B	Nonferrous minerals/metals	0.06	. . .	0.16
07A	Textiles	0.08	. . .	0.26
10B	Hotels/restaurants	0.12	. . .	0.43
05B	Mechanical equipment	0.12	. . .	0.43
07F	Publishing	0.16	0.02	0.52
05C	Electrical equipment	0.20	. . .	0.70
07E	Paper	0.26	. . .	0.86
08B	Construction	0.44	. . .	1.48
04A	Ferrous minerals/metals	0.44	. . .	1.46
09B	Telecommunications	0.98	1.36	. . .
03B	Electricity	1.23	1.56	0.51
03C	Petroleum	2.50	2.73	1.97
05E	Ships/planes/weapons	2.56	0.79	6.69
10A	Real estate	2.62	2.67	2.41
03A	Coal	3.68	5.13	0.02
10C	Services, miscellaneous	4.75	4.30	5.97
01	Agriculture	5.70	. . .	19.32
02	Food/tobacco	6.25	0.01	21.50
06B	Chemicals/rubber	18.54	25.96	0.29
11	Wholesale/retail trade	20.90	15.91	32.88
09A	Transport services	28.27	39.57	1.63

Sources: INSEE C4; and INSEE C20.

* Less than 0.005 percent.

a. 1962 SNA. Industries defined according to ENF (see appendix C). SOEs identified in table F-5. Measured subsidy defined in appendix F. Mean values for the period.

Table A-38. Share of Measured Subsidies to Nonfinancial Enterprises (GEN Excluded), by Industry, 1967–81[a]
Percent

Code	Industry	Mean	Minimum	Maximum	Code	Industry	Mean	Minimum	Maximum
T32	Telecommunications	*	*	*	T14	Mechanical equipment	0.77	0.28	1.64
T29	Auto sales/repair	0.02	*	0.21	T12	Chemical products n.e.c.	0.80	0.31	1.81
T04	Coal	0.02	*	0.11	T07	Ferrous minerals/metals	0.82	0.10	1.89
T28	Retailing, nonfood	0.07	*	0.28	T05	Petroleum	0.87	*	3.11
T10	Glass	0.07	*	0.19	T16	Ground transport equipment	1.00	0.14	2.20
T19	Leather	0.08	*	0.26	T06	Electricity	1.14	0.58	2.87
T27	Retailing, food	0.10	*	0.37	T22	Publishing	1.17	0.86	1.40
T08	Nonferrous minerals/metals	0.15	*	0.41	T15A	Electrical equipment, business	1.23	0.10	4.04
T23	Rubber/plastics	0.21	*	0.49	T24	Construction	1.80	1.05	3.93
T26	Wholesaling, nonfood	0.22	*	1.06	T17	Ships/planes	4.39	2.68	6.30
T09	Building materials	0.23	*	0.73	T33	Business services	4.39	3.15	6.00
T15B	Electrical equipment, home	0.27	*	0.65	T03	Foods n.e.c.	5.55	1.18	8.70
T30	Hotels/restaurants	0.32	*	0.53	T02	Meat/dairy	5.68	0.82	8.77
T20	Wood/miscellaneous mfg	0.32	*	0.73	T35	Real estate	6.07	4.88	8.42
T13	Metallic products	0.35	*	1.03	T31	Transport services	6.59	4.70	8.72
T11	Bulk chemicals	0.37	*	0.87	T34	Consumer services	11.33	7.47	14.10
T18	Textiles/apparel	0.47	*	1.10	T01	Agriculture	15.28	9.78	26.63
T21	Paper	0.48	0.37	0.73	T25	Wholesaling, food	27.39	15.74	36.96

Sources: INSEE C78, and INSEE, comptes des entreprises par secteur d'activité, level T (unpublished).
* Less than 0.005 percent.
a. 1972 SNA. Industries defined according to NAP-T (see appendix C). GEN listed in appendix table F-6.

Table A-39. Subsidies Received as Percent of Expenditures, by Nonfinancial State-Owned Enterprise, 1959–69[a]

Name[b]	1959	1960	1961	1962	1963	1964	1965	1966	1967	1968	1969	Mean
Alcool	1	0	0	0	0	0	0	0	0	0	0	0
GDF	1	1	1	1	1	1	1	1	1	1	1	1
EDF	1	1	1	1	1	1	1	1	1	0	0	1
IN	0	0	0	0	0	0	0	0	0	0	20	2
PTT	0	0	1	2	8	8	0	0	1	0	0	2
AF	3	4	4	6	5	3	0	0	0	7	0	3
CNR	2	2	2	4	2	2	1	6	14	9	10	5
CGT	5	8	7	5	8	11	9	9	6	8	7	8
CDF	1	2	3	4	11	7	9	11	16	24	27	11
AP	9	11	15	14	17	16	15	13	10	8	3	12
MM	10	11	10	15	17	14	14	13	13	14	19	14
SNPE	13	10	17	11	8	24	15	20	22	11	13	15
SNCF	19	18	18	12	22	24	27	28	29	31	28	23
RATP	31	30	23	29	31	39	42	49	42	45	54	38
CEA	78	62	57	61	73	77	66	67	66	61	65	67
ONERA	92	82	68	67	68	74	84	79	77	79	70	76
10C[c]	7	5	5	5	5	5	5	6	7	7	7	6
10A[c]	5	5	6	6	6	5	6	6	5	6	8	6
03C[c]	20	28	22	22	19	16	25	28	31	22	13	22
11[c]	33	38	75	72	62	67	64	89	71	81	87	67

Sources: INSEE C4; INSEE C20; and INSEE E11.
a. 1962 SNA. Abbreviations of names explained in appendix B. Subsidy ratio defined in appendix F.
b. In eleven nonfinancial SOEs (SEITA, TRAPIL, SNECMA, Nord, SCC, MDPA, Havas, SNPA, RNUR, Sud, and APC), subsidies received amounted to 0 percent of total outlays during each year of observation. Unobserved are MDPA in 1969 and SCC in 1959–67.
c. Industry-level groups defined according to ENF (see appendix C). SOEs in each group identified in appendix table F-5.

Table A-40. Subsidies Received as Percent of Expenditures, by Grande Entreprise Nationale, 1959–76[a]

Year	RATP	SNCF	CDF	AI	AF	PTT	GDF	EDF
1959	11	11	1	. . .	3	2	1	1
1960	13	10	2	. . .	3	2	1	1
1961	10	9	3	. . .	4	2	1	1
1962	19	12	4	. . .	6	3	1	1
1963	23	14	12	0	5	9	1	1
1964	33	15	8	0	2	8	1	1
1965	36	21	10	8	0	2	1	1
1966	45	19	12	6	0	2	1	1
1967	37	21	17	4	0	1	1	1
1968	41	24	26	8	8	2	1	0
1969	52	21	28	3	0	2	1	0
1970	43	14	23	3	0	1	1	1
1971	40	15	22	0	0	1	1	1
1972	42	14	21	0	0	1	1	0
1973	41	16	26	0	0	2	0	0
1974	39	15	17	5	0	2	0	0
1975	40	17	15	0	0	2	1	0
1976	40	19	19	1	0	1	0	1
Mean	34	16	15	3	2	2	1	1

Source: INSEE E57.
a. 1971 SNA. Enterprises identified and subsidy ratio defined in appendix F.

Table A-41. Private Nonfinancial Enterprises, Subsidies Received as Percent of Expenditures, by Industry, 1959–69[a]

Code	Industry	Mean	Minimum	Maximum	Code	Industry	Mean	Minimum	Maximum
08A	Building materials	*	*	*	05C	Electrical equipment	0.2	*	0.5
07B	Apparel	*	*	*	07F	Publishing	0.2	0.1	0.4
07G	Miscellaneous manufactures	*	*	0.1	03C	Petroleum	0.3	0.1	0.4
07D	Wood	*	*	0.1	04A	Ferrous minerals/metals	0.4	0.3	0.5
05A	Fabricated metals	*	*	0.1	07E	Paper	0.4	0.3	0.6
06A	Glass	*	*	0.2	09A	Transport services	0.4	0.2	0.9
05D	Road vehicles	*	*	0.1	10C	Miscellaneous services	0.5	0.3	0.7
07A	Textiles	*	*	0.1	11	Wholesale/retail trade	0.5	0.4	0.7
06B	Chemicals/rubber	*	*	0.2	03A	Coal	0.7	*	6.4
05B	Mechanical equipment	0.1	*	0.2	02	Food/tobacco	1.6	0.7	2.4
07C	Leather	0.1	*	0.3	03B	Electricity	1.6	1.0	2.2
08B	Construction	0.1	0.1	0.2	10A	Real Estate	2.3	0.8	4.5
10B	Hotels/restaurants	0.1	*	0.5	01	Agriculture	2.7	2.3	3.3
04B	Nonferrous minerals/metals	0.1	*	1.1	05E	Ships/planes/weapons	4.4	3.0	6.2

Sources: INSEE C4; and INSEE C20.
* Less than 0.05 percent.
a. 1962 SNA. Industries defined according to ENF (see appendix C). Subsidy ratio defined in appendix F.

Table A-42. Nonfinancial Enterprises (GEN Excluded), Subsidies Received as Percent of Expenditures, by Industry, 1967–81ᵃ

Code	Industry	Mean	Minimum	Maximum	Code	Industry	Mean	Minimum	Maximum
T32	Telecommunications	*	*	*	T16	Ground transport equipment	0.2	*	0.6
T29	Auto sales/repair	*	*	0.1	T07	Ferrous minerals/metals	0.3	*	0.7
T28	Retailing, nonfood	*	*	0.1	T15B	Electrical equipment, home	0.3	*	1.0
T27	Retailing, food	*	*	0.1	T12	Chemical products	0.4	0.2	0.9
T26	Wholesaling, nonfood	*	*	0.1	T15A	Electrical equipment, business	0.4	*	1.4
T13	Metallic products	0.1	*	0.5	T21	Paper	0.4	0.2	0.6
T08	Nonferrous minerals/metals	0.1	*	0.4	T22	Publishing	0.7	0.4	0.9
T19	Leather	0.1	*	0.3	T33	Business services	0.7	0.5	1.1
T11	Bulk chemicals	0.1	*	0.4	T03	Food n.e.c.	1.0	0.2	2.1
T23	Rubber/plastics	0.1	*	0.4	T04	Coal	1.2	*	6.6
T30	Hotels/restaurants	0.1	*	0.3	T02	Meat/dairy	1.7	0.3	2.5
T10	Glass	0.2	*	0.4	T31	Transport services	1.7	1.2	2.6
T18	Textiles/apparel	0.2	*	0.4	T25	Wholesaling, food	2.6	1.3	3.6
T20	Wood/miscellaneous mfg.	0.2	*	0.4	T34	Consumer services	2.8	2.2	4.0
T09	Building materials	0.2	*	0.6	T06	Electricity	2.9	1.4	9.4
T14	Mechanical equipment	0.2	0.1	0.4	T17	Ships/planes	3.0	2.0	4.5
T05	Petroleum	0.2	*	0.6	T01	Agriculture	3.1	1.8	5.5
T24	Construction	0.2	0.1	0.6	T35	Real estate	5.0	3.9	6.9

Sources: INSEE C78; and INSEE, comptes des entreprises par secteur d'activité, level T (unpublished).
* Less than 0.05 percent.
a. 1971 SNA. Industries defined according to NAP-T (see appendix C). Subsidy ratio defined in appendix F.

Table A-43. *Measured Subsidies and Indemnities for Wartime Damage, by Industry, 1951*[a]
Millions of new francs

Code	Industry	Operating, capital, and stabilization subsidies	Indemnities for wartime damage	Code	Industry	Operating, capital, and stabilization subsidies	Indemnities for wartime damage
29	Railroads	686	191	22	Textiles	*	20
35	Wholesale/retail trade	412	6	10	Metallurgy	*	12
36	Services	374	*	23	Apparel	*	5
11	Machinery, except electrical	170	10	17	Building materials	*	4
02	Agriculture	136	447	15	Electrical equipment	*	3
34	Telecommunications	92	*	08	Metallic ores	*	2
06	Petroleum	36	27	13	Automobiles	*	2
05	Water/steam	35	*	18	Construction	*	1
32	Air transport	25	3	12	Ships	*	1
03	Electricity	22	5	25	Wood	*	1
21	Food	20	*	28	Road transport	*	1
26	Paper	13	7	16	Handcrafted machinery	*	*
09	Chemicals	11	7	19	Rubber	*	*
14	Aircraft	11	*	20	Tobacco products	*	*
31	Maritime transport	7	337	24	Leather	*	*
30	Inland water transport	5	19	27	Miscellaneous manufactures	*	*
04	Natural gas	4	*	33	Transport-related services	*	*
01	Fish	1	20		Unallocated	610	350
07	Coal	1	5		Total	2,671	1,486

Source: Ministère des Affaires Economiques et Financières, *Tableau Economique de l'Année 1951*, pp. 230–303, 315.
* Less than Fr 500,000 in subsidies or Fr 500,000 in indemnities.
a. Code is that used in source. Discrepancies between totals here and in source (p. 315) are due to differences in rounding procedure.

Table A-44. Subsidies and Indemnities Received as Percent of Expenditures, by Industry, 1951[a]

Code	Industry	Subsidies and indemnities	Subsidies only	Code	Industry	Subsidies and indemnities	Subsidies only
16	Handcrafted machinery	*	*	09	Chemicals	0.3	0.2
19	Rubber	*	*	04	Natural gas	0.4	0.4
20	Tobacco	*	*	26	Paper	0.4	0.3
24	Leather	*	*	35	Wholesale/retail trade	0.5	0.5
27	Miscellaneous manufactures	*	*	08	Metallic minerals	0.7	*
33	Transport-related services	*	*	03	Electricity	0.7	0.6
37	Banking/insurance	*	*	11	Mechanical equipment	1.3	1.2
18	Construction	*	*	06	Petroleum	1.4	0.8
25	Wood	*	*	14	Aircraft	1.6	1.6
13	Automobiles	*	*	36	Services n.e.c.	2.7	2.7
28	Road transport	0.1	*	02	Agriculture	5.5	1.3
23	Apparel	0.1	*	32	Air transport	5.6	5.0
15	Electrical equipment	0.1	*	34	Telecommunications	5.7	5.7
21	Food	0.1	0.1	01	Fish	7.7	0.4
12	Ships	0.1	*	30	Freshwater transport	13.8	2.9
22	Textiles	0.1	*	29	Rail transport	13.8	10.8
10	Metallurgy	0.2	*	31	Maritime transport	17.6	0.4
17	Building materials	0.2	*	05	Water/steam	19.8	19.8
07	Coal	0.2	*				

Source: Ministère des Affaires Economiques et Financières, *Tableau Economique de l'Année 1951*, comptes des entreprises, pp. 230–303.
* Less than 0.05 percent.
a. Code is that used in source. Expenditure comprises purchases of goods and services, remuneration of labor, indirect taxes, and gross investment.

Table A-45. *Financial Enterprises, Subsidies Received as Percent of Expenditures, 1959–80*[a]

Year	Credit institutions (S40)	Insurance companies (S50)	Year	Credit institutions (S40)	Insurance companies (S50)
1959	1	1	1970	2	1
1960	2	1	1971	3	2
1961	2	1	1972	3	2
1962	3	1	1973	3	2
1963	2	1	1974	2	2
1964	3	1	1975	2	3
1965	3	1	1976	3	3
1966	3	1	1977	2	3
1967	3	1	1978	3	2
1968	2	1	1979	2	4
1969	2	1	1980	2	2
			Mean	2	2

Sources: INSEE C67–68; and INSEE, *Rapport sur les Comptes de la Nation* (annual), comptes détaillés des secteurs institutionnels.
a. 1971 SNA. Subsidy ratio defined in appendix F.

Table A-46. *Credit Institutions, Operating Subsidies Received as Percent of Interest Paid, 1959–80*[a]

Year	All (S40)	Monetary (S41)	Other (S42)	Year	All (S40)	Monetary (S41)	Other (S42)
1959	3.0	n.a.	n.a.	1970	4.3	4.7	3.6
1960	3.9	n.a.	n.a.	1971	5.9	7.7	3.6
1961	4.3	n.a.	n.a.	1972	6.1	7.8	3.6
1962	6.1	n.a.	n.a.	1973	4.6	5.6	3.1
1963	5.5	n.a.	n.a.	1974	3.2	3.5	2.6
1964	6.5	n.a.	n.a.	1975	3.9	4.7	2.7
1965	6.6	n.a.	n.a.	1976	4.8	5.9	3.0
1966	7.2	n.a.	n.a.	1977	3.9	4.4	3.1
1967	5.9	n.a.	n.a.	1978	4.7	5.3	3.6
1968	4.9	n.a.	n.a.	1979	3.8	4.3	2.8
1969	4.5	n.a.	n.a.	1980	2.8	2.8	2.7
				Mean (1959–80)	4.8	n.a.	n.a.
				Mean (1970–80)	4.4	5.1	3.1

Sources: INSEE, C67–68; and INSEE, *Rapport sur les Comptes de la Nation* (annual).
n.a. Not available.
a. 1971 SNA.

Table A-47. Nonfinancial Enterprises, Payroll Taxes as Percent of Labor Compensation, by Industry and Type of Enterprise, 1962–69ᵃ

Code	Industry	All	Private	State-owned	Code	Industry	All	Private	State-owned
10B	Hotels/restaurants	10.4	10.4	...	04B	Nonferrous minerals/metals	21.0	21.0	...
01	Agriculture	12.9	12.9	...	04A	Ferrous minerals/metals	21.1	21.1	...
09B	Telecommunications	15.7	...	15.7	07B	Apparel	21.1	21.1	...
03C	Petroleum	18.8	17.7	26.5	07G	Miscellaneous manufactures	21.1	21.1	...
06B	Chemicals/rubber	18.9	19.3	16.6	05D	Road vehicles	21.2	20.9	22.0
07F	Publishing	19.2	19.2	20.0	07E	Paper	21.2	21.2	...
10C	Services, miscellaneous	19.8	19.0	22.1	02	Food/tobacco	21.8	21.9	21.0
06A	Glass	19.8	19.8	...	07C	Leather	22.0	22.0	...
05C	Electrical equipment	19.8	19.8	...	08A	Building material	22.4	22.4	...
05E	Ships/planes/weapons	20.0	20.6	19.3	07D	Wood	23.5	23.5	...
11	Wholesale/retail trade	20.1	20.1	16.5	08B	Construction	23.5	23.5	...
10A	Real estate	20.8	19.1	24.8	03A	Coal	24.3	25.2	24.3
05B	Mechanical equipment	20.9	20.9	...	03B	Electricity	30.7	21.5	31.8
05A	Fabricated metals	20.9	20.9	...	09A	Transport services	33.1	23.1	38.4
07A	Textiles	21.0	21.0	...					
						Mean	20.9	20.4	23.0

Source: INSEE C20.

a. 1962 SNA. Industries defined according to ENF (see appendix C). Payroll tax is employers' social security contribution (variable 702 of 1962 SNA). Labor compensation is the sum of variables 701, 702, and 716 of 1962 SNA. Mean values for the period.

Table A-48. *Nonfinancial Enterprises, Indirect Taxes as Percent of Output, by Industry and Type of Enterprise, 1959–69*[a]

Code	Industry	All	Private	State-owned
01	Agriculture	1.5	1.5	...
09B	Telecommunications	2.2	...	2.2
10C	Services, miscellaneous	3.0	3.0	2.3
04B	Nonferrous minerals/metals	3.3	3.3	...
11	Wholesale/retail trade	3.7	3.7	−8.7
10A	Real estate	3.7	2.9	4.8
05E	Ships/planes/weapons	4.1	4.3	3.9
04A	Ferrous minerals/metals	5.5	5.5	...
03A	Coal	6.1	5.7	6.1
08B	Construction	6.1	6.1	...
09A	Transport services	6.3	6.1	6.5
07F	Publishing	6.4	6.5	0.4
06B	Chemicals/rubber	6.5	7.0	2.2
05D	Road vehicles	6.8	6.4	8.2
03B	Electricity	7.1	6.9	7.1
10B	Hotels/restaurants	7.3	7.3	...
05B	Mechanical equipment	7.3	7.3	...
07A	Textiles	7.9	7.9	...
05C	Electrical equipment	7.9	7.9	...
07E	Paper	8.6	8.6	...
07C	Leather	8.6	8.6	...
05A	Fabricated metals	9.1	9.1	...
07B	Apparel	9.1	9.1	...
06A	Glass	9.7	9.7	...
07D	Wood	10.1	10.1	...
07G	Miscellaneous manufactures	10.3	10.3	...
08A	Building materials	10.3	10.3	...
02	Food/tobacco	13.0	7.7	211.6
03C	Petroleum	41.3	43.3	3.1
	Mean	6.6	n.a.	n.a.

Sources: INSEE C4; and INSEE C20.

n.a. Not available.

a. 1962 SNA. Industries defined according to ENF (see appendix C). Indirect taxes are the sum of variables 735, 736, 737, 738; output is the sum of *production nonstockée* and *variations de stocks*. Output is net of indirect taxes. It is negative in 1959 for SOEs in industry 11. Mean values for the period.

Table A-49. Corporate Income Tax Paid as Percent of Cash Flow, by Industry and Type of Enterprise, 1962–69[a]

Code	Industry	All	Private	State-owned	Code	Industry	All	Private	State-owned
09B	Telecommunications	*	...	*	10C	Services, miscellaneous	14.8	18.9	0.6
03A	Coal	0.2	17.0	*	02	Food/tobacco	14.9	14.6	13.2
03B	Electricity	2.7	14.5	1.0	07A	Textiles	15.2	15.2	...
04A	Ferrous minerals/metals	3.6	3.6	...	06A	Glass	15.5	15.5	...
09A	Transport services	3.8	10.5	0.1	10B	Hotels/restaurants	15.6	15.6	...
06B	Chemicals/rubber	7.4	14.6	0.1	08A	Building materials	15.7	15.7	...
05E	Ships/planes/weapons	8.1	11.6	4.1	05A	Fabricated metals	16.3	16.3	...
10A	Real estate	8.2	22.1	*	05C	Electrical equipment	17.2	17.2	...
03C	Petroleum	9.8	13.7	2.0	07C	Leather	18.5	18.5	...
04B	Nonferrous minerals/metals	10.8	10.8	...					
08B	Construction	11.3	11.3	...	05B	Mechanical equipment	18.6	18.6	...
05D	Road vehicles	11.8	12.8	5.0	07G	Miscellaneous manufactures	19.1	19.1	...
07E	Paper	12.4	12.4	...	07B	Apparel	19.7	19.7	...
07D	Wood	14.2	14.2	...	11	Wholesale/retail trade	22.5	23.3	*
07F	Publishing	14.4	14.6	*		Weighted average	11.8	n.a.	n.a.

Source: INSEE C20.

n.a. Not available.

* Less than 0.05 percent.

a. 1962 SNA. Industries defined according to ENF (see appendix C). Cash flow is sum of corporate income tax paid (variable 731), gross corporate saving (variable 8a), and corporate dividends paid (variable 722). Mean values for the period.

Table A-50. Regression of Effective Rate of Corporate Income Tax on Capital Intensity of Production, Examination of Residuals[a]
Percent

Code	Industry	Tax rate Residual	Tax rate Actual	Code	Industry	Tax rate Residual	Tax rate Actual
04A	Ferrous minerals/metals	−7.9	3.6	05A	Fabricated metals	0.7	16.3
05E	Ships/planes/weapons	−3.6	11.6	06B	Chemicals/rubber	1.2	14.6
04B	Nonferrous minerals/metals	−3.0	10.8	05C	Electrical equipment	1.6	17.2
05D	Road vehicles	−2.7	12.8	07C	Leather	1.6	18.5
03C	Petroleum	−2.4	13.7	07B	Apparel	2.4	19.7
07D	Wood	−1.7	14.2	07G	Miscellaneous mfg	3.1	19.1
07E	Paper	−1.7	12.4	05B	Mechanical equipment	3.3	18.6
02	Food/tobacco	−1.5	14.6	03A	Coal	3.7	17.0
07F	Publishing	−1.2	14.6	06A	Glass	3.8	15.5
07A	Textiles	−0.1	15.2	08A	Building materials	4.5	15.7

Sources: INSEE C4; and INSEE C20.

a. 1962 SNA. Industries defined according to ENF (see appendix C). Actual tax rate is ratio of corporate income tax paid (variable 731) to corporate cash flow as defined in table A-49. Residual tax rate is difference between actual rate and rate predicted in regression of actual rate on ratio of gross corporate investment in plant and equipment (variable 6c) to output (*production distribuée* plus increase in inventory). Tax rate is mean value for 1962–69. Ratio of investment to output is mean value for 1959–69. Sample is private corporations in all industries (except agriculture, which has no corporate sector) that produce goods rather than services.

Table A-51. Share of Value Added in Manufacturing, by Industry, Selected Countries, 1982
Percent

Code[a]	Industry	France	Germany	Italy	United Kingdom
31	Food	16.9	10.4	5.7	14.9
32	Textiles	6.9	4.6	12.6	5.9
33	Wood	2.1	2.8	3.2	3.0
34	Paper/publishing	5.2	4.0	5.8	9.5
35	Chemicals	16.9	20.0	16.5	15.7
351	Industrial chemicals	5.2	6.5	n.a.	5.0
352	Other chemicals	3.4	5.0	n.a.	5.0
353	Petroleum refining	4.7	5.0	1.4	1.9
354	Other petroleum products	0.1	n.a.	n.a.	0.3
355	Rubber	1.6	1.2	1.8	1.2
356	Plastics products	1.8	2.2	2.4	2.3
36	Nonmetallic minerals	3.5	3.8	7.4	4.8
37	Basic metals	6.5	6.1	8.5	4.5
38	Fabricated metals	40.6	47.7	39.5	40.7
381	Metal products	5.0	6.8	6.0	6.4
382	Machines n.e.c.	14.3	14.6	10.4	12.2
383	Electrical machinery	7.7	12.3	9.3	9.8
384	Transport equipment	12.6	12.4	11.5	10.7
385	Professional goods	1.0	1.6	2.3	1.5
39	Other manufactures	1.4	0.6	0.9	0.9

Source: OECD, *Industrial Structure Statistics, 1984.*

n.a. Not available.

a. International standard industrial classification.

Table A-52. *Share of Value Added, by Sector, Selected Countries, 1960, 1980*

Percent

Sector	France	Germany	Italy	United Kingdom
Agriculture				
1960	10.6	5.8	12.3	3.4
1980	4.1	2.1	6.4	1.8
Industry[a]				
1960	39.0	53.1	41.3	42.8
1980	35.9	42.7	42.8	37.5
Services				
1960	50.4	41.0	46.4	53.8
1980	60.0	55.2	50.9	60.6
Manufacturing				
1960	29.1	40.3	28.6	32.1
1980	26.3	32.6	30.5	24.0

Source: OECD, *Historical Statistics, 1960–1985*, tables 5.1–5.4.
a. Mining; manufacturing; electricity, gas, and water; and construction.

Table A-53. *Distributions of Manufacturing and Nonmanufacturing Industries by Ratio of Imports to Consumption, 1959, 1980*[a]

Ratio of imports to consumption (percent)	Manufacturing industries				Nonmanufacturing industries			
	Number		Percent of consumption[b]		Number		Percent of consumption[c]	
	1959	1980	1959	1980	1959	1980	1959	1980
Less than 5	23	4	53	9	20	18	71	74
5–9	10	4	21	5	1	1	4	7
10–14	8	5	15	25	4	2	19	10
15–19	1	5	5	6	1	2	1	3
20–29	1	12	2	27	2	1	3	0
30 or more	3	16	3	27	4	8	2	6

Source: INSEE input-output tables in current prices, level S (unpublished).
a. Ratio of imports to consumption (exposure to imports) is $100 (M+T)/(Q+M+T-X)$, where M is imports c.i.f., T is tariff collected, Q is output (*production distribuée*), and X is exports f.o.b. Industries defined according to NAP-S79 (see appendix C). Industry S56 omitted.
b. Domestic consumption of manufactures.
c. Domestic consumption of nonmanufactures.

Table A-54. *Change in Ratio of Imports to Consumption,*
Manufacturing and Nonmanufacturing Industries,
Selected Periods, 1959–80[a]
Percent except final two columns

(1)		(2)		Mean difference (2)−(1)	Standard deviation (2)−(1)	t-ratio[b]
Period	Mean ratio	Period	Mean ratio			
Manufacturing						
1959	8.4	1980	25.3	16.9[c]	13.2	8.7
1959	8.4	1969	15.8	7.4[c]	8.3	6.0
1970	16.7	1980	25.3	8.7[c]	6.9	8.6
1959	8.4	1966	12.4	3.9[c]	5.0	5.3
1973	19.1	1980	25.3	6.2[c]	5.9	7.2
1959–69[d]	7.4	1970–80[d]	8.7	1.3	6.9	1.3
1973–80[d]	3.9	1973–80[d]	6.2	2.3[e]	5.6	2.8
Nonmanufacturing						
1959	13.1	1980	19.7	6.6[f]	17.7	2.1
1959	13.1	1969	15.4	2.4	7.4	1.8
1970	16.4	1980	19.7	3.4[f]	9.0	2.1
1959	13.1	1966	14.6	1.5	5.2	1.7
1973	17.5	1980	19.7	2.2	7.3	1.7
1959–69[d]	2.4	1970–80[d]	3.4	1.0	6.4	0.9
1973–80[d]	1.5	1973–80[d]	2.2	0.6	6.0	0.6

Source: INSEE input-output tables in current prices, level S (unpublished).
a. Ratio of imports to consumption (exposure to imports) is $100 (M+T)/(Q+M+T-X)$, where M is imports c.i.f., T is tariff collected, Q is output (*production distribuée*), and X is exports f.o.b. Means and standard deviations relate to forty-six manufacturing and thirty-two nonmanufacturing industries defined according to NAP-S79 (see appendix C). Industry S56 omitted.
b. Relates to hypothesis that mean change is 0.
c. Differs from 0 at the .001 level of significance in a one-tail test.
d. Mean ratio is mean difference in ratio between last and first years of period.
e. Differs from 0 at the .01 level of significance in a one-tail test.
f. Differs from 0 at the .05 level of significance in a one-tail test.

Table A-55. *Distributions of Manufacturing and Nonmanufacturing*
Industries by Change in Ratio of Imports to Consumption, 1959–80[a]

Change in ratio	Manufacturing industries			Nonmanufacturing industries		
	Number	Percent of output[b]		Number	Percent of output[c]	
		1959	1980		1959	1980
Less than 0	1	1	0	8	22	14
0–4	8	23	26	17	69	79
5–9	6	19	15	3	6	6
10–19	14	35	33	0	0	0
20 or more	17	22	26	4	3	1

Source: INSEE input-output tables in current prices, level S (unpublished).
a. Ratio of imports to consumption (import exposure) is $100 (M+T)/(Q+M+T-X)$, where M is imports c.i.f., T is tariff collected, Q is output (*production distribuée*), and X is exports f.o.b. Industries defined according to NAP-S79 (see appendix C). Industry S56 omitted.
b. Output of manufactures.
c. Output of nonmanufactures.

Table A-56. *Manufacturing Industries in Which Ratio of Imports to Consumption Increased Less Than 10 Percentage Points, 1959–80*[a]
Percent

Code	Industry	1959	1980	Change 1959–80
402	Sugar	33.6	16.2	−17.3
38-9	Grain mill products	1.9	3.5	1.5
36	Dairy products	3.2	4.8	1.6
19	Drugs	2.2	4.2	2.0
32	Ships	4.2	6.6	2.3
41	Beverages	5.5	8.0	2.5
20	Foundry products	1.5	4.3	2.8
053	Petroleum products	6.5	11.4	4.9
51	Printing/publishing	3.4	8.4	5.0
15	Building materials	5.9	11.6	5.7
312	Railway vehicles	3.0	9.9	6.9
35	Meat	4.2	12.5	8.3
26	Military products	2.6	11.0	8.4
52	Rubber products	11.9	20.8	8.9
21	Metallic products	3.8	12.9	9.1

Source: INSEE input-output tables in current prices, level S (unpublished).

a. Ratio of imports to consumption (exposure to imports) is $100\ (M + T)/(Q + M + T - X)$, where M is imports c.i.f., T is tariff collected, Q is output (*production distribuée*), and X is exports f.o.b. Industries defined according to NAP-S79 (see appendix C). Change is measured in percentage points.

Table A-57. *Manufacturing Industries in Which Ratio of Imports to Consumption Failed to Exceed 5 Percent, 1959*
Percent

Code	Industry	1959	1980	Change 1959–80
49	Furniture	1.2	17.8	16.6
42	Tobacco products	1.4	15.6	14.2
20	Foundry products	1.5	4.3	2.8
46	Shoes	1.6	31.6	30.1
38-9	Grain mill products	1.9	3.5	1.5
47	Apparel	1.9	19.1	17.1
452	Leather products	2.0	25.2	23.1
19	Drugs	2.2	4.2	2.0
26	Military products	2.6	11.0	8.4
442	Knitwear	2.9	37.7	34.8
312	Railway vehicles	3.0	9.9	6.9
36	Dairy products	3.2	4.8	1.6
443	Woven textiles	3.3	39.3	35.9
16	Glass	3.3	24.4	21.1
51	Printing/publishing	3.4	8.4	5.0
53	Plastics products	3.5	21.0	17.5
21	Metallic products	3.8	12.9	9.1
311	Road vehicles	4.0	26.8	22.8
35	Meat	4.2	12.5	8.3
32	Ships	4.2	6.6	2.3
18	Chemical products nec	4.3	21.7	17.3
43	Manmade fibers	4.4	60.1	55.8
28	Electrical equipment	4.4	20.9	16.5

Source: INSEE input-output tables in current prices, level S (unpublished).

a. Ratio of imports to consumption (exposure to imports) is $100\,(M+T)/(Q+M+T-X)$, where M is imports c.i.f., T is tariff collected, Q is output (*production distribuée*), and X is exports f.o.b. Industries defined according to NAP-S79 (see appendix C). Change is measured in percentage points.

Table A-58. *Distributions of Manufacturing and Nonmanufacturing Industries by Ratio of Exports to Output, 1959, 1980*[a]

Ratio of exports to output (percent)	Manufacturing industries				Nonmanufacturing industries			
	Number		Percent of output[b]		Number		Percent of output[c]	
	1959	1980	1959	1980	1959	1980	1959	1980
Less than 5	4	2	16	2	24	20	91	76
5–9	15	6	34	27	2	2	5	1
10–14	12	3	16	9	1	4	0	14
15–19	7	7	14	12	0	3	0	8
20–29	6	9	18	10	2	2	2	0
30 or more	2	19	2	40	3	1	2	1

Source: INSEE input-output tables in current prices, level S (unpublished).

a. Ratio of exports to output (propensity to export) is $100\,(X/Q)$, where X is exports f.o.b. and Q is output (*production distribuée*). Industries defined according to NAP-S79 (see appendix C). Industry S56 omitted.

b. Output of manufactures.

c. Output of nonmanufactures.

Table A-59. *Change in Ratio of Exports to Output, Manufacturing and Nonmanufacturing Industries, Selected Periods, 1959–80*[a]

Percent

(1)		(2)		Mean difference (2)−(1)	Standard deviation (2)−(1)	t-ratio[b]
Period	Mean ratio	Period	Mean ratio			
Manufacturing						
1959	13.5	1980	26.5	13.0[c]	10.5	8.4
1959	13.5	1969	16.2	2.7[d]	7.0	2.6
1970	18.5	1980	26.5	8.0[c]	7.1	7.6
1959	13.5	1966	14.1	0.6	4.9	0.8
1973	21.2	1980	26.5	5.3[c]	4.9	7.3
1959–69[e]	2.7	1970–80[e]	8.0	5.3[c]	9.8	3.6
1956–66[e]	0.6	1973–80[e]	5.3	4.7[c]	6.9	4.6
Nonmanufacturing						
1959	8.9	1980	8.4	−0.5	7.7	−0.4
1959	8.9	1969	7.7	−1.2	5.6	−1.2
1970	7.7	1980	8.4	0.7	4.7	0.8
1959	8.9	1966	8.2	−0.7	3.3	−1.3
1973	7.9	1980	8.4	0.5	3.8	0.7
1959–69[e]	−1.2	1970–80[e]	0.7	1.9	6.8	1.5
1956–66[e]	−0.7	1973–80[e]	0.5	1.2	4.8	1.4

Source: INSEE input-output tables in current prices, level S (unpublished).

a. Ratio of exports to output (propensity to export) is 100 (X/Q), where X is exports f.o.b. and Q is output (*production distribuée*). Means and standard deviations relate to forty-six manufacturing and thirty-two nonmanufacturing industries defined according to NAP-S79 (see appendix C). Industry S56 omitted.

b. Relates to hypothesis that mean change is 0.

c. Differs from 0 at the .001 level of significance in a one-tail test.

d. Differs from 0 at the .05 level of significance in a one-tail test.

e. Mean ratio is mean difference in ratio between last and first years of period.

Table A-60. *Distributions of Manufacturing Industries by Change in Ratio of Exports to Output, 1959–80*[a]

Change in ratio	Number	Percent of manufacturing output	
		1959	1980
Less than 0	2	2	3
0–4	7	15	21
5–9	11	34	25
10–19	16	36	35
20 or more	10	12	16

Source: INSEE input-output tables in current prices, level S (unpublished).

a. Ratio of exports to output (propensity to export) is 100 (X/Q), where X is exports f.o.b. and Q is output (*production distribuée*). Industries defined according to NAP-S79 (see appendix C).

Table A-61. *Distribution of Manufacturing Industries, by Exposure to Direct Foreign Investment, 1962, 1980*[a]

	1962			1980	
Exposure (percent)[b]	Number of industries	Percent of sales[c]	Exposure (percent)[b]	Number of industries	Percent of value added[d]
0–4	23	38	0–4	1	4
5–9	8	18	5–9	7	14
10–19	7	33	10–19	8	30
20–29	1	2	20–29	9	29
30 or more	4	9	30–49	9	18
			50 or more	3	6

Sources: Ministère de l'Economie et des Finances, "Recensement des Investissements Etrangers en France," table 3; and Ministère de l'Industrie et de la Recherche, *9 Ans d'Implantation Etrangère dans l'Industrie, 1er Janvier 1973–1er Janvier 1981,* pp. 103–27.

a. 1962: industries defined according to NAE-2 (see appendix C). 1980: industries defined according to NAP-100 (see appendix C); source for 1980 omits industries 26, 35–38, 41, 42.

b. In 1962, exposure is sales of French companies under foreign control divided by sales of all French companies (percent). In 1980, exposure is value added in French companies under foreign control divided by value added in all French companies (percent).

c. Sales of these forty-three industries.

d. Value added in these thirty-seven industries.

Table A-62. *Distributions of Industries, by Percentage Change in Prices, 1959–64, 1959–69*[a]

	1959–64				1959–69		
Change in price (percent)[b]	Number of industries	Percent of total output[c]		Change in price (percent)[d]	Number of industries	Percent of total output[c]	
		1959	1964			1959	1969
Decrease				*Decrease*			
20 or more	2	0.2	0.1	20 or more	3	0.5	0.3
10–19	4	1.4	1.5	10–19	5	1.8	1.9
1–9	5	4.2	3.9	0–9	4	3.8	3.6
Increase				*Increase*			
0–9	12	9.5	8.8	1–9	6	4.3	3.4
10–19	28	32.9	30.5	10–19	10	9.6	7.9
20–29	16	28.2	30.1	20–29	13	18.9	17.8
30–39	10	21.8	22.7	30–39	15	24.2	21.9
40 or more	2	1.8	2.4	40–49	7	6.8	6.5
				50–59	3	8.5	10.6
				60–69	6	6.4	6.8
				70–79	4	13.4	15.8
				80 or more	3	1.9	3.6

Source: INSEE input-output tables in current prices and 1970 prices, level S (unpublished).

a. Industries defined according to NAP-S79 (see appendix C).

b. Change in price is $100 \, [(Q64/QR64)/(Q59/QR59) - 1]$, where Q is *production distribuée* in current prices, QR is *production distribuée* in 1970 prices, and $Q64$ is *production distribuée* in 1964.

c. Output is *production distribuée* measured in current prices.

d. Change in price is $100 \, [(Q69/QR69)/(Q59/QR59) - 1]$, where Q is *production distribuée* in current prices, QR is *production distribuée* in 1970 prices, and $Q69$ is *production distribuée* in 1969.

Table A-63. *Share of French Exports to OECD Countries, by Type of Commodity, 1983*
Percent

SITC Code	Section	Share of French exports[a]	Share exported to OECD[b]
0	Food/animals	13	68
1	Beverages/tobacco	3	85
2	Raw materials n.e.c.	4	92
3	Mineral fuels/lubricants	4	86
4	Animal/vegetable oils	0	58
5	Chemicals/related products	13	74
6	Manufactures by material	19	71
7	Machinery/transport equipment	34	61
8	Miscellaneous manufactures	9	72
9	Commodities/transactions n.e.c.	1	56
	All	100	69

Source: OECD, *Foreign Trade by Commodities, 1983*, series C, vol. I: *Exports*.
a. Share is 100 (Xk/X), where Xk is French exports of goods in SITC section k, and X is total French exports.
b. Share is 100 ($XOECDk/Xk$), where $XOECDk$ is French exports to OECD of goods in SITC section k.

Table A-64. *Share of French Exports to OECD Countries, by Type of Commodity, Selected Years, 1952–83*[a]
Percent

SITC Code	Section	1952	1958	1963	1968	1973	1978	1983
0	Food/animals	34	39	58	73	76	77	67
1	Beverages/tobacco	50	63	79	80	81	80	80
2	Raw materials n.e.c.	83	82	86	85	86	85	84
3	Mineral fuels/lubricants	42	51	67	87	91	87	79
4	Animal/vegetable oils	31	17	43	63	61	57	56
5	Chemicals/related products	39	39	54	59	65	67	67
6	Manufactures by material	33	42	64	68	72	68	67
7	Machinery/transport equipment	26	39	55	54	65	58	54
8	Miscellaneous manufactures	35	37	63	70	75	70	67
9	Commodities/transactions n.e.c.	12	20	31	46	47	68	53
	All	37	44	62	65	71	67	64

Sources: 1952: OEEC, *Foreign Trade*, series II: *Foreign Trade by Areas and by Commodity Categories* (Sept. 1953). 1958: OEEC, *Foreign Trade*, series B: *Analytical Abstracts, Jan.-Dec. 1959*, no. 1. 1963: OECD, *Foreign Trade*, series C: *Trade by Commodities, Jan.-Dec. 1963*, vol. I: *Exports*. 1968: OECD, *Statistics of Foreign Trade*, series B: *Analytical Abstracts, Jan.-Dec. 1968*, no. 1. 1973: OECD, *Statistics of Trade*, series B: *Trade by Commodities, Country Summaries, Jan.-Dec. 1973*, no. 1. 1978: OECD, *Statistics of Foreign Trade*, series C: *Trade by Commodities, Market Summaries: Exports, Jan.-Dec. 1978*. 1983: OECD, *Foreign Trade by Commodities, 1983*, series C, vol. I: *Exports*.
a. Measured as 100 ($XOECDk/Xk$), where $XOECDk$ is French exports to OECD of goods in SITC section k and Xk is French exports to all countries of goods in SITC section k. OECD excludes Australia, Finland, Japan, New Zealand, and Spain.

Table A-65. *Distribution of Manufacturing Industries by Reliance on OECD for Export Markets, 1983*

Reliance on OECD (percent)[a]	Number of industries[b]	Share of exports (percent)[c]
0–29	0	0
30–49	7	20
50–59	4	13
60–69	7	19
70–79	10	28
80–89	7	20
90 or more	0	0
All	35	100

Source: OECD, *Foreign Trade by Commodities, 1983*, series C, vol. I: *Exports*.
a. Reliance is 100 $(XOECDk/Xk)$, where $XOECDk$ is French exports to OECD of goods in SITC division k, and Xk is French exports to all countries of goods in SITC division k.
b. Industries are manufacturing divisions of SITC, revision 2. Manufactures are goods in SITC sections 5-8.
c. Share of French exports of manufactures.

Table A-66. *French Manufacturing Industries Sending Less Than 50 Percent of Their Exports to OECD Countries, 1983*[a]

		SITC division k manufactures		
SITC Code	Division	Percent of manufacturing exports[b]	Percent to OECD[c]	Percent to French Overseas Union[d]
54	Medicinals/pharmaceuticals	2.0	50	36
69	Manufactures of metal n.e.c.	3.9	50	21
57	Explosives	0.1	48	21
79	Transport equipment except road vehicles	5.4	47	7
73	Metalworking machinery	0.8	46	10
74	General industrial machinery	5.8	45	18
76	Telecommunications/sound equipment	2.0	37	16

Source: OECD, *Foreign Trade by Commodities, 1983*, series C, vol. I: *Exports*.
a. Manufacturing industries are the two-digit divisions of SITC, revision 2, sections 5-8.
b. Percent of French exports of goods in SITC sections 5-8.
c. Percent of all exports of goods assigned to this SITC division.
d. See appendix G.

Table A-67. Exposure to Imports and to Foreign Investment, Concentrated Industries in Mining and Manufacturing, 1980[a]
Percent

Code	Industry	Four-firm producer concentration ratio[b]	Ratio of imports to consumption[c]	Foreign control of domestic value added[d]
13	Nonferrous metals	52	52	35
32	Ships	52	7	18
31	Ground transport equipment	58	26	15
10	Crude steel	60	29	16
52	Rubber products	64	21	21
33	Aerospace equipment	66	37	2
5	Petroleum	69	44	42
40	Foods nec	72	29	37
9	Ferrous minerals	76	72	23
14	Nonmetallic minerals	77	44	17
12	Metallic minerals, nonferrous	82	86	27
27	Office equipment	91	74	91
39	Grain mill products	96	6	44
43	Manmade fibers	97	60	32

Sources: Ministère de l'Industrie et de la Recherche, *La Concentration dans l'Industrie de 1974 à 1980*; INSEE input-output tables in current prices, level S (unpublished); and Ministère de l'Industrie et de la Recherche, *9 Ans d'Implantation Etrangère dans l'Industrie, 1er Janvier 1973-1er Janvier 1981*, pp. 81–127.

a. Manufacturing and mining industries in which the four-firm producer concentration ratio exceeds 50 percent. Industries defined according to NAP-100 (see appendix C). One source or more omits industries 26, 35-38, 41-42.

b. Ratio is $100(Q4/Q)$, where Q is output (*production distribuée*) of all domestic producers and $Q4$ is output of four largest domestic producers.

c. Ratio is $100 (M+T)/(Q+M+T-X)$, where M is imports c.i.f., T is tariff collected, Q is *production distribuée*, and X is exports f.o.b.

d. Ratio is $100 (VAF/VA)$, where VAF is value added in French companies under foreign control, and VA is value added in all French companies.

Table A-68. French Manufacturing Subsidiaries of Foreign Companies, Extent and Ownership of Residual Equity Capital
Percent

Parent control[a]	Parent home United States	Other	Residual owner[b]	Parent home United States	Other
95 or more	57	42	French private party	68	70
51–94	22	28	Other private party	9	19
50	7	9	French government	0	3
25–49	8	14	Widely dispersed	23	8
5–24	7	7			

Source: Vaupel and Curhan, *The World's Multinational Enterprises*, cross-tabulations 10.1.1, 10.1.2, 12.1.1, 12.1.2.

a. Parent control is parent-owned fraction of subsidiary's equity capital. Based on 209 subsidiaries of U.S. multinationals and 380 subsidiaries of other multinationals.

b. Based on 53 subsidiaries of U.S. multinationals and 67 subsidiaries of other multinationals.

Table A-69. *Distribution of French Manufacturing Industries by Extent of U.S. Direct Investment, 1962*

U.S. control[a]	Number of industries	Share of sales[b]
0–4	21	61
5–9	2	11
10–19	3	18
20–32	2	10
33 or more	0	0
All	28	100

Source: Ministère de l'Economie et des Finances, "Recensement des Investissements Etrangers en France," tables 1, 3. Industries defined according to NAE-2 (see appendix C). Source includes industries 10, 16, 18–21, 25–30, 32, 35–36, 37–39, 42–44, 46–47, 53–55, 57, 58, 61.

a. Control is 100 $(SUSk/Sk)$, where $SUSk$ is sales of American-controlled companies in industry k, and Sk is sales of all companies in industry k.

b. Percentage of sales in all twenty-eight industries.

Table A-70. *Distribution of French Manufacturing Industries by Extent of U.S. Direct Investment, 1980*

U.S. control[a]	Number of industries	Share of value added[b]
0–4	12	35
5–9	7	33
10–19	4	15
20–32	5	14
33 or more	1	2
All	29	100

Source: Ministère de l'Industrie et de la Recherche, *9 Ans d'Implantation Etrangère dans l'Industrie, 1er Janvier 1973–1er Janvier 1981*. Industries defined according to NAP-100 (see appendix C). Source includes industries 5, 10, 13, 15–25, 27–29, 31–32, 34, 43–45, 47, 50–54.

a. Control is 100 $(VAUSk/VAk)$, where $VAUSk$ is value added in American-controlled companies in industry k, and VAk is value added in all companies in industry k.

b. Percentage of value added in all twenty-nine industries.

Table A-71. *Foreign Manufacturing Subsidiaries of French Companies, by Location, as of January 1, 1971*[a]
Percent

Location	Share	Location	Share
North America	7.1	Middle East	2.1
United States	5.0	Africa	16.8
Canada	2.1	French North Africa	7.3
Latin America	17.0	Other French Africa	7.1
Europe	50.6	Asia and Oceania	6.2
Germany	9.4	Japan	0.7
Spain	9.2	All	100.0
Belgium-Luxembourg	8.5		
Italy	8.0		
United Kingdom	4.7		
Netherlands	3.3		

Source: Vaupel and Curhan, *The World's Multinational Enterprises*, cross-tabulation 1.21.1, amended version, in files of Raymond Vernon.

a. Based on 424 subsidiaries. Share is measured in terms of number of subsidiaries. Areas defined as in source, except Pakistan assigned here to Asia.

Table A-72. *Share of Household Expenditure on Food, by Type of Retailer, 1962–84*
Percent

Year	Small independent general stores	Small independent specialty stores	Small chain stores	Variety stores	Supermarkets	Hypermarkets	Other retailers	Nonretailers
1962	31.3	36.1	13.6	3.1	1.0	*	1.1	13.8
1963	30.8	36.5	13.2	3.4	1.6	*	1.1	13.4
1964	30.5	36.5	13.3	3.5	2.1	0.1	1.1	12.9
1965	29.7	36.6	13.3	3.7	2.7	0.1	1.2	12.7
1966	29.0	37.0	13.4	3.8	3.2	0.1	1.3	12.2
1967	28.2	36.8	13.5	4.0	3.8	0.3	1.2	12.2
1968	27.1	36.6	13.5	4.1	4.5	0.8	1.2	12.2
1969	26.2	34.8	14.2	4.3	6.1	1.5	1.2	11.7
1970	25.3	33.4	13.3	4.4	7.7	3.4	1.3	11.2
1971	23.5	33.3	13.5	4.3	8.6	4.3	1.5	11.0
1972	22.2	32.8	12.7	4.1	9.0	6.3	1.2	11.7
1973	21.1	32.1	12.1	4.0	9.9	7.6	1.2	12.0
1974	20.4	30.7	11.5	3.9	10.9	9.1	1.2	12.3
1975	20.4	30.3	10.4	3.7	11.3	10.0	1.2	12.7
1976	19.2	30.4	9.9	3.4	11.8	11.0	1.2	13.1
1977	19.0	30.0	9.8	3.2	12.1	11.5	1.2	13.1
1978	18.2	29.9	8.7	3.1	12.8	12.1	1.4	13.8
1979	16.9	29.5	8.3	3.1	13.6	12.8	1.3	14.5
1980	15.8	29.5	8.2	3.3	14.3	13.6	1.3	14.0
1981	15.1	28.9	7.6	3.3	15.3	14.6	1.3	13.9
1982	14.4	28.6	7.2	3.3	15.9	15.2	1.2	14.2
1983	14.2	28.3	6.8	3.2	16.6	15.6	1.2	14.1
1984	13.9	27.8	6.2	3.1	17.5	16.6	1.1	13.8

Sources: Guillement, *Le Commerce de Détail de 1962 à 1979*, pp. 18–19; INSEE C122, p. 17; and INSEE C128, p. 22.
* Less than 0.05 percent.

Table A-73. *Number of Large Retail Food Establishments, 1957–84*

Year	Supermarket	Hypermarket	Year	Supermarket	Hypermarket
1957	1	0	1971	2,069	143
1958	2	0	1972	2,330	211
1959	18	0	1973	2,587	259
1960	49	0	1974	2,694	291
1961	121	0	1975	2,846	305
1962	207	0	1976	3,157	339
1963	323	1	1977	3,302	369
1964	449	2	1978	3,492	387
1965	566	3	1979	3,710	407
1966	673	4	1980	3,962	426
1967	821	12	1981	4,261	460
1968	1,045	26	1982	4,510	493
1969	1,453	71	1983	4,906	521
1970	1,828	114	1984	5,279	549

Source: INSEE C128, pp. 54–55.

Table A-74. Share of Household Expenditure on Nonfood Merchandise, by Type of Retailer, 1962–84
Percent

Year	Food retailers				Nonfood retailers			
	Small food retailers	Supermarkets	Variety stores	Hypermarkets	Department stores	General stores	Specialty stores	Nonretailers
1962	4.4	0.2	1.9	*	4.3	2.3	66.4	20.5
1963	4.2	0.3	2.1	*	4.3	2.2	66.4	20.5
1964	4.3	0.5	2.2	*	4.3	2.2	66.0	20.5
1965	4.2	0.6	2.4	*	4.4	2.1	65.4	20.9
1966	4.2	0.7	2.4	0.1	4.4	2.1	65.2	20.9
1967	4.0	0.8	2.5	0.1	4.3	2.1	65.0	21.2
1968	3.7	0.9	2.5	0.3	4.1	2.0	64.7	21.8
1969	3.8	1.2	2.6	0.6	4.1	2.1	63.9	21.7
1970	3.8	1.5	2.5	1.3	4.2	2.2	62.5	22.0
1971	3.2	1.7	2.5	2.1	4.0	2.2	62.3	22.0
1972	2.4	1.8	2.2	3.0	3.7	2.3	63.1	21.5
1973	1.8	1.9	2.1	3.7	3.6	2.3	63.5	21.1
1974	1.8	2.0	2.0	4.2	4.1	2.2	62.3	21.4
1975	2.0	2.2	1.9	4.6	4.0	2.2	62.4	20.7
1976	2.0	2.4	1.8	5.0	3.9	2.2	61.8	20.9
1977	2.0	2.5	1.8	5.5	3.7	2.4	60.8	21.3
1978	2.1	2.8	1.7	5.8	3.7	2.5	60.1	21.3
1979	2.0	2.9	1.6	6.0	3.5	2.5	59.8	21.7
1980	1.9	3.1	1.7	6.3	3.3	2.5	59.3	21.9
1981	1.8	3.2	1.6	6.6	3.2	2.6	58.9	22.1
1982	1.7	3.3	1.6	6.8	3.3	2.5	58.8	22.0
1983	1.7	3.3	1.6	6.9	3.2	2.6	58.6	22.1
1984	1.6	3.5	1.6	7.2	3.1	2.6	58.2	22.2

Sources: Guillement, Le Commerce de Détail 1962 à 1979, pp. 23-24; INSEE C122, p. 18; and INSEE C128, p. 23.
* Less than 0.05 percent.

Table A-75. *Gross Markups in Food and Nonfood Retailing, by Size of Retailer, 1971–76*[a]
Percent

Number of salaried employees	1971	1972	1973	1974	1975	1976
Food retailing[b]						
0	22.0	22.5	24.8	22.8	24.8	25.6
1–9	24.2	24.1	24.1	26.5	29.1	29.9
10–99	19.0	20.7	20.2	21.3	22.5	22.0
100–999	23.1	23.2	23.3	22.8	24.7	23.4
1,000 or more	28.3	26.5	26.5	25.8	28.9	25.4
0 or more	24.6	24.2	24.3	24.6	27.1	25.6
Nonfood retailing[b]						
0	40.2	40.1	47.1	27.8	40.4	36.7
1–9	41.6	41.8	41.8	40.1	48.9	46.2
10–99	40.6	43.1	42.4	42.2	50.2	46.5
100–999	52.1	50.8	52.1	47.5	53.8	52.5
1,000 or more	57.7	47.6	58.3	54.5	54.6	53.5
0 or more	43.7	43.8	44.7	42.5	50.1	47.4

Sources: INSEE E34, E38, E49, E51, E60, and E72.
a. Gross markup is sales revenue (*chiffre d'affaires hors taxes*) less purchases of goods (*achats de matières et marchandises*), divided by purchases of goods.
b. Companies in NAP T27 (food) or NAP T28 (nonfood). Includes companies (incorporated or not) filing standard-form tax returns (BIC-*réel*).

Table A-76. *Index of Retail Prices for Selected Foods, by Type of Store, 1976*[a]

Type of store	All products	Nonalcoholic beverages	Fluid milk	Fresh fruit
Large enterprises	97.5	96.8	99.7	98.7
Hypermarkets	94.1	91.5	98.0	94.1
Supermarkets	98.5	98.7	100.9	98.6
Other chains	100.2	99.1	99.0	102.9
Other cooperatives	96.1	97.0	102.2	101.6
Miscellaneous	100.9	102.6	95.9	97.1
Small Enterprises	101.9	107.2	100.5	101.0
Open-air markets	100.3	101.1	100.7	94.5
Specialty shops	104.1	106.9	99.2	107.7
General stores	100.5	107.2	100.7	104.0
All	100.0	100.0	100.0	100.0

Source: Rempp, "Les Différences de Prix entre le Petit et le Grand Commerce," table 2.
a. Based on a survey of 133 narrowly defined foods. Miscellaneous large enterprises are department and variety stores. Source includes relative price data for additional categories of products.

Table A-77. *Profitability of Food and Nonfood Retailing,
by Size of Retailer, 1971–76*[a]
Percent

Number of salaried employees	1971	1972	1973	1974	1975	1976
Food retailing[b]						
0	38.9	37.6	39.7	52.6	59.4	66.3
1–9	33.0	33.5	36.2	39.5	41.6	45.6
10–99	19.8	16.2	16.7	19.7	20.3	20.2
100–999	14.4	14.4	15.8	17.7	15.2	15.0
1,000 or more	19.6	18.3	19.2	21.0	20.9	21.2
0 or more	23.0	21.9	23.2	26.1	27.0	28.5
Nonfood retailing[b]						
0	29.8	31.8	28.3	45.6	43.4	47.1
1–9	37.7	39.0	38.5	43.1	44.2	43.6
10–99	25.5	28.7	31.1	36.4	33.0	31.7
100–999	19.8	18.9	24.7	27.2	27.8	21.7
1,000 or more	12.6	14.4	11.4	14.7	13.2	16.5
0 or more	28.8	30.3	31.1	35.9	36.2	35.9

Sources: INSEE E34, E38, E49, E51, E60, and E72.

a. Profitability is the ratio of gross operating profit (*excédent brut d'exploitation*) to gross fixed assets (*immobilisations brutes*).

b. Companies in NAP T27 (food) or NAP T28 (nonfood). Includes companies (incorporated or not) filing standard-form tax returns (BIC-*réel*).

Table A-78. *Unemployment Rates for Large European Economies, by Age and Sex, 1983–86*[a]

Percent

Category	1983	1984	1985	1986
Entire labor force				
France	7.5	9.4	9.9	10.1
Germany	6.8	7.1	7.4	7.1
Italy	8.6	9.8	9.2	10.0
United Kingdom	11.1	10.9	10.7	10.9
Men 25 and older				
France	4.3	5.3	5.8	6.0
Germany	5.2	5.3	5.7	5.3
Italy	2.4	2.9	2.8	3.2
United Kingdom	9.3	9.1	8.9	9.1
Women 25 and older				
France	7.0	8.1	8.8	9.8
Germany	6.6	7.5	8.0	8.4
Italy	7.9	8.5	7.9	8.4
United Kingdom	7.2	7.8	7.7	8.2
Men under 25				
France	14.6	20.4	21.3	20.4
Germany	11.2	10.5	10.1	9.1
Italy	23.4	26.8	26.0	26.3
United Kingdom	22.6	20.7	20.4	19.8
Women under 25				
France	22.1	28.1	27.6	25.7
Germany	11.4	11.5	11.2	11.2
Italy	33.8	39.0	38.6	42.4
United Kingdom	17.6	16.8	16.6	16.3

Source: Statistical Office of the European Communities, *Employment and Unemployment 1987*, p. 179.
a. Based on EC labor force surveys designed to ensure international comparability.

Appendix B
Abbreviations

AF	Compagnie Nationale Air France
AGF	Assurances Générales de France
AI	Lignes Aériennes Intérieures Air Inter
Alcool	Régie Commerciale des Alcools
ANVAR	Agence Nationale de Valorisation de la Recherche
AP	Aéroports de Paris
APC	Azote et Produits Chimiques
ATIC	Association Technique de l'Importation Charbonnière
BFCE	Banque Française du Commerce Extérieur
BNCI	Banque Nationale pour le Commerce et l'Industrie
BNP	Banque Nationale de Paris
BRGM	Bureau de Recherches Géologiques et Minières
BRP	Bureau de Recherches de Pétrole
CCCHCI	Caisse Centrale de Crédit Hotelier, Commercial et Industriel
CDC	Caisse des Dépôts et Consignations
CDF	Charbonnages de France
CEA	Commissariat à l'Energie Atomique
CEP	Compagnie d'Exploration Pétrolière
CEPME	Crédit d'Equipement des Petites et Moyennes Entreprises
CFP	Compagnie Française des Pétroles
CGP	Commissariat Général du Plan
CGT	Compagnie Générale Transatlantique
CIC	Crédit Industriel et Commercial

CII	Compagnie Internationale pour l'Informatique
CMB	Compagnie des Machines Bull
CMLR	*Common Market Law Reports*
CNCA	Caisse Nationale de Crédit Agricole
CNE	Caisse Nationale d'Epargne
CNEP	Comptoir National d'Escompte de Paris
CNES	Centre National d'Etudes Spatiales
CNEXO	Centre National pour l'Exploitation des Océans
CNME	Caisse Nationale des Marchés de l'Etat
CNP	Caisse Nationale de Prévoyance
CNR	Compagnie Nationale du Rhône
COB	Commission des Opérations de Bourse
COFACE	Compagnie Française d'Assurance pour le Commerce Extérieur
DTAT	Direction Technique des Armements Terrestres
DTCA	Direction Technique des Constructions Aéronautiques
DTCN	Direction Technique des Constructions Navales
EC	European Communities
ECR	*European Court Reports*
ECSC	European Coal and Steel Community
EEC	European Economic Community
EDF	Electricité de France
EMC	Entreprise Minière et Chimique
ENF	Entreprises non financières (appendix C)
ERAP	Entreprise de Recherches et d'Activités Pétrolières
FDES	Fonds de Développement Economique et Social
FIRS	Fonds d'Intervention et de Régularisation du Marché du Sucre
FORMA	Fonds d'Orientation et de Régularisation des Marchés Agricoles
FOU	French Overseas Union (appendix G)
FRT	Fonds de la Recherche et de la Technologie
GAN	Groupe des Assurances Nationales
GDF	Gaz de France

GEN	Grandes Entreprises Nationales (AF, AI, CDF, EDF, GDF, PTT, RATP, and SNCF)
GIAT	Groupement Industriel des Armements Terrestres
Havas	Agence Havas
HLM	Habitation à loyer modéré
IDI	Institut de Développement Industriel
IFP	Institut Français du Pétrole
IN	Imprimerie Nationale
INSEE	Institut National de la Statistique et des Etudes Economiques
JOCE	*Journal Officiel des Communautés Européennes*
JORF	*Journal Officiel de la République Française*
MDPA	Mines de Potasse d'Alsace (Mines Domaniales de Potasse d'Alsace)
MGF	Mutuelles Générales de France
MM	Compagnie des Messageries Maritimes
NAC	Nomenclature des Entreprises, Etablissements, et Toutes Activités Collectives 1949 (appendix C)
NAE	Nomenclature des Activités Economiques 1959 (appendix C)
NAP	Nomenclatures d'Activités et de Produits 1973 (appendix C)
NORD	Nord-Aviation
OECD	Organization for Economic Cooperation and Development
OEEC	Organization for European Economic Cooperation
OJEC	*Official Journal of the European Communities*
ONERA	Office National d'Etudes et de Recherches Aérospatiales
ONIA	Office National Industriel de l'Azote
ONIC	Office National Interprofessionnel des Céréales
ORTF	Office de la Radiodiffusion Télévision Française
PREPA	Société de Prospection et d'Exploitations Pétrolières en Alsace
PTT	Postes et Télécommunications

RAP	Régie Autonome des Pétroles
RATP	Régie Autonome des Transports Parisiens
RCN	*Rapport sur les Comptes de la Nation*
REC	*Recueil de la Jurisprudence de la Cour de Justice des Communautés Européennes*
RNUR	Régie Nationale des Usines Renault
RPM	Resale price maintenance
SCC	Société Chimique des Charbonnages
SDR	Société de Développement Régional
SEITA	Service d'Exploitation Industrielle des Tabacs et des Allumettes
SITC	Standard International Trade Classification
SMIC	Salaire Minimum Interprofessionnel de Croissance
SMIG	Salaire Minimum Interprofessionnel Garanti
SNA	System of national accounts
SNCF	Société Nationale des Chemins de Fer Français
SNEA	Société Nationale Elf-Aquitaine
SNECMA	Société Nationale d'Etude et de Construction de Moteurs d'Aviation
SNIAS	Société Nationale Industrielle Aérospatiale
SNPA	Société Nationale des Pétroles d'Aquitaine
SNPE	Société Nationale des Poudres et Explosifs
SOE	State-owned enterprise
SUD	Sud-Aviation
TRAPIL	Société des Transports Pétroliers par Pipe-Line
UAP	Union des Assurances de Paris
UGP	Union Générale des Pétroles
VAT	Value-added tax

Appendix C
Industrial Classifications

Since World War II, France has employed three different schemes of industrial classification—the Nomenclature des Entreprises, Etablissements, et Toutes Activités Collectives, or NAC (1947–59); the Nomenclature des Activités Economiques, or NAE (1960–73); and the Nomenclatures d'Activités et de Produits, or NAP (since 1974). NAC and NAE differ mildly, but NAE and NAP can diverge sharply.[1] Hence the absence of consistent economic information at the industry level for the postwar period as a whole. See Guibert, Laganier, and Volle, "Essai sur les Nomenclatures Industrielles"; and Rousseau, "Pourquoi Change-t-On de Nomenclature?"

NAC-2

Two-digit industries of NAC. See INSEE, *Nomenclature des Entreprises, Etablissements, et Toutes Activités Collectives;* and INSEE, *Annuaire Statistique de la France, 1952,* pp. 340–43.

NAE-2

Two-digit industries of NAE. See INSEE E43, p. 240.

01 Fish
02 Forest products
03 Agricultural crops
04 Livestock
05 Agriculture-related activities
06 Electricity

07 Gas
08 Water and steam
09 Miscellaneous sources of energy
10 Petroleum
11 Solid fuels
12 Ferrous minerals

1. A rough correspondence between three-digit NAE and two-digit NAP appears in INSEE E43, pp. 252–58.

13 Nonferrous metallic minerals
14 Building materials
15 Miscellaneous minerals
16 Steel
17 Nonferrous metals
18 Metallurgy
19 Semifinished metals
20 Foundry products, boilers, mechanical engines, pumps
21 Machinery for agriculture, industry, and railways
22 General mechanical engineering
23 Metallic products I
24 Metallic products II
25 Ships
26 Motor vehicles and bicycles
27 Aerospace equipment
28 Electrical and electronic equipment
29 Precision goods
30 Glass
31 Ceramic products
32 Building materials not elsewhere classified
33 Construction I
34 Construction II
35 Chemicals I
36 Chemicals II
37 Rubber and asbestos
38 Tobacco products and matches
39 Oils and fats
40 Grain mill products
41 Freshly baked goods
42 Sugar, distilled products, beverages
43 Dairy products
44 Preserved foods
45 Miscellaneous food products
46 Ice and other frozen products
47 Textile products
48 Textile-related activities
49 Apparel
50 Furs
51 Leather
52 Shoes
53 Wood and furniture

54 Paper
55 Printing and publishing
56 Jewelry and related products
57 Toys, games, and sporting goods
58 Musical instruments, audio equipment, records
59 Ornaments for home and office; brushes
60 Miscellaneous products
61 Plastics products
62 Public road transport
63 Railway transport and mass transit
64 Inland water transport
65 Maritime transport
66 Air transport
67 Transport-related activities
68 Communications
69 Wholesaling and retailing of food I
70 Wholesaling and retailing of food II
71 Chain stores and stores not elsewhere classified
72 Mobile wholesaling and retailing
73 Wholesaling and retailing of raw materials, energy products, hardware, machinery, and vehicles I
74 Wholesaling and retailing of raw materials, energy products, hardware, machinery, and vehicles II
75 Wholesaling and retailing of textiles, apparel, and leather
76 Miscellaneous wholesaling and retailing
77 Hotels
78 Restaurants and cafés
79 Scrap products
80 Business services I
81 Business services II
82 Rental, sale, and leasing of real estate, plant, and equipment
83 Finance
84 Insurance
85 Public administration: economic and financial
86 Radio and television broadcasting

87 Movie production
88 Amusements
89 Personal care services
90 Household servants
91 Health care
92 Public administration: general
93 Police and the judicial system
94 Religious activities

95 Education
96 Sports and recreation
97 Liberal professions
98 Public administration: socioeconomic
99 Military services
00 Activities conducted outside France

ENF

ENF is entreprises non financières, based on NAE. See "Méthodes de la Comptabilité Nationale," pp. 191–94; or INSEE E43, pp. 241–43.

1 Agriculture
2 Food, drink, and tobacco products
3A Coal
3B Electricity, gas (except natural gas), and water
3C Petroleum and natural gas
4A Iron ore, iron, and crude steel
4B Crude nonferrous metals and their ores
5A Semifinished and finished metals
5B Mechanical equipment, machine tools, precision goods, and office equipment
5C Electrical and electronic equipment
5D Road vehicles
5E Ships, aerospace equipment, military products
6A Glass
6B Chemicals, rubber products, nonmetallic minerals

7A Textiles
7B Apparel
7C Leather, including shoes
7D Wood, including furniture
7E Paper
7F Printing and publishing
7G Miscellaneous manufactures, including plastics products
8A Building materials
8B Construction
9A Transport services
9B Telecommunications, including mail
10A Real estate development (construction management, rental, and sale of whole buildings and apartments)
10B Hotels, cafés, restaurants
10C Miscellaneous services, business and personal
11 Wholesale and retail trade

MCBCND

MCBCND is branches de la comptabilité nationale détaillée, based on NAE. See INSEE D67, pp. 77–78.

01 Agriculture
02 Food, drink, and tobacco products

03 Coal
04 Gas, except natural gas

05 Electricity and water
06 Petroleum and natural gas
07 Building materials, including
   ceramics
08 Glass
09 Iron ore, iron, and crude steel
10 Crude nonferrous metals and their
   minerals
11 Semifinished and finished metals
12 Mechanical equipment, including
   machine tools, precision goods,
   and office equipment
13 Electrical and electronic
   equipment
14 Road vehicles
15 Ships, aerospace equipment,
   military products
16 Chemicals, rubber products,
   nonmetallic minerals
17 Textiles
18 Apparel
19 Leather, including shoes
20 Wood, including furniture
21 Paper
22 Printing and publishing

23 Miscellaneous manufactures,
   including plastics products
24 Construction
25 Transport services
26 Telecommunications, including
   mail
27 Real estate development
   (construction management,
   rental, and sale of whole
   buildings and apartments)
28 Miscellaneous services, business
   and personal
29 Wholesale and retail trade
30 Financial institutions
31 National government, except
   military services
32 Military services
33 Local government, quasi-
   governmental organizations
34 Social security
35 Private, foreign, and international
   organizations
36 Household servants
37 Miscellaneous

NAP-100

Two-digit industries of NAP. See Ministère de l'Economie et des Finances, *Nomenclatures d'Activités et de Produits, 1973.*

00 Agricultural products not grown
   in France
01 Agriculture
02 Forest products
03 Fish
04 Coal
05A Crude petroleum and natural gas
05B Petroleum products
06 Electricity
07 Gas, except natural gas
08 Water and steam
09 Ferrous minerals
10 Crude steel
11 Semifinished steel

12 Nonferrous metallic minerals
13 Nonferrous metals, unfinished
14 Nonmetallic minerals
15 Building materials, including
   ceramics
16 Glass
17 Bulk chemicals
18 Chemical products not elsewhere
   classified
19 Drugs
20 Foundry products
21 Metallic products
22 Agricultural equipment
23 Machine tools

24 Mechanical equipment I
25 Mechanical equipment II
26 Military products
27 Office equipment, including computers
28 Electrical equipment
29A Electronic equipment, business
29B Electronic equipment for households
30 Household equipment not elsewhere classified
31 Ground transport equipment
32 Ships
33 Aerospace equipment
34 Precision goods
35 Meat
36 Dairy products
37 Preserved foods
38 Freshly baked goods
39 Grain mill products
40 Foods not elsewhere classified
41 Beverages
42 Tobacco products
43 Manmade fibers
44 Textiles
45 Leather and leather products, except shoes
46 Shoes
47 Apparel
48 Wood
49 Furniture
50 Paper
51 Printing and publishing
52 Rubber products
53 Plastics products
54 Miscellaneous manufactures
55 Construction
56 Scrap products
57 Wholesale trade in food
58 Wholesale trade in consumers goods except food
59 Wholesale trade for industry
60 Trade-related services
61 Large-scale retailing (primarily food)
62 Small-scale retailing in food

63 Large-scale retailing (primarily nonfood)
64 Specialized retailing except food
65 Sale and repair of automobiles
66 Miscellaneous repair services
67 Hotels, cafés, restaurants
68 Rail transport services, intercity
69 Road transport services, including urban mass transit
70 Freshwater transport
71 Maritime transport
72 Air transport
73 Transport terminals
74 Transport-related services not elsewhere classified
75 Telecommunications, including mail
76 Holding companies
77 Consulting services
78 Finance-related services
79 Real estate development
80 Rental and leasing of equipment
81 Rental and leasing of buildings, business and residential
82 Education, private
83 Research and development, private
84 Health care, private
85 Social services, private
86 Leisure services, private
87 Miscellaneous services, private
88 Insurance
89 Finance
90 General government
91 Social security
92 Education, public
93 Research and development, public
94 Health care, public
95 Social services, public
96 Leisure services, public
97 Miscellaneous services, public
98 Household servants
99 Foreign diplomats and delegates to international organizations in France

NAP-S89

NAP, S-level aggregation, used since 1970. Identical to NAP-100 except in the following respects:

041	Coal and lignite	442	Knitwear
042	Coke	443	Woven goods
051	Crude petroleum	451	Leather
052	Natural gas	452	Leather products except shoes
053	Petroleum products	57-4	NAP-100 57-64
171	Bulk inorganic chemicals	691	Intercity trucking
172	Bulk organic chemicals	692	Other road transport
291	Electronic equipment for business	73-4	NAP-100 73-74
		76-9	NAP-100 76-79
292	Electronic equipment for households	811	Rental of residential buildings
		812	Rental of commercial and industrial buildings
311	Road vehicles		
312	Railway vehicles	82-3	NAP-100 82-83
401	Edible oils and fats	85-7	NAP-100 85-87
402	Sugar	90-8	NAP-100 90-99
403	Food products not elsewhere classified	99	Intermediate consumption not allocated among activities (imputed banking services)
441	Yarn and thread		

NAP-S79

NAP, S-level aggregation, used between 1959 and 1969. Identical to NAP-100 except in the following respects:

041	Coal and lignite	401	Edible oils and fats
042	Coke	402	Sugar
051	Crude petroleum	441	Yarn and thread
052	Natural gas	442	Knitwear
053	Petroleum products	443	Woven goods
171	Bulk inorganic chemicals	451	Leather
172	Bulk organic chemicals	452	Leather products except shoes
22-5	NAP-100 22-25	57-4	NAP-100 57-64
27	NAP-100 27 and NAP-S89 291	68-0	NAP-100 68-70
292	Electronic equipment for households	71-2	NAP-100 71-72
		73-4	NAP-100 73-74
311	Road vehicles	76-9	NAP-100 76-79
312	Railway vehicles	811	Rental of residential buildings
37	NAP-100 37 and NAP-S89 403	812	Rental of commercial and industrial buildings
38-9	NAP-100 38-39		

82-3 NAP-100 82-83
85-7 NAP-100 85-87
90-8 NAP-100 90-99

99 Intermediate consumption not allocated among activities (imputed banking services)

NAP-T

NAP, T-level aggregation. See INSEE E64, pp. 165–71; or INSEE E43, pp. 245–47.

T01 Agriculture, forest products, fish
T02 Meat and dairy products
T03 Food not elsewhere classified and tobacco products
T04 Coal
T05 Petroleum and natural gas
T06 Electricity, gas (except natural gas), and water
T07 Iron ore, iron, crude and semifinished steel
T08 Crude and semifinished nonferrous metals and their ores
T09 Building materials and nonmetallic minerals
T10 Glass
T11 Bulk chemicals, manmade fibers
T12 Chemical products, including drugs, personal and home care products, fertilizers, paint, and explosives
T13 Metallic products
T14 Mechanical equipment, machine tools, precision goods
T15A Electrical equipment; office equipment; electronic equipment for business
T15B Electronic equipment for households; household equipment not elsewhere classified

T16 Ground transport equipment
T17 Ships, aerospace equipment, military products
T18 Textiles and apparel
T19 Leather, including shoes
T20 Wood (including furniture), miscellaneous manufactures
T21 Paper
T22 Printing and publishing
T23 Rubber and plastics products
T24 Construction
T25 Wholesale trade in food
T26 Wholesale trade except in food
T27 Retail trade in food
T28 Retail trade except in food
T29 Sale and repair of automobiles
T30 Hotels, cafés, restaurants
T31 Transport services
T32 Telecommunications, including mail
T33 Business services, including real estate development, equipment leasing, consulting, and holding companies
T34 Consumer services
T35 Rental of buildings (business and residential)
T36 Insurance
T37 Finance
T38 Government

Appendix D
Treaties and Legislation

The European Communities

An official source is European Communities, *Treaties Establishing the European Communities, Treaties Amending These Treaties, Documents Concerning the Accession*. An excellent compendium of treaties, conventions, protocols, and regulations is Stein, Hay, and Waelbroeck, *Documents for European Community Law and Institutions in Perspective*.

French Antitrust Law

The best official source for the period analyzed in this book is *Concurrence et Prix: Textes Généraux*. English versions of French legislation, regulations, circulars, and opinions appear in OECD, *Guide to Legislation on Restrictive Business Practices*.

The new antitrust law, ordinance 86-1243 of December 1, 1986, appears in *Journal Officiel de la République Française* (December 8, 1986); it is reprinted in Ministère de l'Economie, des Finances et de la Privatisation, "Liberté des Prix et Nouveau Droit de la Concurrence," pp. 39–46. Given the importance attached in chapter 5 of this book to the prohibition of refusal to sell, I translate below the relevant sections of the new law.[1]

---

1. The advisory opinions and quasi-judicial decisions of the new Conseil de la Concurrence during its first year of operation are summarized in Balladur. *Une France Plus Forte*, pp. 54–55. Several involved selective selling.

ARTICLE 7

It is illegal for an enterprise, or a group of enterprises, to abuse:

1. A dominant position in the domestic market, or in a substantial part thereof;

2. A state of economic dependence experienced by suppliers or customers who lack equivalent opportunities.

These abuses might consist in particular of refusal to sell, tying, or discrimination, as well as termination of relationship solely for refusal to submit to unjustified commercial practices.

ARTICLE 10

Exempt from articles 7 and 8 are practices shown to result:

1. From the application of statute or regulation;

2. In economic progress, an equitable share of which is reserved for customers. Under no circumstances, however, can competition be eliminated in respect of a substantial part of the commerce involved; nor can the restraints in question exceed those indispensable to the achievement of progress. . . .

ARTICLE 11

The Competition Council acts on its own initiative or on that of the minister of economic affairs, a business enterprise, or an organization specified in article 5(2).

The Council examines practices which might be prohibited under articles 7 and 8, and which might be justified by article 10. Where necessary, it issues administrative penalties [*sanctions*] and injunctions.

The Council transmits to a state prosecutor [*procureur de la République*] infractions warranting application of article 17.

ARTICLE 13

The Competition Council can . . . impose administrative penalties. In the case of corporations, the maximum penalty is 5 percent of the corporation's sales revenue (excluding value-added tax) during the last full accounting period. . . .

ARTICLE 17

Individuals who fraudulently play major roles in the conception or execution of practices violating articles 7 and 8 are punishable by six months to four years in prison and/or a fine of Fr 5,000 to Fr 500,000.

ARTICLE 32

Article 1(1) of law 63-628 of July 2, 1963, is replaced by the following:

Retailers who resell a commodity at a price below the effective purchase price are punishable by fines of Fr 5,000 to Fr 100,000. The effective purchase price is presumed to be the invoiced price plus sales tax, other specific taxes, and, where relevant, the cost of transport.

ARTICLE 36

Producers, traders, industrialists, and artisans engaging in the following practices must repair the harm caused by their actions:

1. Discrimination not justified by real circumstances and creating competitive advantages or disadvantages.

2. Refusal to sell in cases where the request is not abnormal, where it is made in good faith, and where the refusal is not justified by article 10.

3. Tying the sale or purchase of one good or service to the sale or purchase of other goods or services.

Proceedings pursuant to this article are initiated in civil or commercial jurisdictions by the party alleging harm, by the examining magistrate [*parquet*], by the minister in charge of the economy, or by the president of the Competition Council. . . .

Appendix E
Finance

MOST OF THE financial statistics on which I rely appear in the national income accounts.[1] They measure net annual *flows* of funds between broad sectors of the economy—nonfinancial corporations, financial enterprises, insurance companies, government, private nonprofit institutions, households, and the rest of the world. Also available, however, are data on *stocks* of debt and securities outstanding.[2]

National accounts data overstate the reliance of nonfinancial enterprises on domestic financial credit. In the first place, they ignore loans extended by one nonfinancial enterprise to another (henceforth, nonfinancial credit, which includes both commercial credit linking buyer and seller and intraenterprise credit linking members of a family of companies. Families of companies, or *groupes*, appear frequently on the French industrial landscape). And yet, one study found that nonfinancial credit amounted to half of short-term loans, and 36 percent of all loans, received by nonfinancial enterprises.[3] Another study found that reliance on nonfinancial credit, as measured by nonfinancial credit received less nonfinancial credit offered, varies greatly among industries.[4]

1. The *tableau des opérations financières* has existed since 1953; see Carré, Dubois, and Malinvaud, *La Croissance Française*, p. 419, note 2. Bourdon and Sok, *Tableaux des Opérations Financières et Endettement des Entreprises par Secteur, 1959–1976*, presents the 1971 SNA version of the tableau for 1959–76; for later years, see the annual *Rapport sur les Comptes de la Nation*.
2. Valued at historical cost. See Goldet, Nicolas, and Séruzier, "L'Endettement des Entreprises et des Ménages de 1954 à 1974," tables 1 and 2.
3. See Gresh, "L'Endettement des Secteurs de 1971 à 1974," p. 25.
4. In 1975, the difference between nonfinancial credit received and nonfinancial credit offered constituted at least 10 percent of total liabilities in retailing of food, retailing except food, construction, and ships, planes, and weapons; see Vannoise, "Le Crédit Commercial Interentreprises," table 3.

The second reason national accounts data overestimate the reliance of nonfinancial enterprises on domestic financial credit is partial neglect of funds raised abroad. During the decade and a half that followed World War II, French enterprises made little use of foreign saving. In 1961, however, nonfinancial corporations (except GEN) began to float bonds abroad.[5] The GEN followed suit in 1967. Between 1961 and 1978, nonfinancial corporations (except GEN) placed 8 percent to 29 percent of their bonds on foreign markets (depending on the year); between 1967 and 1978 the GEN placed 0 percent to 34 percent of their bonds on foreign markets. Less important quantitatively than nonfinancial credit, financial resources supplied from abroad are too significant after 1960 to monitor only roughly.

The nationalized banks and insurance companies, acquired in 1945–46 and 1982, functioned much like private enterprises. In contrast, certain banks created by government had no counterparts in the private sector. Their activities warrant brief description here.

Direction du Trésor

Between 1948 and 1960 the French government received substantial transfers of capital from the United States, most under the Marshall Plan. Before 1955 these transfers constituted 10 percent to 20 percent of government receipts.[6] Initially, Marshall monies were placed in a treasury account created specially for the purpose (the Fonds de Modernisation et d'Equipement) and employed to finance productive investments. Between 1948 and 1955 a number of similar accounts were created, each with a different clientele. In 1955 the several accounts were merged to form the Fonds de Développement Economique et Social. Although deprived of foreign aid, FDES has continued to lend money to a variety of customers.

In its youth FDES devoted most of its resources to development of economic infrastructure, colonial as well as domestic. Frequently,

5. The following information is taken from INSEE, *Le Mouvement Economique en France, 1949–1979*, pp. 351, 361.

6. *Recettes définitives.* See INSEE, *Le Mouvement Economique en France, 1949–1979*, pp. 233–34.

therefore, its clients were local governments, foreign governments, or state-owned enterprises (SOEs).[7] Recently, FDES has directed substantial resources toward the private sector. Even so, it has rarely dealt directly with private enterprises. Typically, an interministerial committee has decided who should receive loans, FDES has set the terms and borne the risk, and financial intermediaries have handled the administration.

Treasury also provided certain public enterprises with equity capital, and it guaranteed repayment of some of their borrowing.[8] The guarantees permitted SOEs to borrow on attractive terms; hence they amounted to subsidies of the projects so financed. The guarantees had the added virtue of impinging modestly on the national budget.[9]

Caisse des Dépôts et Consignations (CDC)

Formed in 1816 to maintain escrow accounts for private parties and to facilitate repayment of government debt, CDC eventually dominated the supply of saving to several parts of the economy. Its current importance stems from its role as allocator of funds collected by the checking, savings, and insurance networks operated partly through the post office.[10]

7. A cumulative distribution of loans extended by type of beneficiary appears in Fonds de Développement Economique et Social, *Rapport pour 1969–1970 du Conseil de Direction*, app. 2, table 1.

8. Not all SOEs benefited from such favors. According to Stoffaës, *Politique Industrielle*, p. 235, during the first eighteen years of its existence as a public enterprise, Renault received neither infusions of equity nor loan guarantees from the national government: "In no way did government favor Renault's access to public financial institutions."

9. The most general authority to commit the state to guarantee repayment is vested in the minister of finance. Early in the postwar period, when saving was scarce, this power was used frequently. Private as well as public enterprises benefited from the guarantees. Subsequently, however, guaranteed repayment of credit was used only sparingly to shape the composition of investment. See Dony, Giovaninetti, and Tibi, *L'Etat et le Financement des Investissements Privés*, pp. 225–26.

10. At the end of World War II, funds collected by the caisses d'épargne and caisses de prévoyances accounted for 70 percent and 22 percent, respectively, of CDC liabilities; deposits in escrow and other accounts contributed the remaining 8 percent. In 1970 the caisses still acounted for 88.4 percent of CDC liabilities. See Dusart, *La Caisse des Dépôts et Consignations*, p. 24.

At the end of World War II, CDC's assets consisted primarily of loans to national government.[11] During the years that followed, CDC tailored its investment strategy to the goals of indicative planning. During the first plan (1947–52), it invested half its resources in reconstruction of basic industries—partly through purchases of government bonds and partly through funds made available to Crédit National. During the second plan (1953–57), CDC redirected its funds toward local governments (40 percent of its portfolio) and housing. Starting with the third plan (1958–61), it increased its role in business finance by investing in corporate securities and by lending, directly and through Crédit National, to nonfinancial enterprises.

As of 1970, CDC's portfolio of assets differed markedly from its antecedent of 1944. Loans to local governments now accounted for 41 percent, finance of housing for 20 percent, national debt for 11 percent, stocks and bonds for 9 percent, and loans to industry and agriculture for 7 percent. CDC lent directly to nonfinancial SOEs and indirectly to their private counterparts.[12] The largest by far of France's institutional investors, it also owned stock in several hundred unquoted companies.[13]

Crédit National

Crédit National was created in 1919 to finance reconstruction after World War I. Following World War II, it became the principal conduit of long-term funds from government to nonfinancial enterprises. Initially, most of its funds financed domestic investment in plant and equipment. Gradually, it broadened both the forms and the uses of its finance.[14] Apart from lending its own resources, Crédit

11. Ibid. Seventy-six percent of the total; the balance went to industry and agriculture (10 percent), to local governments (5 percent), and for housing (3 percent).

12. Ibid.; and Choinel and Rouyer, *Le Système Bancaire Français*, p. 87.

13. At the end of 1982 it accounted for 13.6 percent of the market value of bonds and 3.1 percent of the market value of stocks listed on French exchanges; ibid., pp. 87–88. More generally, miscellaneous credit institutions (S42) and insurance companies (S50), many of them owned by government, purchased 48 percent of the net new issues of share capital during 1980; INSEE, *Rapport sur les Comptes de la Nation de l'Année 1983*, tableau détaillé des opérations financières.

14. Since 1972 it finances investments outside France, and since 1980 it supplies funds in return for remuneration that depends on the success of the project (*prêts participatifs*); Choinel and Rouyer, *Le Système Bancaire Français*, pp. 100–02.

National managed loans to business and to foreign governments that were funded by FDES or ECSC; it endorsed requests made of the central bank by other banks to refinance their receivables, and it counselled such agencies of government as ANVAR on the wisdom of granting investment subsidies for particular projects.

Early in the postwar period, Crédit National relied heavily on FDES resources. It culled most of its other funds from bonds floated on French securities markets. During the early 1980s, bond issues accounted for virtually all of Crédit National's resources; a considerable fraction of its bonds were issued in foreign currencies.[15]

Banque Française du Commerce Extérieur

BFCE was created in 1920 to finance French exports. Disintegration of the international trading system between the world wars prevented BFCE from achieving significance until after its reorganization in 1947.

Like so many of the special banks under government control, BFCE engaged in banking operations on its own account and also on behalf of government. It loaned money at long term to French exporters and to foreign buyers of French products, endorsed export-related financial assets for discount at the central bank, and assembled packages of loans and foreign aid (*crédits mixtes*) for foreign governments purchasing French goods and services. BFCE raised money on the bond market. Government facilitated the bank's operations by guaranteeing repayment of its debt securities and by offering the bank interest subsidies.

Compagnie Française d'Assurance du Commerce Extérieur (COFACE)

Created in 1948, COFACE insured French enterprises against a variety of risks associated with international trade. These included failure to win orders after prospecting in foreign markets, unexpected increases in the cost of producing goods, changes in exchange rates,

15. At the end of 1982, advances from FDES amounted to 1 percent of direct loans outstanding. Twenty percent were issued in foreign currencies in 1980, 37 percent in 1982. Ibid., p. 100.

and failure of foreign buyers to repay trade credit. During 1979 COFACE insurance covered 30 percent of French exports; but the incidence of such insurance varied greatly by type and destination of merchandise.[16] The proportion of exports covered by COFACE was 56 percent in capital goods but 19 percent in consumption goods; it was 68 percent for exports to developing countries, and 60 percent for those to the Eastern bloc, but 15 percent for those to developed countries.

Banque de France

The French central bank engaged actively in discounting. In choosing among projects to refinance, it cared less about the health of the bank at the window than about the use to which the original loan was put.[17]

The Bank of France discounted both short- and medium-term credit. Decisions concerning the medium term were made before approval of the original loan. Operationally, the prospective lender would seek endorsement of the project by a government agency, such as the Commissariat Général du Plan or by a public financial enterprise such as Crédit National. In principle, endorsement was granted to projects consistent with the current economic plan. The project, along with the endorsement, was then submitted to the Bank of France. The bank usually refinanced any project that was suitably endorsed.

Discounting of short-term credit followed a different procedure. For each financial enterprise, the Bank of France established a ceiling on the amount of credit it would discount.[18] As a percentage of the beneficiary's credit outstanding, the ceiling varied among financial enterprises.

16. Les Echos, *L'Economie de A à Z*, p. 117.

17. Until 1970, the central bank also discounted receivables owned by nonfinancial enterprises; ibid., p. 272.

18. This procedure was adopted in 1948. Since 1951 this volume has been more a target than a ceiling. The bank discounted credit in excess of target at progressively higher rates, known as hell and hell-plus (*enfer* and *super enfer*).

Appendix F
Measured Subsidies

GOVERNMENTS subsidize private parties in myriad ways. In addition to unilateral transfers of money, subsidies include supply of goods and services at below-market prices, selective relief from taxation and regulation, and payment of above-market prices for goods and services received. Although simple to specify conceptually, subsidies can be difficult to measure in practice.[1] Unsurprisingly frequently, government statistics fail to quantify accurately the subsidy equivalence of government policies.

To emphasize the imperfect correspondence between concept and data, I refer to subsidies registered in national income accounts as *measured* subsidies. This appendix describes French data on measured subsidies; it also explains the variable used in chapter 3 to proxy the likely impact of subsidies on recipient industries or enterprises.

Measured Subsidies, Transfers, and Hidden Subsidies

In France's system of national accounts (SNA), business enterprises receive several types of transfers labeled *subventions*. Together these constitute the measured subsidies discussed in the text. The 1962 SNA distinguished operating subsidies, stabilization subsidies, and capital subsidies.[2] The 1971 SNA distinguished operating subsidies

---

1. Numerous examples of the problem, and some ingenious methods of overcoming it, appear in Le Pors, *Les Transferts Etat-Industrie en France et dans les Pays Occidentaux;* and Le Foll, "Les Aides Publiques à l'Industrie."

2. Respectively, *subventions d'exploitation* (742), *subventions d'équilibre* (743), and *subventions d'équipment* (744), where parenthetical numbers refer to the nomenclature of transactions in the national accounts. The nomenclature appears, for example, in INSEE, *Comptes Nationaux de la Base 1956, Séries 1949–1959; Séries Longues Macroéconomiques,* pp. 78–80.

and capital subsidies.[3] In principle, capital subsidies promote investment in productive assets, while operating subsidies compensate enterprises for selling at low prices or buying at high ones. In practice, however, certain operating subsidies such as interest subsidies (*bonifications d'intérêt*) relate more to investment than to production. Most measured subsidies involve the transfer of cash, but a few, such as the special credit on value-added tax accorded to certain investments during 1975, involve tax expenditure.

Measured subsidies flow to business from one of two sources: domestic government or the European Communities.[4] Before 1970 virtually all measured subsidies originated in domestic government.[5] Since 1970 the role of the European Communities has increased, especially in the agricultural sphere; nevertheless, as of 1982, domestic government still provided more than three-quarters of all measured subsidies.

Unfortunately for the analyst, not all subsidies to business are contained in a category labeled subsidy. Unmeasured subsidies are treated in various ways: some appear in another category of transfers from government to business; others appear as transfers from government to economic agents outside the business sector; still others appear as payments for services rendered by business to government.

SUBSIDIES CATEGORIZED AS NONSUBSIDY TRANSFERS TO BUSINESS

Grants to repair wartime damage and cancellation of debts owed to government fall in this category. In the 1962 SNA, reconstruction grants constituted a distinct category of transfer (*dommages de guerre*)

3. Respectively *subventions d'exploitation* (R30) and *aides à l'investissement* (R71), where parenthetical expressions refer to the nomenclature of transactions in the national accounts. The nomenclature appears, for example, in INSEE, *Rapport sur les Comptes de la Nation de l'Année 1982*. The stabilization subsidies of the 1962 SNA are classified as operating subsidies in the 1971 system.

4. In the 1962 SNA, international and foreign governments were classified as "government;" in the 1971 system, they were assigned to "rest of the world."

5. For 1959–70 see INSEE C67-68, tableaux économiques d'ensemble; for 1971–82 see INSEE, *Rapport sur les Comptes de la Nation* (annual), vol. 3, comptes détaillés des secteurs institutionnels. Before 1971 the EC never contributed as much as 1 percent of subsidies paid to business; between 1971 and 1982 it paid 11 percent to 19 percent of such subsidies.

while forgiveness of debts was classified with miscellaneous transfers (*opérations diverses de répartition*). In the 1971 system both were classified as miscellaneous capital transfers (*autres transferts en capital*).

If all transfers received by business were government subsidies, one could use total transfers received as a proxy for subsidies received. Unfortunately, many transfers to business are not government subsidies; they originate in the private sector. For example, when French companies receive goods and services from abroad and fail to pay for their imports until a subsequent accounting period, they are considered to have received a current transfer from their foreign suppliers. Such "gifts" account for a large fraction of miscellaneous current transfers (*transferts courants divers*) received by nonfinancial corporations.[6] Of the miscellaneous capital transfers received by nonfinancial corporations, a considerable fraction is received by developers of real estate; these transfers amount to subsidized housing provided by other corporations for their employees. Among the various categories of transfer not labeled as subsidy, the 1962 version of war reparations is closest to being a government subsidy of business and the 1971 version of miscellaneous current transfers is the farthest from being such a subsidy.

To appreciate the consequences of extending the domain of subsidy to include other transfers, one must examine the quantitative significance of the various transfers received by business enterprises. At the beginning of the postwar period, reparations accounted for a large fraction of transfers received by nonfinancial enterprise (table F-1). Their importance declined steadily, however, and by 1957 their share had fallen permanently below 10 percent. Between 1959 and 1979 measured subsidies always accounted for more than 75 percent of transfers received by nonfinancial business enterprise (table F-2). In the financial sector, however, miscellaneous capital transfers to credit institutions (table F-3) or miscellaneous current transfers to insurance companies (table F-4) accounted for considerable shares of transfers received.

6. INSEE C78, p. 64.

Table F-1. *Transfers Received, by Type, Nonfinancial Enterprises,*
1949–59[a]
Percent unless otherwise specified

	Type of transfer					
Year	Operating subsidy (742)	Stabilization subsidy (743)	Capital subsidy (744)	War reparations (745)	Miscellaneous (77)	Millions of francs
1949	24.8	11.3	12.3	45.6	6.1	4,080
1950	27.7	12.5	12.2	40.1	7.5	4,410
1951	32.3	14.2	13.5	34.3	5.8	4,310
1952	34.7	15.7	14.9	29.2	5.4	4,960
1953	34.6	18.5	18.5	22.8	5.6	5,690
1954	40.8	19.3	14.0	20.9	5.1	6,280
1955	48.7	18.4	10.8	17.7	4.3	7,590
1956	51.9	17.4	15.2	11.9	3.6	8,290
1957	53.2	14.3	18.5	9.4	4.5	8,590
1958	51.9	13.9	19.6	7.6	6.9	8,500
1959	46.3	8.7	25.4	7.2	12.3	7,780

Source: INSEE, *Comptes Nationaux de la Base 1956, Séries 1949–1959: Séries Longues Macroéconomiques,* tableaux économiques d'ensemble and comptes d'affectation des entreprises nonfinancières.
a. 1956 SNA.

SUBSIDIES CATEGORIZED AS TRANSFERS TO PARTIES OUTSIDE THE BUSINESS SECTOR

Several transfers to parties outside business involved the SNCF. One involved compensation for charging special fares to certain customers; another involved government contributions to employee retirement benefits. In the 1962 SNA, both types of transfer were considered operating subsidies received by the SNCF. In the 1971 system, however, neither was considered a subsidy to the railroad. The first was treated as a transfer from government to the favored users of SNCF services. It appeared in the national accounts as subsidies to large families and war veterans, as labor compensation to members of the armed forces, and as intermediate consumption by government in connection with its guardianship of prisoners. The consequent omission from SNCF's measured subsidy exceeded Fr 1 billion during 1971.[7] The second subsidy—payment of retirement benefits—appeared in the 1971 SNA as a transfer from national government to the social security system. During 1971 the amount

7. INSEE C60, p. 108.

Table F-2. *Transfers Received, by Type, Nonfinancial Enterprises, 1959–80*[a]
Percent unless otherwise specified

	Measured subsidies			Other transfers			
Year	Operating (R30)	Capital (R71)	All	Miscellaneous current (R69)	Miscellaneous capital (R79)	All	Millions of francs
1959	69.8	14.2	84.0	3.2	12.9	16.0	5,298
1960	66.1	13.0	79.1	9.2	11.7	20.9	6,282
1961	65.0	12.4	77.4	11.8	10.8	22.6	7,601
1962	65.4	9.7	75.0	18.0	7.0	25.0	9,599
1963	72.8	10.0	82.9	12.0	5.2	17.1	10,468
1964	71.9	12.9	84.8	9.7	5.5	15.2	10,541
1965	72.5	13.4	85.9	9.1	5.0	14.1	11,984
1966	69.3	17.9	87.3	7.9	4.8	12.7	13,506
1967	69.3	19.0	88.3	6.7	4.9	11.7	15,083
1968	73.2	15.7	88.9	7.2	3.8	11.1	17,464
1969	71.3	16.3	87.6	7.8	4.6	12.4	18,475
1970	71.1	16.5	87.6	8.4	4.0	12.4	17,241
1971	73.0	15.2	88.2	7.4	4.4	11.8	17,699
1972	69.1	15.3	84.3	11.5	4.2	15.7	20,699
1973	70.1	15.0	85.1	10.3	4.6	14.9	24,368
1974	66.2	14.2	80.5	12.9	6.6	19.5	29,537
1975	65.1	16.3	81.4	13.3	5.3	18.6	39,441
1976	58.3	26.0	84.4	9.5	6.1	15.6	54,109
1977	71.6	13.1	84.7	9.3	6.0	15.3	54,741
1978	71.2	11.6	82.8	10.7	6.5	17.2	59,289
1979	66.9	10.6	77.5	16.4	6.2	22.5	69,197
1980	60.5	9.4	70.0	24.6	5.4	30.0	85,775

Sources: 1959–69: INSEE C67-68. 1970–80: INSEE, *Rapport sur les Comptes de la Nation* (annual), comptes détaillés des secteurs institutionnels.
a. 1971 SNA. Nonfinancial enterprises are sectors S10 and S81.

in question exceeded Fr 2 billion. In 1969 these two categories of subsidy amounted to 39 percent of SNCF's measured subsidy (capital and operating) using the 1962 SNA.[8]

HIDDEN SUBSIDIES

The final category of unmeasured subsidies is the most difficult to detect because it fails to appear as transfers to anyone. Two examples will make the point. In 1971 the government contributed Fr 237

8. INSEE E11, p. 114.

Table F-3. *Transfers Received, by Type, Credit Institutions,*
1959–80[a]
Percent unless otherwise specified

	Measured subsidies			Other transfers			
Year	Operating (R30)	Capital (R71)	All	Miscellaneous current (R69)	Miscellaneous capital (R79)	All	Millions of francs
1959	48.3	*	48.3	*	51.7	51.7	240
1960	58.7	*	58.7	*	41.3	41.3	315
1961	62.0	*	62.0	*	38.0	38.0	361
1962	71.2	*	71.2	*	28.8	28.8	535
1963	66.5	*	66.5	*	33.5	33.5	532
1964	68.8	*	68.8	*	31.2	31.2	703
1965	69.7	*	69.7	*	30.3	30.3	856
1966	72.5	*	72.5	*	27.5	27.5	1,052
1967	72.0	*	72.0	*	28.0	28.0	1,051
1968	72.4	*	72.4	*	27.6	27.6	1,125
1969	77.3	*	77.3	*	22.7	22.7	1,508
1970	79.3	*	79.3	*	20.7	20.7	1,845
1971	74.7	*	74.7	*	25.3	25.3	2,895
1972	54.4	*	54.4	33.5	12.2	45.6	4,862
1973	48.7	*	48.7	41.2	10.1	51.3	6,379
1974	76.8	*	76.8	1.1	22.2	23.2	4,366
1975	71.5	*	71.5	2.3	26.1	28.5	5,624
1976	75.4	0.1	75.5	1.4	23.1	24.5	7,334
1977	59.7	*	59.7	13.5	26.8	40.3	9,053
1978	54.0	0.2	54.2	31.4	14.4	45.8	14,001
1979	64.3	*	64.3	16.2	19.5	35.7	12,123
1980	71.9	0.2	72.1	2.6	25.2	27.9	11,018

Sources: 1959–69: INSEE C67-68. 1970–80: INSEE, *Rapport sur les Comptes de la Nation* (annual), comptes détaillés des secteurs institutionnels.
* Less than 0.05 percent.
a. 1971 SNA. Credit institutions are sector S40.

million to research and development activity in the computer industry;
it was classified in the 1971 SNA as a payment for services rendered
in R&D activity even though the 1962 SNA would have considered
it a capital subsidy. Similarly, in 1971 the government gave Fr 200
million to ERAP; it was classified in the 1971 SNA as an infusion of
equity even though the 1962 SNA would have considered it a capital
subsidy.[9]

9. INSEE C60, p. 110.

Table F-4. *Transfers Received, by Type, Insurance Companies, 1959–80*[a]
Percent unless otherwise specified

	Measured subsidies			Other transfers			
Year	Operating (R30)	Capital (R71)	All	Miscella- neous current (R69)	Miscella- neous capital (R79)	All	Millions of francs
1959	42.0	*	42.0	58.0	*	58.0	238
1960	34.6	*	34.6	65.4	*	65.4	217
1961	39.3	*	39.3	60.7	*	60.7	242
1962	35.0	*	35.0	65.0	*	65.0	237
1963	38.2	*	38.2	61.8	*	61.8	262
1964	39.5	*	39.5	60.5	*	60.5	281
1965	46.4	*	46.4	53.6	*	53.6	334
1966	43.6	*	43.6	56.4	*	56.4	328
1967	51.3	*	51.3	48.7	*	48.7	394
1968	39.3	*	39.3	60.7	*	60.7	338
1969	41.4	*	41.4	58.6	*	58.6	394
1970	53.5	*	53.5	46.5	*	46.5	585
1971	65.8	*	65.8	33.6	0.7	34.2	876
1972	68.9	*	68.9	30.4	0.6	31.1	1,091
1973	66.6	0.1	66.7	32.7	0.7	33.3	1,215
1974	59.6	*	59.6	38.2	2.2	40.4	1,490
1975	72.7	*	72.7	27.2	0.1	27.3	2,286
1976	80.7	*	80.7	19.2	0.1	19.3	3,066
1977	77.3	*	77.3	22.6	0.1	22.7	3,065
1978	71.9	1.8	73.6	26.2	0.2	26.4	2,619
1979	84.4	*	84.4	15.6	*	15.6	4,800
1980	74.1	*	74.1	25.9	0.1	25.9	3,264

Sources: 1959–69: INSEE C67-68. 1970–80: INSEE, *Rapport sur les Comptes de la Nation* (annual), comptes détaillés des secteurs institutionnels.
* Less than 0.05 percent.
a. 1971 SNA. Insurance companies are sector S50.

Meaning of Business Enterprise

Several enterprises straddle the boundary between government and business. Like businesses they produce goods and services; like governments they sometimes fail to sell their output in markets, they regulate and coordinate private enterprises, and they receive earmarked revenues from special taxes (*taxes parafiscales*). Examples of such entities are

—CEA, created to develop French nuclear weapons and then expanded to develop French nuclear power;

—DTAT, a branch of the defense ministry engaged in the production of weapons;

—FDES, an arm of the treasury promoting investments in infrastructure, plant, and equipment;

—IFP, a scientific and economic research organization supporting the petroleum industry; and

—ONIC, an agricultural stabilization board.

These organizations could be considered business enterprises, agencies of government, or private nonprofit institutions. Unless they are assigned to the business sector, much of the bounty they receive from government will not be included in measured subsidies.

In the 1962 SNA many such quasi enterprises were assigned to the business sector (table F-5): Thus IFP was designated a private nonprofit institution, while FDES was considered part of national government; the others mentioned above were classified as nonfinancial enterprises. In the 1971 system, however, most were assigned to government (table F-6): thus CEA, DTAT, FORMA, Imprimerie Nationale, ONERA, ONIC, the Paris Opera, Opéra Comique, Comédie Française, and the passenger transport authorities owned by regional and local governments were all reclassified from nonfinancial enterprise to government. Since many were subsidized heavily, measured subsidies to nonfinancial enterprise appeared far larger in the 1962 system than in its successor.

Although the 1962 system defined nonfinancial enterprise broadly, it failed to treat financial enterprises (purveyors of credit or insurance) as part of the business sector. In this respect it defined business more narrowly than did its 1971 counterpart.

The assignment of financial enterprises to the business sector affected substantially the calculation of their measured subsidies.[10] For example, in 1971 Caisse Nationale de Crédit Agricole received Fr 1,591 million in subsidies according to 1971 procedures that were not treated as such in the 1962 system. Corresponding amounts for

10. Most subsidies received by financial enterprises are *bonifications*. These are considered operating subsidies. By convention, however, only business enterprises can receive operating subsidies. As a result, such transfers were assigned in the 1962 SNA to a nonsubsidy category.

Table F-5. *Nonfinancial State-Owned Enterprises, 1962 SNA*[a]

Industry	Enterprise	Industry	Enterprise
2	Régie Commerciale des Alcools	6B	Commissariat à l'Energie
2	SEITA		Atomique
3A	Charbonnages de France	7F	Imprimerie Nationale
3B	Electricité de France	9A	Société Nationale des Chemins de
3B	Gaz de France		Fer Français
3B	Compagnie Nationale du Rhône	9A	Régie Autonome des Transports
3C	ERAP		Parisiens
3C	Société Nationale des Pétroles	9A	Compagnie Nationale Air France
	d'Aquitaine	9A	Various municipal and regional
3C	PREPA		bus systems
3C	Compagnie d'Exploitation Pétro-	9A	Aéroport de Paris
	lière	9A	Compagnie Générale Transatlan-
3C	TRAPIL		tique
5D	Régie Nationale des Usines	9A	Compagnie des Messageries Mari-
	Renault		times
5E	SNECMA	9B	Postes et Télécommunications
5E	Nord-Aviation	9B	Compagnie Française de Câbles
5E	Sud-Aviation		Sous-Marins et de Radio
5E	ONERA	10A	Various pulic housing authorities
5E	Direction Technique des Arme-	10C	Agence Havas
	ments Terrestres	10C	ORTF
6B	Société Chimique des Charbon-	10C	Various public theater companies
	nages	10C	Various public hospitals and
6B	Entreprise Minière Chimique		related institutions
6B	Mines de Potasse d'Alsace	10C	Union Générale Cinémato-
6B	Azote et Produits Chimiques		graphique
6B	Service des Poudres	11	FORMA
		11	ONIC

Source: INSEE C20, pp. 3–4.

a. Principal activity of the enterprise defined according to ENF (see appendix C). Acronyms identified in appendix B.

other financial institutions were also large: Caisse de Prêts aux Organismes d'HLM, Fr 571 million; COFACE, Fr 478 million.[11]

Allocation of Subsidy among Business Enterprises

National income accounts aim above all at accurate depiction of the macroeconomic landscape. Division of aggregate magnitudes into industry- or company-specific components plays a secondary role in the exercise. Accordingly, some variables are measured only for the economy as a whole. Others are measured at the industry as well as

11. INSEE C60, p. 108.

Table F-6. *Nonfinancial State-Owned Enterprises, 1971 SNA*[a]

Industry	Enterprise
T04	Charbonnages de France
T06	Electricité de France
T06	Gaz de France
T31	Compagnie Nationale Air France
T31	Air Inter
T31	Régie Autonome des Transports Parisiens
T31	Société Nationale des Chemins de Fer Français
T32	Postes et Télécommunications

Source: INSEE E57, p. 13.
a. The *grandes entreprises nationales* (GEN). Principal activity of the enterprise defined according to NAP-T (see appendix C). Acronyms identified in appendix B.

the aggregate level. Still others are measured at the aggregate level and broken down arbitrarily into industry-level estimates. Only the second type of variable is useful to those interested in observing variations among activities in economic structure, behavior, or performance.

In both the 1962 and the 1971 SNAs, data on transfers, including transfers in the form of subsidies, are available at the industry level. The 1962 approach employs categories of activity based on NAE (see appendix C). The 1971 approach employs categories based on NAP-T.[12] In both systems of accounting, industry-level measured subsidies are observed directly, using information in government budgets and enterprise accounts.[13] On the other hand, both SNAs distribute aggregate estimates of miscellaneous transfers among industries using mechanical formulae. Thus under 1971 rules, the

12. With one exception, the categories conform to NAP-T. The exception concerns T35 (rental and leasing activities), part of which is assigned to nonfinancial enterprise, and part of which is assigned to financial enterprise. In the data presented in chapter 3, T35 refers strictly to the nonfinancial component.

13. INSEE C5, p. 89; and INSEE C78, pp. 61–62. In the 1962 SNA, subsidies associated with imports are *not* observed at the industry level. In fact, INSEE did not even estimate the distribution of such subsidies among activities; it simply reported an aggregate figure for each year. Between 1959 and 1969 such unallocated subsidies never amounted to as much as 2 percent of measured subsidies. (Calculations based on INSEE C4, pp. 81–83; and INSEE C20, pp. 34, 35, 38). Over this eleven-year period the importance of rebates on import duties declined, perhaps owing to formation of the EEC. In any event, unallocated subsidies do not appear to be important during this period. Such is not the case, however, for 1951. As appendix table A-43 reveals, 23 percent of total subsidies and 24 percent of total indemnities were not allocated among activities.

aggregate volume of miscellaneous current transfers is allocated among industries in proportion to imports for the component relating to imports and in proportion to sales for the rest.[14] Sales revenue is also the criterion for allocating miscellaneous capital transfers in the 1971 system, and for allocating miscellaneous transfers in the 1962 system.[15]

Given the method by which miscellaneous transfers are calculated at the industry level, it is hardly appropriate to employ such data in interindustry analysis. Although government subsidies sometimes travel to business in the form of miscellaneous transfers, I ignore such transfers in chapter 3.

MEASURING THE DEGREE OF SUBSIDY

To gauge the impact of subsidy on recipient behavior, one should compare choices made in the presence of subsidies with choices made in their absence. The choices relate, for example, to quantities of factors employed, quantities of goods produced, and amounts of investments undertaken. This impact will depend on such factors as the amount of the subsidy, the terms of the subsidy, the goals of the enterprise, and the constraints apart from subsidy that impinge on the enterprise, constraints that relate, for example, to production technology and the terms on which the enterprise can buy and sell in various markets. In other words, the impact of a subsidy cannot be measured by its volume alone.

In studies of particular subsidies to particular enterprises, it may be possible to engage in formal and precise modeling of impact. In studies like this, however, both subsidies and enterprises appear in casts of thousands, obstructing all possibility of theoretical satisfaction. As a first step toward appraisal of subsidy impact, I relate the subsidies received by an enterprise to the expenses they are designed to defray. I shall refer to this percentage as DS, the degree of subsidy associated with the enterprise or group of enterprises under examination. Without companion evidence on elasticities of response to subsidies received, DS can over- or underestimate true impact.

14. INSEE C78, p. 65.
15. INSEE C78, p. 65; and INSEE C5, p. 94. In the 1962 SNA, war compensation was allocated among activities on the basis of government budget data (INSEE C5, p. 90). The distribution of compensation among activities thus matched in quality the distribution of measured subsidies among activities.

In tables based on the 1962 SNA the numerator of DS is measured as

(1) $100(V742 + V744),$

where V742 = operating subsidies received (including stabilization subsidies received) and V744 = capital subsidies received. Variable numbers correspond to the nomenclature of transactions in the 1962 SNA.

In tables based on the 1971 SNA the numerator of DS is measured as

(2) $100(R30 + R71),$

where R30 = operating subsidies received and R71 = capital subsidies received. Variable numbers correspond to the nomenclature of transactions in the 1971 SNA.

The denominator of DS varies slightly as a function of data source. The several versions are specified in the next section. The quantitative consequences of these differences in definition are slight.

Availability of Data on Business Subsidies

For all nonfinancial enterprises combined, data on subsidies and transfers are available since 1949. The period 1949–59 is covered according to the 1956 SNA.[16] Starting with 1959, data appear according to the 1971 SNA.[17] The 1971 SNA offered subsidy and transfer information on financial as well as nonfinancial enterprises. Among nonfinancial enterprises, the 1971 SNA distinguished three groups: *grandes entreprises nationales* (S11), other corporations (S12), and unincorporated enterprises (S81). Among financial enterprises, the 1971 SNA separated purveyors of credit (S40) from purveyors of insurance (S50).

In tables constructed using macroeconomic data based on the 1971 SNA, the denominator of DS is measured as

16. INSEE, *Comptes Nationaux de la Base 1956, Séries 1949–1959; Séries Longues Macroéconomiques*.

17. For 1959–70, see INSEE C67–68; thereafter, INSEE, *Rapport sur les Comptes de la Nation* (annual).

(3)   P20 + R10 + R22 + R41 + R43 + R44 + R45 + R46
$$+ \text{ R51 + R61 + R64 + R66 + R69 + P41,}$$

where P20 = intermediate consumption, R10 = compensation paid to employees, R22 = indirect taxes paid, R41 = interest paid, R43 = rentals and royalties paid, R44 = dividends paid, R45 = compensation paid to entrepreneurs, R46 = bonuses paid to employees, R51 = insurance premiums paid, R61 = direct taxes paid, R64 = services provided to employees, R66 = current transfers paid to private nonprofit organizations, R69 = miscellaneous current transfers paid, and P41 = gross investment in plant and equipment. Variable numbers correspond to the nomenclature of transactions in the 1971 SNA.

At the industry level, using the 1962 SNA, two documents covering 1959–69 divide nonfinancial enterprises into twenty-nine activities and provide detailed financial information on each activity.[18] Within activities, enterprises are separated into public and private ventures. Public enterprise is defined relatively broadly (table F-5).

The corresponding publication using the 1971 SNA covers 1967–75.[19] Comparable data for 1976–81 are available from INSEE in unpublished form. Nonfinancial enterprises are divided into thirty-six activities, largely according to NAP-T, but only the GEN (table F-6) are distinguished from other corporations. One other publication provides information at the industry level using the 1971 SNA. It covers the period 1959–70 and decomposes nonfinancial enterprise into twelve activities.[20]

In tables constructed using industry-level data based on the 1962 SNA, the denominator of DS is measured as

(4)   A + 701 + 702 + 716 + 721 + 723 + 735 + 736
$$+ \text{ 737 + 738 + 742 + 7511 + 77 + 6c,}$$

where A = purchases of goods and services, 701 = gross wages and salaries, 702 = social security contributions of employers, 716 = social services provided by employers, 721 = interest paid, 723 = rental and royalty fees paid, 735 = sales taxes paid, 736 = special taxes paid, 737 = wage-based taxes (excluding social security), 738

18. INSEE C4; and INSEE C20. The nomenclature is ENF (see appendix C).
19. INSEE C78.
20. INSEE C67–68. The nomenclature is NAP-U.

= other indirect taxes, 742 = operating subsidies paid, 7511 = insurance premiums paid, 77 = miscellaneous transfers paid, and 6c = gross investment in plant and equipment.[21]

In tables constructed using industry-level data based on the 1971 SNA, the denominator of DS is measured as

(5)   CI + R10 + R22 + R41 + R43 + R44 + R45 + R46
$$+ R51 + R61 + R642 + R66 + R69 + P41,$$

where CI = intermediate consumption, R10 = compensation of employees, R22 = indirect taxes, R642 = services provided to employees, and each other variable is defined as in equation 3.[22]

At the company level, INSEE has published SNA-compatible information for public enterprises only. One publication examines twenty-six public enterprises during 1959–69 using the 1962 SNA.[23] The other examines the GEN during 1959–76 using the 1971 SNA.[24]

In tables constructed from data defined according to 1962 SNA, the denominator of DS is measured as

(6) A + S + CS + PS + I + II + IARD + ODR + ED + GE,

where A = purchases of goods and services, S = gross wages and salaries, CS = employers' contributions to social security, PS = services provided to employees, I = interest paid, II = indirect taxes paid, IARD = insurance premiums paid, ODR = miscellaneous transfers paid, ED = purchase of plant and equipment, and GE = expenditure on major repairs.

In tables constructed from data defined according to 1971 SNA, the denominator of DS is measured as

(7)   PB20 + R10 + R22 + R41 + R43 + R44 + R51
$$+ R61 + R64 + R66 + R69 + P41,$$

where PB20 = intermediate consumption and each other variable is defined as in equation 3.

21. INSEE C4; and INSEE C20. Variable numbers correspond to the nomenclature of transactions in the 1962 SNA.

22. INSEE C78. Variable numbers correspond to the nomenclature of transactions in the 1971 SNA.

23. INSEE E11.

24. INSEE E57.

Appendix G
International Trade
and Investment

Exposure to Imports, Propensity to Export

At the industry level the best information on imports in relation to consumption and on exports in relation to production appears in input-output tables associated with the national income accounts. For 1959–82 input-ouput tables have been published according to NAP-T; available but unpublished are NAP-S tables (see appendix C). I have used the S-level tables here.

For 1949–59 INSEE has published input-output tables compatible with the 1956 SNA. These tables do not bear close comparison with those described in the previous paragraph. In the first place, they decompose the economy into just sixteen industries, defined according to NAE. In the second place, the concepts employed to construct the input-output tables differ from those of the 1971 SNA. (For example, the earlier input-output scheme expresses variables inclusive of value-added tax; the later scheme expresses them net of value-added tax.)

Industry-level exposure to international trade between 1949 and 1959 is observed best in 1951, using the input-output table constructed specially for that year.[1] Not only does it decompose the economy into 157 activities, but it distinguishes trade with the French Overseas Union from trade with other countries. Once again, methodological discrepancy prevents close comparisons between the 1951 table and those covering 1949–59 and 1959–82.

---

1. Ministère des Affaires Economiques et Financières, *Tableau Economique de l'Année 1951.*

International Investment

France publishes two types of information on direct foreign investment. The first and oldest is balance of payments statistics. For my purposes, this series has several defects: it does not extend all the way back to World War II.[2] It is not disaggregated by industry, it identifies the nationality of immediate but not of ultimate parents and subsidiaries, and it does not take account of the foreign investor's recourse to host-country finance.[3] The last of these defects is critical. It ensures that inward direct foreign investment, expressed as a proportion of productive investment in the host industry, will understate foreign control of the domestic industry's activity.

The best information culled from balance of payments statistics covers 1965–78.[4] It reports flows of direct investment and of long-term loans between France and each of nine other rich countries— Belgium-Luxembourg, Canada, West Germany, Italy, the Netherlands, Spain, Switzerland, the United Kingdom, and the United States. Disinvestments, as well as investments, are tabulated; and country totals are disaggregated into twelve broad industries, five of which span manufacturing.

The second type of information on direct foreign investment reports by industry the sales, employment, value added, and investment of French companies under foreign control. The position of the foreigners is then expressed as a percentage of total domestic activity. The earliest evidence of this type resulted from a government census undertaken in 1962.[5] Foreign control was defined as foreign ownership of 20 percent or more of the domestic company's equity capital. Industries were defined according to NAE. Since 1974, annual

---

2. Before the 1960s, the official data did not always distinguish direct investment, portfolio investment, and long-term loans. The sources of data for this period are described well in Bertin, *L'Investissement des Firmes Etrangères en France (1945–1962)*.

3. In addition to retaining earnings in its subsidiary, the foreign investor can borrow money and float securities in the host country. None of these funds is detected in balance of payments statistics.

4. Arnaud-Ameller and Marnata, *Les Flux d'Investissement Direct entre la France et l'Extérieur, 1965–1978*.

5. See "Recensement des Investissements Etrangers en France," pp. 321–28.

evidence of this type is published by the ministry of industry.[6] It applies only to industries overseen by the ministry of industry; so commerce, services, most foods, tobacco products, and military products are excluded. Industries are defined according to NAP.

The ministry of industry considers a domestic company as entirely controlled, partially controlled, or uncontrolled by foreigners, depending on whether foreigners own a majority of its share capital, between 20 percent and 50 percent (inclusive), or less than 20 percent. If the company is entirely controlled by foreigners, then all of its activity is attributed to foreigners. If the company is uncontrolled by foreigners, then none of its activity is attributed to foreigners. If the company is partially controlled by foreigners, then the share of its activity attributed to foreigners is the share of its capital they own. Given the scarcity of French companies owned 20 percent to 50 percent by foreigners, this index is highly correlated with the share of industry employment attributable to companies owned at least 50 percent by foreigners.

The ministry of industry data cannot be compared with those based on the 1962 census. The system of industrial classification differs, as does the measure of business activity.

In addition to government data, private information has been compiled in the context of academic research. For the period before World War II, the reader should consult the work of Maurice Lévy-Leboyer and, for the colonial dimension, that of Jacques Marseille.[7] These studies emphasize outward not inward investment. Based primarily on securities listings, they do not always permit separation of direct from other forms of foreign investment.

The Harvard Business School studies directed by Raymond Vernon examined the foreign manufacturing subsidiaries of 413 of the world's largest nonfinancial corporations. The sample, established on the basis of *Fortune's* listings of the world's largest corporations inside and outside the United States, consisted of 187 parent companies based in the United States, 136 in Western Europe, 67 in Japan, 11 in Canada, and 12 in various other countries. Among the European

6. Ministère de l'Industrie et de la Recherche, *9 Ans d'Implantation Etrangère dans l'Industrie, 1er Janvier 1973–1er Janvier 1981.*

7. Lévy-Leboyer, ed., *La Position Internationale de la France;* and Marseille, *Empire Colonial et Capitalisme Français,* p. 98.

parent companies, 48 were British, 32 German, 21 French, 9 Swedish, 8 Italian, 7 Swiss, 6 Belgian or Luxembourgeois, and 5 Dutch. As of January 1, 1971, the parent companies based outside the United States controlled 5,680 foreign manufacturing companies; and on January 1, 1968, the U.S. parents controlled 4,246 foreign manufacturing companies.[8]

For each foreign subsidiary, Vernon's databank contains such information as national location, date of entry into the parent's entourage, date of exit from the entourage, and principal line of business. Vernon gathered his information through surveys of existing enterprises. Since many of France's colonial companies died prior to his investigation, the data may understate the importance of colonial investment earlier in the century. In any event, they are best suited to analysis of the postwar period.

Composition of the French Overseas Union (FOU)

Throughout chapter 4, FOU is defined to include territory now belonging to the following thirty-one countries or dependencies:

Algeria
Bénin
Burkina-Faso
Cameroon
Central African Republic
Chad
Comoro Islands
Congo
Djibouti
French Guiana
Gabon
Guadeloupe (including Marie-Galante, Désirade, St. Barthélémy, and St. Martin, north)
Guinea
Ivory Coast
Kampuchea
Laos

Madagascar
Mali
Martinique
Mauritania
Morocco
New Caledonia (including Wallis and Futuna)
Niger
Polynesia (including French territories in Oceania)
Réunion (including Southern and Antarctic territories)
Saint Pierre and Miquelon
Sénégal
Togo
Tunisia
Vanuatu
Viet Nam

8. Vaupel and Curhan, *The World's Multinational Enterprises*, tabulation 1.1, and cross-tabulation 1.21.1.

Bibliography

Adams, William James. "Firm Size and Research Activity: France and the United States." *Quarterly Journal of Economics*, vol. 84 (August 1970).

————. "International Differences in Corporate Profitability." *Economica*, vol. 43 (November 1976).

————. "Market Structure and Corporate Power: The Horizontal Dominance Hypothesis Reconsidered." *Columbia Law Review*, vol. 74 (November 1974).

————. "Producer-Concentration as a Proxy for Seller-Concentration: Some Evidence from the World Automotive Industry." *Journal of Industrial Economics*, vol. 29 (December 1980).

————. "Should Merger Policy Be Changed? An Antitrust Perspective." In *The Merger Boom*, edited by Lynn E. Browne and Eric S. Rosengren. Conference Series, 31. Boston: Federal Reserve Bank of Boston, 1988.

Adams, William James, and Christian Stoffaës, eds. *French Industrial Policy*. Washington: Brookings Institution, 1986.

Aftalion, Florin. "The Political Economy of French Monetary Policy." In *The Political Economy of Monetary Policy: National and International Aspects*, edited by Donald R. Hodgman. Conference Series, 26. Federal Reserve Bank of Boston, 1983.

Aggarwal, Sumer C. "MRP, JIT, OPT, FMS? Making Sense of Production Operations Systems." *Harvard Business Review*, vol. 63 (September 1985).

Albert, Michel. *Le Pari Français: Le Nouveau Plein-Emploi*. Paris: Éditions du Seuil, 1982.

Aldcroft, Derek H. *The Inter-War Economy: Britain, 1919-1939*. London: B. T. Batsford, 1970.

Aldcroft, Derek H., ed. *The Development of British Industry and Foreign Competition, 1875–1914: Studies in Industrial Enterprise*. London: George Allen and Unwin, 1968.

Ardaugh, John. *France in the 1980s*. New York: Penguin Books, 1982.

Arnaud-Ameller, Paule. *La France à l'Epreuve de la Concurrence Internationale, 1951–1966*. Paris: Armand Colin, 1970.

Arnaud-Ameller, Paule, and F. Marnata. *Les Flux d'Investissement Direct entre la France et l'Extérieur, 1965–1978*. Paris: Centre National de la Recherche Scientifique, 1981.

Artus, Patrick, Claude Bismut, and Michèle Debonneuil. "La Pénétration Etrangère sur le Marché Français: Vingt Années Plus Une." *Economie et Statistique*, no. 135 (July 1981).

Asselain, Jean-Charles, and Christian Morrisson. "Economic Growth and Interest Groups: The French Experience." In *The Political Economy of Growth*, edited by Dennis C. Mueller. New Haven: Yale University Press, 1983.

Atreize. *La Planification Française en Pratique*. 2d ed. Paris: Editions Economie et Humanisme, Les Editions Ouvrières, 1976.

Aujac, Henri. "La Hiérarchie des Industries dans un Tableau des Echanges Inter-Industrielles." *Revue Economique*, vol. 11 (March 1960).

———. "An Introduction to French Industrial Policy." In *French Industrial Policy*, edited by William James Adams and Christian Stoffaës. Washington: Brookings Institution, 1986.

Auquier, Antoine A. *French Industry's Reaction to the European Common Market*. New York: Garland, 1984.

———. "Sizes of Firms, Exporting Behavior, and the Structure of French Industry." *Journal of Industrial Economics*, vol. 29 (December 1980).

Azéma, Jacques. *Le Droit Français de la Concurrence*. Paris: Presses Universitaires de France, 1981.

Bairoch, Paul. *Commerce Extérieur et Développement Economique de l'Europe au XIXe Siècle*. Paris: Mouton, 1976.

———. "Commerce Extérieur et Développement Economique: Quelques Enseignements de l'Expérience Libre-Echangiste de la France au XIXe Siècle." *Revue Economique*, vol. 21 (January 1970).

Balassa, Bela A. *The First Year of Socialist Government in France*. Washington: American Enterprise Institute for Public Policy Research, 1982.

———. "La Politique Economique Socialiste: L'An III." *Commentaire*, vol. 7 (Spring 1984).

———. "Selective versus General Economic Policy in Postwar France." In *French Industrial Policy*, edited by William James Adams and Christian Stoffaës. Washington: Brookings Institution, 1986.

———. "Whither French Planning?" *Quarterly Journal of Economics*, vol. 79 (November 1965).

———, ed. *European Economic Integration*. Amsterdam: North-Holland, 1975.

Balladur, Edouard. *Une France Plus Forte: Liberté Economique et Réforme Financière, 1986–1988*. Paris: Ministère de l'Economie, des Finances et de la Privatisation, 1988.

———. *Je Crois en l'Homme Plus qu'en l'Etat*. Paris: Flammarion, 1987.

Balladur, Jean-Pierre. "Les Echanges Extérieurs de la France entre 1960 et 1970." *Economie et Statistique*, no. 31 (February 1972).

Balladur, Jean-Pierre, and Antoine Coutière. "France." In *The Value-Added Tax: Lessons from Europe*, edited by Henry J. Aaron. Washington: Brookings Institution, 1981.

Banque de France. *Les Principaux Mécanismes de Distribution du Crédit*. 8th ed. Paris: Banque de France, 1983.

Barbichon, G. "Mutation et Migration des Agriculteurs." *Revue d'Economie Politique,* vol. 79 (March 1969).

Barre, Raymond. "Quelques Aspects de la Régulation du Pouvoir Economique." *Revue Economique,* vol. 9 (November 1958).

Barrère, Alain. "La Politique du Crédit en France depuis 1945." *Revue Economique,* vol. 2 (September 1951).

Barzini, Luigi. *The Europeans.* New York: Simon and Schuster, 1983.

Bastiat, Frédéric. *Economic Sophisms.* New York: Van Nostrand, 1964.

―――. *Selected Essays on Political Economy.* New York: Van Nostrand, 1964.

Bauer, Michel. *Les 200: Comment On Devient Patron.* Paris: Editions du Seuil, 1987.

Baum, Warren C. *The French Economy and the State.* Princeton: Princeton University Press, 1958.

Beaud, Michel, Pierre Danjou, and Jean David. *Une Multinationale Française: Pechiney Ugine Kuhlmann.* Paris: Editions du Seuil, 1975.

Belloc, Brigitte. "Non-Salariés des Secteurs Non Agricoles: Une Population Stable depuis Dix Ans." *Economie et Statistique,* no. 209 (April 1988).

Bellon, Bertrand. *Le Pouvoir Financier et l'Industrie en France.* Paris: Editions du Seuil, 1980.

―――. "La Reconquête du Marché Extérieur." *Revue d'Economie Industrielle,* no. 23 (issue 1, 1983).

Bellon, Bertrand, and Jean-Marie Chevalier, eds. *L'Industrie en France.* Paris: Flammarion, 1983.

Berger, Suzanne. "D'une Boutique à l'Autre: Changes in the Organization of the Traditional Middle Classes from the Fourth to Fifth Republics." *Comparative Politics,* vol. 10 (October 1977).

―――. "Lame Ducks and National Champions: Industrial Policy in the Fifth Republic." In *The Fifth Republic at Twenty,* edited by William G. Andrews and Stanley Hoffmann. Albany: State University of New York Press, 1981.

―――. *Peasants against Politics: Rural Organization in Brittany, 1911–1967.* Cambridge: Harvard University Press, 1972.

―――. "Reflections on Industrial Society: The Survival of the Traditional Sectors in France and Italy." In *Dualism and Discontinuity in Industrial Societies,* edited by Suzanne Berger and Michael J. Piore. New York: Cambridge University Press, 1980.

―――, ed. *Organizing Interests in Western Europe: Pluralism, Corporatism and the Transformation of Politics.* New York: Cambridge University Press, 1981.

Bergsten, Eric E. "The Administration of Economic and Social Programs in France by the Use of the Contractual Technique." *Southern California Law Review,* vol. 48 (1975).

Berthelot, Yves. "Comment." In *Trade Policy in the 1980s,* edited by William R. Cline. Washington: Institute for International Economics, 1983.

Bertin, Gilles Y. *L'Investissement des Firmes Etrangères en France (1945–1962).* Paris: Presses Universitaires de France, 1963.

Bertrand, Hugues, Cyrille Mansuy, and Michel Norotte. "Vingt Groupes Industriels Français et le Redéploiement." *Economie et Prévision,* no. 51 (issue 6, 1981).

Bied-Charreton, François, and Jean Raffegeau. *Guide Pratique du Financement des Entreprises.* 2d ed. Paris: Francis Lefebvre, 1984.

Blair, John M. *The Control of Oil.* New York: Pantheon, 1976.

Blanc, Jacques, and Chantal Brulé. *Les Nationalisations Françaises en 1982.* Notes et Etudes Documentaires, 4721-22. Paris: La Documentation Française, 1983.

Bloch-Lainé, François. *Profession Fonctionnaire: Entretien avec Françoise Carrière.* Paris: Editions du Seuil, 1976.

Bloch-Lainé, François, and Jean Bouvier. *La France Restaurée, 1944–1954: Dialogues sur les Choix d'une Modernisation.* Paris: Librairie Arthème Fayard, 1986.

Bloch-Lainé, François, and Pierre de Vogüé. *Le Trésor Public et le Mouvement Général des Fonds.* Paris: Presses Universitaires de France, 1960.

Bloch-Lainé, Jean-Michel, and Bruno Moschetto. *La Politique Economique de la France.* Paris: Presses Universitaires de France, 1981.

Boissonnade, Prosper. *Colbert: Le Triomphe de l'Etatisme, la Fondation de la Suprématie Industrielle de la France, la Dictature du Travail, 1661–1683.* Paris: M. Rivière, 1932.

———. *Le Socialisme d'Etat: L'Industrie et les Classes Industrielles en France pendant les Deux Premiers Siècles de l'Ere Moderne, 1453–1661.* Paris: H. Champion, 1927.

Bok, Derek C. *The First Three Years of the Schuman Plan.* Princeton Studies in International Finance, 5. Princeton: Princeton University, Department of Economics and Sociology, International Finance Section, 1955.

Boltanski, Luc. *Les Cadres: La Formation d'un Groupe Social.* Paris: Les Editions de Minuit, 1982.

Boltho, Andrea, ed. *The European Economy: Growth and Crisis.* New York: Oxford University Press, 1982.

Bonnefous, Edouard, and Jacques Blanc. *A la Recherche des Milliards Perdus.* Paris: Presses Universitaires de France, 1980.

Boublil, Alain. *Le Socialisme Industriel.* Paris: Presses Universitaires de France, 1977.

Boudoul, Jacques, and Jean-Paul Faur. "Depuis 1975, les Migrations Interrégionales Sont Moins Nombreuses." *Economie et Statistique,* no. 180 (September 1985).

Bourdon, Françoise, and Hach Sok. *Tableaux des Opérations Financières et Endettement des Entreprises par Secteur, 1959–1976.* Paris: Economica, 1983.

Boyer, Robert. "The Current Economic Crisis: Its Dynamics and Its Implications for France." In *The Mitterrand Experiment: Continuity and Change in Modern France,* edited by George Ross, Stanley Hoffmann, and Sylvia Malzacher. New York: Oxford University Press, 1987.

———. "Industrial Policy in Macroeconomic Perspective." In *French Industrial Policy,* edited by William James Adams and Christian Stoffaës. Washington: Brookings Institution, 1986.

————. "Is France Declining Relative to the OECD?" Paper presented at Harvard University, Center for European Studies, November 5, 1987.

Boyer, Robert, and Jacques Mistral. *Accumulation, Inflation, Crises.* 2d ed. Paris: Presses Universitaires de France, 1983.

Boyer, Robert, and Pierre Ralle. "Croissances Nationales et Contrainte Extérieure avant et après 1973." *Economies et Sociétés: Cahiers de l'Institut de Sciences Mathématiques et Economiques Appliques,* series P, no. 29 (1986).

Brémond, Janine, ed. *Les Nationalisations.* 3d ed. Paris: Hatier, 1977.

Brewer, Anthony. "Turgot: Founder of Classical Economics." *Economica,* vol. 54 (November 1987).

Brocard, Renaud, and Jean-Marie Gandois. "Grandes Entreprises et PME." *Economie et Statistique,* no. 96 (January 1978).

Brochier, Hubert. "Etude Statistique du Comportement des Entreprises vis-à-vis du Marché Financier." *Revue Economique,* vol. 7 (July 1956).

Brothwood, Michael. "The Court of Justice on Article 90 of the EEC Treaty." *Common Market Law Review,* vol. 20 (August 1983).

Browne, Lynn E., and Eric S. Rosengren, eds. *The Merger Boom.* Conference Series, 31. Boston: Federal Reserve Bank of Boston, 1988.

Byé, Maurice. "L'Opération des 27-28 Décembre 1958." *Revue Economique,* vol. 10 (March 1959).

Cable, Vincent. *Protectionism and Industrial Decline.* London: Hodder and Stoughton in association with the Overseas Development Institute, 1983.

Caffet, Jean-Pierre, and others. "L'Economie Française à l'Horizon 1991: La Recherche du Carré Magique." *Economie et Statistique,* no. 195 (January 1987).

Cahen, L. "Evolution de la Population Active en France depuis 100 Ans d'après les Recensements Quinquennaux." *Etudes et Conjoncture,* vol. 8 (May 1953).

Cahiers Français. "Les Entreprises Publiques: La France à l'Heure de Choix," no. 150 (September 1971).

————. "La Politique Industrielle," no. 212 (July 1983).

————. "Le Tissu Industriel," no. 211 (May 1983).

Callies, Jean-Marie. "Quatre Entreprises sur Dix Créés depuis 1981: Le Tissu Productif Se Renouvelle Rapidement." *Economie et Statistique,* no. 206 (January 1988).

Camus, Benjamin, and others. *La Crise du Système Productif.* Paris: INSEE, 1981.

Caron, François. *An Economic History of Modern France.* New York: Columbia University Press, 1979.

Carré, Jean-Jacques, Paul Dubois, and Edmond Malinvaud. *La Croissance Française: Un Essai d'Analyse Economique Causale de l'Après-Guerre.* New ed. Paris: Editions du Seuil, 1972.

Carter, Edward C., II, Robert Forster, and Joseph N. Moody, eds. *Enterprise and Entrepreneurs in Nineteenth- and Twentieth-Century France.* Baltimore: Johns Hopkins University Press, 1976.

Casson, Mark. *The Firm and the Market: Studies on Multinational Enterprise and the Scope of the Firm.* Cambridge: MIT Press, 1987.

Castel, Michel, and Jean-André Masse. *L'Encadrement du Crédit*. Paris: Presses Universitaires de France, 1983.

Castells, Manuel, and Francis Godard. *Monopolville: Analyse des Rapports entre l'Entreprise, l'Etat, et l'Urbain à Partir d'une Enquête sur la Croissance Industrielle et Urbaine de la Région de Dunkerque*. Paris: Mouton, 1974.

Catherine, Robert, and Pierre Gousset. *L'Etat et l'Essor Industriel: Du Dirigisme Colbertien à l'Economie Concertée*. Paris: Editions Berger-Levrault, 1965.

Catinat, Michel, Jean Pisani-Ferry, and Katheline Schubert. "Les Incidences d'une Dévaluation du Franc Ont-Elles Varié depuis Vingt Ans?" *Economie et Statistique*, no. 178 (June 1985).

Caves, Richard E. *American Industry: Structure, Conduct, Performance*. 6th ed. Englewood Cliffs, N.J.: Prentice-Hall, 1987.

———. *International Trade, International Investment, and Imperfect Markets*. Special Papers in International Economics, 10. Princeton: Princeton University, Department of Economics, International Finance Section, 1974.

———. *Multinational Enterprise and Economic Analysis*. New York: Cambridge University Press, 1982.

———. *Trade and Economic Structure: Models and Methods*. Cambridge: Harvard University Press, 1960.

———, ed. *Britain's Economic Prospects*. Washington: Brookings Institution, 1968.

Caves, Richard E., and Lawrence B. Krause, eds. *Britain's Economic Performance*. Washington: Brookings Institution, 1980.

Caves, Richard E., Michael E. Porter, and A. Michael Spence, with John T. Scott. *Competition in the Open Economy: A Model Applied to Canada*. Cambridge: Harvard University Press, 1980.

Cazes, Bernard. "Preface." In Anne-Robert Jacques Turgot, *Ecrits Economiques*. Paris: Calmann-Lévy, 1970.

Centre d'Etudes Prospectives et d'Informations Internationales (CEPII). *Economie Mondiale: La Montée des Tensions*. Paris: Economica, 1983.

Cerny, Philip G., and Martin A. Schain, eds. *Socialism, the State and Public Policy in France*. London: Frances Pinter, 1985.

Cézard, Michel, and Daniel Rault. "La Crise A Freiné la Mobilité Sectorielle." *Economie et Statistique*, no. 184 (January 1986).

Chamberlain, Muriel E. *Decolonization: The Fall of the European Empires*. New York: Basil Blackwell, 1985.

Charbonneau, Simon, and Jean G. Padioleau. "La Mise en Oeuvre d'une Politique Publique Réglementaire: Le Défrichement des Bois et Forêts." *Revue Française de Sociologie*, vol. 21 (January 1980).

Chardonnet, Jean. *L'Economie Française: Les Grandes Industries*. Paris: Dalloz, 1971.

———. *L'Economie Française: Les Grandes Industries* (2e Partie). Paris: Dalloz, 1974.

———. *L'Economie Française: L'Industrie* . 2d ed. Paris: Dalloz, 1970.

Chatagner, François, and Bernard Allain, eds. *Les Banques*. Profil Dossier, 546. Paris: Hatier, 1983.

Chenot, Bernard. *Les Entreprises Nationalisées*. Paris: Presses Universitaires de France, 1956.

Chevalier, Alain. "Le Ministère des Finances." *Revue Economique*, vol. 13 (November 1962).

Chevalier, Jean-Marie. *L'Echiquier Industriel*. Paris: Hachette, 1980.

———. "L'Energie." In *L'Industrie en France*, edited by Bertrand Bellon and Jean-Marie Chevalier. Paris: Flammarion, 1983.

Choinel, Alain, and Gérard Rouyer. *Le Système Bancaire Français*. 2d ed. Paris: Presses Universitaires de France, 1985.

Clément, B. "An Appraisal of French Antitrust Policy." *Antitrust Bulletin*, vol. 19 (Fall 1974).

Cline, William R., ed. *Trade Policy in the 1980s*. Washington: Institute for International Economics, 1983.

Clough, Shepard B. "Economic Planning in a Capitalist Society: France from Monnet to Hirsch." *Political Science Quarterly*, vol. 71 (December 1956).

———. *France: A History of National Economics*. New York: Charles Scribner's Sons, 1939.

———. "Retardative Factors in French Economic Development in the Nineteenth and Twentieth Centuries." *Journal of Economic History*, vol. 6 (supplement 1946).

Cohen, Elie, and Michel Bauer. *Les Grandes Manoeuvres Industrielles*. Paris: Pierre Belfond, 1985.

Cohen, Jean-Claude, and Philippe Fondanaiche. "Les Participations Etrangères dans l'Industrie Française en 1971." *Economie et Statistique*, no. 52 (January 1974).

Cohen, Stephen S. *Modern Capitalist Planning: The French Model*. Cambridge: Harvard University Press, 1969.

Cohen, Stephen S., James K. Galbraith, and John Zysman. "Credit Policy and Industrial Policy in France." In U.S. Congress, Joint Economic Committee, *Monetary Policy, Selective Credit Policy, and Industrial Policy in France, Britain, West Germany, and Sweden*. Staff Study, 97th Congress, 1st session. Washington: Government Printing Office, 1981.

Cohen, Stephen S., and Peter A. Gourevitch, eds. *France in the Troubled World Economy*. Boston: Butterworth Scientific, 1982.

Colbert, Jean-Baptiste. *Testament Politique*. The Hague: Henry van Bulderen, 1694 (first published in 1693).

Cole, Charles W. *Colbert and a Century of French Mercantilism*. New York: Columbia University Press, 1939.

———. *French Mercantilism, 1683–1700*. New York: Columbia University Press, 1943.

———. *French Mercantilist Doctrines before Colbert*. New York: R. R. Smith, 1931.

Colin, Philippe, Gilles Gervaise, and Thierry Lamorlette. *Fiscalité Pratique des Affaires*. Paris: Economica, 1976.

"Commerce: Concurrence Accrue en 1984." *Economie et Statistique*, no. 174 (February 1985).

Commissariat Général du Plan, "Aides à l'Industrie." Paris: CGP, April 1982.

Commission de la Concurrence. *Rapport au Ministre pour l'Année* (1979–86). Paris: Imprimerie Nationale, 1980–81; and Direction des Journaux Officiels, 1982–87.

Commission of the European Communities. *Completing the Internal Market: White Paper from the Commission to the Council.* Luxembourg: Office for Official Publications of the European Communities, 1985.

———. *Thirteenth Report on Competition Policy.* Luxembourg: Office for Official Publications of the European Communities, 1983.

———. *XXIst General Report on the Activities of the European Communities.* Luxembourg: Office for Official Publications of the European Communities, 1988.

Comte, Philippe. *Les Contrats de Programme: O.R.T.F., Electricité de France, S.N.C.F. (1970–1974).* Notes et Etudes Documentaires, 4167–68. Paris: La Documentation Française, 1975.

Concurrence et Prix: Textes Généraux. Brochure 1443. Paris: Imprimerie des Journaux Officiels, 1980.

Conseil Economique et Social. "L'Analyse des Circuits et des Coûts de Transformation et de Distribution de Produits Agro-Alimentaires et Leur Eventuel Aménagement." *Journal Officiel de la République Française—Avis et Rapports du Conseil Economique et Social,* no. 4 (February 16, 1983).

———. "La Conversion des Entreprises Industrielles." *Journal Officiel de la République Française—Avis et Rapports du Conseil Economique et Social,* no. 22 (August 17, 1979).

———. *Les Industries de Biens d'Equipement.* Brochure 4081. Paris: Imprimerie des Journaux Officiels, 1987.

———. "Les Investissements Français à l'Etranger et les Investissements Etrangers en France." *Journal Officiel de la République Française—Avis et Rapports du Conseil Economique et Social,* no. 3 (February 25, 1981).

———. "La Politique Charbonnière Nationale dans la Politique Energétique Française." *Journal Officiel de la République Française—Avis et Rapports du Conseil Economique et Social,* no. 5 (March 26, 1986).

———. *Les Prêts et Aides aux Entreprises: Procédures et Circuits de Distribution.* Brochure 4049. Paris: Imprimerie des Journaux Officiels, 1986.

Conseil National du Crédit. *Rapport Annuel.* Paris: Banque de France.

Cossé, Pierre-Yves. "Nationalisations." *Regards sur l'Actualité,* no. 79 (March 1982).

Cotta, Alain. *Le Corporatisme.* Paris: Presses Universitaires de France, 1984.

———. *La France et l'Impératif Mondial.* Paris: Presses Universitaires de France, 1978.

Cotteret, Jean-Marie, and Claude Emeri. *Le Budget de l'Etat.* 4th ed. Paris: Presses Universitaires de France, 1983.

Coupaye, Pierre. *Les Banques Françaises: Bilan d'une Réforme.* Notes et Etudes Documentaires, 4470-71. Paris: La Documentation Française, 1978.

"La Croissance du Commerce en 1987: Toujours les Hypermarchés." *Economie et Statistique,* no. 209 (April 1988).

"La Croissance Confisquée." *Observations et Diagnostics Economiques: Revue de l'Observatoire Français de Conjoncture Economique,* no. 19 (April 1987).

Cunéo, Philippe. "L'Impact de la Recherche et Développement sur la Productivité Industrielle." *Economie et Statistique,* no. 164 (March 1984).

Cunéo, Phillipe, Françoise Dupont, and Sylvie Mabile. "1980–1985: Des Mutations Sectorielles Plus Profondes Que Prévu," *Economie et Statistique,* no. 201 (July 1987).

Dacier, Pierre, Jean-Louis Levet, and Jean-Claude Tourret. *Les Dossiers Noirs de l'Industrie Française: Echecs, Handicaps, Espoirs.* Paris: Librairie Arthème Fayard, 1985.

Dalloz, Jacques. *La France de la Libération (1944–1946).* Paris: Presses Universitaires de France, 1983.

Darbel, Alain. "L'Evolution Récente de la Mobilité Sociale." *Economie et Statistique,* no. 71 (October 1975).

Davenport, Michael. "The Economic Impact of the EEC." In *The European Economy: Growth and Crisis,* edited by Andrea Boltho. New York: Oxford University Press, 1982.

Davies, Stephen, and Richard E. Caves. *Britain's Productivity Gap.* New York: Cambridge University Press, 1987.

Défossé, Gaston. *Le Commerce Intérieur: Données, Evolution, Structure, Organisation.* Paris: Presses Universitaires de France, 1944.

Défossé, Gaston, and Yves Flornoy. *La Bourse des Valeurs.* 12th ed. Paris: Presses Universitaires de France, 1984.

Delapierre, Michel, ed. *Nationalisations et Internationalisation: Stratégies des Multinationales Françaises dans la Crise.* Paris: La Découverte/Maspero, 1983.

Delapierre, Michel, and Charles-Albert Michalet. *Les Implantations Etrangères en France: Stratégies et Structures.* Paris: Calmann-Lévy, 1976.

De La Torre, Jose. *Clothing Industry Adjustment in Developed Countries.* Thames Essay 38. London: Trade Policy Research Centre, 1984.

Delattre, Michel. "1979–1984: Une Nouvelle Donne pour les Branches de l'Industrie." *Economie et Statistique,* no. 186 (March 1986).

———. "Points Forts et Points Faibles du Commerce Extérieur Industriel." *Economie et Statistique,* no. 157 (July 1983).

Delavennat, Christine. "Qui A Peur de la Concurrence?" *Express,* June 27, 1986.

Delestré, Henri, and Jacques Mairesse. *La Rentabilité des Sociétés Privées en France, 1956–1975, Dossier Statistique.* Paris: INSEE, 1978.

Delion, André G., and Michel Durupty. *Les Nationalisations, 1982.* Paris: Economica, 1982.

Delorme, Robert, and Christine André. *L'Etat et l'Economie: Un Essai d'Explication de l'Evolution des Dépenses Publiques en France, 1870–1980.* Paris: Editions du Seuil, 1983.

Demailly, Dominique, and Alain Tranap. *Rétropolation 1959–1969 de Comptes Détaillés des Biens et des Services.* Archives et Documents, 164. Paris: INSEE, 1986.

Denuc, Jules. "Structures des Entreprises." *Revue d'Economie Politique*, vol. 53 (January 1939).

De Roux, Xavier, and Dominique Voillemot. *Le Droit de la Concurrence de la C.E.E.* 4th ed. Paris: Juridictionnaires Joly, 1982.

————. *Le Droit Français de la Concurrence et de la Consommation.* 2 vols. Paris: Juridictionnaires Joly, 1986.

Desplanques, Guy. "Les Migrations Intérieures entre 1968 et 1975: La Ville ou la Campagne?" *Economie et Statistique*, no. 107 (January 1979).

Desrosières, Alain. "La Dimension des Etablissements Industriels Français: Comparaison avec Six Pays." *Economie et Statistique*, no. 2 (June 1969).

Dessert, Daniel, and Jean-Louis Journet. "Le Lobby Colbert: Un Royaume ou une Affaire de Famille." *Annales: Economies, Sociétés, Civilisations*, vol. 30 (November 1975).

Dessirier, Jean. "Secteurs 'Abrité' et 'Non-Abrité' dans le Déséquilibre Actuel de l'Economie Française." *Revue d'Economie Politique*, vol. 49 (July 1935).

Deville, Jean-Claude. "Les Migrations Intérieures entre 1968 et 1975: Près d'un Français sur Dix A Changé de Région." *Economie et Statistique*, no. 107 (January 1979).

Didier, Michel. "Crise et Concentration du Secteur Productif." *Economie et Statistique*, no. 144 (May 1982).

————. "L'Evolution Récente des Fusions d'Entreprises en France." *Etudes et Conjoncture*, vol. 24 (February 1969).

Diebold, William, Jr. *The Schuman Plan: A Study in Economic Cooperation, 1950–1959.* New York: Praeger, 1959.

————. *Trade and Payments in Western Europe: A Study in Economic Cooperation, 1947–1951.* New York: Harper and Brothers, 1952.

Dietsch, Michel. "La Fonction Financière du Crédit Commercial Interentreprises." *Economie et Statistique*, no. 174 (February 1985).

Dillard, Dudley. *Economic Development of the North Atlantic Community.* Englewood Cliffs, N.J.: Prentice-Hall, 1967.

Direction de la Sécurité Sociale. *La Sécurité Sociale en France.* Paris: La Documentation Française, 1975.

Dixit, Avinash. "International Trade Policy for Oligopolistic Industries." *Economic Journal*, vol. 94 (supplement 1984).

Domberger, Simon. *Industrial Structure, Pricing and Inflation.* Oxford: Martin Robertson, 1983.

Dominick, Mary F. "Adjudicating European Steel Policy: Judicial Review of the State Aids and Production Quota Systems in 1985." *Common Market Law Review*, vol. 23 (Summer 1986).

Donges, Jürgen. "Comment." In *Trade Policy in the 1980s*, edited by William R. Cline. Washington: Institute for International Economics, 1983.

Dony, Jean, Alain Giovaninetti, and Bernard Tibi. *L'Etat et le Financement des Investissements Privés.* Paris: Editions Berger-Levrault, 1969.

Dore, Ronald P. *Flexible Rigidities: Industrial Policy and Structural Adjustment in the Japanese Economy, 1970–80.* Stanford: Stanford University Press, 1986.

Dreyfus, Pierre. *La Liberté de Réussir.* Paris: Jean-Claude Simoën, 1977.

Dubarry, Jean-Pierre, and Philippe Meunier. "Pénétration du Marché Intérieur et Effort à l'Exportation: Approche Géographique." *Economie et Statistique,* no. 142 (March 1982).

Dubarry, Jean-Pierre, and Antoine Sanson-Carette. "Les Entreprises Françaises sur le Marché des Grands Equipements." *Economie et Statistique,* no. 116 (November 1979).

Dubois, Paul. "Le Financement des Sociétés Industrielles et Commerciales au Cours des Dix Dernières Années." *Economie et Statistique,* no. 99 (April 1978).

———. "La Rupture de 1974." *Economie et Statistique,* no. 124 (August 1980).

———. "Ruptures de Croissance et Progrès Technique." *Economie et Statistique,* no. 181 (October 1985).

Duchêne, Georges. *L'Empire Industriel: Histoire Critique des Concessions Financières et Industrielles du Second Empire.* Paris: Librairie Centrale, 1869.

Dufau, Jean. *Les Entreprises Publiques.* Paris: Editions de l'Actualité Juridique, 1973.

Dumez, Hervé, and Alain Jeunemaître. "Diriger l'Economie: L'Etat et les Prix en France, 1936–1986." Paris: Ecole Polytechnique, Centre de Recherche en Gestion, September 1987.

———. "Le Jeu des Tarifs Publics en France," *Revue Française d'Economie,* vol. 2 (Autumn 1987).

Dunham, Arthur L. *The Anglo-French Treaty of Commerce of 1860 and the Progress of the Industrial Revolution in France.* Ann Arbor: University of Michigan Press, 1930.

Du Pont, Pierre. *L'Etat Industriel.* Paris: Sirey, 1961.

Dupoux, Jean, and Bernard Grosgeorge. *Les Marchés Publics en France.* Paris: Presses Universitaires de France, 1977.

Durand, Brigitte, and Hervé Passeron. "L'Incidence Macroéconomique des Dépenses d'Investissement: L'Exemple de la RATP." *Economie et Statistique,* no. 181 (October 1985).

Dusart, Gérard. *La Caisse des Dépôts et Consignations.* Notes et Etudes Documentaires, 4577-78. Paris: La Documentation Française, 1980.

Dussauze, Elizabeth. *L'Etat et les Ententes Industrielles: Quelques Expériences.* Paris: Librairie Sociale et Economique, 1938.

Dutailly, Jean-Claude. "Aides aux Entreprises: 134 Milliards de Francs en 1982." *Economie et Statistique,* no. 169 (September 1984).

Dutailly, Jean-Claude, and Michel Hannoun. "Les Secteurs Sensibles de l'Industrie." *Economie et Statistique,* no. 120 (March 1980).

Earle, Edward M., ed. *Modern France: Problems of the Third and Fourth Republics.* Princeton: Princeton University Press, 1951.

Les Echos. *L'Economie de A à Z.* Paris: Editions Ramsay, 1982.

Ehrmann, Henry W. *Organized Business in France.* Princeton: Princeton University Press, 1957.

Elbaum, Mireille. "Continuités et Ruptures des Evolutions d'Emploi dans l'Industrie et le Commerce." *Economie et Statistique,* no. 206 (January 1988).

Elie, Pierre. "Structure de la Population Totale au Recensement de 1968." *Economie et Statistique*, no. 45 (May 1973).

Encaoua, David. "Pouvoir de Monopole et Groupes Industriels: Un Essai d'Economie Industrielle Appliqué à la France." Ph.D. dissertation. Université de Paris I, 1982.

Encaoua, David, and Alexis Jacquemin. "Organizational Efficiency and Monopoly Power: The Case of French Industrial Groups." *European Economic Review*, vol. 19 (September 1982).

Encaoua, David, and Bernard Franck. "Performances Sectorielles et Groupes de Sociétés." *Revue Économique*, vol. 31 (May 1980).

Encaoua, David, and Philippe Michel. *Dynamique des Prix Industriels en France.* Paris: Economica, 1986.

Estrin, Saul, and Peter Holmes. *French Planning in Theory and Practice.* London: George Allen and Unwin, 1983.

European Coal and Steel Community. *CECA, 1952–1962: Résultats, Limites, Perspectives.* Luxembourg: ECSC, 1963.

European Communities. *Treaties Establishing the European Communities, Treaties Amending These Treaties, Documents Concerning the Accession.* Luxembourg: Office for Official Publications of the European Communities, 1978.

Eymard-Duvernay, François. "Les Secteurs de l'Industrie et Leurs Ouvriers." *Economie et Statistique*, no. 138 (November 1981).

Fabius, Laurent. *Le Coeur du Futur.* Paris: Calmann-Lévy, 1985.

Fabre, François, and Claude Taffin. "Qui A Déménagé entre 1973 et 1978, et Pourquoi?" *Economie et Statistique*, no. 133 (May 1981).

Faure, Edgar. *La Disgrâce de Turgot, 12 Mai 1776.* Paris: Gallimard, 1961.

———. *La Politique Française du Pétrole.* Paris: Editions de la Nouvelle Revue Critique, 1938.

Fayolle, Jacky. "L'Attitude des Entreprises Face à la Concurrence Etrangère." *Economie et Statistique*, no. 124 (August 1980).

Febvay, M. "La Population Agricole Française: Structure Actuelle et Evolution." *Etudes et Conjoncture*, vol. 11 (August 1956).

Fonds de Développement Economique et Social. *Rapport pour 1969–1970 du Conseil de Direction.* Paris: Imprimerie Nationale, 1970.

Fort, Agnès, and Michel Guillement. *Formes de Vente et Parts de Marché dans le Commerce de Détail.* Archives et Documents, 47. Paris: INSEE, 1982.

Fourastié, Jean. *Les Trente Glorieuses ou la Révolution Invisible de 1946 à 1975.* Paris: Librairie Arthème Fayard, 1979.

Fourquet, François. *Les Comptes de la Puissance: Histoire de la Comptabilité Nationale et du Plan.* Paris: Encres, 1980.

Franck, Louis R. "Planisme Français et Démocratie." *Revue Economique*, vol. 4 (March 1953).

François, Jean-Paul, and Jean-Luc Grosbois. *Le Secteur Public dans l'Industrie avant et après les Nationalisations.* Traits Fondamentaux du Système Industriel Français, 25. Paris: La Documentation Française, n.d.

François-Marsal, Frédéric. *Le Dépérissement des Entreprises Publiques.* Paris: Calmann-Lévy, 1973.

Franko, Lawrence G. *The European Multinationals: A Renewed Challenge to American and British Big Business.* New York: Harper and Row, 1976.

Freyche, Michel. "Export Promotion as Industrial Policy." In *French Industrial Policy,* edited by William James Adams and Christian Stoffaës. Washington: Brookings Institution, 1986.

Freyssenet, Michel. *La Sidérurgie Française, 1945–1979: L'Histoire d'une Faillite, les Solutions Qui S'Affrontent.* Paris: Savelli, 1979.

Galambert, Patrice. *Les Sept Paradoxes de la Politique Industrielle.* Paris: Les Editions du Cerf, 1982.

Galbraith, John Kenneth. *American Capitalism: The Concept of Countervailing Power.* Boston: Houghton Mifflin, 1952.

Gauron, André. *Histoire Economique et Sociale de la Cinquième République,* vol. 1: *Le Temps des Modernistes.* Paris: La Découverte/Maspero, 1983.

Gelpi, Rosa-Maria. "La Formation des Taux et le Mécanisme de la Distribution des Crédits dans le Système Bancaire Français avant et après la Réforme de 1965–1967." *Revue Economique,* vol. 28 (May 1977).

Gervais, Jacques. *La France Face aux Investissements Etrangers: Analyse par Secteurs.* Paris: Editions de l'Entreprise Moderne, 1963.

Gervais, Michel, Claude Servolin, and Jean Weil. *Une France sans Paysans.* Paris: Editions du Seuil, 1965.

Ghersi, G., M. C. Allaya, and M. Allaya. *Etude sur la Concentration, les Prix et les Marges dans la Distribution des Produits Alimentaires—Evolution de la Concentration et des Prix dans la Distribution Alimentaire en France.* Série Evolution de la Concentration et de la Concurrence, 45. Brussels: Commission of the European Communities, 1980.

Gilbert, Milton C., and Irving B. Kravis. *An International Comparison of National Products and the Purchasing Power of Currencies: A Study of the United States, the United Kingdom, France, Germany, and Italy.* Paris: Organization for European Economic Cooperation, 1954.

Gillespie, Robert W. "The Policies of England, France, and Germany as Recipients of Foreign Direct Investment." In *International Mobility and Movement of Capital,* edited by Fritz Machlup, Walter S. Salant, and Lorie Tarshis. New York: Columbia University Press, 1972.

Gilpin, Robert G., Jr. *France in the Age of the Scientific State.* Princeton: Princeton University Press, 1968.

Glaude, Michel, and Mireille Moutardier. "L'Evolution des Niveaux de Vie de 1966 à 1979." *Economie et Statistique,* no. 142 (March 1982).

Glickmann, David L. "The British Imperial Preference System." *Quarterly Journal of Economics,* vol. 61 (May 1947).

Goldet, Hélène, François Nicolas, and Michel Séruzier. "L'Endettement des Entreprises et des Ménages de 1954 à 1974." *Economie et Statistique,* no. 73 (December 1975).

Golob, Eugene O. *The Méline Tariff: French Agriculture and Nationalist Economic Policy.* New York: Columbia University Press, 1944.

Gorgé, Jean-Pierre. "Concentrations d'Entreprises: Ralentissements en 1973." *Economie et Statistique*, no. 58 (July 1974).

Gormley, Laurence W. *Prohibiting Restrictions on Trade within the EEC: The Theory and Application of Articles 30–36 of the EEC Treaty*. Amsterdam: North-Holland, 1985.

Goubert, Pierre. *100000 Provinciaux au XVIIe Siècle: Beauvais et le Beauvaisis de 1600 à 1730*. Paris: Flammarion, 1968.

———. *Louis XIV et Vingt Millions de Français*. Paris: Librairie Arthème Fayard, 1966.

Gourevitch, Peter A. *Politics in Hard Times: Comparative Responses to International Economic Crises*. Ithaca: Cornell University Press, 1986.

Goux, Christian. "Parliament Should Play a Larger Role in Industrial Policy." In *French Industrial Policy*, edited by William James Adams and Christian Stoffaës. Washington: Brookings Institution, 1986.

Grais, Bernard. "L'Evolution des Structures de la Population Active: Analyse des Résultats des Enquêtes sur l'Emploi d'Octobre 1962 et 1964." *Etudes et Conjoncture*, vol. 23 (March 1968).

Gravier, Jean-François. *Paris et le Désert Français: Décentralisation, Equipement, Population*. Paris: Le Portulan, 1947.

———. *Paris et le Désert Français en 1972*. Paris: Flammarion, 1972.

Gremion, Catherine. "Decentralization in France: A Historical Perspective." In *The Mitterrand Experiment: Continuity and Change in Modern France*, edited by George Ross, Stanley Hoffmann, and Sylvia Malzacher. New York: Oxford University Press, 1987.

Gresh, Hani. "L'Endettement des Secteurs de 1971 à 1974." *Economie et Statistique*, no. 99 (April 1978).

———. "Les Entreprises Publiques et la Création de Filiales." *Economie et Statistique*, no. 65 (March 1975).

Grey, Rodney de C. "A Note on US Trade Practices." In *Trade Policy in the 1980s*, edited by William R. Cline. Washington: Institute for International Economics, 1983.

Gruson, Claude. *Origine et Espoirs de la Planification Française*. Paris: Dunod, 1968.

———. *Programmer l'Espérance*. Paris: Stock, 1976.

Guibert, Bernard, Jean Laganier, and Michel Volle. "Essai sur les Nomenclatures Industrielles." *Economie et Statistique*, no. 20 (February 1971).

Guillaumont-Jeanneney, Sylviane. *Politique Monétaire et Croissance Economique en France, 1950–1966*. Paris: Librairie Armand Colin, 1969.

Guillement, Michel. *Le Commerce de Détail de 1962 à 1979*. Archives et Documents, 9. Paris: INSEE, 1980.

Guinchard, Philippe. "Productivité et Compétitivité Comparées des Grands Pays Industriels." *Economie et Statistique*, no. 162 (January 1984).

Guyénot, Jean. *Le Droit des Ententes Industrielles*. Paris: Presses Universitaires de France, 1972.

Hall, Peter A. "The Evolution of Economic Policy under Mitterrand." In *The Mitterrand Experiment: Continuity and Change in Modern France*, edited by

George Ross, Stanley Hoffmann, and Sylvia Malzacher. New York: Oxford University Press, 1987.

———. *Governing the Economy: The Politics of State Intervention in Britain and France.* New York: Oxford University Press, 1986.

Hansen, Alvin H. *Economic Policy and Full Employment.* New York: McGraw-Hill, 1947.

Hardy-Hémery, Odette. *De la Croissance à la Désindustrialisation: Un Siècle dans le Valenciennois.* Paris: Presses de la Fondation Nationale des Sciences Politiques, 1984.

Harris, André, and Charles Sedouy. *Les Patrons.* Paris: Editions du Seuil, 1977.

Hatton, Georges. *Le Commerce Extérieur de la France.* Paris: Editions Berger-Levrault, 1968.

Haudeville, Bernard. "Politique Industrielle et Politique Economique Générale: Réflexion sur le Cas Français." *Revue d'Economie Industrielle,* no. 23 (issue 1, 1983).

Hauser, Henri. "Colonies et Métropole." *Revue d'Economie Politique,* vol. 53 (January 1939).

———. *La Pensée et l'Action Economiques du Cardinal de Richelieu.* Paris: Presses Universitaires de France, 1944.

Hayward, Jack E. *The State and the Market Economy: Industrial Patriotism and Economic Intervention in France.* Brighton: Wheatsheaf Books, 1985.

Hayward, Jack E., and Michael Watson, eds. *Planning, Politics, and Public Policy: The British, French, and Italian Experience.* New York: Cambridge University Press, 1975.

Heilbroner, Robert. "Reflections: Hard Times." *New Yorker,* September 14, 1987.

Hernandez, Claude, Brigitte Peskine, and Alain Saglio. "La Pénétration Etrangère dans l'Industrie Française." *Economie et Statistique,* no. 72 (November 1975).

Hexner, Ervin. *International Cartels.* Chapel Hill: University of North Carolina Press, 1945.

Hillman, Arye L., and Eliakim Katz. "Risk-Averse Rent Seekers and the Social Cost of Monopoly Power." *Economic Journal,* vol. 94 (March 1984).

Hine, R. C. *The Political Economy of European Trade: An Introduction to the Trade Policies of the EEC.* New York: St. Martin's Press, 1985.

Hirschman, Albert O. *The Strategy of Economic Development.* New Haven: Yale University Press, 1958.

Hodgman, Donald R. *National Monetary Policies and International Monetary Cooperation.* Boston: Little, Brown, 1974.

———. *Selective Credit Controls in Western Europe.* Chicago: Association of Reserve City Bankers, 1976.

Hoffmann, Stanley. *Decline or Renewal? France since the 1930s.* New York: Viking Press, 1974.

———. *Le Mouvement Poujade.* Paris: Librairie Armand Colin, 1956.

———. "Paradoxes of the French Political Community." In Stanley Hoffmann and others, *In Search of France.* Cambridge: Harvard University Press, 1963.

Horne, Alistair. *A Savage War of Peace: Algeria, 1954–1962.* New York: Penguin Books, 1985.

Hoselitz, Bert F. "Entrepreneurship and Capital Formation in France and Britain since 1700." In Universities-National Bureau Committee for Economic Research, *Capital Formation and Economic Growth*. Princeton: Princeton University Press, 1955.

Houssiaux, Jacques. *Concurrence et Marché Commun*. Paris: Editions M. T. Genin, 1960.

―――. "Distorsions de Structures et Adaptations Structurelles en France de 1789 à 1914." *Revue Economique*, vol. 9 (September 1958).

―――. *Le Pouvoir de Monopole*. Paris: Sirey, 1958.

Houssiaux, Jacques, and C. Amoy. "L'Evolution de la Concentration dans les Industries Françaises: L'Exemple de l'Industrie Textile." *Revue d'Economie Politique*, vol. 75 (March 1965).

Huet, Maryse. "Résultats du Recensement de la Population de 1975: Emploi et Activité entre 1968 et 1975." *Economie et Statistique*, no. 94 (November 1977).

INSEE. *Annuaire Statistique de la France*. Paris: INSEE, annual. [Unless otherwise noted, INSEE is the publisher of its own documents.]

―――. *Comptes Nationaux de la Base 1956, Séries 1949–1959: Séries Longues Macroéconomiques*. Archives et Documents, 23. 1981.

―――. *Les Entreprises et Leurs Etablissements au 1er Janvier 1983*. 1983.

―――. *Les Etablissements Industriels, Artisanaux et Commerciaux en France en 1958*. Paris: Imprimerie Nationale, 1959.

―――. "Les Etablissements Industriels et Commerciaux du Secteur Privé en France en 1950." *Bulletin Mensuel de Statistique*, new series (April 1952, supplement).

―――. *Les Etablissements Industriels et Commerciaux en France en 1954*. Paris: Imprimerie Nationale, 1956.

―――. *Les Etablissements Industriels et Commerciaux en France en 1962*. Paris: Imprimerie Nationale, 1963.

―――. *Le Mouvement Economique en France, 1949–1979: Séries Longues Macroéconomiques*. 1981.

―――. *Nomenclature des Entreprises, Etablissements, et Toutes Activités Collectives*. 2d ed. Paris: Imprimerie Nationale, 1949.

―――. *Rapport sur les Comptes de la Nation* (annual).

―――. *Recensement Général de la Population de Mai 1954: Population Légale (Résultats Statistiques)*. Paris: Imprimerie Nationale, 1956.

―――. *Recensement Général de la Population de Mai 1954: Résultats du Sondage au 1/20ème, Population-Ménages-Logements, France Entière*. Paris: Imprimerie Nationale, 1956.

―――. *Recensement Général de la Population de 1962: Résultats du Sondage au 1/20 pour la France Entière, Population Active*. Paris: Imprimerie des Journaux Officiels, 1964.

―――. *Recensement Général de la Population de 1968: Résultats du Sondage au 1/20 pour la France Entière, Population Active*. Paris: Imprimerie Nationale, 1971.

————. *Recensement Général de la Population de 1982: France Métropolitaine, Structure de la Population Totale*. Paris: Imprimerie Nationale, n.d.

————. *Recensement Général de la Population de 1982: Métropole, Tableaux Statistiques de Population Légale*. Paris: Imprimerie Nationale, 1983.

————. *Recensement Général de la Population de 1982: Population de la France (Métropole et Départements d'Outre-Mer), Régions, Départements, Arrondissements, et Cantons*. 1982.

————. *Recensement de l'Industrie, 1963: Résultats pour 1962*. 5 vols. Paris: Imprimerie Nationale, 1965–68.

————. *Résultats Statistiques du Recensement Général de la Population Effectué le 10 Mars 1946*, vol. 3: *Population Active*, part 1: *Ensemble de la Population Active*. Paris: Imprimerie Nationale, 1952.

———— C4. *Les Comptes de la Nation, Base 1962: Les Comptes des Entreprises par Secteurs, Séries 1959–1966*. 1969.

———— C5. *Sources et Méthodes d'Evaluation de la Comptabilité Nationale: Les Comptes des Entreprises par Secteurs*. 1970.

———— C20. *Les Comptes de la Nation, Base 1962: Les Comptes des Entreprises par Secteurs, Séries 1962–1969*. 1973.

———— C46. *Le Commerce en France de 1968 à 1974*. 1976.

———— C60. *L'Ancien et le Nouveau Système de Comptabilité Nationale: Comparaison Chiffrée sur l'Année 1971*. 1978.

———— C67-68. Marc Beudaert, Léna Lori, and Michel Séruzier. *Rétropolation des Comptes Nationaux dans le Nouveau Système de Comptabilité Nationale Française—Séries 1959–1970*. 1978.

———— C78. *Sources et Méthodes d'Elaboration des Comptes Nationaux: Les Comptes des Entreprises par Secteur d'Activité, Séries 1967–1975*. 1979.

———— C106. *Le Commerce en 1981: Rapport de la Commission des Comptes Commerciaux de la Nation—Juin 1982*. 1982.

———— C122. *Le Commerce en 1983: Rapport de la Commission des Comptes Commerciaux de la Nation—Juin 1984*. 1984.

———— C128. *Le Commerce en 1984: Rapport de la Commission des Comptes Commerciaux de la Nation—Juin 1985*. 1985.

———— D4. Michel Schiray. *Migrations entre Régions et au Niveau Catégorie de Commune de 1954 à 1962*. 1970.

———— D30. Marie-Claude Gérard. *Aspects Démographiques de l'Urbanisation: Analyse 1968, Evolution 1954–1962 et 1962–1968*. 1974.

———— D32. Richard Pohl, Claude Thélot, and M. F. Jousset. *L'Enquête Formation-Qualification Professionnelle de 1970*. 1974.

———— D52. *Principaux Résultats du Recensement de 1975*. 1977.

———— D67. Françoise Guillot, Nicole Schmitz, and Laurent Thévenot. *Recensement Général de la Population de 1975: Population Active*. 1979.

———— D91. Richard Pohl and Jeanine Soleilhavoup. *Mobilité Professionnelle—Enquête Formation-Qualification Professionnelle de 1977*. 1982.

———— D97. *Recensement Général de la Population de 1982: Principaux Résultats, Sondage au 1/20e—France Métropolitaine*. 1984.

—— D100. Françoise Guillot. *Recensement Général de la Population de 1982: France Métropolitaine, Population Active.* 1984.

—— D123. *Population Active, Emploi et Chômage depuis 30 Ans.* 1987.

—— E1. Jean-Pierre Nioche. "Taille des Etablissements Industriels dans Sept Pays Développés. In *Deux Etudes sur la Dimension des Entreprises Industrielles.* 1969.

—— E11. Eric Huret and others. *Les Entreprises Publiques de 1959 à 1969.* 1972.

—— E19. Michel Hannoun. *La Démographie des Très Grands Etablissements Industriels, 1961–1970.* 1973.

—— E31-32. Bernard Guibert and others. *La Mutation Industrielle de la France: Du Traité de Rome à la Crise Pétrolière.* 2 vols. 1975.

—— E34. Michel Tardieu and Michel Pierre. *Les Comptes Intermédiaires des Entreprises en 1971.* 1976.

—— E38. Michel Blanc and Michel Pierre. *Les Comptes Intermédiaires des Entreprises en 1972.* 1976.

—— E43. Chantal Leprêtre. *La Concentration des Etablissements Industriels Français en 1962 et 1972.* 1976.

—— E44. *Les Statistiques d'Entreprises, Sources.* 1977.

—— E46-47. Jean-Paul Girard, Monique Gombert, and Michel Petry. *Les Agriculteurs,* vol. 1: *Clés pour une Comparaison Sociale.* 1977.

—— E49. Michel Blanc and Michel Pierre. *Les Comptes Intermédiaires des Entreprises en 1973.* 1977.

—— E51. Michel Blanc and Michel Pierre. *Les Comptes Intermédiaires des Entreprises en 1974.* 1978.

—— E57. Georges Borie and others. *Les Grandes Entreprises Nationales de 1959 à 1976.* 1978.

—— E60. Michel Blanc and Michel Pierre. *Les Comptes Intermédiaires des Entreprises en 1975.* 1979.

—— E64. Renaud Brocard. *Les Entreprises Françaises: Concentration et Grandes Entreprises des Secteurs et des Branches.* 1979.

—— E71. *Les Groupes de Sociétés dans le Système Productif Français, Année 1974.* 1980.

—— E72. Jean-François Loué and Pierre Müller. *Les Comptes Intermédiaires des Entreprises en 1976.* 1980.

—— E96. Didier Castille, Denis Cavaud, and Pierre Müller. *Les Comptes du Secteur Public Concurrentiel, Séries 1981–1983.* 1985.

—— E98. Jean Alain Monfort and Laurent Vassille. *La Concentration des Activités Economiques: Les Etablissements, les Entreprises, et les Groupes.* 1985.

—— E103. Michel Dietsch. *Le Crédit Interentreprises.* 1986.

—— E108. Eric Vert. *L'Agriculture dans la C.E.E.,* vol. 2: *Emploi et Activité.* 1987.

—— E110. Jean Thibaud. *Petites Entreprises de l'Artisanat, du Commerce et des Services.* 1988.

———— M95. Marie-Annick Mercier. *Consommation et Lieux d'Achat des Produits Alimentaires en 1979.* 1982.

International Monetary Fund. *Balance of Payments Yearbook.* Washington: IMF, various years.

————. *Direction of Trade Statistics Yearbook.* Washington: IMF, various years.

————. *Direction of Trade Annual, 1958–1962.* Washington: IMF, 1962.

Jackson, John H. *Legal Problems of International Economic Relations.* Saint Paul: West Publishing, 1977.

————. *World Trade and the Law of GATT: A Legal Analysis of the General Agreement on Tariffs and Trade.* Indianapolis: Bobbs-Merrill, 1969.

Jackson, John H., Jean-Victor Louis, and Mitsuo Matsushita. "Implementing the Tokyo Round: Legal Aspects of Changing Economic Rules." *Michigan Law Review,* vol. 81 (December 1982).

Jacquemin, Alexis. *The New Industrial Organization: Market Forces and Strategic Behavior.* Cambridge: MIT Press, 1987.

Jacquemin, Alexis, Elisabeth de Ghellinck, and Christian Huveneers. "Concentration and Profitability in a Small Open Economy." *Journal of Industrial Economics,* vol. 29 (December 1980).

Jacquemin, Alexis, and Michel Rainelli. "Filières de la Nation et Filières de l'Entreprise." *Revue Economique,* vol. 35 (March 1984).

Jaikumar, Ramchandran. "Postindustrial Manufacturing." *Harvard Business Review,* vol. 86 (November 1986).

Jeanneney, Jean-Marcel. *Forces et Faiblesses de l'Economie Française, 1945–1959.* 2d ed. Paris: Librairie Armand Colin, 1959.

————. *Pour un Nouveau Protectionnisme.* Paris: Editions du Seuil, 1978.

Jenny, Frédéric. "Rapport sur la Relation Pouvant Exister entre les Pratiques de Certains Types de Distributeurs et la Pénétration Croissante de Notre Marché par les Produits Etrangers." Paris: Commission de la Concurrence, March 1984.

Jenny, Frédéric, and André-Paul Weber. "Aggregate Welfare Loss Due to Monopoly Power in the French Economy: Some Tentative Estimates." *Journal of Industrial Economics,* vol. 32 (December 1983).

————. "Concentration Economique et Fonctionnement des Marchés," *Economie et Statistique,* no. 65 (March 1975).

————. *Concentration et Politique des Structures Industrielles.* Paris: La Documentation Française, 1974.

————. "French Antitrust Legislation: An Exercise in Futility?" *Antitrust Bulletin,* vol. 20 (Fall 1975).

Johnson, Chalmers. *MITI and the Japanese Miracle: The Growth of Industrial Policy, 1925–1975.* Stanford: Stanford University Press, 1982.

Johnstone, Allan W. *United States Direct Investment in France: An Investigation of the French Charges.* Cambridge: MIT Press, 1965.

Jouvenel, Bertrand de. *L'Economie Dirigée: Le Programme de la Nouvelle Génération.* Paris: Librairie Valois, 1928.

————. *Napoléon et l'Economie Dirigée: Le Blocus Continental.* Brussels and Paris: Les Editions de la Toison d'Or, 1942.

Jublin, Jacques, and Jean-Michel Quatrepoint. *French Ordinateurs: De l'Affaire Bull à l'Assassinat du Plan Calcul.* Paris: Alain Moreau, 1976.

Kahler, Miles. *Decolonization in Britain and France: The Domestic Consequences of International Relations.* Princeton: Princeton University Press, 1985.

Keeler, John T. S. "Corporatist Decentralization and Commercial Modernization in France: The Royer Law's Impact on Shopkeepers, Supermarkets and the State." In *Socialism, the State and Public Policy in France,* edited by Philip G. Cerny and Martin A. Schain. London: Frances Pinter, 1985.

Kemp, Tom. *Economic Forces in French History.* London: Dennis Dobson, 1971.

———. *Industrialization in Nineteenth Century Europe.* 2d ed. London: Longman, 1985.

Kilborn, Peter T. "U.S. Rearranging Its Top Priorities for Trade Policy: More Protectionist Line." *New York Times,* April 29, 1988.

Kindleberger, Charles P. *Economic Growth in France and Britain, 1851–1950.* Cambridge: Harvard University Press, 1964.

———. *Marshall Plan Days.* London: George Allen and Unwin, 1987.

———. "The Postwar Resurgence of the French Economy." In Stanley Hoffmann and others, *In Search of France.* Cambridge: Harvard University Press, 1963.

King, Anthony S. *Britain Says Yes: The 1975 Referendum on the Common Market.* Washington: American Enterprise Institute for Public Policy Research, 1977.

Knickerbocker, Frederick T. *Oligopolistic Reaction and Multinational Enterprise.* Boston: Harvard University Graduate School of Business Administration, 1973.

Kramer, Jane. *Unsettling Europe.* New York: Vintage Books, 1981.

———. "Letter from Europe." *New Yorker,* January 18, 1982.

Krause, Lawrence B. "Import Discipline: The Case of the United States Steel Industry." *Journal of Industrial Economics,* vol. 11 (November 1962).

Kravis, Irving B., Alan Heston, and Robert Summers. *World Product and Income: International Comparisons of Real Gross Product.* Baltimore: Johns Hopkins University Press, 1982.

Krier, Henri, and Joël Jallais. *Le Commerce Intérieur.* Paris: Presses Universitaires de France, 1985.

Kuisel, Richard F. *Capitalism and the State in Modern France: Renovation and Economic Management in the Twentieth Century.* New York: Cambridge University Press, 1981.

———. *Ernest Mercier: French Technocrat.* Berkeley: University of California Press, 1967.

Kuznets, Simon. *Modern Economic Growth: Rate, Structure, and Spread.* New Haven: Yale University Press, 1966.

Lafay, Gérard. *Dynamique de la Spécialisation Internationale.* Paris: Economica, 1979.

La Genière, Renaud de. *Le Budget.* Paris: Presses de la Fondation Nationale des Sciences Politiques, 1976.

La Gorce, Paul-Marie de. *L'Après-Guerre, 1944–1952: Naissance de la France Moderne.* Paris: B. Grasset, 1978.

Landes, David S. "French Business and the Businessman: A Social and Cultural Analysis." In *Modern France: Problems of the Third and Fourth Republics,* edited by Edward M. Earle. Princeton: Princeton University Press, 1951.

———. "French Entrepreneurship and Industrial Growth in the Nineteenth Century." *Journal of Economic History,* vol. 9 (May 1949).

———. "Observations on France: Economy, Society, and Polity." *World Politics,* vol. 9 (April 1957).

———. "Religion and Enterprise: The Case of the French Textile Industry." In *Enterprise and Entrepreneurs in Nineteenth- and Twentieth-Century France,* edited by Edward C. Carter II, Robert Forster, and Joseph N. Moody. Baltimore: Johns Hopkins University Press, 1976.

Lang, Gérard, and Claude Thélot. "Taille des Etablissements et Effets de Seuil." *Economie et Statistique,* no. 173 (January 1985).

Laroque, Guy. "La Fin des Restrictions: 1946–1949." *Economie et Statistique,* no. 129 (January 1981).

Lassudrie-Duchêne, Bernard, and Jean-Louis Mucchielli. "Les Echanges Intra-Branche et la Hiérarchisation des Avantages Comparés dans le Commerce International." *Revue Economique,* vol. 30 (May 1979).

Lattre, André de. *Les Finances Extérieures de la France (1945–1958).* Paris: Presses Universitaires de France, 1959.

Lauber, Volkmar. *The Politics of Economic Policy: France, 1974-1982.* New York: Praeger, 1983.

Laulhé, Pierre. "Se Mettre à Son Compte: Des Installations Plus Nombreuses mais Plus Fragiles." *Economie et Statistique,* no. 209 (April 1988).

Lawrence, Robert A., and Charles L. Schultze, eds. *Barriers to European Growth: A Transatlantic View.* Washington: Brookings Institution, 1987.

Lebedel, Claude. "La Pénétration des Produits Français sur les Marchés Etrangers." *Economie et Statistique,* no. 26 (September 1971).

Leclerc, Edouard. *Ma Vie pour un Combat.* Paris: Pierre Belfond, 1974.

Le Foll, Jean. "Les Aides Publiques à l'Industrie: Eléments d'Evaluation," *Economie et Prévision,* no. 70 (issue 4, 1985).

Le Franc, Jean-Daniel. *Industrie: Le Péril Français.* Paris: Editions du Seuil, 1983.

Lehoucq, Thérèse, and Jean-Paul Strauss. "Les Industries Françaises de Haute Technologie: Des Difficultés à Rester dans la Course." *Economie et Statistique,* no. 207 (February 1988).

Lemperière, J. "Structure et Evolution des Exportations des Pays du Marché Commun et de la Grande-Bretagne depuis 1951." *Etudes et Conjoncture,* vol. 15 (May 1960).

Le Pors, Anicet. *Les Béquilles du Capital: Transferts Etat-Industrie, Critère de Nationalisation.* Paris: Editions du Seuil, 1977.

———. "Transferts Etat-Industrie." *Statistiques et Etudes Financières* (issue 2, 1971).

———. *Les Transferts Etat-Industrie en France et dans les Pays Occidentaux.* Notes et Etudes Documentaires, 4303. Paris: La Documentation Française, 1976.

Le Pors, Anicet, and Jacques Prunet. "Les 'Transferts' entre l'Etat et l'Industrie." *Economie et Statistique*, no. 66 (April 1975).

Lévy, Raymond. "Industrial Policy and the Steel Industry." In *French Industrial Policy*, edited by William James Adams and Christian Stoffaës. Washington: Brookings Institution, 1986.

Lévy-Lambert, Hubert. *La Vérité des Prix*. Paris: Editions du Seuil, 1975.

Lévy-Leboyer, Claude. *L'Ambition Professionnelle et la Mobilité Sociale*. Paris: Presses Universitaires de France, 1971.

Lévy-Leboyer, Maurice. "Innovation and Business Strategies in Nineteenth- and Twentieth-Century France." In *Enterprise and Entrepreneurs in Nineteenth- and Twentieth-Century France*, edited by Edward C. Carter II, Robert Forster, and Joseph N. Moody. Baltimore: Johns Hopkins University Press, 1976.

————. "The Large Corporation in Modern France." In *Managerial Hierarchies: Comparative Perspectives on the Rise of the Modern Industrial Enterprise*, edited by Alfred D. Chandler and Herman Daems. Cambridge: Harvard University Press, 1980.

————. *Le Patronat de la Seconde Industrialisation*. Paris: Editions Economie et Humanisme, Les Editions Ouvrières, 1979.

————. "Le Patronat Français A-t-Il Eté Malthusien?" *Le Mouvement Social*, no. 88 (July 1974).

————, ed. *La Position Internationale de la France: Aspects Economiques et Financiers, XIXe–XXe Siècles*. Paris: Editions de l'Ecole des Hautes Etudes en Sciences Sociales, 1977.

Lister, Louis. *Europe's Coal and Steel Community: An Experiment in Economic Union*. New York: Twentieth Century Fund, 1960.

Loup, Jacques. "La Concentration dans l'Industrie Française d'après le Recensement de 1963." *Etudes et Conjoncture*, vol. 24 (February 1969).

Loustalet, Bruno. "L'Assurance." In *L'Industrie en France*, edited by Bertrand Bellon and Jean-Marie Chevalier. Paris: Flammarion, 1983.

Lubell, Harold. "The Role of Investment in Two French Inflations." *Oxford Economic Papers*, new series, vol. 7 (February 1955).

Luethy, Herbert. *France against Herself: A Perceptive Study of France's Past, Her Politics, and Her Unending Crises*. New York: Praeger, 1955.

Lukoff, F. L. "European Competition Law and Distribution in the Motor Vehicle Sector: Commission Regulation 123/85 of 12 December 1984." *Common Market Law Review*, vol. 23 (Winter 1986).

McArthur, John H., and Bruce R. Scott. *Industrial Planning in France*. Boston: Harvard University Graduate School of Business Administration, 1969.

Maddison, Angus. "Growth and Slowdown in Advanced Capitalist Countries." *Journal of Economic Literature*, vol. 25 (June 1987).

————. *Phases of Capitalist Development*. New York: Oxford University Press, 1982.

Madinier, Philippe. "La Mobilité du Travail aux Etats-Unis et en France." *Revue Economique*, vol. 10 (July 1959).

Magniez, Jacques. "La Production Industrielle N'A Pas Suivi la Demande Intérieure." *Economie et Statistique,* no. 159 (October 1983).

Maier, Charles S. *Recasting Bourgeois Europe: Stabilization in France, Germany, and Italy in the Decade after World War I.* Princeton: Princeton University Press, 1975.

Maillet, Pierre. "Disparités Sectorielles dans la Croissance Economique: Influence de la Demande Finale et de l'Evolution Technologique en France entre 1950 et 1963." *Revue d'Economie Politique,* vol. 75 (March 1965).

――――. *La Politique Industrielle.* Paris: Presses Universitaires de France, 1984.

Maillet, Pierre, and Monique Maillet. *Le Secteur Public en France.* Paris: Presses Universitaires de France, 1964.

Marchal, André. "Marché Commun Européen et Zone de Libre-Echange." *Revue Economique,* vol. 9 (March 1958).

Marcy, Gérard. "Libération Progressive des Echanges et Aide à l'Exportation en France depuis 1949." *Cahiers de l'Institut de Science Economique Appliquée,* series P, no. 2 (May 1959).

――――. "Quelques Aspects de l'Evolution de la Réglementation Française du Commerce Extérieur depuis 1945: Contrôle des Changes et Règlements Internationaux." *Revue Economique,* vol. 9 (May 1958).

Marenco, Claudine, and Claude Quin. *Structures et Tendances de la Distribution Française: Tableau de Bord, 1980–1981.* Paris, Ministère du Commerce et de l'Artisanat, n.d.

Marenco, Giuliano. "Public Sector and Community Law." *Common Market Law Review,* vol. 20 (October 1983).

Markham, James M. "France at Crossroads: Le Pen Vote Shatters Unity of Right and Threatens Nation's Social Peace." *New York Times,* April 26, 1988.

――――. "Outsiders' Candidate: The French Try to Explain Le Pen—and His Appeal." *New York Times,* May 1, 1988.

Marseille, Jacques. *Empire Colonial et Capitalisme Français: Histoire d'un Divorce.* Paris: Albin Michel, 1984.

Martin, Germain. *La Grande Industrie sous le Règne de Louis XIV (Plus Particulièrement de 1660 à 1715).* New York: Burt Franklin, 1971 (first published in 1899).

Martin, Roger. *Patron de Droit Divin.* Paris: Gallimard, 1984.

Mason, Edward S. "Saint-Simonism and the Rationalization of Industry." *Quarterly Journal of Economics,* vol. 45 (August 1931).

Massé, Pierre. *Le Plan ou l'Anti-Hasard.* Paris: Gallimard, 1965.

Mathieu, Edouard. *Aides Régionales et Structures Industrielles: Sept Années de Primes de Développement Régional (1974–1980).* Traits Fondamentaux du Système Industriel Français, 29. Paris: Ministère de l'Industrie et de la Recherche, n.d.

Mathieu, Edouard, and Maryse Suberchicot. "Marchés Publics et Structures Industrielles." *Economie et Statistique,* no. 96 (January 1978).

――――. *Marchés Publics et Structures Industrielles.* Traits Fondamentaux du Système Industriel Français, 3. Paris: La Documentation Française, n.d.

Mathieu, Gilbert. "Le 'Rapport Hannoun' Souligne la Forte Concentration et la

Faible Efficacité des Aides Publiques à l'Industrie." *Le Monde*, September 27, 1979.

Mathis, Jean, and Jacques Régniez. "L'Industrie Française dans l'Echange International: 1970–1979." *Economie et Prévision*, no. 46 (issue 1, 1981).

Maurice, Marc, François Sellier, and Jean-Jacques Silvestre. *Politique d'Education et Organisation Industrielle en France et en Allemagne: Essai d'Analyse Sociétale*. Paris: Presses Universitaires de France, 1982.

Mazier, Jacques. "La Politique Industrielle, 1974–1981—Essai de Bilan." Paris: Commissariat Général du Plan, 1982.

Meade, James E., H. H. Liesner, and S. J. Wells. *Case Studies in European Economic Union: The Mechanics of Integration*. New York: Oxford University Press, 1962.

Mehl, Lucien, and Pierre Beltrame. *Le Système Fiscal Français*. 2d ed. Paris: Presses Universitaires de France, 1985.

Mendès-France, Pierre. *Choisir: Conversations avec Jean Bothorel*. Paris: Stock, 1974.

Mentré, Paul. "The French Economy Should Be Deregulated." In *French Industrial Policy*, edited by William James Adams and Christian Stoffaës. Washington: Brookings Institution, 1986.

Mény, Yves. "The Socialist Decentralization." In *The Mitterrand Experiment: Continuity and Change in Modern France*, edited by George Ross, Stanley Hoffmann, and Sylvia Malzacher. New York: Oxford University Press, 1987.

Merrill, William C., and Norman Schneider. "Government Firms in Oligopoly Industries: A Short-Run Analysis." *Quarterly Journal of Economics*, vol. 80 (August 1966).

Messerlin, Patrick. *La Révolution Commerciale*. Paris: Bonnel Editions, 1982.

"Méthodes de la Comptabilité Nationale: Cadres et Définitions de la Base 1959." *Etudes et Conjoncture*, vol. 21 (March 1966).

Meynaud, Jean. "Les Banques Face à la Politique du Crédit." *Revue Economique*, vol. 8 (July 1957).

Michalet, Charles-Albert. "Nationalisations-Internationalisation: Un Faux Dilemme." *Revue d'Economie Industrielle*, no. 23 (issue 1, 1983).

———. *Les Placements des Epargnants Français de 1815 à Nos Jours*. Paris: Presses Universitaires de France, 1968.

Michalet, Charles-Albert, and Michel Delapierre. *La Multinationalisation des Entreprises Françaises*. Paris: Gauthier-Villars, 1973.

———. *The Multinationalization of French Firms*. Chicago: Academy of International Business, 1975.

Michel, Henri. *La Défaite de la France: Septembre 1939–Juin 1940*. Paris: Presses Universitaires de France, 1980.

Milner, Helen V. *Resisting Protectionism: Global Industries and the Politics of International Trade*. Princeton: Princeton University Press, 1988.

Milward, Alan S. *The Reconstruction of Western Europe, 1945–1951*. Berkeley: University of California Press, 1984.

Ministère des Affaires Economiques et Financières. *Tableau Economique de l'Année 1951*. Paris: Imprimerie Nationale, 1957.

Ministère de l'Economie et des Finances, *Nomenclatures d'Activités et de Produits 1973.* Paris: Imprimerie des Journaux Officiels de la République Française, 1980.

———. "Recensement des Investissements Etrangers en France." *Statistiques et Etudes Financières,* red series, no. 219 (March 1967).

Ministère de l'Economie, des Finances et du Budget. *Créer, Investir, Innover, Reprendre, Transmettre: Mesures Récentes Prises en Faveur des Entreprises.* Paris: Ministère des Finances, 1986.

———. "Les Dépenses Fiscales." *Notes Bleues,* no. 236 (July 15, 1985).

———. "Les Dépenses Fiscales." *Statistiques et Etudes Financières,* no. 381 (July 1981).

———. *Livre Blanc sur la Réforme du Financement de l'Economie.* Paris: La Documentation Française, 1986.

———. "Les Mesures Fiscales Nouvelles." *Notes Bleues,* no. 266 (February 10, 1986).

———. "La Politique Monétaire en 1985." *Notes Bleues,* no. 200 (November 5, 1984).

———. "Le Recensement Economique des Marchés Publics: Résultats pour 1983." *Notes Bleues,* no. 252 (November 4, 1985).

———. "Les Statistiques de la Direction Générale des Impôts pour 1980." *Statistiques et Etudes Financières,* no. 396 (January 1982).

Ministère de l'Economie, des Finances et de la Privatisation. "Liberté des Prix et Nouveau Droit de la Concurrence." *Notes Bleues,* supplement to no. 310 (December 15, 1986).

———. "Les Mesures Fiscales Adoptées au Cours de l'Année 1987." *Notes Bleues,* no. 369 (February 1, 1988).

———. "1987: Une Année d'Action Economique et Financière." *Notes Bleues,* no. 368 (January 25, 1988).

———. "La Réforme Fiscale, 1986–1988." *Notes Bleues,* no. 375 (March 14, 1988).

Ministère des Finances. *Inventaire de la Situation Financière (1913–1946).* Paris: Imprimerie Nationale, 1946.

Ministère de l'Industrie. *La Concentration des Entreprises Industrielles de 1972 à 1976.* Traits Fondamentaux du Système Industriel Français, 13. Paris: La Documentation Française, n.d.

———. *La Recherche Développement dans les Entreprises Industrielles en 1975.* Traits Fondamentaux du Système Industriel Français, 8. Paris: Ministère de l'Industrie, n.d.

Ministère de l'Industrie, du Commerce et de l'Artisanat. *Déconcentration Industrielle et Productivité.* Etudes de Politique Industrielle, 19. Paris: La Documentation Française, 1977.

Ministère de l'Industrie et de la Recherche. *Colloque sur le Redéploiement Industriel, 27-28-29 Mai 1975.* Etudes de Politique Industrielle, 6. Paris: La Documentation Française, 1975.

———. *La Concentration dans l'Industrie de 1974 à 1980.* Traits Fondamentaux du Système Industriel Français, 26. Paris: La Documentation Française, n.d.

————. *L'Industrie Française.* 2 vols. Paris: La Documentation Française, 1975–76.

————. *Les Marchés Publics en 1974 dans l'Industrie.* Traits Fondamentaux du Système Industriel Français, 2. Paris: La Documentation Française, 1977.

————. *9 Ans d'Implantation Etrangère dans l'Industrie, 1er Janvier 1973–1er Janvier 1981.* Traits Fondamentaux du Système Industriel Français, 28. Paris: La Documentation Francaise, n.d.

————. *Une Politique Industrielle pour la France: Actes des Journées de Travail des 15 et 16 Novembre 1982.* Paris: La Documentation Française, n.d.

————. *Le Secteur Public Industriel en 1982.* Traits Fondamentaux du Système Industriel Français, 38. Paris: Ministère de l'Industrie, n.d.

Mistral, Jacques. "125 Ans de Contrainte Extérieure: L'Expérience Française." Discussion paper 8505. Centre d'Etudes Prospectives d'Economie Mathématique Appliquées à la Planification, 1985. Published partially under the same title in *Economies et Sociétés: Cahiers de l'Institut de Sciences, Mathématiques et Economiques Appliquées,* series P, no. 29 (1986).

————. "Compétitivité et Formation de Capital en Longue Période." *Economie et Statistique,* no. 97 (February 1978).

————. "Les Dépendances de la France en Matièrc dc Bicns d'Equipement." *Revue d'Economie Industrielle,* no. 23 (issue 1, 1983).

————. "La Diffusion Internationale de l'Accumulation Intensive et sa Crise." In *Economie et Finance Internationales,* edited by Jean-Louis Reiffers. Paris: Dunod, 1982.

————. "Vingt Ans de Redéploiement du Commerce Extérieur." *Economie et Statistique,* no. 71 (October 1975).

"La Mobilité Sociale et la Mobilité Professionnelle." *Premiers Résultats,* no. 66 (July 1986).

Molinier, Jean. "L'Evolution de la Population Agricole du XVIIIe Siècle à Nos Jours." *Economie et Statistique,* no. 91 (July 1977).

Monfort, Jean. "A la Recherche des Filières de Production." *Economie et Statistique,* no. 151 (January 1983).

Monnet, Jean. *Mémoires* . Paris: Librairie Arthème Fayard, 1976.

Morin, François. *La Structure Financière du Capitalisme Français.* Paris: Calmann-Lévy, 1974.

Mormiche, Pierre. *Données sur les Grands Etablissements Industriels.* Archives et Documents, 117. Paris: INSEE, 1984.

Morris, Brian, and Klaus Boehm. *The European Community: A Practical Directory and Guide for Business, Industry, and Trade.* 2d ed. Detroit: Gale Research, 1986.

Morvan, Yves. "La Politique Industrielle Française depuis la Libération: Quarante Années d'Interventions et d'Ambiguïtés." *Revue d'Economie Industrielle,* no. 23 (issue 1, 1983).

Mucchielli, Jean-Louis, and Jean-Pierre Thuillier. *Multinationales Européennes et Investissements Croisés.* Paris: Economica, 1982.

Murat, Inès. *Colbert.* Paris: Librairie Arthème Fayard, 1980.

Musgrave, Richard A. *Fiscal Systems.* New Haven: Yale University Press, 1969.

Néel, A. "Effets de Structure et Effets de Concurrence: La Part des Produits Manufacturés d'Origine Française dans les Importations de Quelques-uns des Principaux Clients de la France (1951–1958)." *Etudes et Conjoncture,* vol. 15 (May 1960).

Nef, John U. *Industry and Government in France and England, 1540–1640.* Ithaca: Cornell University Press, 1964 (first published in 1940).

Nelson, James R., ed. *Marginal Cost Pricing in Practice.* Englewood Cliffs, N.J.: Prentice-Hall, 1964.

Nême, Colette. "Les Possibilités d'Abolition du Contrôle des Changes Français." *Revue d'Economie Politique,* vol. 96 (March 1986).

Nême, Jacques, and Colette Nême. *Economie Européenne.* Paris: Presses Universitaires de France, 1970.

Newman, Howard II. "Strategic Groups and the Structure-Performance Relationship." *Review of Economics and Statistics,* vol. 60 (August 1968).

Nicolas, Alain, and Didier Bury. "Les Grands Groupes Commerciaux Français de 1972 à 1979." *Economie et Prévision,* no. 49 (issue 4, 1981).

Nord, Philip G. *Paris Shopkeepers and the Politics of Resentment.* Princeton: Princeton University Press, 1986.

O'Brien, Patrick, and Caglar Keyder. *Economic Growth in Britain and France, 1780–1914: Two Paths to the Twentieth Century.* London: George Allen and Unwin, 1978.

OECD Economic Outlook, no. 41 (June 1987).

Official Journal of the European Communities. Luxembourg: Office for Official Publications of the European Communities.

Oliver, Peter. "A Review of the Case Law of the Court of Justice on Articles 30 to 36 EEC in 1983." *Common Market Law Review,* vol. 21 (March 1984).

Olson, Mancur. *The Logic of Collective Action: Public Goods and the Theory of Groups.* Cambridge: Harvard University Press, 1971.

———. *The Rise and Decline of Nations: Economic Growth, Stagflation, and Social Rigidities.* New Haven: Yale University Press, 1982.

Organization for Economic Cooperation and Development. *Foreign Trade by Commodities, 1983,* series C, vol. 1: *Exports.* Paris: OECD, 1985.

———. *Foreign Trade,* series C: *Trade by Commodities, Jan.–December 1963,* vol. I: *Exports.* Paris: OECD, n.d.

———. *France.* OECD Economic Surveys. Paris: OECD, 1987.

———. *Guide to Legislation on Restrictive Business Practices.* Paris: OECD, 1983.

———. *Historical Statistics, 1960–1985.* Paris: OECD, 1987.

———. *The Industrial Policy of France.* Paris: OECD, 1974.

———. *Industrial Structure Statistics, 1984.* Paris: OECD, 1986.

———. *Japan.* OECD Economic Surveys. Paris: OECD, 1985.

———. *National Accounts of OECD Countries, 1950–1979,* vol. 1: *Main Aggregates.* Paris: OECD, 1981.

———. *National Accounts, 1960–1985,* vol. 1: *Main Aggregates.* Paris: OECD, 1987.

———. *National Accounts, 1960–1986*, vol. 1: *Main Aggregates*. Paris, OECD, 1988.

———. *National Accounts, 1970–1985*, Supplement to vol. 1: *Purchasing Power Parities*. Paris: OECD, 1987.

———. *Statistics of Foreign Trade*, series B: *Trade by Commodities, Analytical Abstracts, Jan.-Dec. 1968,*. no. 1. Paris: OECD, n.d.

———. *Statistics of Foreign Trade*, series B: *Trade by Commodities, Country Summaries, Jan.-Dec. 1973*. no. 1. Paris: OECD, n.d.

———. *Statistics of Foreign Trade*, series C: *Trade by Commodities, Market Summaries: Exports, Jan.-Dec. 1978*. Paris: OECD, n.d.

———. *Statistics of National Accounts, 1950–1961*. Paris: OECD, 1964.

Organization for European Economic Cooperation. *European Economic Cooperation: A Survey*. Paris: OEEC, 1951.

———. *Foreign Trade*, Series II: *Foreign Trade by Areas and by Commodity Categories, 1952*. Paris: OEEC, September 1953.

———. *Foreign Trade*, series B: *Analytical Abstracts, Jan.-Dec. 1959*, no. 1. Paris: OEEC, n.d.

———. *OEEC Statistical Bulletins, Foreign Trade, Series IV, Member Countries Combined, 1952*. Paris: OEEC, 1953.

Orléan, André. "L'Insertion dans les Echanges Internationaux: Comparaison de Cinq Grands Pays Développés." *Economie et Statistique*, no. 184 (January 1986).

Ottenwaelter, Benoît, and Etienne Turpin. "Les Difficultés de l'Industrie N'Epargnent Pas les Entreprises Publiques." *Economie et Statistique*, no. 157 (July 1983).

Ouin, Marc. "The Establishment of the Customs Union." In *American Enterprise in the European Common Market: A Legal Profile*, edited by Eric Stein and Thomas L. Nicholson. Vol. 2. Ann Arbor: University of Michigan Press, 1960.

Padieu, René. "Les Bas Salaires." *Economie et Statistique*, no. 39 (November 1972).

Padioleau, Jean G. *Quand la France S'Enferre: La Politique Sidérurgique de la France depuis 1945*. Paris: Presses Universitaires de France, 1981.

———. *L'Etat au Concret*. Paris: Presses Universitaires de France, 1982.

Pasqualaggi, Gilles. "Les Ententes en France: Leurs Principaux Aspects, les Problèmes Que Pose Leur Contrôle." *Revue Economique*, vol. 3 (January 1952).

Passeron, Hervé, and Paul Zagame. "Modernisation Industrielle et Politique Macroéconomique: Le Cas de l'Automobile." *Economie et Statistique*, no. 182 (November 1985).

Patterson, Gardner. "The European Community as a Threat to the System." In *Trade Policy in the 1980s*, edited by William R. Cline. Washington: Institute for International Economics, 1983.

Pelkmans, Jacques. *Market Integration in the European Community*. The Hague: Martinus Nijhoff, 1984.

Perrin-Pelletier, François. "Industrial Policy and the Automobile Industry." In

French Industrial Policy, edited by William James Adams and Christian Stoffaës. Washington: Brookings Institution, 1986.

Perroux, François. "Les Formes de la Concurrence dans le Marché Commun." *Revue d'Economie Politique,* vol. 68 (January 1958).

—————. *Pouvoir et Economie.* Paris: Dunod, 1974.

Petersmann, Ernst-Ulrich. "International and European Foreign Trade Law: GATT Dispute Settlement Proceedings against the EEC." *Common Market Law Review,* vol. 22 (September 1985).

Petit, Pascal. "Full-Employment Policies in Stagnation: France in the 1980s." *Cambridge Journal of Economics,* vol. 10 (December 1986).

Philippe, M. *Le Rôle de l'Etat dans le Financement de l'Entreprise.* Paris: Dunod, 1970.

Picard, Roger. "Structure Commerciale." *Revue d'Economie Politique,* vol. 53 (January 1939).

Piens, Bertrand, and André Viguier. *Le Commerce en 27 Secteurs, 1974–1981: Comptes, Marges par Produits, Investissements.* Archives et Documents, 81. Paris: INSEE, 1983.

Piettre, André. *Economie Dirigée d'Hier et d'Aujourd'Hui: Du Colbertisme à Notre Temps.* Paris: Librairie de Médicis, 1947.

—————. *L'Evolution des Ententes Industrielles en France depuis la Crise.* Paris: Librairie du Recueil Sirey, 1936.

Piore, Michael J. "Historical Perspectives and the Interpretation of Unemployment." *Journal of Economic Literature,* vol. 25 (December 1987).

Piore, Michael J., and Charles F. Sabel. *The Second Industrial Divide: Possibilities for Prosperity.* New York: Basic Books, 1984.

Plaisant, Robert. "France." In *World Law of Competition,* edited by Julian O. von Kalinowski. Vol. B3. New York: Matthew Bender, 1980.

Pohl, Richard, and Jeanine Soleilhavoup. "La Transmission du Statut Social sur Deux ou Trois Générations." *Economie et Statistique,* no. 144 (May 1982).

Poinat, François, and Jean Thibaud. *Les Petites Entreprises Industrielles en 1983.* Archives et Documents, 133. Paris: INSEE, 1985.

Ponssard, Jean-Pierre. "Marchés Publics et Innovation: Concurrence ou Régulation?" *Revue Economique,* vol. 32 (January 1981).

Porter, Michael E. *Competitive Advantage: Creating and Sustaining Superior Performance.* New York: The Free Press, 1985.

Pose, Alfred. "Structure et Méthodes Bancaires." *Revue d'Economie Politique,* vol. 53 (January 1939).

Poujade, Pierre. *J'Ai Choisi le Combat.* St. Céré (Lot): Société Générale des Editions et des Publications, 1955.

Praderie, Michel. "La Population Active Employée par Branche entre 1954 et 1962." *Etudes et Conjoncture,* vol. 19 (March 1964).

Praderie, Michel, and Jean-Jacques Carré. "La Population Active par Secteur d'Etablissement." *Etudes et Conjoncture,* vol. 19 (April 1964).

Praderie, Michel, and Monique Passagez. "La Mobilité Professionnelle en France entre 1959 et 1964." *Etudes et Conjoncture,* vol. 21 (October 1966).

Precheur, Claude. *1968, Les Industries Françaises à l'Heure du Marché Commun.* Paris: Société d'Edition d'Enseignement Supérieur, 1969.

Price, Roger. *The Modernization of Rural France: Communications Networks and Agricultural Market Structures in Nineteenth Century France.* New York: St. Martin's Press, 1984.

Price Waterhouse. *Accounting Principles and Reporting Practices: A Survey in 46 Countries.* New York: Price Waterhouse, 1975.

Pryor, Frederic L. "The Size of Production Establishments in Manufacturing." *Economic Journal,* vol. 82 (June 1972).

Quatrepoint, Jean-Michel. *Histoire Secrète des Dossiers Noirs de la Gauche.* Paris: Editions Alain Moreau, 1986.

Rabier, Jacques-René. "Cinq Ans de Marché Commun du Charbon et de l'Acier." *Revue Economique,* vol. 9 (March 1958).

Rapport Annexe sur l'Etat de la Recherche et du Développement Technologique: Activités en 1982 et 1983, Perspectives 1984. Projet de Loi de Finances pour 1984. Paris: Imprimerie Nationale, 1983.

Rapport au Parlement sur les Aides à l'Industrie, Annexe au Projet de Loi Portant Règlement Définitif du Budget de 1984. Paris: Imprimerie Nationale, 1987.

Rapport au Parlement sur les Fonds Publics Attribués à Titre d'Aides aux Entreprises Industrielles, Annexe au Projet de Loi Portant Règlement Définitif du Budget. Paris: Imprimerie Nationale, 1979–82, 1984.

Rapport sur les Disparités entre les Prix Français et Etrangers (Nathan report). Paris: Imprimerie Nationale, 1954.

Rapport sur les Entreprises Publiques (Nora report). Paris: La Documentation Française, 1967.

Rapport sur les Obstacles à l'Expansion Economique (Armand-Rueff report). Paris: Imprimerie Nationale, 1960.

Ratcliffe, Barrie M. "The Tariff Reform Campaign in France, 1831–1836." *Journal of European Economic History,* vol. 7 (Spring 1978).

Rattin, Solange. "Un Chef d'Exploitation Agricole sur Trois A Plus de 60 Ans." *Economie et Statistique,* no. 185 (February 1986).

Rault, Daniel. "Secteurs d'Activité: L'Evolution des Structures de la Main-d'Oeuvre." *Economie et Statistique,* nos. 171–72 (November-December 1984).

Reid, Donald. *The Miners of Decazeville: A Genealogy of Deindustrialization.* Cambridge: Harvard University Press, 1985.

Reiffers, Jean-Louis, ed. *Economie et Finance Internationales.* Paris: Dunod, 1982.

Reignier, Elisabeth. "La Pluriactivité en Agriculture." *Economie et Statistique,* no. 173 (January 1985).

Rempp, Jean-Michel. "Les Différences de Prix entre le Petit et le Grand Commerce." *Economie et Statistique,* no. 106 (December 1978).

Reuter, Paul. "A Propos des Ententes Industrielles et Commerciales." *Droit Social,* vol. 15 (July 1952), vol. 15 (September 1952), and vol. 16 (January 1953).

Richardson, George B. *Information and Investment: A Study in the Working of the Competitive Economy.* New York: Oxford University Press, 1960.

Rivero, Jean. "Action Economique de l'Etat et Evolution Administrative." *Revue Economique*, vol. 13 (November 1962).

Rivier, Jacques. "La Place des Entreprises Publiques dans l'Economie Nationale." *Economie et Statistique*, no. 6 (November 1969).

Roehl, Richard. "French Industrialization: A Reconsideration." *Explorations in Economic History*, vol. 13 (July 1976).

Ross, George, Stanley Hoffmann, and Sylvia Malzacher, eds. *The Mitterrand Experiment: Continuity and Change in Modern France*. New York: Oxford University Press, 1987.

Ross, Malcolm. "Challenging State Aids: The Effect of Recent Developments." *Common Market Law Review*, vol. 23 (Winter 1986).

Rouilleault, Henri. "Groupes Publics et Politique Industrielle." *Economie et Prévision*, no. 70 (issue 4, 1985).

Rousseau, Roland. "Pourquoi Change-t-On de Nomenclature?" *Economie et Statistique*, no. 70 (September 1975).

Roy, Maurice. *Les Commerçants: Entre la Révolte et la Modernisation*. Paris: Editions du Seuil, 1971.

Rueff, Jacques. *Combats pour l'Ordre Financier: Mémoires et Documents pour Servir à l'Histoire du Dernier Demi-Siècle*. Paris: Librairie Plon, 1972.

Saada, Kathy, and Serge Volkoff. "La Mobilité Professionnelle durant une Année." *Economie et Statistique*, no. 42 (February 1973).

Saboulin, Michel de. "Les Contrastes Démographiques entre Régions." *Economie et Statistique*, no. 124 (August 1980).

Saint-Geours, Jean. *Pouvoir et Finance*. Paris: Librairie Arthème Fayard, 1979.

Salais, Robert, and Laurent Thévenot, eds. *Le Travail: Marchés, Règles, Conventions*. Paris: Economica, 1986.

Sandalow, Terrance, and Eric Stein, eds. *Courts and Free Markets: Perspectives from the United States and Europe*. 2 vols. New York: Oxford University Press, 1982.

Santini, Sylvie. "Livre: La Solution Douce." *Express*, June 27, 1986.

Sautory, Olivier. "Plus de la Moitié de la Population A Changé au Moins une Fois de Commune en Vingt Ans." *Economie et Statistique*, no. 209 (April 1988).

Sautter, Christian. "L'Efficacité et la Rentabilité de l'Economie Française de 1954 à 1974." *Economie et Statistique*, no. 68 (June 1975).

Sauvy, Alfred. *Histoire Economique de la France entre les Deux Guerres*. 3 vols. Paris: Economica, 1984.

Savary, Julien. *Les Multinationales Françaises*. Paris: Presses Universitaires de France, 1981.

Saxonhouse, Gary R. "The Micro- and Macroeconomics of Foreign Sales to Japan." In *Trade Policy in the 1980s*, edited by William R. Cline. Washington: Institute for International Economics, 1983.

Schattschneider, Elmer E. *Politics, Pressures, and the Tariff: A Study of Free Private Enterprise in Pressure Politics, As Shown in the 1929–1930 Revision of the Tariff*. New York: Prentice-Hall, 1935.

Schelling, Thomas C. *The Strategy of Conflict*. Cambridge: Harvard University Press, 1960.

Scherer, Frederic M. *Industrial Market Structure and Economic Performance*. 2d ed. Boston: Houghton Mifflin, 1980.

Schmill, Erick. *Les Investissements Etrangers en France* . Paris: Cujas, 1966.

Schrans, Guy. "National and Regional Aid to Industry under the EEC Treaty." *Common Market Law Review*, vol. 10 (1973).

Schultze, Charles. "Industrial Policy: A Dissent." *Brookings Review*, vol. 2 (Fall 1983).

Schumpeter, Joseph. "The Analysis of Economic Change." *Review of Economic Statistics*, vol. 17 (May 1935).

Scitovsky, Tibor. *Economic Theory and Western European Integration*. Stanford: Stanford University Press, 1958.

Scoville, Warren C. *Capitalism and French Glassmaking, 1640–1789*. Berkeley: University of California Press, 1950.

Sègre, Henri, ed. *Les Entreprises Publiques en France*. Paris: Editions Sociales, 1975.

Servan-Schreiber, Jean-Jacques. *Le Défi Américain*. Paris: Editions Denoël, 1967.

Sheahan, John. "Experience with Public Enterprise in France and Italy." In *Public Enterprise: Economic Analysis of Theory and Practice*, edited by William G. Shepherd. Lexington, Mass.: D.C. Heath, 1976.

———. *An Introduction to the French Economy*. Columbus: C. E. Merrill Publishing, 1969.

———. *Promotion and Control of Industry in Postwar France*. Cambridge: Harvard University Press, 1963.

Shepherd, William G. "What Does the Survivor Technique Show about Economies of Scale?" *Southern Economic Journal*, vol. 34 (July 1967).

Shutt, Harry. *The Myth of Free Trade: Patterns of Protectionism since 1945*. New York: Basil Blackwell, 1985.

Smith, Michael S. *Tariff Reform in France, 1860–1900: The Politics of Economic Interest*. Ithaca: Cornell University Press, 1980.

Snyder, Richard C. "Commercial Policy as Reflected in Treaties from 1931 to 1939." *American Economic Review*, vol. 30 (December 1940).

Soulage, Bernard, and Simon-Pierre Thiery. "Quelles Institutions pour une Nouvelle Politique Industrielle?" *Revue d'Economie Industrielle*, no. 23 (issue 1, 1983).

Spivey, W. Allen. *Economic Policies in France, 1976–81: The Barre Program in a West European Perspective*. Ann Arbor: University of Michigan Graduate School of Business Administration, 1982.

Statistical Office of the European Communities (Eurostat). *Employment and Unemployment, 1983*. Luxembourg: Office for Official Publications of the European Communities, 1983.

———. *Employment and Unemployment, 1987*. Luxembourg: Office for Official Publications of the European Communities, 1987.

———. *National Accounts ESA—Aggregates, 1960–1981*. Luxembourg: Office for Official Publications of the European Communities, 1983.

————. *Structural Data Base, Tables by Branch, 1960–1981.* Studies of National Accounts, 4. Luxembourg: Office for Official Publications of the European Communities, 1984.

Stein, Eric. "The European Community in 1983: A Less Perfect Union?" *Common Market Law Review,* vol. 20 (December 1983).

————. *Harmonization of European Company Laws: National Reform and International Coordination.* Indianapolis: Bobbs-Merrill, 1971.

Stein, Eric, and Peter Hay. *Law and Institutions in the Atlantic Area: Documents.* Indianapolis: Bobbs-Merrill, 1967.

————. *Law and Institutions in the Atlantic Area: Readings, Cases and Problems.* Indianapolis: Bobbs-Merrill, 1967.

Stein, Eric, Peter Hay, and Michel Waelbroeck. *Documents for European Community Law and Institutions in Perspective.* Indianapolis: Bobbs-Merrill, 1976.

————. *European Community Law and Institutions in Perspective: Text, Cases and Readings.* Indianapolis: Bobbs-Merrill, 1976.

Stein, Eric, and Thomas L. Nicholson. *American Enterprise in the European Common Market: A Legal Profile.* 2 vols. Ann Arbor: University of Michigan Press, 1960.

Stern, Robert M. *Foreign Trade and Economic Growth in Italy.* New York: Praeger, 1967.

Stigler, George J. *Capital and Rates of Return in Manufacturing Industries.* Princeton: Princeton University Press, 1963.

————. "The Economies of Scale." *Journal of Law and Economics,* vol. 1 (October 1958).

Stocking, George W., and Myron W. Watkins. *Cartels in Action: Case Studies in International Business Diplomacy.* New York: Twentieth Century Fund, 1946.

Stoffaës, Christian. *Fins de Mondes: Déclin et Renouveau de l'Economie.* Paris: Editions Odile Jacob, 1987.

————. *La Grande Menace Industrielle.* New ed. Paris: Calmann-Lévy, 1978.

————. "Industrial Policy in the High-Technology Industries." In *French Industrial Policy,* edited by William James Adams and Christian Stoffaës. Washington: Brookings Institution, 1986.

————. *Politique Industrielle.* Paris: Les Cours de Droit, 1984.

Stoffaës, Christian, and Jacques Victorri. *Nationalisations.* Paris: Flammarion, 1977.

Stoléru, Lionel. *L'Impératif Industriel.* Paris: Editions du Seuil, 1969.

————. *La France à Deux Vitesses.* Paris: Flammarion, 1982.

Svennilson, Ingvar. *Growth and Stagnation in the European Economy.* Geneva: United Nations Economic Commission for Europe, 1954.

Swann, Dennis. *The Economics of the Common Market.* 5th ed. New York: Penguin Books, 1984.

Tamisier, Marie-Hélène. "Les Restructurations Marquent la Vie des Entreprises et des Groupes." *Economie et Statistique,* no. 158 (September 1983).

Tavitian, Roland. "Les Processus de Distorsions et d'Adaptations Structurelles dans l'Economie Française depuis 1914." *Revue Economique,* vol. 9 (September 1958).

Taylor, Paul G. *The Limits of European Integration.* New York: Columbia University Press, 1983.

Taylor, Stuart, Jr. "High Court Backs Discounter Curbs by Manufacturers." *New York Times,* May 3, 1988.

Teissedre, Jean. "Evolution de la Réglementation Française du Commerce Extérieur (1945 à 1949)." *Droit Social,* vol. 12 (September 1949).

Terreul, Georges-François. *Le Financement des Entreprises en France depuis la Fin du XIXe Siècle à Nos Jours.* Paris: Librairie Générale de Droit et de Jurisprudence, 1961.

Thélot, Claude. "A Propos de la Mobilité Interentreprises: Réactions sur une Note de J. Vincens." *Revue Economique,* vol. 31 (May 1980).

————. "L'Evolution de la Mobilité Sociale dans Chaque Génération." *Economie et Statistique,* no. 161 (December 1983).

————. "Mobilité Professionnelle Plus Forte entre 1965 et 1970 Qu'entre 1959 et 1964." *Economie et Statistique,* no. 51 (December 1973).

Thévenot, Laurent. "Les Catégories Sociales en 1975: L'Extension du Salariat." *Economie et Statistique,* no. 91 (July 1977).

Thomas, Jean-Noël. "Impôt sur les Sociétés et le Comportement Industriel de l'Etat." *Revue d'Economie Industrielle,* no. 7 (issue 1, 1979).

Tibi, Claude. "La Place de l'Algérie dans les Relations Commerciales de la France Métropolitaine." *Etudes et Conjoncture,* vol. 16 (July 1961).

Tilly, Charles. *The Vendée: A Sociological Analysis of the Counterrevolution of 1793.* Cambridge: Harvard University Press, 1964.

Torem, Charles, and William L. Craig. "Control of Foreign Investment in France." *Michigan Law Review,* vol. 66 (February 1968).

"Les Trusts Français aux Colonies." *Economie et Politique,* vol. 1, nos. 5-6 (1954).

Turgot, Anne-Robert Jacques. *Ecrits Economiques.* Paris: Calmann-Lévy, 1970.

Uri, Pierre. *Changer l'Impôt (pour Changer la France).* Paris: Editions Ramsay, 1981.

————. "Harmonisation des Politiques et Fonctionnement du Marché." *Revue Economique,* vol. 9 (March 1958).

U.S. Department of Commerce, Bureau of the Census. *1970 Census of Population: Mobility for States and the Nation.* Subject reports, PC(2)-2B. Washington: Government Printing Office, 1973.

————. *1970 Census of Population: Occupation and Residence in 1965.* Special reports, PC(2)-7E. Washington: Government Printing Office, 1973.

————. Bureau of Economic Analysis. *Selected Data on U.S. Direct Investment Abroad, 1950–1976.* Washington: Department of Commerce, 1982.

————. *Survey of Current Business.*

Usher, Abbot P. "Colbert and Governmental Control of Industry in Seventeenth Century France," *Review of Economic Statistics,* vol. 16 (November 15, 1934).

Vangrevelinghe, Gabriel. "Les Niveaux de Vie en France, 1956 et 1965." *Economie et Statistique,* no. 1 (May 1969).

Vannoise, Robert de. "Le Crédit Commercial Interentreprises: 400 Milliards en 1975." *Economie et Statistique*, no. 99 (April 1978).

Vaupel, James W., and Joan P. Curhan. *The World's Multinational Enterprises: A Sourcebook of Tables Based on a Study of the Largest U.S. and Non-U.S. Manufacturing Corporations*. Boston: Harvard University Graduate School of Business Administration, 1973.

Vedel, Georges. "Euratom." *Revue Economique*, vol. 9 (March 1958).

Vernier-Palliez, Bernard. "Preface." In *French Industrial Policy*, edited by William James Adams and Christian Stoffaës. Washington: Brookings Institution, 1986.

Vernon, Raymond, ed. *Big Business and the State: Changing Relations in Western Europe*. Cambridge: Harvard University Press, 1974.

Vernon, Raymond, and Debora Spar. *Beyond Globalism: Remaking American Foreign Economic Policy*. New York: Free Press, 1989.

Vernon, Raymond, and Debora L. Spar. *Beyond Globalism: Remaking American Foreign Economic Policy*. New York: Free Press, 1989.

Vert, Eric. "Les Revenus Non Agricoles des Agriculteurs, Choix ou Nécessité?" *Economie et Statistique*, no. 182 (November 1985).

Vibert, Paul. *La Concurrence Etrangère: Les Industries Nationales; Celles Qui Naissent et Grandissent, Celles Qui Meurent ou Se Transforment*. Paris: C. Bayle, 1887.

Vincent, L.-A. "Population Active, Production et Productivité dans 21 Branches de l'Economie Française (1896-1962)." *Etudes et Conjoncture*, vol. 20 (February 1965).

———. "Les Progrès de Productivité et Leur Utilisation à l'Electricité de France de 1952 à 1962." *Etudes et Conjoncture*, vol. 20 (January 1965).

Vincent, Micheline. "Vingt Ans de Textile-Habillement." *Economie et Statistique*, no. 138 (November 1981).

Walter, François. "Note sur Divers Procédés d'Incitation Fiscale à l'Investissement." *Revue Economique*, vol. 7 (July 1956).

Weber, André-Paul. "Entreprise Multinationale et Pratiques Restrictives." *Revue Economique*, vol. 23 (July 1972).

Weber, Eugen. *Peasants into Frenchmen: The Modernization of Rural France*. Stanford: Stanford University Press, 1976.

Weiller, Jean. "Les Degrés de l'Intégration et les Chances d'une 'Zone de Coopération' Internationale." *Revue Economique*, vol. 9 (March 1958).

———. "De la Protection Rigide aux Contrôles Souples." *Revue Economique*, vol. 9 (May 1958).

———. "Echanges Extérieurs." *Revue d'Economie Politique*, vol. 53 (January 1939).

———. "Les Tendances de Longue Durée des Echanges Extérieurs de la France." *Revue Economique*, vol. 2 (May 1951).

Wells, Louis T., Jr. "Automobiles." In *Big Business and the State: Changing Relations in Western Europe*, edited by Raymond Vernon. Cambridge: Harvard University Press, 1974.

Wexler, Imanuel. *The Marshall Plan Revisited: The European Recovery Program in Economic Perspective.* Westport, Conn.: Greenwood Press, 1983.

Who Owns Whom: Continental Europe. New York: Dun & Bradstreet, 1986.

Wickham, Sylvain. *Concentration et Dimensions.* Paris: Flammarion, 1966.

Wright, Gavin. "American Industrial Leadership, 1879–1940: Trade in Manufactures." CEPR Discussion Paper 108. Stanford: Stanford University, Center for Economic Policy Research, October 1987.

Yacono, Xavier. *Les Etapes de la Décolonisation Française.* 3d ed. Paris: Presses Universitaires de France, 1982.

———. *Histoire de la Colonisation Française.* Paris: Presses Universitaires de France, 1973.

Zeldin, Theodore. *France, 1848–1945: Ambition and Love.* New York: Oxford University Press, 1979.

———. *France, 1848–1945: Anxiety and Hypocrisy.* New York: Oxford University Press, 1981.

———. *France, 1848–1945: Intellect and Pride.* New York: Oxford University Press, 1980.

———. *France, 1848–1945: Politics and Anger.* New York: Oxford University Press, 1979.

———. *France, 1848–1945: Taste and Corruption.* New York: Oxford University Press, 1980.

Zentz, P. "Le Rôle de la Caisse Nationale des Marchés de l'Etat pour l'Octroi de Crédits de Rééquipement dans le Cadre Professionnel." *Revue Economique,* vol. 2 (September 1951).

Zinsou, Lionel. *Le Fer de Lance: Essai sur les Nationalisations Industrielles.* Paris: Olivier Orban, 1985.

Zukin, Sharon, ed. *Industrial Policy: Business and Politics in the United States and France.* New York: Praeger, 1985.

Zysman, John. *Governments, Markets, and Growth: Financial Systems and the Politics of Industrial Change.* Ithaca: Cornell University Press, 1983.

———. *Political Strategies for Industrial Order: State, Market, and Industry in France.* Berkeley: University of California Press, 1977.

Index

New Caledonia, 179
New Hebrides, 179
New Zealand, 204
Nicoud movement, 114, 241, 243
Norway, 145
Nuclear industry: industrial policy, 51; government subsidies, 82, 84, 113, 116; SOEs, 62

Occupational mobility. *See* Labor mobility
OECD. *See* Organization for Economic Cooperation and Development
OEEC. *See* Organization for European Economic Cooperation
Office equipment industry: export propensity, 160–61, 181; foreign investment, 188, 193; government research support, 79, 80; imports exposure, 158
Office National d'Etudes et de Recherches Aérospatiales (ONERA), 85–86
Office National Interprofessionnel des Céréales (ONIC), 82, 84–86
Oligopoly, 12, 98–99, 150, 152, 170, 185, 189, 200, 238
Olivetti, 188
Organization for Economic Cooperation and Development (OECD), 6, 100, 144, 180–84, 245, 257, 259
Organization for European Economic Cooperation (OEEC), 130–32, 140
Ottawa agreements, 203
Ouin, Marc, 132
Output: indirect taxes and, 93; foreign investment and, 163–65; industrial, 17–18, 20; government subsidies and, 55, 81; total per capita amounts, 4

Pareto optimality, 49–50, 54, 117
Paribas, 59
Payroll taxes, 93
Pechiney-Ugine Kuhlmann, 60, 167
Personal income taxes, 96–97; tax complémentaire, 208–09
Petroleum industry: corporate income taxes, 96; employment, 33, 34; foreign investment, 166, 193; government procurement, 78; government subsidies, 85–86, 113, 116; imports exposure, 156–57, 159; indirect taxes, 94; SOEs, 65–66; wartime damage indemnities, 87

Peugeot, 153
Pharmaceuticals industry: export propensity, 182; foreign subsidiaries, 166; government subsidies, 116; imports exposure, 157
Piore, Michael, 33, 248, 259, 268
Planning. *See* Government policy
Plant and equipment: government financing, 73, 105; investment tax incentives, 10; modernization, 3, 13
Plastics industry: employment, 31; government subsidies, 116
Politique de créneaux. *See* Strategy of niches
Politique de filières. *See* Strategy of vertical streams
Pompidou, Georges, 86n, 229
Population growth, 36–40
Poron, 227
Portugal, 140, 145
Poujade movement, 114, 241, 243
Precision goods industry: export propensity, 182; foreign investment, 193; government research support, 80
Price regulation, 3, 98–100, 120, 206, 213, 231; under ECSC, 125–27; resale price maintenance, 218–19, 226, 228, 231–32
Prices: alignment, 235–38; discriminatory, 63–64, 139; imports, 167–77; markups, 234–35; sensitivity, 185; SOEs, 62–64, 68
Productivity, 19, 44, 107–08
Profitability, 238–39, 247
Promotion of domestic enterprise, 51–53, 87, 94
Protectionism, 3, 11, 14, 197–98, 261–62, 265, 266–67
PTT, 85–86
Public enterprise. *See* State-owned enterprise (SOE)

Radar, 221
Railway industry: coal and steel transport costs, 127–28; employment, 33; government subsidies, 82, 84, 87, 113, 116; SOEs, 62, 65–66; wartime damage indemnities, 87
Real estate industry: corporate income taxes, 95; government subsidies, 84; SOEs, 70